The Welfare of Children

SECOND EDITION

DUNCAN LINDSEY

OXFORD
UNIVERSITY PRESS

2004

OXFORD
UNIVERSITY PRESS

Oxford   New York
Auckland   Bangkok   Buenos Aires   Cape Town   Chennai
Dar es Salaam   Delhi   Hong Kong   Istanbul   Karachi   Kolkata
Kuala Lumpur   Madrid   Melbourne   Mexico City   Mumbai   Nairobi
São Paulo   Shanghai   Taipei   Tokyo   Toronto

Copyright © 1994, 2004 by Oxford University Press, Inc.

Published by Oxford University Press, Inc.
198 Madison Avenue, New York, New York 10016

www.oup.com

Oxford is a registered trademark of Oxford University Press

Library of Congress Cataloging-in-Publication Data
Lindsey, Duncan.
The welfare of children / Duncan Lindsey.—2nd. ed.
p. cm.
Includes bibliographical references and indexes.
ISBN 0-19-513670-5; ISBN 0-19-513671-3 (pbk.)
1. Child welfare—United States—History. 2. Child welfare—
North America—History. 3. Child abuse—United States—Prevention—Finance.
4. Child abuse—North America—Prevention—Finance. I. Title.
HV741 .L527 2003
362.7'0973—dc21   2003006097

1 3 5 7 9 8 6 4 2

Printed in the United States of America
on acid-free paper

The Welfare of Children

To Betty McDaniel, M.S.W.

who has devoted her life to child welfare

Preface

Most children in America are well cared for by parents who have the necessary resources and love. But many children are not so fortunate. Millions grow up in homes where the basic resources of food and clothing and, sometimes, even love are not available. They live in dilapidated housing and blighted neighborhoods. The adults who care for them are barely able to care for themselves. These adults are struggling to make a living and to keep food on the table. The attention to the needs of their children and even basic child care are too often neglected. This is life for the millions of children living in poverty.

Today, the typical family for such children is a single parent, most often a lone mother, who, although she may love her children, does not have the resources, time, energy, or education to properly provide for them. The wages of her full-time job are often so low that paying for child care takes most of her paycheck. Her children's father too often provides little or no support, and is unlikely to be materially or emotionally involved in his children's lives.

What support will this mother receive from society, from government and charitable organizations? Very little or none. In earlier times the public child welfare system would have assisted her with supportive services, but that system no longer exists, replaced by a child protection system whose sole concern is finding and removing a relatively few children from situations of severe child abuse. The child who is simply poor and disadvantaged is not the client of the child protection system.

The United States is the wealthiest country in the world. We have unlimited possibilities. Most children are raised in families that will be able to provide for the futures of their children. The United States in recent decades has adopted policies and programs that have led to increased inequality. The enormous new wealth created has not been distributed widely to all. One of the consequences of this inequality is that the situation for the poor has deteriorated. The economic circumstances for poor children have declined. These children cannot be expected to alter their situation. They are, after all, just children; they rely on their parents. But their parent, the single mother who is working full-time to provide for them and their home and to earn a living is under stress and strain that are unlikely to allow for the care and nurturing needed to ensure their future.

It is not too late. We can reverse this situation by developing policies and programs that support these parents and reduce their poverty and stress, thereby aiding their children. We must develop a public child welfare system that truly lifts children's hopes and aspirations and produces a different outcome for all disadvantaged and poor children. In doing so we will be ensuring that the creators of the future no longer include large numbers of bitter and disappointed youth. Only then can we hope for a stable, secure, and harmonious society for generations to come. To this end, this book is about our children and our collective obligation to them.

Acknowledgments

This work is the result of conversation and friendship with many colleagues concerned with improving our collective effort on behalf of children. The field of child welfare is a truly wonderful and exciting place. Our work is important and our effort makes a difference.

I have struggled with the issues examined here for the last several decades. During this period, I have had the fortune of founding and editing *Children and Youth Services Review,* the major research journal in the child welfare field. This experience has allowed me to be near the center of a broad professional debate during a period of great creative ferment. The ideas and approaches debated in the pages of the *Review* have been the wellspring of my own thinking and have driven the analysis presented here. I am grateful to all who have participated.

There are so many people to thank. I began writing the first edition of this book at the University of California at Berkeley where I was a visiting scholar. Berkeley was an extraordinary place—a vibrant research community. It was the ideal environment to pursue the development of this study. The delight at Berkeley for me was getting to know George Bennett, Eileen Gambrill, Neil Gilbert, Jill Duerr Berrick, Mark Courtney, and Mary Ann Mason.

The University of Oregon allowed me to pursue the study of child welfare in a learned community situated in a beautiful setting. I was at the University for more than a decade and a half. I want to acknowledge the contribution of Marie Harvey, Wes Hawkins, Michele Hawkins, Judy and Mike Hibbard, Mary and Steve Ickes, Virginia Low, and Paul Nicholson. I have also studied at the Faculty of Social Work at the University of Toronto. My close friends Lynn McDonald, Cheryl Regehr and Nico Trocmé have been a source of inspiration and knowledge.

This second edition was written at the School of Public Policy at the University of California at Los Angeles. I want to thank Rosina Becerra, Rachel Bentley, Julie Cederbaum, Khush Cooper, Diane de Anda, Jenny Doh, Robert Goldstein, Zeke Hasenfield, Neal Halfon, Joel Handler, Alfreda Iglehart, Todd Franke, Sacha Klein Martin, Ailee Moon, Farah Orap Silver, Kimi Thompson, and others for their support. While finishing this edix

tion I served as Chair of the UCLA Academic Senate where I shared thoughts with numerous colleagues including Cliff Brunk, Judy Brunk, Steve Cederbaum, Luisa Crespo, John Edmond, David Kaplan, Kathy Komar, Michele Mehaffey, Boni Mendez, Kathy Speers, John Tucker, William Worger, Steven Yeazell, and the many others who make the Senate such a great part of UCLA.

I want to thank all of the students I have had the great pleasure of working with over the last decade at UCLA. The classroom experience has been a forum to examine and challenge ideas and, in this process, been an incomparable joy. I would like to thank Laura Batres, Heather Beasley, Corinna Benn, Tuyen Bui, Jennifer Carew, Bethany Daly, Hildy Dimarzio, Corinne Ear, Gloria Escamilla, Katherine Ford, Rhona Gardner, Alicia Garoupa, Maria Gil, Maria Guerrero, Yvonne Guzman, Joyce Johnson, Michelle Koenig, Melinda London, Cynthia Long, Ngu-Mui Lu, Sean Lynch, Kai Martin, Tisa McGhee, Laura Mooiman, Abigail Nelson, Catheryne Nguyen, Michele Palmer-Bray, Tracy Peeples, Minh-Thuy Pham, Martin Raya, Sherri Reeves, Teresa Rubio, Nao Saadi, Jenny Schulman, Lylia Segovia, Amy Stansel, Natalie Stewart, Michelle Tally, Peter Tran, Deborah Ujfalusy, Nicole Viola, Shana Votaw, Amber Wiley, Cynthia Wu and the many other students who have engaged the issues presented here.

While writing this and the earlier edition I have sent versions to various friends and colleagues. I am grateful to those who provided comments and criticisms, including Victor Groze, Elizabeth Hutchison, Alfred Kadushin, Thomas McDonald, Leroy Pelton, Lois Pierce, Aron Shlonsky, and Ted Stein. Several other colleagues and friends were generous with their interest and concern. I particularly want to thank Marianne Berry, Douglas Besharov, Andrew Bridge, Edythe and Eli Broad, Emily Bruce, Sheldon Danziger, Robert Dingwall, Jane and Michael Eisner, William Epstein, David Fanshel, David Gil, Jessica Huang, Diane Jacobs, Henry S. Maas, Rosemary Sarri, Ira Schwartz, Margaret Sherraden, Michael Sherraden, Paul Stuart, Michael Wald, and Stan Witkin.

The first and second editions of this book took shape with the help of Howard H. Wade. Before it was drafted Howard and I debated and discussed these issues for endless hours. While assembling the study Howard's analytic and editorial skill was tremendous. I cannot adequately express my gratitude for his contributions both as architect and builder of what you now see as a book.

In addition, I have had the great fortune of working with David Roll and later, Nancy Hoagland, Maura Roessner, and Joan Bossert at Oxford University Press. The book that emerged following their editorial leadership is considerably different from what I started with. I am grateful for their tireless effort and encouragement.

My mother has provided the most important ingredient of this study. I am eternally grateful for all she has taught me and for all she has done. It has taken many years to realize the sacrifices she made to raise my brother and me. But now I am beginning to understand and appreciate all she has done. I hope in some small way this book is a testament to that understanding.

My family has been my haven. They have provided the context for everything I do, including the writing of this book. My identical twin brother, Buck, and I have engaged in a dialogue since we could first talk and which continues to this day. His careful reading and critique of the ideas presented here have been essential—even when we disagreed. My wife, Debbie, more than anyone, has nurtured and encouraged this study. She is the center of my world. Our children, Ethan and Sierra, debated many of the issues discussed here. I owe so much of my understanding of children and young people to them. They have been the source of my inspiration and perseverance in completing this work. Other family members who have shared their views with me include Jerry McDaniel, Paul and Paula McDaniel, John and René McDaniel, Jenny Lindsey, Merlin Kaufman, Dana Diller, Marci and Paul Cauthorn, and Danny and Kirsten Kaufman. I would also like to thank Garrett and Sean Lindsey, Ann Marie, Aaron, and Rebecca McDaniel, Luke, and Aiden Kaufman, and all our children.

Betty McDaniel, my wife's mother, has been a child welfare social worker (MSW from the University of Chicago) throughout her career. Her life has been dedicated to children. She has lived what she believes and has provided an example for all who know her of heartfelt commitment. I have dedicated the second edition of this book to her. There is no person I love and admire more.

Contents

The Welfare of Children

Introduction

The Talmud, emphasizing the importance of each individual life, says, "If during the course of your own life, you have saved one life, it is as if you have saved all humankind." Few occupations give us the opportunity of participating in the saving of a life. The everyday life of the child welfare worker is concerned with just that—reclaiming a child for life.

Alfred Kadushin, *Child Welfare Services*

When we examine how a society cares for its children, especially its disadvantaged children, we are peering into the heart of a nation. The United States, the wealthiest country in the world, has more children living in poverty than any other industrialized nation. Millions of children wake up to dangerous neighborhoods, dilapidated and violent schools, impoverished and stressful homes, and futures void of opportunity. While poverty has essentially been eliminated for groups such as the elderly, it continues to blight the lives of millions of children with little change in the last several decades. Further, the country that pioneered strategies to prevent child abuse and now spends more money fighting it than do all other industrialized countries has the highest rate of child abuse in the world. In fact, more children are reported for child abuse and neglect in the United States than in all the other industrialized nations combined.

In our society we assign primary responsibility for the care and nurturing of children to the family. Collective responsibility for children is restricted to reclaiming children from situations where the family is unable to meet its obligation. This approach was adequate when most families were able to meet their children's needs. However, in the last several decades major social change has left large numbers of families unable to meet those needs. The TV family of the 1950s where father goes off to work while mother stays home and cares for the children has become less common while the single mother struggling to raise two, three, or more children on a minimum-wage job, without child care, health care, or the support of an extended family, has become more common. For the millions of children living in this latter family structure, poverty is the prevailing condition.

Impoverished families who are unable to meet the needs of their children are, in overwhelming numbers, looking to the child welfare system for

1

help. Yet the child welfare system, which has been transformed in the last several decades into a child protection system directed toward investigating abuse and neglect, and removing children from families and placing them in foster care, is no longer prepared to assist in solving the problems of child poverty.

From its inception over a century ago the child welfare system has focused on the "residual" [1] group of children who were "left out" (the residue or leftovers of a productive society), that is, those who were orphaned, abandoned, neglected, or impoverished. In the early years of child welfare such children were cared for in orphanages and later in foster families. As long as the problem could be confined to a limited, identifiable group of children, services could be developed to meet their needs. In recent decades, economic and social demands have narrowed this definable group to such an extent that the residual approach no longer makes sense. Today, child welfare social workers no longer try to alleviate poverty and its impact but instead spend most of their time investigating reports of child abuse, and trying to rescue children from crises, when they should be working in a framework that will effectively prevent those crises.

Critics like to think that child welfare professionals are themselves the culprits. If only they could... well, do their job more effectively. But social workers are not miracle workers, and it is hard to imagine how they could do more, given their crushing caseloads and shrinking resources. Struggling daily to aid multitudes of children caught in a web of social disintegration, poverty, substance abuse, and despair, most are doing all that is humanly possible. Increasingly, child abuse regulations are placing these professionals in a position where they can do little more than conduct criminal abuse investigations—something for which most lack the training, aptitude, and authority.

The problem lies with the *residual* perspective that guides current understanding of what can be accomplished. This approach demands that aid should be invoked only after the family is in crisis and other support groups (kin, neighborhood) have failed to meet a child's minimal needs. In this perspective the child welfare agency becomes a kind of triage, a battle-front hospital where casualties are sorted and only the most seriously wounded receive attention. But because the damage to children is so great

---

[1] Merriam-Webster's dictionary defines *residual* as "remainder" such as "of, relating to, or characteristic of a residue." The residual approach focuses on dealing with the residue separate from the whole of which it was a part. For example, *residual oil* is defined as "fuel oil that remains after the removal of valuable distillates (as gasoline) from petroleum." In the context of child welfare the "residual approach" examines the left over children separate from the larger society of which they are a part and which contributed to their circumstance.

by the time they enter the system, the number who survive and benefit is minimal. A growing proportion of children are being left to fend for themselves in an increasingly competitive high-technology market economy.

By every standard the residual perspective and the system it spawned have failed to make progress for children. Overall the residual model has not adapted to the major social and institutional changes that have occurred. In critical ways it lacks the instruments to effectively solve the problems confronting impoverished children today. While the residual approach may stave off the most brutal and horrific instances of abuse and poverty, it cannot return the millions of children who live in poverty to the economic and social mainstream.

It is significant to note that the situation children face is not tolerated in other areas of our society. For example, government is quick to provide the technology, infrastructure, and resources that businesses require to compete in the global economy. Entrepreneurs and investors routinely look to government to provide a suitable environment for their economic enterprises. Likewise, through Social Security and Medicare, senior citizens have seen poverty ended among their ranks.

In 2003 more than 13 million children live in poverty in the United States. This poverty is heavily concentrated among children of color. There are few federal programs which address this problem. Further, the few limited programs that deal with child poverty have not proven effective in reducing it. The current programs that deal with it are ill-conceived and outdated. The major barrier continues to be social policies and programs guided by a perspective that requires we wait until severe problems emerge before we act. However, when millions of children live in poverty, with no end in sight, we must begin looking for the root causes and solutions that will prevent disaster before it happens.

The current approach is that resources are allocated to society's less fortunate only when they can be identified. While such a residual approach may have been sufficient in the nineteenth and early twentieth centuries, it is not suited to the social conditions to which our society has evolved. What is needed are innovative and imaginative solutions that will address the problems poor and disadvantaged children face in a postindustrial market economy.

To the extent that the problems which children in poverty face are structural (i.e., induced by external socioeconomic forces and circumstances), they must be approached at that level. During the Great Depression, instead of viewing social problems as the product of the dysfunctional behavior of individuals, social reformers struggled to alter dysfunctional social structures. In the 1950s poverty was greatest among seniors. However, universal coverage of all seniors by way of Social Security and Medicare has dramatically reduced poverty among the elderly. Today rates of poverty among the elderly are among the lowest of all groups.

In the same way, if there is to be any hope of developing workable solutions to child poverty, the child welfare system must begin looking to the wider social and economic problems which families face. We must begin looking for long-term solutions that can be as effective at addressing child poverty as Social Security and Medicaid have been in addressing senior poverty.

The problems that confront the public child welfare system are not insurmountable. Children in poverty can be helped. Their safety and opportunity can be significantly improved. The high rates of poverty that have persisted among them for decades can be substantially reduced. All of this is possible given strategies that account for new realities. The government of the United Kingdom has committed to reducing child poverty by 50 percent in the next ten years and ending child poverty within the next 20 years. They have embarked on major reform to achieve this goal.

Organization of the Second Edition

The second edition of *The Welfare of Children* takes into account two major changes since the publication of the first edition in 1994—one legislative and the other technological. First, the welfare reform legislation of 1996 has fundamentally altered the public child welfare system as broadly understood. The implications of this reform are examined. Second, the internet has emerged as a major source of information on child welfare programs at both the state and federal levels. Throughout the text I provide links to these web based resources. Further, supplementary and updated materials found in the book are now made available at the book's Web site at www.childwelfare.com/book. This allows for continual and periodic updating of the statistics and other material found in the second edition.

Some material only tangential to the thesis has been shortened or removed, while other material more central to the thesis has been expanded for clarification or emphasis. As well, the order of argument has been slightly restructured. Of course, statistical data have been updated while other material and points of view that either had not yet appeared ten years ago or that I was not aware of have been included.

As before, this book is divided into two parts. Part I (chapters 2–7) provides a history of the child welfare system, examining specifically the residual model, which is the form collective responsibility for children has taken from the time the field emerged around 1850, until now. I analyze changes in our society and in the practice of child welfare that have led to the problems we now face. I also provide an overview of what researchers have learned about the effectiveness of child welfare programs. Only when we understand the knowledge base that informs current child welfare practices are we ready to examine their limitations and look toward long-term solutions. Overall, part I seeks to provide the necessary foundation for understanding and critically assessing the public child welfare system and to develop broad new policy initiatives.

Chapter 1 reviews the first century of development in child welfare (roughly 1850 to 1960) which ended, after World War II, with a renewed commitment to child welfare research and to the development of institutions to support that research.

Chapter 2 examines research on the effectiveness of casework—the main approach used by child welfare social workers to serve their clients.

Chapter 3 examines research aimed at improving the effectiveness of the public child welfare agency. Since the 1970s there have been several major child welfare demonstration programs which paved the way for comprehensive reform of child welfare services. We review these studies.

Chapter 4 examines how the child welfare system has adapted to the changing conditions of American families. After World War II mothers began a long steady entry back into the labor force that would continue for the next half century. Increasingly, women with preschool children were expected to work outside the home. Although education (and thus child care) was provided for children ages six to eighteen, very little was available for children under six. The failure to provide universal day care placed increasing demands on the mothers of these children.

Chapter 5 explores the transformation of the public child welfare system into a child protection system. In 1962, in the *Journal of the American Medical Association* C. Henry Kempe and his colleagues reported on hundreds of children under three years of age who had been "battered," and whose broken bones or cranial injuries could not be adequately or consistently explained. The dramatic image of infants being battered horrified the public. Child protection advocates passed mandatory child abuse reporting laws, with the result that annual child abuse reports have risen in the United States from 10,000 in 1962 to more than 3 and a quarter million in 2002. In the ensuing decades, the child welfare system has been redirected from aiding disadvantaged children to investigating child abuse reports.

Critical to the functioning of the child welfare system is the process of decision-making. Which children should be removed from their families and placed in foster care? When should they be removed? These questions are central to effective decision-making of the child welfare system. What process is used to make these decisions? How precise is our knowledge which guides this decision-making by social workers? As will be seen in chapter 6 these critical decisions are rarely made with scientific precision and accuracy.

Chapter 7 questions the soundness of child abuse remaining the principal focus of decision-making. I describe how efforts to protect children from alleged physical and sexual assault have absorbed virtually all the resources of the child welfare system. I argue that the proper place for the investigation and prosecution of physical and sexual assault of children is with the police and judicial system. If the police were to play their appropriate role, the child welfare system could return to its original mandate—serving disadvantaged and deprived children. Child welfare social workers lack the investigative training and coercive authority required to deal with the physical and sexual assault of children. Placing responsibility for protection from abuse with child welfare mires the profession in a morass it cannot solve.

Part II (chapters 8-12) points the way toward long-term solutions for child welfare based upon the needs of children in an advanced global economy in the postindustrial society. This section reviews the major programs and policies that affect children, and explores structural approaches and investments in our social infrastructure that may help to break the cycle of child poverty, neglect, and abuse. It attempts to identify those child welfare problems that are best treated through a structural approach, while redefining and clarifying those services that must continue to be addressed through a residual approach.

Chapter 8 analyzes the distribution of resources in the U.S. and other industrialized market economies, identifying those economic and social assumptions that drive our free market system. How much wealth and income is produced? How are these distributed? How much goes to children, especially children in poverty? With what consequences?

Chapter 9 explores the root causes of many child welfare problems. When young people start a family before they have the resources and maturity to be self supporting they are forced to rely on welfare. For most, the consequence will be a life of poverty and despair. How much of this is part of a larger cycle of poverty stemming from the lack of opportunity for poor children? I examine the development of the welfare system and the criticisms made of it. I suggest approaches that I believe could lead us out of the woods of the too long unresolved welfare debate.

Chapter 10 examines the effects of the most important event affecting poor children in the last several decades—welfare reform of 1996. It is now possible to examine the consequences of this reform for children. Proponents of the reform herald the dramatic drop in the welfare caseload. In most states, the number of children receiving welfare has been cut in half. Several states have achieved a more than three-quarters reduction. What has been the consequence of this dramatic end of welfare as we know it? In this chapter I examine the economic circumstance of poor children post welfare reform.

Chapter 11 examines social policy initiatives and programs designed to alter the current structural arrangements responsible for the condition of poor children. If the families served by child welfare agencies suffer from severe economic hardship, and this hardship is a factor that contributes to the problems child welfare is attempting to solve, social and economic policy changes that address this hardship should be pursued. Further, solutions to these problems do not necessarily require more money as much as rethinking and redesigning policies and programs that have proven ineffective and out of date. For example, children suffer because of an ineffective and obsolete court administered child support collection system. They also suffer because of inequities in the form of the children's allowance program developed in the United States. I review these programs and suggest needed reforms.

Chapter 12 proposes a "social savings" approach that would break the continuing "cycle of poverty" among children. This is essentially the same approach that was used to end poverty among the elderly. In 2003, Britain implemented a Child Trust Fund that uses this approach. No doubt the Child Future Savings Account proposal has limitations, but it suggests the kinds of strategies, within a broader structural understanding of child welfare, that might solve the problems children face. Ending child poverty will take more than providing immediate relief of hardship. Long-term solutions designed to break the cycle of poverty are required.

The closing chapter brings the arguments together and presents a summary of the analysis and a discussion of future directions.

While part II speaks to the current state of affairs in the American child welfare system, it nevertheless rests upon a conceptual foundation established by part I. Understanding the history of child welfare informs the discussion of long-term solutions I believe are necessary and suitable for the problems we face in the twenty-first century. If you are not interested in the historical development of the child welfare system, but would like to examine various approaches designed to ameliorate child poverty, begin with part II. Later, if interest leads you, return to part I.

The child welfare system we know today emerged in its current form during the 1850s. Chapter 1 begins the story.

Part I

The Child Welfare System

> The maltreatment syndrome of children is an intolerable disease and can be eradicated through definite measures and through cooperative integrated efforts by the medical, social and legal disciplines of our society.
>
> V. J. Fontana and D. J. Besharov, *The Maltreated Child*

Child welfare has historically responded to the needs of dependent and neglected children with common sense, energy, and practicality and has been motivated by a sense of moral responsibility and compassion, like the charity movement that preceded it. Lacking a tradition of scientific research, help relied on good intentions and high moral purpose. This approach was satisfactory for only so long in an age of research and science. My interest in part I is to examine what is known from research in the field of child welfare. Has a credible and serviceable knowledge base developed that would permit building an effective child welfare service system?

The Medical Model

There are certain historical and present-day parallels between the child welfare and the medical professions. Prior to the late 1800s, the medical profession was essentially nonscientific. Medical practice was transformed into a respected profession because of the development of scientific knowledge and technology for the treatment of medical problems. Physicians were authorized to prescribe treatment regimens based on their professional judgment as to what would work for a given patient with a particular set of problems (Starr, 1982).

In the second half of the nineteenth century, major advances in medicine occurred. Understanding of human physiology, the autonomic nervous system, the cardiovascular system, and other major components of the human anatomy and organism was greatly advanced. Procedures for surgery were also advanced.

9

The contribution of Joseph Lister provides an illustration. Before Lister's research, people feared surgery—and for good reason—since many didn't survive. The simplest surgery could lead to infection and often death. In fact, death after surgery ranged as high as 50 percent. The research by Louis Pasteur set the stage for Lister's work by focusing on bacteria. After Pasteur discovered that bacteria caused fermentation, Lister discovered that fermentation of pus was also due to germs (bacteria). At first, Lister used carbolic acid spray to kill the bacteria in the air. However, Lister soon realized that the surgeon's hands and medical instruments were principally responsible for carrying bacteria. To prevent the spread of bacteria, Lister urged the use of antiseptics to kill germs on the surgeon's hands and instruments. He demonstrated that following this approach greatly reduced the likelihood of deaths after surgery. In 1880, Lister introduced the use of "catgut gloves" as an additional way to reduce the transmission of bacteria. Mortality after major surgery fell from as high as 50 percent to 5 percent, largely as a result of the application of antiseptics advanced by Lister.

Where is the child welfare field in the development of a scientifically validated knowledge base? Part I examines the current state of knowledge development in the child welfare field. As with medicine, so it is possible in child welfare to develop empirically tested and measured programs and intervention strategies, a scientific discipline and profession that would allow for better service to children and families in need (Desowitz, 1987; Lindblom and Cohen, 1979; Epstein, 1999). I examine the progress the child welfare field has made in this regard.

Taken as a whole part I provides the necessary understanding of the field and background information required to develop broad policy initiatives in the child welfare field. It is written for those who have an interest in understanding how the child welfare system emerged and why it has come to take the form it has. It provides an understanding of the problem that the solutions in part II address.

1

Emergence of the Modern
Child Welfare System

Of Child-Birth. When labour proves tedious and difficult; to prevent inflammations, it will be proper to bleed...She should lose at least half a pound of blood from the arm. Her drink ought to be barley water sharpened with juice of lemon.

William Buchan, M.D., *Domestic Medicine*

Prior to the mid-nineteenth century the practice of medicine was essentially nonscientific, which is to say that the causes of most medical problems were unknown. It was not until the last half of the nineteenth century that germs, viruses, and the host of genetic and functional causes of illness were discovered. Even the mechanisms associated with obvious traumas were known only in a very gross way: "broken bones heal correctly only if reset properly and immobilized." The medical profession was, by and large, restricted to minor symptomatic treatment where that was possible, and palliative "supportive therapy" that consisted primarily of comforting and giving hope. Seriously ill people went to the hospital, such as it was, to die. The beds were arranged so the patients could see the altar and join in the celebration of daily mass. Instead of nurses, the hospital staff was comprised of nuns. The staff administered medicine made from herbs gathered from the wild or cultivated in the convent gardens to relieve the suffering of the patients in their final days.

Given this state of medical development, it was not surprising that even mild illnesses and injuries could prove fatal, especially among the poor. A fall from a roof, resulting only in broken bones, could mean death a few days later. A minor flesh wound in war often festered into an injury that took the soldier's life. What today might be regarded as a routine complication of child birth frequently carried away the mother. A mild flu or cold could escalate into a fever that within hours or days consumed the patient.

Throughout the nineteenth century, and as late as the first decades of the twentieth century, large numbers of children lost their parents in just this fashion, and so became wards of the state. In 1920, more than 750,000 orphaned children—children whose parents had died—could be found in the United States, a number that would decline to less than 2,000 fifty years later. Until the mid-nineteenth century, provision for the welfare of orphaned or abandoned children took the form of institutional custodial care. Children were lodged, as had been the practice since the seventeenth century in Europe, in infirmaries and almshouses (poorhouses) alongside the aged, infirm, and insane. The conditions under which young orphan children were condemned to live were often appalling:

> In no less than three different infirmaries, we found little boys confined, for constraint or punishment, with the insane. In one instance, a little deaf and dumb boy was locked in a cell, in the insane department, opposite a cell in which a violently insane woman was confined. This woman had been casting her own filth, through the shattered panels of her door, at this little boy, the door of whose cell was all bespattered. He was crying bitterly, and, on being released, made signs indicating that he was very hungry. He was locked here to prevent him from running off. This little boy is something over 10 years of age. His father was killed in the war of the rebellion; his mother is an inmate of a lunatic asylum. He (the boy) is of sound body and mind. (*Children in Ohio Infirmaries,* 1867, Albert G. Byers, Secretary of Ohio Board of State Charities, p. 249)

> Last spring I was much attracted by a little girl in the poorhouse, three years old, whose parents were respectable people. The father had been drowned, the mother had an arm so wasted by rheumatism that she was unable to support herself and child. Notwithstanding the painful surroundings, she being one of three respectable women in a room otherwise filled with women of bad character, the love of the mother and child, the one so tender and patient, the other so clinging and affectionate, brought a redeeming flood of light into the darkened room. Shortly after, the mother died. Last autumn I saw the little girl. In the interval she had changed to stone. Not a smile nor a word could be drawn from her. The bright look had faded utterly. She was now under the care of the old pauper-woman. I had known this old woman for more than a year, and ought not therefore to have been surprised at the change in little Mary, and yet I did not recognize the child at first. I could not believe such a change possible. . . . A member of our Committee on Children, Mr. Charles L. Brace, when informed of the condition of these children, offered, as Secretary of the Children's Aid Society, to take all these children, including the little babies, free of charge, and provide them with [foster] homes in the West. But the superintendents declined this offer. They

wished the children to remain in the county, where, as they said, they could see them themselves, look after them, know what became of them. Alas! we know only too well what becomes of children who live and grow up in the poorhouse. (*Children in Westchester County Poorhouse,* New York, 1872, Miss Schuyler, State Charities Aid Association, First Annual Report, 1873, p. 251)

Investigations and exposés of the conditions of almshouses gave rise to a reform movement to place children in more humane surroundings, such as children's orphanages, large custodial institutions that provided food and shelter to sometimes hundreds of children of all ages in a single building. Although expensive to operate, they nevertheless removed children from the abuse, neglect, and despair of the poor houses, and placed them in an environment where their needs could be more adequately addressed. Many children entered the orphanage as infants and left as young adults. Although orphanages were regarded as cold, people-processing institutions lacking the warmth and loving care of a family, they continued to proliferate throughout the 1800s, until by the end of the nineteenth century they housed probably in excess of 100,000 children.[1]

Invention of Foster Care

In New York in 1853, Charles Loring Brace, a young Yale-educated theologian, believed a better way could be found to provide for the children and youth wandering the streets of New York City. As an alternative to life in large custodial institutions such as orphanages and almshouses, Brace founded the Children's Aid Society and developed the "placing-out system" (or foster care) in which orphaned and abandoned children from New York were sent to farm homes in Ohio, Michigan, Illinois, and Indiana (Brace, 1859). The children were sent in groups of about a hundred to designated locations where farmers and their families would gather to receive them. Between 1853 and 1890 the Children's Aid Society alone placed more than 92,000 children from the almshouses, orphanages, and slums of New York City to family farms in the Midwest (Leiby, 1978).

---

[1] In 1882, Hastings Hart presented a census of public institutions for children (Bruno, 1957: 69). According to Hart the total number of children in public and private institutions was 100,000. There were 74,000 children in orphanages; 15,000 were in reformatories, 5,000 in institutions for the feebleminded, 4,500 in institutions for the deaf, and 1,500 in institutions for the blind.

Brace argued that placing children not only provided farm families with needed labor, it gave the children wholesome work and a caring family. Placement represented more than just care and provision of orphaned and abandoned children; it was an avenue of upward mobility and a way for the children to escape poverty. "The very constitution, too, of an agricultural and democratic community favors the probability of a poor child's succeeding. When placed in a farmer's family, [the child] grows up as one of their number, and shares in all the social influences of the class. The peculiar temptations to which he has been subject—such, for instance, as stealing and vagrancy—are reduced to a minimum; his self-respect is raised, and the chances of success held out to a laborer in this country, with the influence of school and religion soon raise him far above the class from which he sprang" (Brace, 1880).

Brace's experiment was favorably received by many people concerned with the problem of orphaned children, and soon became widely used. By the turn of the century the emerging "system" of child welfare consisted not only of numerous large custodial orphanages, but of many foster care agencies that sought to place[2] orphaned and abandoned children out with farm families.[3]

Challenges to Brace

Those who operated orphanages were, not surprisingly, critical of the placing-out system. Was foster care, they asked, really an improvement over an orphanage? Custodial institutions offered professional attention to the needs of the children, which foster families, lacking the training, could not provide. Children placed in orphanages were not dispersed all over the country where their care could not be supervised. The proponents of institutional care were concerned that children placed out in foster homes were too often regarded by their caretakers as indentured servants or even slaves. And, no doubt, some farm families certainly exploited their foster children for their labor.

---

[2] In 1891, J. J. Kelso developed the "placing out" approach in Canada and founded the Toronto Children's Aid Society. Kelso has been viewed as the chief architect of Ontario's, and to a lesser extent, Canada's child welfare system (Bellamy and Irving, 1986; Jones and Rutman, 1981).

[3] Preceding the development of family foster care was the policy of sending vagrant and homeless street children from Britain to colonies around the world.

On the other side, foster care advocates argued that placing out provided a nonrestrictive family home environment in which the children might receive love and care in a manner not found in orphanages. Such arguments were, of course, based not on empirical research but on commonsense views of what was best for children. While Brace received support from New York City officials who facilitated his efforts by pointing to the decline in the number of juveniles arrested—from 5,880 in 1860 to 1,666 in 1876—others voiced concern about where the juveniles were ending up. In 1879, at a national conference on social work, Albert G. Byers of Ohio claimed that Brace simply dumped carloads of delinquents in the Midwest without concern for the welfare of either the children or the states receiving them. John Early of Indiana echoed Byers's concern and declared that many of the children sent from New York ended up in state penitentiaries. Every placed out child from New York that he knew about, with the exception of one, Early said, had gone "to the bad." In 1882, at a national social work conference, a delegate from North Carolina claimed that the farmers receiving the children used them as slaves.

In 1876, stung by accusations by the New York Prison Association that Midwestern prisons were filled with former wards of his placing-out system, Brace sponsored a series of studies to investigate the allegations. He assigned investigators to visit prisons and reformatories in Illinois, Indiana, and Michigan. In 1894, after several years of tracking down and interviewing thousands of people who had been involved in the placing-out experiment, he was able to proclaim, "It was found that in Michigan and Illinois, where 10,000 children had been sent for foster care placement, not a single boy or girl could be found in all their prisons and reformatories!" (Brace, 1894: 348).

In 1894, Hastings Hart, secretary of the Minnesota State Board of Charities, examined the fates of 340 children sent from New York in the previous three years. According to Hart, more than 58 percent of the children either turned out badly or could not be located. Hart found that a few seriously delinquent children had been placed, perhaps without the knowledge of the Children's Aid Society, but placed nonetheless. In addition, Hart found that many children had been hastily placed without adequate supervision to ensure their protection. Hart concluded his study with recommendations that would prevent the placing out of dangerous children and ensure the proper protection of all children once they were placed.

Brace responded to these criticisms by improving the procedures used to place children. However, it was long after Brace's death before the Children's Aid Society implemented procedures to ensure supervision of chil-

dren placed out in distant farm homes. What eventually distinguished foster care, as initiated by Brace and Kelso, from indentured servitude, was
that the children were placed in homes where a Children's Aid Society
caseworker had conducted a "home study" to make sure the family would
provide a suitable home for the child placed in their care. In addition, the
Children's Aid Society periodically reviewed the homes where the children
were placed to monitor their progress. If children were exploited or mistreated, they would, at least in theory, be removed and placed in another,
more suitable home.

The Early Studies of Foster Care

Although questions on the placing-out system lingered, no significant studies on the effectiveness of foster care versus institutional care, or for that
matter any aspect of the emerging child welfare "system," were undertaken
for some 25 years following publication of the last Brace-sponsored studies
(Wolins and Piliavin, 1964). Then, in 1924, Theis published a study entitled, *How Foster Children Turn Out,* which examined a sample of 797
children who at one time had been placed in foster care. After interviewing
two-thirds of the children Theis concluded that "of those whose present
situation is known 77.2 percent are 'capable' persons, individuals able to
manage their affairs with average good sense and who live in accordance
with good standards in their communities" (p. 161). In other words, foster
care, Theis concluded, did not prevent children from becoming responsible
members of the community.

An immediate criticism of Theis's study, one reflected in the foreword
by Holmer Folks, was that it lacked a comparison group of children in institutional care. In 1930, Trotzkey rectified this in a study that included a
sample of 1,214 foster children and a comparison group of 2,532 children
in institutional care. Trotzkey examined the physical and psychological
development of the children and concluded that "both types of care are doing good work and are needed." Trotzkey argued against the critics of institutional care and suggested that to abolish institutions would result in "a
distinct and irreparable loss both to the child and the community" (Trotzkey, 1930: 107).

Following the studies by Theis and Trotzkey, no other significant research on foster care would be attempted until the early 1950s when a consistent effort at conducting research in child welfare would emerge. To
guide the research efforts the child welfare field would need to develop a

consensus on its purpose and domain. Once a definition was agreed upon, practitioners and researchers could begin developing the necessary scientifically tested knowledge base required for professional practice and effective services.

The Redirection of Foster Care: Not Just for Orphans

As the new century neared, and the number of orphans declined, foster care began to be directed toward children whose mothers were viewed as being unable to properly provide for them. Clements, who examined the history of children in foster care in late-nineteenth-century Philadelphia, found that most came from families who were either "too poor or too vicious" to care for them. The children were removed from impoverished lone mothers and placed in "good Christian homes" in the country, which were viewed as providing a clean wholesome environment far removed from the deleterious influences of the urban squalor they came from. The children were returned home only when the mother was able to demonstrate she had the economic resources to properly care for the child (Clement, 1978; Gordon, 1988). Costin (1992: 191) cites a letter from the period (1916) that indicates the patronizing and authoritative attitudes of child welfare workers:

Dear Sir,

During the last week we have heard from several neighbors and numerous friends of yours that you have been drinking a great deal. We also heard that you are partly to blame for your wife's recent conduct [due to your alcoholism]. We urge you to stop drinking, as we are seriously thinking that the home environment is not what it should be for the children.

We hope you will give us no further opportunity to warn and reprimand you.

Very truly yours,
The Associated Charities

Thus, as the number of orphans declined, foster care would come to serve primarily children whose mothers were viewed as being unable to provide for them. It should be noted that the primary concern was not to assist the mothers, but to aid the children. The bias throughout North

America during this period derived from the Puritan tradition that viewed the poor and unemployed as "lazy" and "undeserving" (Sinanoglu, 1981), while mothers of children born out of wedlock were "sinful." Thus, the children placed in foster homes were being rescued by the early social reformers from an immoral and unhealthy environment and placed where clean air, middle-class values, and strong religious guidance were believed to be abundant.[4]

Early Residual Approach to Child Welfare

It is important to note that from the beginning the problem of orphaned and abandoned children was viewed from a *residual perspective*.[5] Without family or resources, abandoned or orphaned children constituted the social "leftovers" (or residual children) who had fallen beyond the economic and social pale. That this may have happened through no fault of their own was of no consequence. They were to be provided for, if at all, as inexpensively and conveniently as possible, enough to satisfy the social conscience but no more. At best, child welfare services were viewed as a grudging handout. As Kadushin and Martin (1988: 673) noted, "In general, arrangements to provide institutional care for children were made for the convenience of the community, not out of the concern for the individual child. Provision of minimal care in the cheapest way was considered adequate care."

Within this residual perspective, numerous internal debates would arise. One question that arose early on was this: which was better, foster care or life in an orphanage? (Barth, 2002; McKenzie, 1999; Wolins and Piliavin, 1964). Later, when the number of orphans and orphanages declined, and foster care emerged as the dominant choice of child welfare intervention,

---

[4]The effort to rescue children from "unsuitable" conditions also characterized the wave of child exports from England during the same period (roughly 1850 to 1950). Altogether about 150,000 homeless and wayward youth were gathered up in urban centers of England and sent to rural farm outposts in Canada, the United States, South Africa, and Australia (Bean and Melville, 1989).

[5] The residual perspective regards state intervention as a measure of last resort to be used only after the resources of the family, kinship network, and neighborhood have been exhausted (Wilensky and Lebeaux, 1965). The residual approach holds that individuals who need help should look first to their family and kinship networks and then to their friends and immediate community. Only if all these sources of support fail should the individual turn to the wider society (government) for help. When the government does help, the residual approach suggests it should be minimal, time-limited, and confined to highly selective forms of help directed to specific categories of need.

the questions would become: How effective is foster care? How and when should it be used? How can children be kept out of it? As we shall see, such questions would guide the direction of research in the field for the next century. However, the underlying premise that neglected, abandoned, and orphaned children were a social problem to be dealt with in a residual fashion would continue unexamined.

The Children's Bureau—The Beginning of a System

[The purpose of the Bureau was to investigate and report] upon all matters pertaining to the welfare of children and child life among all classes of our people. [It was charged to investigate] infant mortality, the birth rate, orphanage, juvenile courts, desertion, dangerous occupations, accidents and diseases of children, employment, and legislation affecting children.

   Dorothy Bradbury and Martha Eliot, *History of the Children's Bureau*

By the turn of the century child welfare had begun shifting from institutional care and placing out of children to a broader definition of what child welfare should involve. The Children's Bureau, established in 1912, was heralded, along with the establishment of the juvenile court, as a major achievement of the Progressive Era. A federal agency, it was responsible for research and dissemination of information about children. In its early years it focused on infant mortality, maternal and child health, child labor, and the promotion of mothers' pensions.

Infant Mortality

In 1900, almost one in five children did not live to the end of the first year. In fact, many children died during birth, and it was not uncommon for the mother to die also, especially if she was poor and the birth was difficult or complicated in any way. Those children who survived were confronted with other threats: pneumonia, diarrhea, cholera, bacterial infections, diphtheria, measles, convulsions, and more. Most deaths were preventable and largely the result of poverty and unsanitary conditions.

   After studying the problem of infant mortality and identifying its causes, the bureau mounted a national campaign advocating sanitary conditions, improvements in well-baby care, prenatal check-ups, and higher standards for milk. Mothers were warned of the dangers of raw milk and informed of the value of breast-feeding. The bureau's efforts brought dramatic success, and a rapid decline in infant mortality continued for the next several decades.

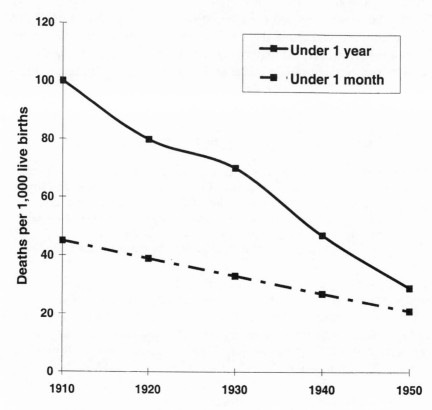

Figure 1.1 Infant Mortality in the United States, 1915–1950

Without question, the efforts of the Children's Bureau resulted in dramatic improvements in the general health of all children. The efforts begun more than 75 years ago continue to impact the lives of children. Today, the rate of maternal and infant mortality is one-fifth what it was when the bureau began (see figure 1.1). Through the bureau's efforts federal legislation to protect the health of mothers and infants was enacted calling for the availability of public health nurses, hospital and medical care for mothers and infants, instruction in hygiene, and centers for advising mothers on child health and development issues. The legislation, passed in 1921 and known as the Sheppard-Towner Bill, provided for federal grants-in-aid to the states to implement its provisions. Regrettably, the bill was repealed seven years later as being too intrusive into affairs of the family.

Child Labor

> Through the eyes of the Bureau, the United States began to see the long procession of her toiling children—grimy, dirty boy workers in mines picking slate from coal, small children working far into the night in tenement homes on garments or artificial flowers, where home was a workshop; groups of small children toiling in fields under a hot summer sun setting onions, picking cotton, topping beets; children picking shrimp and working in canneries; youngsters working at machines in factories.
>
> Dorothy Bradbury and Martha Eliot, *History of the Children's Bureau*

In addition, the Children's Bureau organized research and investigations of the exploitation of children in the labor market. At the turn of the century children could be found working in the coal mines of Kentucky and Tennessee, in the factories of the industrial states, and in agriculture in virtually every state. Early reform efforts brought attention to the exploitation of children for their labor and led to legislation at both the federal and state levels limiting child labor.[6] Overall, as a result of the efforts of the Children's Bureau and the leadership of Julia Lathrop, Edith and Grace Abbot, and others, the exploitation of children for their labor was substantially reduced.

Mother's Pensions—The First Family Preservation Movement

> The power to maintain a decent family living standard is a primary essential in child welfare.
>
> Julia Lathrop

In the 1890s concern had focused on protecting children from cruelty and neglect at the hands of their parents. In the Progressive Era of the early twentieth century this concern was challenged by a family preservation movement critical of the large number of children who were ending up in institutions and foster homes. At a 1909 White House Conference on Children a consensus was reached that children should never be removed from their parents "for reasons of poverty." Mary Richmond (1901) argued that "the cry of 'Save the children' must be superseded by the new cry 'Save the Family,' for we cannot save one without the other." Virtually all the families served by the early "child-savers" had been impoverished widows or mothers raising children by themselves. For the first time, the customary

---

[6] Of course, the mechanization of the modern farm and the resulting decline in demand for child labor was also responsible for progress against the exploitation of children for their labor.

view that indolence or lack of character resulted in poverty was being challenged by social workers.

The child welfare system must, according to social workers, focus on keeping families together and preventing the problems that lone mothers faced. In 1899, the Committee on Neglected and Dependent Children urged the importance of family preservation:

> Do not be in a hurry to send the children to an institution until you are convinced of the hopelessness of preserving the home. Remember that, when the home is broken up, even temporarily, it is no easy task to bring it together again, and that a few dollars of private charity, a friendly visit, a kind word and a helping hand will lift up the courage of the deserving poor; and this is half the battle, because discouragement begets carelessness. (*Report of the Committee on Neglected and Dependent Children.* Proceedings of the 26th National Conference on Charities and Corrections.)

The general child protection attitude that "if child rescue is the object, stick to that and that alone" began giving way to the view that protecting children meant trying to preserve the fragile family unit of the poor mother and her children. Central to preserving the family was the view that poor mothers needed public aid so that they could avoid the conditions that would lead to removal of their children. In 1911, Illinois became the first state to provide aid to dependent children in their own homes through a program of mothers' pensions.

In 1914, the Children's Bureau joined the effort to promote mothers' pension programs with the first of a series of studies demonstrating the value of this approach. The studies included research on the use of mothers' pensions in Denmark, New Zealand, and several of the states. Within the next two years virtually all states were considering mothers' pension schemes to provide aid to dependent children. By 1920, mothers' pension programs had been enacted in 40 states. They became the major mechanism for ensuring that poor mothers could keep their children and preserve their families. In 1921, more than 45,000 families with 120,000 children were receiving assistance through such programs, which would become the precursor of Aid to Dependent Children enacted in 1935 as part of the Social Security Act.

AFDC (Welfare) and Child Welfare

During the Great Depression social welfare became an institutionalized function of government, with the Social Security Act forming the foundation of the modern welfare state in America. Provisions of the act provided income protection (or welfare) not only for the elderly (Old Age Assistance) and the disabled (Aid to the Permanently and Totally Disabled [APTD]), but also families headed by mothers (Aid to Dependent Children [ADC] and later Aid to Families with Dependent Children [AFDC]). The Social Security Act also provided federal support for foster care (through Title IV) for poor families. Despite this shared goal, the administration and control of income protection programs (AFDC and later TANF) remained separate from the child welfare system, including foster care.[7]

The Modern Child Welfare System

By the 1950s the modern child welfare system began to emerge as a major public institution, with child welfare agencies becoming professional state agencies providing foster care and an assortment of other services.[8] In 1956, the Children's Bureau reported that 5,628 staff were employed in public child welfare agencies (Low, 1958). Six states had more than 200 child welfare workers, while only eight states had less than 25 staff. During the 1950s thirty-five states and the District of Columbia passed their first legislation giving local public welfare agencies responsibility for child welfare services. Within the next decade the staff of public child welfare agencies in the United States nearly tripled (see figure 1.2). By 1977, the professional employees in state and local child welfare agencies had doubled again to more than 30,000. Further, child welfare agencies were separate from public welfare agencies, a circumstance that added to the popular support and professional prestige of the child welfare system.

---

[7] In the first edition of his classic textbook on child welfare Kadushin (1967) devoted his longest chapter to the AFDC program. Steiner (1976) posits that since its emergence as a profession child welfare sought to disassociate itself from public assistance, even though these programs accounted for most of the assistance to poor children. Roberts (2002) points out that, "in an attempt to secure bipartisan support for government spending on poor children, liberals such as Senator Walter Mondale abandoned their focus on poverty's harm to children." Nelson (1984) writes, "This was part of a conscious strategy to dissociate efforts against abuse from unpopular poverty programs. The purpose was to describe abuse as an all-American affliction, not one found solely among low-income people."

[8] Foster care has historically been the major expenditure for child welfare agencies. In 1956, 72 percent of total spending for child welfare services by state and local agencies in the United States went for foster care payments (Low, 1958). Analyzing the annual reports of the Ministry of Human Resources in British Columbia between 1978 to 1981, Callahan reported "that funds for 8,700 children in care demanded at least 65 percent of the budget while preventive programs including day care, rehabilitation, special services, and homemakers for 25,000 children received the remaining 35 percent" (1985: 23).

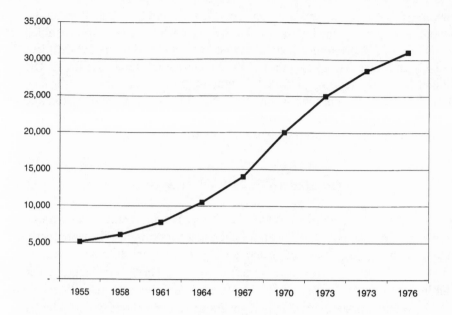

Figure 1.2 Full-time Professional Employees of Public Child Welfare Agencies, 1955 to 1976

As early as 1934 professional organizations had attempted to define the focus of the child welfare field. By 1957, Hagan could write: "Child welfare in social work deals with the problems of the child that result when the needs which parents are ordinarily expected to meet are either unmet or inadequately met." The Child Welfare League of America's (1959) task force on defining child welfare services echoed Hagan's definition. Neither group mentioned child abuse but focused on the needs of disadvantaged children.

Deficit Model

In 1967, Alfred Kadushin, one of the great theorists in the field, published *Child Welfare Services,* his seminal textbook on child welfare. His work, which reflected an encyclopedic knowledge of the research in child welfare at the time, expanded and elaborated on the definition of child welfare proposed by other professionals. It would determine the direction of child welfare for the next three decades. To Kadushin, the child welfare system existed within the traditional residual orientation:

> The approach suggesting that child welfare services are responsible primarily in those situations in which the usual normative social provisions are failing to meet the child's needs adequately is generally called a residual or minimalist orientation to social services. A residual orientation may leave the child without protection until such harm has been done since it is essentially crisis-oriented and reactive rather than proactive, remedial rather than preventive in approach. It is frequently termed a "deficit model," in that it is focused on family breakdown. The aim of this book is to describe the residually oriented activities that child welfare services actually do perform. (Kadushin and Martin, 1988: 7-8)[9]

Operating within the residual perspective, Kadushin maintained that child welfare social workers must look to and understand the parent/child relationship, because it was from problems in this relationship that the need for social work intervention arose. The child welfare system was:

> a network of public and voluntary agencies in social work practice that specialize in the prevention, amelioration, or remediation of social problems related to the functioning of the parent-child relationship through the development and provision of specific child welfare services: services to children in their own home, protective services, day care, homemaker service, foster family care, services to the unwed mother, adoption services, and institutional child care. (Kadushin and Martin, 1988: 24)

The Traditional Residual Model

According to Kadushin, child rearing was the responsibility of parents. He identified a number of role responsibilities that parents had in raising their

---

[9] Kadushin and Martin (1988: 24) recognized that "the contrasting developmental orientation suggests that child welfare services are social utilities, like public schools, libraries, and parks" (see Wilensky and Lebeaux, 1958). Such services, then, should be made available to all children in all families and should be appropriately helpful to all. Child welfare services, rather than being only for the "poor, the troubled, the dependent, the deviant and the disturbed," should also be directed to "average people under ordinary circumstances" to meet "normal living needs" (Schorr, 1974; Kahn and Kamerman, 1975; Kahn, 1976). Nevertheless, Kadushin preferred the residual model.

children.[10] If all went minimally well in these responsibilities, there would be no need for state involvement. He also identified circumstances in which parents failed to fulfill their responsibilities, and which would require the intervention of public child welfare.[11] The child welfare system helped parents meet their responsibilities through the provision of supportive and supplementary services or, when that was not possible, by removing the children and providing substitute care. Kadushin viewed the child welfare system as a system designed to provide services that would assist parents in meeting their obligations to their children. He identified three levels of intervention to characterize the hierarchy of services that child welfare agencies provided:

- *Supportive.* Direct service programs, such as in-home counseling to help parents fulfill their parental responsibilities, were designed to strengthen and preserve the family.
- *Supplementary.* The provision of income assistance (TANF) or in-kind services, such as homemaker services and day care, would help parents carry out their parental role responsibilities.
- *Substitute.* If the parent was unable to meet the essential parental role responsibilities, even with the provision of supportive and supplementary services, services to temporarily replace (or substitute for) the biological parent, such as foster family care, group care, residential treatment and, when appropriate, adoption, would be provided.

Although the traditional model proposed a three-tier service approach, the residual perspective had the effect of ratcheting the system down so that foster care became the heart of child welfare. The residual model, especially in difficult economic times, required limiting services to the most serious cases. Over time the child welfare system became a crisis intervention service where only the most seriously harmed children received attention. The needs of families that did not require the child to be removed

---

[10] The role responsibilities of the parent include providing (1) income (for food, shelter, clothes, etc.); (2) emotional security and love; (3) discipline; (4) protection from harm and danger; (5) education; and (6) socialization.

[11] Problems of role functioning are categorized by Kadushin as (1) parental role unoccupied, e.g., death of parent; (2) parental incapacity, e.g., serious illness, drug addiction; (3) parental role rejection, e.g., neglect or abandonment; (4) intrarole conflict, e.g., neither parent takes responsibility for care and discipline; (5) interrole conflict, e.g., competing demands prevent adequate care of child; (6) child incapacity, e.g., autism, epilepsy, brain injury; (7) deficiency of community resources, e.g., unemployment, economic depression.

would have to wait. Supportive services such as counseling and parent training were usually the first to be cut, while supplementary services such as day care never became a principal concern. Although Kadushin listed these in his textbook, in practice they were rarely provided by child welfare agencies.

During its early history the child welfare system was concerned primarily with supportive and substitute care services. Although originally viewed as central to child welfare, income maintenance programs (such as TANF and social assistance) are now viewed as outside the domain of child welfare (Steiner, 1976: 36–39). Although Kadushin, in his early formulations, was concerned with the importance of income security programs like TANF, he eventually came to view income security programs and issues of economic well-being as outside the scope of the child welfare social worker.[12] Income maintenance and child welfare are now provided by separate agencies and departments, with little formal connection between the two.

The residual perspective assumes that the troubles of those families served by the child welfare system derive from shortcomings in the parents (that is, a moral, psychological, physiological, or some other personal failing) that must be addressed through casework. As Martin (1985: 53) observes, "The residual perspective incorporates the psychological rationale. Underpinning this ideological set is the belief that our society offers opportunities for all families to provide for the physical, emotional, and social needs of their children and, consequently, that failure in these tasks is a failure of the parent(s) or possibly the family as a whole. Service intervention is thus focused on seeking change at the individual or family level." The child is seen as needing protection from these failings. Foster care emerged as the major tool the child welfare system uses to deal with parental and family problems. The agency removes the child and then watches and hopes that the family will sufficiently heal itself to take the child home again. Only occasionally are services provided to the parent.

As a result of the arguments put forth by Kadushin and other child welfare theorists the residual model was cemented into place as the underlying premise on which the entire edifice of traditional child welfare practice rested. During the formative years of the profession, it provided the framework and underlying assumptions for essentially all research that would occur. It shaped the questions to be asked. It narrowed the aspira-

---

[12] This can be seen by Kadushin's treatment of AFDC in the first edition of his textbook (1967). Originally, Kadushin included a major chapter on AFDC. In the fourth edition (1988) this chapter was omitted.

tions and opportunities the child welfare system might have. The major textbooks in the field continue to advocate the residual approach (Kadushin and Martin, 1988; McGowan and Meezan, 1983). McGowan and Meezan (1983: 505) argue:

> We believe it is unrealistic to expect the child welfare field to expand its boundaries to the point where it could assume the responsibility of providing for the welfare of all children, and we would urge a renewed emphasis on its original function of providing services to children whose developmental needs cannot be fully met by their own families, even with the assistance of the community support services available to all families and children. In other words, we view child welfare as essentially a residual service system.

Why did Kadushin and his colleagues choose to define child welfare within a residual perspective? Its major advantage is that it allows the profession to *target* limited services to those most in need. In this sense, the residual perspective differentiated child welfare from other activities that were supportive of the general welfare of children, such as the Girl Scouts, Campfire Girls, and the Boy Scouts. Child welfare was directed toward disadvantaged or needy children. Thus, the choice of the residual perspective was, in large measure, pragmatic. There were many children who could benefit from publicly supported programs (Zeitz, 1964). If services were made available to all children, the amount available to any one child would be limited. Further, it was believed that disadvantaged children were more in need of the limited resources of child welfare than were others.

The choice of the residual perspective was also in keeping with a cherished belief in protecting the privacy of the family. Within this view, "the State should not interfere in the rearing of children unless it can be shown that the child is exposed to a serious risk of harm" (Archard, 1993: 122). The residual perspective conformed to this view. Involvement of agents of the public child welfare system was to be invoked only when the child was at risk of harm because of parental failures. As Goldstein, Freud, and Solnit (1979: 9) argue: "The child's need for safety within the confines of the family must be met by law through its recognition of family privacy as the barrier to state intrusion upon parental autonomy, a child's entitlement to autonomous parents, and privacy—are essential ingredients of 'family integrity.' " The decision of Kadushin and others in the child welfare field to stay with the residual perspective was in keeping with the history of the field. Yet, as we shall learn, this decision was to have profound consequences for the growth and development of the profession.

Development of Institutional Support for Research in Child Welfare

From the start of the century to the years immediately following World War II child welfare social workers had been working to establish themselves as "professionals" responsible for the organization and management of child-serving institutions (both foster and institutional care). Their efforts, as we have seen, were mainly organizational. The charity movement provided its own motive and rationale for child welfare staff in the early period. Limited scientific research had been undertaken to justify or guide their actions. Following World War II this came to be regarded as a great lack, since, with the impetus and prestige given science and technology by the war, a coherent scientific knowledge base was something increasingly necessary for any group wanting to regard itself as "professional" and "scientific."

One reason for the dearth of research in child welfare is that before 1948 no professional journal that might attract research existed. In that year, the Child Welfare League changed its *Bulletin*, which until that time had been essentially a newsletter discussing professional matters, into a professional journal entitled *Child Welfare*. The editor observed, "This first issue of *Child Welfare* . . . marks our rededication to better services for children. The content is particularly appropriate, for each article tells of efforts of social agencies that promise decidedly better service" (Gordon, 1948: 10).

The following year *Child Welfare* published an article entitled "The Challenge to Research" by Gunnar Dybwad (1949: 9), in which the author began: "If we pose as our first question, 'Why do we need research?' the simplest answer might be: To explain and evaluate what we have done in the past; to be able to defend or even to understand what we are doing now; and to plot the guideposts of future planful action." It was, however, difficult to conduct major empirical studies without proper funding. Dybwad pointed out that "in 1947 the Army and Navy together spent $500 million for research, and the Department of Agriculture spent $13 million, of which no less than $1,300,000 worth of research was spent on cows; as contrasted to $50,000 available to the Children's Bureau for research (1/26th of the amount spent for research on cows)."

Although Dybwad chafed at the lack of money, he was aiming in another direction: "As social workers, we must either relinquish the claim of constituting a professional group, or we must acknowledge that one of the basic criteria of a profession is its use of scientific analysis in constant self-evaluation."[13] Dybwad's plea for research was being echoed in the broader field of social work (Abbott, 1942; French, 1949; Karpf, 1931; Todd, 1919). Since the early formation of the profession, social work had been concerned with the development of a method or approach that would allow it to persuade the general public that practitioners should be relied on to solve the problems of the disadvantaged and the poor. The primary method developed by social work was "casework." Casework procedures were particularly suited to the needs of child welfare social workers, since they allowed for the careful tracking of children who became the responsibility of the state. Casework procedures were used to conduct "home studies" to determine the suitability of a prospective foster home. Once children were in care, casework provided a method for monitoring the progress of children.

The casework method promoted by Mary Richmond in the early decades of the century emphasized systematic, efficient, and accurate record keeping along with an attitude of scientific investigation and understanding of the client's problems.[14] Along with developing a professional approach, Richmond identified the need for social work to specify its knowledge base. For Richmond the focus of casework was the individual and his or her problems. Knowledge and theory about human behavior were viewed as central to effective casework practice. In 1917, Richmond published her *Social Diagnosis,* which symbolized the transition "from Darwin to Freud, from environmentalism to the psyche [which] had startling consequences" for the social work field (Wenocur and Reisch, 1989: 69).

Richmond's emphasis on the psychological problems of the disadvantaged and poor offered charity workers the opportunity to move "beyond

---

[13] During its earliest years *Child Welfare* was the major journal in the child welfare field. The journal was published by the Child Welfare League of America (CWLA). The membership of the league was not individual child welfare social workers, but public and private child-serving agencies. Thus, the league was governed by the executives and managers of these agencies. One consequence of this structure was a reluctance to criticize or question the effectiveness of child welfare service agencies (see Lindsey, 1978).

[14] The social work profession emerged from a dialectic between its two major theorists— Jane Addams and Mary Richmond. At the turn of the century there was considerable debate as to the best method or approach for social work. Jane Addams (1910) developed the settlement movement at the Hull House. The settlement house movement advocated a broader community organization and social change approach. Addams (1902) was critical of the approach taken by Richmond because it established the caseworker in a role of "moral guardian" to the disadvantaged and poor. Although this concern was appropriate to understanding the problems of the poor, the needs of orphaned and abandoned children required adult supervision and intervention. Addams also criticized the "negative, pseudo-scientific spirit" of the casework approach. Wenocur and Reisch (1989) argue that the casework approach advocated by Richmond prevailed, owing in part to its sponsorship by the powerful elites such as the Russell Sage Foundation and universities.

benevolence and morality into the sanctified realm of scientific expertise" (Wenocur and Reisch, 1989: 59). But where and how were social workers to focus their research? Children who had been orphaned and placed in foster homes did not require psychological treatment. Fortunately for Richmond, the fundamental premise of child welfare social work was changing. Because of advances in medical care and the broad improvement in living conditions, the number of orphans in the United States began declining sharply. In 1920, there were 38 million children and 750,000 orphans. By 1962, the number of children had increased to 66 million, and the number of orphans had dropped to a mere 2,000. Despite this, the number of children in foster care had increased from 73,000 in 1923 to 177,000 in 1962. *Foster care or institutional care was no longer being provided primarily to orphaned children, but to children who were coming to the attention of the child welfare system for very different reasons.* What were the psychological, sociological, political, and economic reasons that these children were being placed in foster care? The early research comparing foster care with institutional care had made no attempt to address such questions. The 1950s began with a call for research to find the answers.

In 1956, the *Social Service Review* published the proceedings of the Conference on Research in the Children's Field. Present at the conference were many who would participate in constructing an empirical knowledge base for child welfare and serve as architects of the changing child welfare system. Addressing the conferees Alfred Kahn (1956: 343) urged:

> The writer remembers the poet's theme that "free [people] set themselves free." We should do what we can to facilitate research and to create the necessary structures and institutions. But we must do more, as educators, as members of professional associations, and as practitioners, to assure that we become, and help prepare others to become, the kind of social workers who will undertake research because they need to and want to. Such social workers will themselves create the necessary practical arrangements.

Such was the clarion call for the development of a scientific knowledge base that would support, justify, and direct the practice of child welfare. In all of it, however, the assumption that child welfare was a perennial social phenomenon that must be viewed and dealt with in a residual manner continued unchallenged (Brieland, 1965).

The Golden Age of Research in Child Welfare

> Of all the children we studied, better than half of them gave promise of living a major part of their childhood years in foster families and institutions. Among

them were children likely to leave care only when they came of age, often after
having had many homes—and none of their own—for ten or so years.

                    Henry Maas and Richard Engler, Jr., *Children in Need of Parents*

The most important study to signal the era of research in child welfare
came from two researchers at the School of Social Welfare at the University of California, Berkeley—Henry Maas and Richard Engler, one a social
worker, the other a sociologist.

In 1959, after several years of exhaustive study and research of the public and voluntary child welfare system in the United States, Maas and
Engler published *Children in Need of Parents,* the first large-scale study of
foster care as it operated in a representative sample of communities.[15] The
researchers found that children removed from their biological parents and
placed with a foster family on what was to be a "temporary" basis often
lingered in foster care for an indeterminate number of years. Further, most
children experienced multiple placements. Joseph H. Reid (1959) of the
Child Welfare League of America, in the study's call for action, noted that
of the 268,000 children in foster care, "roughly 168,000 children [were] in
danger of staying in foster care throughout their childhood years. And although in a third of the cases at least one parent did visit the child, in approximately half the parents visited infrequently or not at all."

Since the early 1900s the number of orphans had been steadily declining, so that by mid-century foster care was being provided to children with
one or more living parents. Foster care had changed from serving orphaned
children to serving "neglected children."

Maas and Engler reported neglect and abandonment as the most common reason for placement in foster care, followed by death of the parents,
illness, economic hardship, and marital conflict (see table 1.1). (It is important to note that *no mention was made of child abuse as a causative factor*,
an issue we will discuss in a later chapter.)

---

[15] In a market economy consumers hold power because of their ability to choose one product or service over another. The problem in the social services, and child welfare in particular, is that free-market forces do not operate. Instead of freely choosing from among a spectrum of services, clients rarely have any choice. Decisions regarding the type and character
of services offered reside with the agency providing them, a circumstance that too often
voids accountability to the client. In the absence of a market mechanism that would make
the social service delivery system accountable, the child welfare system has had to rely on
other ways to achieve accountability. Evaluation research studies emerged as one solution
to accountability—the best method for monitoring the success or failure of child welfare
programs.

**Table 1.1 Factors Causing Foster Care Placement of Children in the
Maas and Engler Study (1959)**

Causative Factor	Referrals (%)
Neglect and abandonment	29
Death, illness, and economic hardship	25
Marital conflict	10
Unwed motherhood	9
Psychological problems	4
Other	24

Note: No mention of child abuse.

In reviewing the original data collected by Maas and Engler, Dwight
Ferguson (1961: 2) observed that "there was a direct relationship between
the proportion of children who came into foster care because of economic
hardship and the size of the AFDC grant." Those families who received a
sufficient AFDC grant were able to adequately care for their children and
were less likely to have their children removed. However, when the grant
was too small, the families were in danger of losing their children. Ferguson complained, "Children are being separated from their parents where
the primary problem in the family is economic hardship" (1961: 2). Reviewing the findings from the Maas and Engler study, Gordon (1960: 29–
30) observed, "the low economic level of the families, poor housing, low
income, inadequate medical care, lack of educational and employment opportunities particularly for the minority groups were found to be among the
reasons for children needing placement."

Foster care was now commonly viewed as a temporary boarding arrangement for children while their parents could address severe personal,
financial, or relationship problems (with orphaned children being placed
through adoptive services). The intent was to provide casework services to
the parents in order to permit reunification with their child.

The average time spent for children in foster care in the Maas and
Engler study was three years. Apparently child welfare agencies sought to
aid distressed families by removing the children until the families could
demonstrate an ability to adequately provide for them. However, few biological families were able to show enough improvement to warrant returning the children. Thus, the children lingered in "temporary" foster care for
long periods of time, often extending over many years. Joseph Reid termed
such children languishing in foster care *orphans of the living*.

Not only did Maas and Engler provide a critical analysis of the foster care system that had developed in the United States, they provided the first comprehensive scientific look at the nation's child welfare system. They investigated the system at eight broadly representative sites. With national statistics on the child welfare system lacking, their data permitted the first general understanding of how foster care was working across the United States. The research revealed that foster care was no longer a service provided to orphaned children, but rather had been transformed into a holding service provided to living parents who, for a variety of reasons, were unable to care for their children or viewed as such by child welfare caseworkers. Further, foster care often became long-term substitute care.

In 1963 in a national survey of child welfare agencies across the United States, Helen Jeter of the Children's Bureau corroborated many of Maas and Engler's findings. Based on data collected from forty-two states, Jeter (1962) estimated that 115,168 children were in foster care and 63,391 children were living in institutions (51,000 in private voluntary institutions for dependent and neglected children). When she compared the length of time in care for the national sample with the representative sample in the Maas and Engler study, Jeter found them similar (see table 1.2).

Table 1.2 Length of Time in Foster Care Reported in Published Studies

Wires and Drake (1952)	Percent	Shyne and Schroeder (1978)	Percent
5 years or less	65	Up to 1 year	29
6 to 10 years	26	1 to 4 years	36
11 to 15 years	9	4 or more years	34
Maas and Engler (1959)		**Tatara and Pettiford (1985)**	
Up to 1.5 years	28	Up to 1 year	37
1.5 to 5.5 years	44	1 to 2 years	20
5.5 years and over	28	2 to 5 years	22
		5 or more years	18
Jeter (1960)		**Fanshel and Shinn (1978)**	
Up to 1.25 years	31	Up to 1 year	24
1.25 to 5.25 years	41	1 to 2 years	13
5.25 years and more	27	2 to 3 years	8
		3 to 4 years	9
		4 to 5 years	7
		5 or more years	39

Moreover, few of the children in Jeter's sample were orphaned. Only 14 percent of the children had lost one or both parents (compared to 23 percent in 1945), while only 1 percent had lost both parents. Thus, foster care now took on the meaning of "temporary care." Since these children had a living parent, they could go home. Agencies were preparing these children for return to (or reunification with) their parents. This was a major change in child welfare—foster care placement was now understood as *temporary*. Children were placed in foster homes so that their parents could have time to "get back on their feet" and be able to take their children back home. Yet, most of the children studied by Maas and Engler had been lingering in foster care for years even though they had living parents. They were being treated like orphans even though they were not. Again, the children had become in Reid's term *orphans of the living*.

In addition, the Jeter study, reported before the "discovery of the battered child syndrome" by Kempe and his colleagues (1962), found wide variations in the use of foster care, some states having foster care placement rates four times greater than other states. As did Maas and Engler, Jeter examined children's "reason for placement." While children were entering foster care for a variety of reasons (table 1.3), little was being done to address those reasons.

Table 1.3 Problems Presented by Children Receiving Child Welfare Services in the Jeter Study (1960)

Problem	Referrals (%)
Neglect, abuse, or exploitation of child	36
Parents not married to each other	7
Child in need of guardianship	8
Illness of parent	9
Interpersonal relationships	9
Child's behavior or condition	17
Financial need of family	5
Unemployment	2
Other	8

As Maas and Engler had found, children were placed in foster care and simply left. Maas and Engler had made the point that foster care could be harmful to children. Concurrent with their research, psychological research was now revealing that parental love and affection were critical to the healthy development of children.

Attachment Theory: Advances in Psychological Research

Shortly after Maas and Engler published their research on children in foster care, Harry Harlow (1958, 1961; Harlow and Zimmerman, 1959) at the University of Wisconsin Primate Center in Madison began a series of experiments with monkeys that would have profound implications for understanding the potential harm of long-term foster care. Although Harlow was probably unaware of the Maas and Engler study and had little interest in foster care, his work would have major implications for understanding the impact of foster care on children.

An experimental psychologist, Harlow wanted to understand the importance of a mother's nurturing on the growth and development of a child. He examined what happened to an infant monkey that was raised in a wire cage that provided necessary physical nourishment but did not permit any emotional interaction or attachment with other monkeys. The monkey's cage allowed it to see and hear other monkeys but did not allow any physical contact. Harlow observed that the infant raised in the isolated cage suffered from intense neurotic behavior when compared to an infant monkey raised with a cloth surrogate mother. When placed with other monkeys, the isolated monkey would spend most of its time huddled in a corner, rocking and clasping itself. The monkey raised with the cloth surrogate did not develop the same problems. Further, the effects of social isolation continued for the experimental monkey into adulthood.

Harlow's experiments provided dramatic evidence of the importance of parental affection and care to the developing child. The research emphasized the importance of providing children with parental nurturing. Children growing up in institutions or in a series of foster homes were deprived of the essential bonding and attachment that comes from a parent.

The implications of this were further examined by the research of John Bowlby (1965, 1973, and 1980), who discovered that children who had been separated from their parents during the second or third year of life (because of war or other reasons) suffered severe distress. Most had been cared for in hospitals or residential nurseries without a mother or mother substitute. According to Bowlby (1969), the "loss of the mother" during this early period of life generated "depression, hysteria, or psychopathic traits in adults." From his extensive research Bowlby concluded that dis-

ruption of the continuity of the emotional relationship with the parent seriously disrupts the normal development of a child.[16]

The implication of Harlow and Bowlby's research for child welfare
was obvious. Children deprived of parental love and affection not only suffered from stunted psychological development but also experienced dis-
torted and harmful developmental consequences. As the famous child development scholar Urie Bronfrenbrenner points out, parents provide their
children with "irrational love," a commodity they can get nowhere else.
Developmental and child psychiatrists interpreted the results to mean that
removing children from their parents, for whatever reason, was harmful to
their development (Goldstein, Freud, and Solnit, 1978). Foster care could
no longer be considered a harmless intervention applied for the benefit of
the child. If used inappropriately, it could cause severe psychological harm.
Further, the multiple placements many children experienced were especially harmful. Maas and Engler (1959: 1) had observed that "children who
move through a series of families are reared without close and continuing
ties to a responsible adult [and] have more than the usual problems in dis-
covering who they are. These are the children who learn to develop shal-
low roots in relationships with others, who try to please but cannot trust, or
who strike out before they can be let down. These are the children about
whom we were most concerned."

The line of research by Bowlby laid the foundation for the permanency
planning movement, which would follow a decade later and which would
emphasize the importance of ensuring that all children have a sense of
permanency in their life (see chapter 3). Children must not be left to drift in
foster care because such drift would detrimentally impact their emotional
and psychological development. Despite this, caseworkers in child welfare
agencies continued to believe that foster care, in and of itself, was not necessarily harmful to all children. Who was right? Was foster care, by its
very nature, harmful or not? What exactly was the impact of foster care on
children and did it influence their development? To answer these questions,
longitudinal research on the impact of foster care was necessary.

Longitudinal Study of Children in Foster Care

In 1963, the Child Welfare League of America and the National Association of Social Workers sponsored an Institute on Child Welfare Research,

---

[16] Several modern investigators have questioned the research by Bowlby. Rutter (1981) and
Clarke and Clarke (1976) have questioned the importance of mother-infant bonding postulated by Bowlby. Also see Johnson and Fein (1991).

which became a catalyst for basic research on foster care to be carried out by researchers in the School of Social Work at Columbia University (Norris and Wallace, 1965). The resulting study was *Children in Foster Care: A Longitudinal Investigation,* by David Fanshel and Eugene Shinn. This study provided the basic empirical research that laid the ground work for subsequent demonstration programs in child welfare.

In 1965, Fanshel and Shinn examined a sample of 659 children who entered foster care in New York over a five-year period. The researchers found a system that was not guided by any systematic scientific knowledge or principles. Although most children who came into foster care eventually left, they spent years in foster care before getting out. In most cases, the home situation they returned to had not improved. In fact, the economic situation of the family had, in many instances, deteriorated.

The study focused on the impact of foster care on the psychological and social development of children. Using a battery of psychological, intellectual, and emotional measures, the study provided a careful, objective, and comprehensive assessment of the impact of foster care on children. Fanshel and his colleagues found little evidence that foster care had a detrimental impact on children in terms of personality, intellectual growth, or social development and behavior.[17] In fact, most children appeared to improve slightly while in foster care.[18]

The study by Fanshel and Shinn (1978) revealed that the most important determinant of how well children did in foster care was *parental visiting.* Those children who were visited most by their parents while in foster care showed greater improvement and were most likely to be restored to their parent(s). As with earlier studies, Fanshel and Shinn found that many children remained in foster care more than five years, and that many had experienced multiple placements.

According to Fanshel and Shinn (1978), "Of those children who remained in foster care after five years, more than half had not been visited

---

[17] The Fanshel and Shinn (1978) study focused on measuring how the psychological well being of children removed from their parents and placed in foster care changed. The limitation with this approach is that children are malleable and resilient. They adjust to difficult and disruptive situations without evidencing measurable harm. This same problem can be seen in recent studies of the impact of welfare reform on child well being. Most of the studies have been unable to identify significant measurable harm even though the economic situation of many of the children has declined.

[18] These earlier findings are similar to recent research. Buehler, Orme, Post, and Patterson (2000) compared the outcomes of foster children with a matched comparison group and found the groups were similar on almost all indicators of adjustment (see McKenzie, 2003).

by their parents for more than a year."[19] Here again were the orphans of the living decried in the Maas and Engler study. Fanshel and others began to ask why, in the absence of contact with their parents, children were being kept in foster care, which was not a treatment modality, but rather the least restrictive form of out-of-home care, intended only for a temporary period.

The practice of placing out children had been seen by Brace and his contemporaries as a "permanent solution" for orphaned children, even though the Children's Aid Society retained custody of the placed children. Many of the children placed out were orphaned or abandoned and unlikely to return home. Current foster care, on the other hand, was different. Since the 1950s, central to the definition of foster care was the assumption that the child should be reunited with its family as soon as the parent could solve the problems that led to placement (see Goldstein, Freud, and Solnit, 1973).[20]

In 1972 and 1975, Shirley Jenkins and Elaine Norman conducted a collateral study on the same sample of children examined by Fanshel. Jenkins and Norman were concerned with filial deprivation—that is, the impact on parents of having their children taken away. What feelings did the parents experience? How did they cope with the loss? What services were provided them? After all, if their children were being removed, it made sense to assume that services would be provided that would enable them to get their children back.

Jenkins and Norman found, not surprisingly, that the mothers experienced enormous sadness and emotional pain at the loss of their children which lasted for years. For most of the mothers the loss was heartfelt and devastating. Nevertheless, the child welfare agencies provided few services to the mothers. Little effort was made to address the problems that had led to the children's removal. Despite this, most of the children were eventually returned to their parents, even though their circumstances had changed little, and in many cases had even deteriorated.

Overall, the studies illuminated an almost Kafkaesque system, in which removal of children from their parents merely aggravated individual pain and suffering, which the agencies seemed neither to understand nor appre-

---

[19] In a review of the foster care system in New York City by the National Black Child Development Institute it was found that 55 percent of the children who entered care in 1986 were still there four and a half years later. They also reported that 70 percent of black children who entered in 1986 were still in care four years later (Children's Defense Fund, 1983: 43).

[20] In 2000, reunification remained the major stated goal for children in foster care. Foster care was the stated goal for over 50 percent of the children in care who had a goal established (Administration for Children and Families, 2002).

ciate. There was little evidence that systematic efforts were being made to restore foster care children to their parents. The primary method used to restore children consisted of casework, and since few children were being returned home expeditiously, it was reasonable to question the effectiveness of casework services.[21]

Summary and Conclusion

Child welfare arose in the latter half of the nineteenth century as a societal response to the needs of children who were orphaned or abandoned, or whose parents were unable to care for them. It began with orphanages that provided food and shelter and limited instruction. Soon after, "placing out" or foster care emerged as a response to the high cost and limited public satisfaction with large state-operated orphanages. Foster care provided the child a family setting, and was less restrictive and less expensive. Shifting the care of children from large custodial institutions into foster family boarding homes was viewed as progressive reform.

With the decline in the number of orphans, child welfare agencies expanded their focus to a broader concern for the welfare of impoverished and neglected children. They provided services to children whom, it was believed, were not adequately cared for by their parent(s) and needed to be removed to substitute care. Over time these residual services evolved into a safety net to protect those children who were at greatest risk of harm through abandonment or neglect.

By 1950, foster care became the major service provided by public child welfare agencies. At about the same time, an effort to develop an understanding of foster care was initiated. Leaders in child welfare called for research and empirical studies that would examine its effects. One of the first studies by Maas and Engler (1959) indicated that children temporarily placed in foster care underwent numerous placements and lingered in care for years. Nevertheless, later research found little evidence of a distinc-

---

[21] As with any professional discipline, the child welfare field during this time wished to emphasize the depth and breadth of its knowledge base (Costin and Rapp, 1984). But the fact was that child welfare had not built an empirically validated knowledge base as was found in physics, chemistry, or public health. The nature of the discipline did not permit the discovery of immutable laws of nature that could be formalized into exact mathematical equations (see Ravetz, 1971; Glazer, 1974). Nor had child welfare developed any powerful theoretical approaches (as in economics, sociology, and psychology) that provided new insight and understanding into the areas of child welfare. Although the introductory textbooks at the time created the impression that there was a highly developed knowledge base, child welfare was, and remains today, essentially a young and undeveloped field.

tively harmful effect resulting from foster care (Fanshel and Shinn, 1978). Fanshel and Shinn found that one of the most important variables determining a child's progress while in foster care was the extent of parental visiting, which affected both the length of stay and how well the child adjusted while in foster care.

Overall, the basic research conducted during the early history of child welfare provided a framework for understanding the child welfare system and the efficacy of approaches designed to serve children. Other research was also under way, research that questioned the single method at the very heart of child welfare—casework—as well as research that attempted to reform the system as a whole. In the next chapter we look at research that attempted to answer the question: How effective is casework?

2

Child Welfare Research:
The Effectiveness of Casework

The great method of experimental research [should be as] closely knit into the work of the good school of social welfare as research has been embodied in the program of the modern medical school.

Edith Abbott, *Social Welfare and Professional Education*

They do things that the Food and Drug Administration (FDA) would never allow you to do with a drug! . . . They're administering a drug—a program, an intervention—and when they're told it doesn't work, they ignore that. Programs should not be implemented on the basis of good marketing and deep pockets. There should be some scientific quality control.

Richard Gelles, "The Children's Crusaders"

What Is Casework?

The core skill available to the child welfare social worker operating within the residual model has been the casework method. First created and implemented by Mary Richmond in the early twentieth century, it allows the social worker to examine the family's problem and to develop a plan to address the family's needs. Casework proceeds on the assumption that underlying the family are certain fundamental "psychodynamic" principles of human relationship and being, both individual and collective, which in the case of the troubled family have gone awry. The caseworker's task is to unravel the complexities of these problems—social and psychological—and so help the family reestablish a stable functionality (Richmond, 1917).

From its beginning, child welfare has been ideally suited to the casework method. The placing-out or foster care approach introduced by Charles Loring Brace lent itself to the features provided by casework. The need for developing a case plan for each child in foster care and monitoring their progress was best achieved by a caseworker who was responsible for completing a "home study" before a child would be placed in a prospective foster family. One hundred years later, the caseworker is still responsible for the child's placement and supervision, as well as working toward restoring (reunification) the child to his or her biological parents as soon as that is possible, or, if that is not possible, developing a plan for "terminating parental rights" and freeing the child for adoption.

The Modern Caseworker

Today, what happens between the client and the child welfare caseworker is at the heart of child welfare services. Although the duties of a modern caseworker vary from agency to agency, a general pattern of what casework involves in a practical way can be described. The caseworker is responsible for collecting information, analyzing and investigating the situation of the parent and child who have, for one reason or another, come to the attention of the child welfare agency (Gambrill, 1997). The original term for this task was "social diagnosis" which also included an examination of the social context of the family's problems.

The premise underlying casework is that the caseworker can identify the family's problem and develop a plan to fix it. Formulating this plan will first involve assessing the client's eligibility for services, usually through an investigation of the client's current situation. This may involve interviewing all concerned parties—biological parents, children, school officials, neighbors, professionals (such as police involved in the case, clergy, and others). The plan will ultimately identify what activities and services—such as job training, parenting and homemaking skills, drug or alcohol treatment and rehabilitation programs, remedial education—will meet the client's needs. In brief, the plan will formulate objectives and the steps to achieve those objectives.[1]

What Casework Is Up Against

> Social workers should not be the secular priests in the church of individual repair; they should be the caretakers of the conscience of the community.
> Harry Specht and Mark Courtney, *Unfaithful Angels*

---

[1] Casework is not generally viewed as a psychotherapeutic method. Although Freudian analysis and traditional psychotherapy were influential in the intellectual development of the field (Trattner, 1990; Wenocur and Reisch, 1989), social workers are generally not trained to be skilled psychotherapists (Specht and Courtney, 1997). Many students often enter the field with aspirations of providing psychotherapy to children. Nevertheless, there is little opportunity for this type of work in the modern public child welfare agency.

In theory, casework seems such a practical, reasonable activity that, if applied in a consistent, judicious, and earnest manner, it should be able to unravel almost any human problem. Yet problems often don't work out so simply. Instead, the caseworker daily encounters such obdurate, intransigent, insoluble, difficult human conditions that any success the worker may count in improving them too often fails to solve the larger problems facing the client. The unfortunate reality is that many of the problems placed before child welfare agencies cannot be solved through casework (Mills, 1959). As Reggie Jones (2003) observes, "I really wanted to help people. So I went to college and got a job working in the social services. For the first time, I saw how desperately some people lived: rodent- and bug-infested homes, filthy kids with uncombed hair. But it wasn't until I started working for New Jersey's Division of Youth and Family Services that hell really started."

Take, as a hypothetical example, a young, single mother with two pre-school children. She is impoverished and living in a small apartment in a crime and drug-infested neighborhood. She has limited education and no job. There is no available daycare which might allow her to work. A succession of men, young and old, have come and gone through her life, none of which have taken or will take responsibility to help her, even though they may be the fathers of her children.

She needs and wants assistance, but she is suspicious, distrustful, and sometimes openly hostile toward the social caseworker who knocks at her door. Her general behavior with the caseworker is to say as little as possible, and certainly not anything that might incriminate herself. She trembles that at any slight hint of disrespect the caseworker will take her children. To receive any monetary assistance, she listens mutely and nods politely to the caseworker's suggestions and promises to make some effort to get her life in order. And although the caseworker may put forth helpful suggestions (the casework "plan"), when action is required, the young client by herself can hardly break the prison of environmental, economic, and psychological constraints that surround her. Multiply this imaginary scene by millions, with variations for geographic location, racial and ethnic background, age, and family size and makeup, and we have some idea of the impossible task that faces child welfare caseworkers in the United States.

Professional Constraints to Casework Effectiveness

The minute we turn around to attempt to address the system that is victimizing people, rather than making the victimization palatable, which is what our profession has done, we will have our heads in a noose.

Ann Hartman, *Empowering the Black Family*

A number of factors, inherent in the professional role of caseworker, serve to undermine positive results in child welfare social work. First, the parameters of casework intervention are set not by the individual child welfare professional, but by the governmental organization. The amount of aid available, the requirements for eligibility, the limitations on recipients' activities, the structure of intervention—all such parameters are established through governmental guidelines. Whether working on the child abuse report phone lines, investigating complaints, developing a case plan for a child removed from his or her parents, assessing a foster family, or visiting a child who has been placed in foster care, the caseworker must work within basic parameters established by the local agency.

Such constraints on professional autonomy often make it difficult to be creative and flexible in assembling the financial and human services necessary to help the client. Indeed, the caseworker with large caseloads and heavy work demands has little room to exercise professional judgment or apply professional skills and knowledge. When limited in this fashion, most casework activities require little professional training or expertise, and it is not surprising that casework tasks are often carried out by untrained employees or employees trained in disciplines other than social work. More often than not, caseworkers are viewed as little more than bureaucrats who enforce and administer programs following the rules and regulations established by the government (Piven and Cloward, 1970). Critical of current child protective service practice, Roberts (2002: 99) argues that "child welfare reflects the political choice to address dire child poverty in Black communities by punishing parents instead of confronting the structural reasons for racial and economic inequality."

The "right to prescribe according to one's judgment," the freedom to choose strategies, and the freedom to employ a strategy one thinks is important in the manner one thinks is best are all characteristics of professional autonomy. Doctors, lawyers, dentists, chiropractors, college professors, and other college-trained professionals are not subject to close supervision. The oversight or supervision that does occur is provided by "peer review." In contrast, the caseworker is generally subject to close administrative supervision, which in turn determines his or her professional advancement, job security, merit review, and financial rewards.

Overall, it is easy to see how the regulatory and administrative constraints on professional autonomy limit the decision-making power and thereby the professional satisfaction that comes from exercising professional authority to achieve a desirable and effective end. In this respect, it is significant to note that the professional opportunity structure in child welfare, that is, the professional career path, leads upward and away from direct involvement with clients.

While eligibility screening and administrative overhead tasks (paperwork) have tended in recent years to be shifted to clerical staff, there remains a large administrative function to be carried out which many caseworkers find less important and rewarding than direct work with clients. As well, caseworkers often deal with very difficult clients who suffer from chronic failure. The few individuals who are helped leave and are inevitably replaced in the caseload by chronic cases.

Assessing the Effectiveness of Casework

Beginning in the early 1950s social workers began to employ the scientific method, which had worked so well in medicine, to assess the effectiveness of social casework treatment approaches. One of the earliest studies to examine the effectiveness of casework services for children was conducted by Powers and Witmer (1951). Their evaluation of the Cambridge Somerville Youth Study has been identified as the first to use a control group design (Fischer, 1973). Powers and Witmer examined the effectiveness of intensive casework services in preventing delinquency among young boys. The study compared an experimental group of 325 predelinquent boys who received direct individualized casework services with a matched control group of 325 boys. The experimental group received treatment for an average of almost five years (mean length of contact equaled four years and ten months).

The caseworkers involved in the Powers and Witmer (1951) study believed that their efforts had substantially helped most of the boys. However, when the outcome was measured in terms of court records, police reports, ratings of social adjustment, and psychological inventories, and compared to the matched control group, no significant differences were found between the boys who received services and those who did not on all of the study's major criteria. Fifteen years after Powers and Witmer, McCabe (1967) conducted a similar experiment that targeted small-group services to parents and children and found no significant difference in overall outcome measures.

One of the most ambitious studies to examine the effectiveness of social casework methods was carried out by Meyer, Borgatta, and Jones (1965). Working with about 400 girls identified through tests administered when they entered a vocational high school in New York as "potential problems," the researchers used trained social workers in an agency specializing in services to delinquent girls to provide social casework services. This large experiment lasted six years and involved 189 referrals to the casework agency and 192 controls. The services included both individual and casework services. During the first year, the program consisted primarily of group treatment for the girls. The investigators examined a broad spectrum of outcome indicators encompassing school behavior (including grades and highest grade completed), personality and sociometric measures, and ratings completed by the caseworkers and the girls. Most of the girls received services over a three-year period, although one subgroup received services for two years. After examining all of the outcome data, the investigators (Meyer, Borgatta, and Jones, 1965) reported that "the conclusion must be stated in the negative when it is asked whether social work intervention with potential high school girls was . . . effective."

Although the early evaluation studies of the effectiveness of casework services to reduce or prevent delinquency among children and adolescents found no significant differences between experimental groups receiving treatment compared to control groups, it was reasoned that they would be effective if directed toward the family. Two evaluation studies illustrate the outcome with this population.

In 1968, Brown reported on an experiment that provided intensive casework services to a population of AFDC recipients. From a group of 1,200 AFDC recipients the investigators randomly selected a group of 50 low-income multiproblem families and compared them with two randomly selected control groups of 50 families who received the usual services of the public welfare agency. In addition to the usual services of the public welfare agency, the experimental families received intensive services from professionally trained caseworkers who had reduced caseloads. The program lasted more than two and a half years. At the end of the treatment the investigators found no significant differences between the experimental group and the two control groups on the major outcome measures. In fact, the study found little movement on the measures of family functioning among any of the groups.

In 1970, Mullin, Chazin, and Feldstein reported a similar study designed to test the effectiveness of intensive professional casework services in changing the family functioning of public assistance families. The 88 randomly selected experimental group families were chosen from new public assistance families and compared with 68 randomly selected control group families. Intensive casework services were provided to the experimental group for a period of up to two years. At the conclusion of the study the investigators found no significant differences between the experimental and control groups.

In 1971, Blenkner, Bloom, and Nielsen reported one of the most discouraging findings regarding the impact of casework services. Beginning with a group of 164 elderly referred to a community agency because they were having difficulty caring for themselves, the investigators randomly assigned 76 to an experimental group and 88 to a control group. The experimental group received intensive casework services from professional caseworkers while the control group received routine community services from a variety of agencies. On outcome, measures derived from interviews and observation ratings found no significant differences between the experimental and control group. On measures of concrete assistance and relief of stress to *the family* of the elderly, the experimental group performed better, a circumstance that could perhaps be explained by their higher rate of institutionalization.

In fact, the higher rate of institutionalization for the experimental group concerned the investigators and led them to consider the hypothesis that the intensive casework services may have accelerated the elderly participants' decline. Thus, they conducted a five-year follow-up, in which they reported significant differences between the experimental and control groups on rates of institutionalization and death. Although outcome measures are debated, there is no question that survival was the ultimate criterion variable. Those elderly persons receiving intensive casework services died *significantly sooner* than those who were not receiving services, raising troubling doubts about the beneficial impact of casework services for this population.

Evaluation Reviews

Making sense of the evaluation studies that began with Powers and Witmer required comprehensive analysis of the studies' essential findings. By identifying common themes revealed in many studies, reviewers endeavored to assess the overall effectiveness of casework services. The published reviews provided an overview, allowing caseworkers to see, as it were, the forest for the trees.

In 1972, Mullen and Dumpson reviewed thirteen evaluation studies of social work intervention conducted during the 1960s. Four of these studies found no significant difference between the groups receiving intervention services and those not. Two studies reported limited gains and seven reported findings supportive of hypotheses of gains made by individuals receiving treatment compared with control groups not receiving treatment. However, for those studies reporting positive results the gains were modest and the overall distributions leaned toward nonsuccess.

In January 1973, Joel Fischer published a comprehensive review of all evaluation studies reported in major social work journals, doctoral dissertations, and unpublished agency monographs completed between 1930 and 1970. More than seventy studies on the effectiveness of casework interventions with a variety of client populations were located and examined in detail. Although many of the studies contained useful information, most failed to include a control group that would have gauged the impact of the casework method. This was a critical factor because the central requirement of experimental research is that a controlled environment be established where a group receiving treatment be compared to a control group not receiving treatment (Metcalf and Thornton, 1992). Those studies that did not include a control group were thus excluded from Fischer's review, leaving only eleven studies. Six of the eleven dealt with children as clients and three with low-income multiproblem families. According to Fischer, the overall outcome of these eleven scientifically acceptable research and evaluation studies was clear: "None of the studies revealed that their program had any significant effect on the clients when outcome measures for experimental and control groups were compared" (1973: 10). "This review of the available controlled research strongly suggests that at present lack of evidence of the effectiveness of professional casework is the rule rather than the exception" (19). In fact, Fischer observed that in about half of the eleven studies clients receiving casework services tended to deteriorate.

Several months earlier Segal (1972) had published similar findings from his review of social work therapeutic interventions, especially with poor clients. Segal concluded that "the evidence with respect to the effectiveness of social work therapeutic intervention remains equivocal. The trends in the data, however, point strongly in the negative direction" (15). In summary, the research was showing that the therapeutic interventions used by caseworkers with troubled families were having little or no measurable beneficial effect. All three major reviews concluded that no substantial evidence existed demonstrating the effectiveness of casework methods (see table 2.1).

Nevertheless, the debate about the effectiveness of social casework intervention continued. In 1980, Reid and Hanrahan published a review of twenty-two controlled experimental studies of direct practice reported since the Mullen and Dumpson, Fischer, and Segal reviews. Their findings were more encouraging: "No recent study that involved a comparison between treated and untreated groups failed to yield at least some positive effects of social work intervention" (1980: 331). Yet even this cautious optimism was met with skepticism from others regarding the significance of the difference observed (Fischer, 1983; Epstein, 1983).

In 1985, Rubin reviewed twelve research studies that appeared after the Mullen and Dumpson, Fischer, and Segal reviews and that included random assignment to control or nonequivalent control groups (see Campbell and Stanley, 1963). As with the Reid and Hanrahan review, Rubin found "further grounds for optimism about the effective forms of practice."

Table 2.1 Summary of Experimental Studies: The Assessment of Casework

---

Powers and Witmer (1951) Evaluated Cambridge Somerville Youth Study
   325 predelinquent boys received intensive casework services for an average of 5 years. 325 boys in a matched control group that did not receive casework. **Findings**: No significant differences on the measures that were hypothesized to change as a result of treatment (i.e., court records, police contacts, ratings of social adjustment, psychological inventories, etc.).

McCabe (1967) The Pursuit of Promise
   Conducted a similar study that targeted small-group services on parents and children (group work).
Findings: No significant differences on measures thought to be influenced by the treatment.

Meyer, Borgata, and Jones (1965) Girls in Vocational High
   Began with 400 girls that tests had identified as "potential problems." Used trained social workers to provide individual and group casework services. 189 in experimenal group. 192 in matched control group. Most girls received treatment over 3 years.
Findings: No difference between experimental and control on a variety of measures including school performance (grades), personality tests, and indications of behavioral problems (delinquency reports).

Brown (1968) Services to Multiproblem Families
   50 low-income families and two control groups were selected from 1,200 AFDC families. Experimental families received intensive casework services from trained social workers. Treatment was administered over a 2.5-year period.
Findings: No difference between the groups. In fact, all the families seemed to have changed little over the period of the study.

Mullin, Chazin, and Feldstein (1970) Preventing Chronic Dependency
   88 subjects randomly assigned to experimental group, 68 to control group. Experimental group received intensive casework services for up to 2 years.
Findings: No statistically significant differences at end of study between the groups.

Blenkner, Bloom, and Nielsen (1971) Protective Services for the Elderly
   Began with 164 elderly persons referred to a community agency because they were having difficulty caring for themselves. 76 were randomly assigned to experimental group, 88 to control group. The experimental group received intensive casework services, while the control group received routine services.
Findings: No significant differences at outcome. Yet there seemed to be a higher rate of institutionalization for the experimental group. What might be the consequence of this, the investigators asked. Thus, they conducted a 5-year follow-up. On the most fundamental measure—whether the elderly person was still alive (the ultimate criterion)—there was a significant difference between the groups, but it favored the control group.

Evaluation Reviews

Mullen and Dumpson (1972) Review of Evaluation Studies
A comprehensive review of available studies found that casework had little impact.

Fischer (1973) Is Casework Effective?
Established criterion for selecting best available studies—use of a control group. Examined literature between 1930 and 1970. Found 11 studies that met this requirement.
Findings: None of the studies revealed that their program had any significant impact.

Segal (1972) Therapeutic Intervention
Reviewed studies that used social workers in a therapeutic setting. What impact did the administered treatment have?
Findings: "The evidence with respect to the effectiveness of social work therapeutic intervention remains equivocal. The trends in the data, however, point strongly in the negative direction."

Sheldon (1986) Social Work Effectiveness Experiments
Reviewed progress since reviews of Mullen and Dumpson (1972), Fischer (1973), and Segal (1972).
Findings: Expressed concern that "progress" in demonstrating effectiveness in recent years may be "at the expense of general relevance."

Again, several authors were critical of Rubin's review. Ezell and McNeece (1986) challenged Rubin's optimistic conclusion, citing that his review was based on studies in which casework intervention had not been performed by actual social workers. The issue involved the definition of casework around which there has always been substantial disagreement (Fischer, 1971). Although, as Hartman (1971) pointed out, "no one has been elected to determine the definition" of casework, it can be defined simply as the services provided by professional caseworkers. In fact, this is the definition Fischer had used to identify the studies for his review.

Ezell and McNeece (1986:402) observed that of the twelve studies Rubin reviewed, interventions in three "were conducted by social work students, social workers were in the minority of workers in two other studies, and there was no mention of social work involvement in five other studies. Another study provided a complete description of the therapists, and none were social workers. There were only two studies in which the majority of personnel delivering a service or providing therapy were social workers, and in one of those, there were no significant differences between the experimental and comparison groups!" (See Rubin, 1986 for his response.)

On balance, it is fair to say that there has been limited evidence of the effectiveness of casework intervention. As reviews by Thomlison (1984) and Sheldon (1986) suggested, social workers need to take seriously the importance of identifying what works and what doesn't on the basis of rigorous empirical research. Sheldon (1986: 238), examining the second wave of experimental evaluations of casework intervention conducted since the reviews by Fischer and Segal, cautions:

> It will be seen that, although there are some strong signs that social work is increasingly able to demonstrate its effectiveness, it may be doing so, in the case of a few studies, at the expense of general relevance. Were it to continue, this would be a profound mistake. It would invite the conclusion that when social workers conducted large-scale experiments on problems of genuine concern to the community, they did rather poorly; when they moved on to much smaller scale problems and used less strict tests of outcome, they did rather better.

The evaluation studies have not produced definitive evidence of the effectiveness of casework as applied to the kinds of problems laid at the doorstep of the child welfare profession (Lindsey and Kirk, 1992).[2] Part of the problem relates again to limitations of the residual perspective. The casework evaluation studies have, in the main, failed to consider the fact that individuals selected to receive casework services often confront structural and institutional barriers that the caseworker has little or no means of changing. Further, providing individuals with casework services whose problems are not strictly personal often stigmatizes them.

---

[2] The concern with the effectiveness of social intervention programs has not been limited to clinical work (Berlin, 1992). After reviewing a number of social experiments Rossi and Wright (1984: 331) wrote that the main lesson learned from research "is that the expected effect of social programs hovers around zero, a devastating discovery for the social reformers." While the negative income tax experiments that shaped Rossi's view produced only minor results, it does not follow that social programs in general can be expected to have little effect. Critics were concerned that a negative income tax would greatly reduce the work effort of those who received a guaranteed minimum income. Further, Rossi's (1987) "iron law" fails to explain the success of the many social programs that have worked well. Since 1930, Social Security in Britain and North America has raised millions out of poverty. The GI Bill in the United States allowed hundreds of thousands of men and women to obtain a college education who might otherwise have never set foot on a campus (Skocpol, 1992, 2000). In the United States Medicare and Medicaid provides a much needed, although inadequate, safety net for the elderly, while in Britain and Canada national health care provides needed health care on a universal basis. Business and industry lobby for programs to create incentives to invest in new machinery and research. Few challenge the role of government policies to support industry. Finally, as we shall see, government policies and programs can have substantial influence on the distribution of wealth and income.

Family Preservation: Intensive Casework Services

The latest effort to assess the impact of casework occurred with the evaluations of family preservation services. As a result of the findings from research on the importance of parental bonding and attachment, the emphasis in modern child welfare has centered on preventing children from being removed from their families. Thus, the fundamental axiom of family preservation, as with all of modern child welfare, is that children should be kept with their biological family whenever possible. The concern is that too many children are removed when, instead, intensive services from a child welfare caseworker might be able to prevent placement. The earliest research to test this intensive casework approach to avert placement was reported by Homebuilders in the state of Washington (Kinney, Madsen, Fleming, and Haapala, 1977). It is important to stress that what is unique with "family preservation" is not its goal but the method used to achieve it—intensive casework services.

Homebuilders developed an approach that allowed for intensive case management services provided by a professional caseworker with a limited case load—usually no more than five active cases at a time. In addition, services were provided within 24 hours and at the convenience of the family being served. Services were viewed as crisis intervention and were concentrated within a time frame of four to six weeks. Homebuilders attempted to identify children who were in imminent need of placement and targeted services to them in order to prevent placement. The early success reported by Homebuilders was remarkable—more than 97 percent avoided placement (Kinney, et al., 1977). This spectacular success rate is reminiscent of that reported by Brace (where he reported that not one child in 10,000 he placed in foster care ended up in jail, prison, or a reformatory).

The enthusiastic supporters and advocates of family preservation have consistently reported favorable results but with major design limitations (Rossi, 1994). The methodological flaw of these early evaluation studies centered on the absence of a control group for the Washington study and a "crippled" overflow control group (nonresponse for a third of the control group) for the Utah study with small sample sizes (27 families in the control condition).[3] But the more fundamental limitation is that these studies represent "advocacy research" rather than conventional impartial science (see Gilbert, 1994 for a discussion of "advocacy research"). As such, the

---

[3] The early research design limitations of Homebuilders were corrected with the use of a matched control group in the Washington and Utah studies reported by Fraser and colleagues (1991).

research effort of family preservation advocates has been to prove the effectiveness of this approach rather than to critically assess its impact.

In recent years there have been more than 35 evaluations of family preservation in one form or another.[4] The essential requirement of an unbiased test of an experimental study is, as we learned from Fischer's (1973) work, the use of a randomized control group.[5] In this regard, three "intensive casework" family preservation studies stand out for their use of randomized control groups with sufficient sample size to test for experimental effects. In California, New Jersey, and Illinois, randomized experimental designs were used with sample sizes in the experimental conditions of 338, 117, and 995 subjects respectively. These three studies provide the most rigorous and unbiased tests of family preservation. All found small or insignificant differences as a result of intensive casework services.

The Illinois Study. The most comprehensive test of family preservation approach has been the *Illinois study* conducted by a team of child welfare researchers at Chapin Hall at the University of Chicago. This study stands out for its care in documenting exactly what services the experimental group received in comparison to the control group. It involved multiple sites with data collected over a three-year period. Family preservation was understood to be intensive casework services provided to a family where there was a likelihood a child might be removed. Services were provided by a caseworker who was limited to five cases at any one time (the normal caseload for caseworkers in the control group was fifty cases). Families

---

[4] These studies include Bergquist, Szwejda, and Pope, 1993; Berry, 1990, 1991, 1992; Chess et al., 1993; Collier and Hill, 1993; Cunningham and Smith, 1990; Feldman, 1990 and 1991; Fraser, Pecora, and Haapala, 1991; Halper and Jones, 1981; Henggler et al., 1992; Hennepin County Community Services Department, 1981; Jones, Neuman, and Shyne, 1976; Kinney et al., 1977; Kinney et al., 1991; Landsman, 1985; Lyle and Nelson, 1983; Magura, 1981; McDonald and Associates, 1990; Meezan and McCroskey, 1993; Michigan Department of Social Services, 1993; Mitchell, Tovar, and Knitzer, 1989; Nelson, Emlen, Landsman, and Hutchinson, 1988; Nelson and Landsman, 1992; Pecora, Fraser, and Haapala, 1991 and 1992; Scannapieco, 1994; Schafer and Erickson, 1993; Schuerman et al., 1991, 1992, and 1993; Schwartz and AuClaire, 1989; Schwartz, AuClaire, and Harris, 1991; Szykula and Fleischman, 1985; Thieman, Fuqua, and Linnan, 1990; University Associates, 1992 and 1993; Wells and Whittington, 1993; Wheeler, 1992; Wheeler et al., 1992; Willems and DeRubeis, 1981; Wood, Barton, and Schroeder, 1988; and Yuan et al., 1990. See Lindsey, Martin, and Doh (2002) for a comprehensive review of studies. Lindsey, Martin and Doh were awarded the *ProHumanitate Medal* by the Center for Child Welfare Policy in 2003 for this study.

[5] With the increased use of statistical designs to evaluate programs, a skeptical attitude toward research in social work has developed. As critics of the positivist approach point out, research is not the use of statistical procedures to prove a particular point of view. Rather, research is the impartial search for truth and the use of investigative methods designed to limit the influence of personal bias (Cournand and Meyer, 1976; Lindsey, 1978). Research must also allow for the refutation of one's program or point of view (Mahoney, 1976).

were provided with services within 24 hours and their caseworkers met with them at a time and place convenient to the family.

Overall, families in the experimental group received almost ten times more contact hours with a caseworker than did the control group. Even after the families received far more casework services, the researchers found no significant advantages for the experimental families (Schuerman et al., 1993).

Heneghan, Horwitz, and Leventhal (1996) examined 46 program evaluations of family preservation studies (FPS) and found 10 that were scientifically credible. They observed that, "despite current widespread use of FPS to prevent out-of-home placements of children, evaluations of FPS are methodologically difficult and show no benefit in reducing rates of out-of-home placements of children at risk of abuse or neglect in 8 of 10 studies" (p. 535). They conclude, "policy in this area has evolved more on faith than on fact" (p. 542). Summarizing the overall findings from the enormous effort to assess the impact of intensive casework services in child welfare, it is reasonable to suggest that the more rigorous has been the research design, the more convincing the evidence that these services have failed to produce significant improvements for clients.

Schuerman and colleagues (1993) conclude from their large scale research study, "We find little evidence that family preservation programs result in substantial reductions in the placement of children. Claims to the contrary have been based largely on non-experimental studies which do not provide sufficient evidence of program effects."[6] Yet, family preservation may also be viewed as a philosophy of service—children should be kept out of foster care whenever possible. As Peter Rossi (1994) observes, the basis for family preservation's success has more to do with faith or "advocacy research" than science.

In the absence of evidence of its effectiveness, it is remarkable to observe the support that intensive casework services under the rubric of family preservation received at the federal level (Adams, 1992; Epstein, 2003a).[7]

---

[6] To explain the absence of experimental advantage even with almost ten times more contact with social workers, Schuerman and colleagues offer two main suggestions. First, it is very difficult to identify children in imminent need of placement and to target services to this group. Second, many of the problems the families face, such as severe poverty and social dislocation, are not amenable to casework services.

[7] The 1994 federal budget provided $60 million in 1994, rising to $240 million in fiscal 1998 for states to establish family preservation services. Most recent federal and state initiatives seem to be guided by this essentially residual approach even though numerous empirical studies have failed to provide evidence of meaningful success (Rossi, 1992a,b; Schuerman et al., 1993; Yuan, 1990). Adams (1992) has indicated that much of the success achieved by advocates of this approach has derived from the leveraging of substantial fund-

Illustration of Family Preservation

It may seem unfair to criticize a program with anecdotal stories or exceptional cases. Yet, "family preservation" has led to charges of needless serious harm and even fatalities on several occasions (Davis, 1988; Gelles, 1996; *Newsweek*, April 25, 1994; Wexler, 1995). In fact, the major lawsuit brought by the American Civil Liberties Union (ACLU) that brought New York City's child welfare agency under court supervision stemmed from a child abuse death in a family preservation program:

> When Marisol was three and one-half years old, she was discharged from foster care and sent to live with her mother, who had placed the child in foster care at birth. Her mother had a history of drug abuse, for which she had been imprisoned. Nothing in her record indicated that she had been rehabilitated.
>
> In sending the child to live with her mother, the New York City child welfare system ignored reports that Marisol had returned from visits prior to discharge unfed and frightened by violence in the home, suggesting that her mother might still be abusing drugs. Instead, authorities applied the system's current operating principle that all children should be with their biological parents . . . A housing inspector happened upon Marisol, locked in a closet in her mother's apartment, near death. She had been repeatedly abused over an extended period of time, eating black plastic garbage bags and her own feces to survive. After leaving the hospital, Marisol reentered foster care. Her permanency goal: return to mother. The service to be provided to enable her mother to resume custody: parenting classes.
>
> Her care was left unmonitored because the system responsible for her safety and well-being was operating under a "family preservation" principle (Lowry, 1998: 1).

---

ing from two large private foundations—the Anne E. Casey Foundation and the Edna McConnell Clark Foundation (Adams, 1992). Many of these evaluation studies have been funded by the benefactors of this approach. Yet, still the findings have been equivocal.

Rossi (1994) summarizes, "The existing studies all show that there are at best marginal differences in post treatment placement rates or in improved families and more frequently no differences at all between experimental group and control group families." The main research in support of family preservation comes from two studies conducted in Utah and Washington. Although an impressive amount of data was collected in these studies, they were, according to Rossi, "badly flawed." Reviewing the results of the Washington and Utah research reported by Fraser, Pecora, and Haapala (1991) in their *Families in Crisis,* Rossi (1994) asks, "Given what these studies have shown, why is it that the child welfare establishment still enthusiastically advocates family preservation? Analogously, why do otherwise competent and surely intelligent persons publish a volume based on fatally flawed data in order to advance the 'family preservation movement'? Are we witnessing another triumph of faith over data?"

Long-term Impact of Foster Care

A Connecticut study found that 75 percent of the youths in the state's criminal justice system were once in foster care. Eighty percent of Illinois inmates spent time in foster care as children.

. . . the child welfare system . . . is a state-run program that disrupts, restructures, and polices Black families. I hope to capture the injustice of a system that separates thousands of Black children from their parents every year and relegates them to damaging state institutions. There is little evidence that the foster care system has improved the well-being of Black children.

Dorothy Roberts, *Shattered Bonds*

The concern raised by the review studies about the effectiveness of casework focuses principally upon services to the family in order to prevent placement or to facilitate reunification. In other words, have casework services or intensive casework services (family preservation) proven effective in foster care? Have casework services assured us that children in foster care do well later in life? What was foster care's impact on children? What became of the many thousands of young people who had been submerged for so many years in the foster care system? Did they become productive well-adjusted adults? Too often the answer to all of these questions was "no" (Horwitz, Balestracci, and Simms, 2001; Kendrick, 1990). Sosin, Piliavin, and Westerfelt (1991) studied the long-term homeless in Minneapolis and found that 39 percent had experienced foster or institutional care as children. Corbit (1985) interviewed street kids in Calgary and found that 90 percent had been in foster care (crown wards). Hepworth (1985: 38) observes, "It is a sad fact that many children graduate from child welfare services to training schools and even ultimately to prison; this is particularly true for native children" (Native Council of Canada, 1978). Kendrick (1990: 69) questions the child protection system that "turns out uneducated, unemployed, confused, and isolated young people."

The most comprehensive study of outcomes for foster children was conducted by Westat (Cook, 1992). The study followed a representative sample of 810 youth emancipated from foster care and found that two and a half years after discharge their situation was "adequate at best." Cook (1992) reported that 54 percent of the young people leaving foster care had graduated from high school (see Table 2.2). At the time of the interviews, 49 percent of the former foster children were employed, and 38 percent had held a job for more than a year. Looking at the young women leaving foster care in their study they found that 60 percent became unwed mothers.

Table 2.2 Westat Foster Care Outcomes

Outcome	Percent
Completed high school	54
Employed at the time of the interview	49
Maintained a job for at least one year	38
Cost to the community	
(i.e., receiving public assistance, incarcerated, etc.)	40
Homeless for at least one night	25
Completely self-supporting	17

Source: Cook (1992).

Almost two-thirds of the young women were receiving public assistance or otherwise were a "cost to the community." In a recent examination of emancipated foster children the Los Angeles Times (2001) found that the young women leaving foster care seemed to find stability only after becoming pregnant and having children.

Dworksy and Courtney (2000) examined the self-sufficiency of foster youth in Wisconsin. They observed, "By almost any standard, total income from earnings, AFDC/TANF cash assistance and Food Stamps for the first eight quarters after discharge from care was very low among our sample of 1819 former foster youth. Median total income and mean total income for this two year period were $2848 and $5781, respectively—well below the poverty line for a one-person family in 1995, which is the earliest year in which the former foster youth were discharged from care."

The Color of Foster Care

The proportion of Black children in out-of-home care in large states such as California, Illinois, New York, and Texas ranges from three times to more than ten times as high as the proportion of white children. Although only 19 percent of the child population in Illinois is Black, Black children make up more than 75 percent of the foster care population.

. . . The racial imbalance in New York City's foster care population is truly mind-boggling: out of 42,000 children in the system at the end of 1997, only 1,300 are white. . . Yet white children make up only 3 percent of its foster care caseload. Less than 24 percent in foster care are Latino, and the vast majority—73 percent—are African American. Black children are ten times more likely to be placed in foster care in New York City than white children.

Dorothy Roberts, *Shattered Bonds*

Table 2.3 The Color of Foster Care, 2000

	Black Children	
	State Population (%)	Foster Care Population (%)
California	7	33
Florida	21	45
Georgia	34	58
Illinois	19	74
Indiana	10	41
New Jersey	16	63
New York	18	45
Ohio	14	47
Pennsylvania	13	41
Texas	12	29
Wisconsin	8	54

Source: www.childwelfare.com (Foster Care Report Cards, slide 6)

As seen in table 2.3, in most states black children constitute the majority of children in the foster care system. In Illinois, almost three-quarters of the foster care population are black even though they are less than one-fifth of the state's child population. In Wisconsin, black children are less than one-tenth of the state's child population but they represent more than half of the state's foster care population.

In New Jersey black children represent almost two thirds of the foster care population even though they are less than one sixth of the state's child population. In Pennsylvania black children make up one eighth of the state's children but more than half the children in foster care. In Wisconsin they represent less than a twelfth, but are half the children in foster care. In these and most other states black children are substantially overrepresented in the foster care population (Courtney and Skyles, 2003; Hines, Lemon, Wyatt, and Merdinger, forthcoming; Smith and Devore, forthcoming). The major child welfare program provided for these disadvantaged children is removal from their family and placement in foster care.

Comprehensive Child Development Studies

Research on child development has consistently indicated the importance of early intervention targeted at children and their families. In this regard, the federal government invests billions of dollars annually on social intervention programs designed to change the situation for young disadvantaged children.

Despite the substantial funding of various social service programs targeting children in poverty, there seems to be little change in child poverty rates. Debates about these programs often centered around which of the various program approaches was most effective. But this left unanswered the question of whether, taken as a whole, the programs make a difference in the lives of the children and families they serve.

In 1988, Congress passed the Comprehensive Child Development Act to determine whether the programs it funds for at-risk low-income young children and families are effective. After extensive consultation with leading experts, Congress developed an evaluation plan, the Comprehensive Child Development Program (CCDP), which would use the most rigorous experimental research design (see figure 2.1). The act authorized the establishment of a set of programs to operate for five years and provided $25 million per year (St. Pierre, Layzer, Goodson, and Bernstein, 1997).

All relevant federally funded programs were included in the CCDP evaluation. The research was conducted by the consulting firm of Abt Associates. Of 24 eligible projects, 21 participated in the evaluation. Program participants were drawn from both urban and rural communities. The sample for the urban group required 360 families (120 for the experimental program, 120 for the control group, and 120 for the replacement group), while the sample for the rural group required 180 families (60 per group).

The total sample for the 21 groups consisted of 4,410 families with 2,213 assigned to the CCDP programs and 2,197 assigned to the control groups. Obviously, families randomly selected for participation in CCDP could not be forced to enroll in the programs. Most families participated; some participated for less than six months, some for a moderate period (two or three years), and some for the full five years. The mean time for involvement was more than 3.3 years (with a standard deviation of 1.6 years).

CCDP involved extensive data collection on more than 100 different outcome measures for mothers and "focus" children. Data were also obtained for fathers and children born subsequent to the "focus" children (see table 2.4).

The research was well executed with high response rates. All of the families were poor (see table 2.4), and almost 60 percent were single parents. More than half did not finish high school. These program families received comprehensive child development program services including counseling, parent education, and case management services.

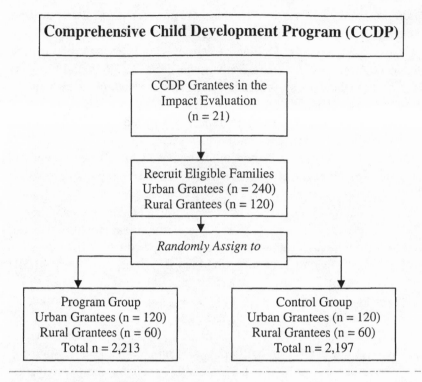

Figure 2.1 The CCDP Evaluation Design
Source: St. Pierre, Layzer, Goodson, and Bernstein (1997).

CCDP Impacts

The CCDP evaluation was conducted for several years, and in 1994 Congress directed a phased closing of the projects by 1998. The 21 programs represented the best comprehensive interventions currently available. The average amount of money spent on these programs was more than $15,000 annually per person (see tables 2.5 and 2.6). What was the impact of CCDP? After an average of more than three years of case management services the evaluators announced their findings:

> "We compared outcomes for CCDP families with outcomes for control group families over a five-year period and reached the following conclusions:
>
> • CCDP had no statistically significant impacts on the economic self-sufficiency of participating mothers, nor on their parenting skills.
> • CCDP had no meaningful impacts on the cognitive or social-emotional development of participating children.

Table 2.4 Comprehensive Child Development Program Sample Characteristics

Race/Ethnicity	Percent	Mother Characteristics	Percent
African American	43	Under 18 for first child	35
Hispanic	26	High school graduate	49
White	26	Annual income under $5,000	44
American Indian	3	Annual income under $10,000	85
Asian	1	Below poverty	100
First Language		Single parent	58
English	84		
Spanish	14		
Other	2		

N = 4,410

Source: St. Pierre, Layzer, Goodson, and Bernstein (1997).

Table 2.5 Summary of the Comprehensive Child Development Program

- Created by Congress in 1988 and funded with $25 million per year.
- Provide intensive case management services to poor families and their children for the first five years of the children's lives.
- 4,410 families randomly assigned to experimental and control groups.
- All families living below the poverty line. Almost 60% were single parents.
- Annual spending for those in the experimental programs was $15,768 (or about $47,000 for each family).

Source: St. Pierre, Layzer, Goodson, and Bernstein (1997).

Table 2.6 After Three Years of Case Management Services Difference Between the Experimental and Control Groups

Experimental Group	Control Group
40% of mothers had jobs	41% of the mothers had jobs
Weekly wages = $254	Weekly wages = $239
68% received food stamps	68% received food stamps
Child vocabulary test = 81.1	Child vocabulary test = 81.0
CCDP annual expense = $15,768	

Source: St. Pierre, Layzer, Goodson, and Bernstein (1997).

- CCDP had no important differential effects on subgroups of participants. Thus, when the data were analyzed across all of the CCDP projects, we see a very convincing and consistent pattern—on average, CCDP did not make a measurable difference in the lives of program participants."

We have spent time reviewing the results of this study because it represents the best research available on the effectiveness of casework. What distinguishes this research is that it identified the best social intervention programs for poor and disadvantaged children and subjected those programs to rigorous scientific review. On virtually every dimension that was examined there was no significant difference (see table 2.6). After years of costly intervention the programs "did not produce any important positive effects on participating families."

The CCDP evaluation (1997: 17) concluded:

There is no question that this six-year effort provided a fair test of this key policy alternative. It has produced important findings—findings showing that *the case management approach does not lead to improved outcomes for parents or children*. This is an important piece of information in the fight against poverty.

Conclusion

Because children's lives are at stake, Child Protective Services cannot stop its work while the public debates its mission, or while researchers discover which interventions might help which families.

> Larner et al., *Protecting Children from Abuse and Neglect*

Black children could be described as involuntary subjects in a government experiment in child rearing with no evidence that they have received any benefit from it.

> Dorothy Roberts, *Shattered Bonds*

In the long view of history, one of the major achievements during the nineteenth century centered around the advances in medicine. Using the methods of science, medicine developed an understanding of the principles of germ theory, the functioning of the circulation system, the biochemical nature of the human body, and the overall functioning of the human organism. During the same period medical science developed vaccinations, surgical techniques, and medical treatments to heal and cure the sick. The principal scientific method used to test medical treatments was the experimental design. Medical treatments were tested by randomly assigning individuals to experimental and control groups and exposing the experimental group to treatment. After the treatment was administered and allowed to have an effect, individuals were assessed to see if there was a difference between the experimental and control group. If the treatment was effective, then those in the experimental group would have improved relative to those in the control group.

When the central method of social work—casework—was examined using experimental designs with random assignment to experimental and control groups, it did not produce significant change.[8] One reason is that casework is not a treatment method. It was not developed as a curative procedure. Rather, casework is essentially a case management approach designed to assess client needs, identify available resources, and monitor client progress. It is an individual case accounting and planning method that suited the needs of the residual approach.

Casework interventions are designed to intervene at the individual level with the hope of changing the life situation of the individual. From the evidence so far, it is clear that effective interventions have not been developed. Why? The difficulties these individuals and families find themselves in are characterized by chronic and severe poverty, and the social service interventions applied to them do not fundamentally address this problem. Further, these individuals often require education and training for effective participation in a highly competitive market economy. It may be that in the future, effective casework intervention technology will be developed that could make a substantial difference in the lives of those served, but it is clear that current casework interventions have not proven effective. The casework evaluations, the family preservation outcome studies, and the CCDP research all failed to find evidence of effectiveness.

---

[8] The discouraging findings from experimental research did not result in a fundamental questioning of the essential method of intervention—casework—as might be expected. Instead, in the years that followed the disappointing findings, a distrust of the scientific method and a questioning of its relevance to social work emerged. Convinced of the efficacy of its involvement with clients, many in social work questioned the definition of effectiveness and the use of experimental and empirical research approaches to the field (Epstein, 1999; Goldstein, 1992; Heineman, 1981). In recent years these scholars have argued that social work has a different philosophical basis than other "science-based" professions, and that it is more like an art and finds its place in the humanities more than the sciences (England, 1986).

3

Child Welfare Reform through Demonstration Research: Permanency Planning

> Of all the children we studied, better than half of them gave promise of living a major part of their childhood years in foster families and institutions. Among them were children likely to leave care only when they came of age, often after having had many homes—and none of their own—for ten or so years.
>
> Henry Maas and Richard Engler, Jr., *Children in Need of Parents*

In the last chapter we examined the effectiveness of casework intervention to bring about change by reforming the individual client using case management, counseling, and therapeutic approaches. Although these approaches have failed to produce evidence of systematic change among clients, this should not lead to the conclusion that research has failed to identify effective methods of intervention. In this chapter we review demonstration research that examines the operation of the child welfare system from an organizational level. The interventions of this research were meant to change the operation of the system altogether in order to meet the needs of clients and to achieve policy goals.

Reforming the Public Child Welfare System—System Intervention

As we have seen, the public child welfare system emerged to ensure care for the children who could not be cared for by their parents—orphans. During the first half of the century, the public child welfare system broadened its focus of concern to include the care of children who were not *adequately* cared for by their parents. The two major services child welfare agencies provided to accomplish this were orphanages and foster care. After World War II orphanages essentially disappeared as foster care emerged as the primary service.

Foster care involves the removal of children from their biological parents and their placement in the "temporary" care of other families. As such, it does not propose to change a client through casework services. Rather, casework services are offered to the family while the child is in care. A major concern with foster care centers on the outcomes for children.

During the 1970s several major demonstration programs in child welfare demonstrated that the existing child welfare system could, through institutional and structural reform based on research, be made more effective at reduced cost. Motivated by a collective need in the profession to force accountability, these research projects instituted changes that illustrated how effective reform could be achieved in the child welfare delivery system.

The traditional child welfare system described by Kadushin and Martin (1988) was as a social service organization where children and their parents (1) entered the system, (2) received care and services, and then (3) left (see figure 3.1).

The federal demonstration projects, which we examine in this chapter, focused on each of these phases. They were part of a broad movement toward permanency planning and are illustrative of the research of the period. The Comprehensive Emergency Services (CES) program proposed major changes to the way children entered the system. The Alameda Project examined what changes could be made in casework services provided to children and families once they entered care. The Oregon Project investigated strategies for reducing the number of children lingering in foster care.

1	2	3
Entry	**Services**	**Exit**
Decision making	Foster care for the child	Restoration to family
Diversion	Service to the biological	Adoption
Emergency services	parent to facilitate restoration	Long-term care

Demonstration Programs		
Comprehensive Emergency Services	**Alameda Project**	**Oregon Project**

Figure 3.1 Structure of the Child Welfare System

Comprehensive Emergency Services Program (CES)

In 1970, the Urban Institute sponsored a study by Marvin Burt and Louis Blair (Burt and Blair, 1971) to examine the adequacy of child welfare delivery services for neglected and abused children. The investigators felt that the system was not functioning well and they hoped to identify problems and to devise and test workable solutions (Gruber, 1978; Vasaly, 1976). The site chosen for the study was Nashville-Davidson County, Tennessee, the home of country music and Vanderbilt University, which was considered to have a fairly typical urban child welfare system.

The study began with a survey of how the county's child welfare services were being delivered. What the investigators found was a fragmented and uncoordinated federation of state, local, and voluntary agencies, in which no single agency had the authority to ensure that children and families were being effectively and comprehensively served. Children were often shuttled from the police to the courts to the social service agency and then into a mix of out-of-home care facilities. Little continuity existed, and at any one time, no one could explain why one child was being treated differently than another. A hodgepodge of agencies provided services to selected categories of needs, and children and families were dealt with only when they matched a particular category; otherwise they were dismissed or dealt with summarily in a manner that did not fit the circumstance. For example, a mother of two is suddenly hospitalized, and the father, a trucker, is away from home. Called to the home by neighbors, the police have no other choice but to take the children into custody and initiate court action placing them in state custody. In a short time, the children have ended up in a foster home or a residential, locked-door treatment facility.

Further, most children and families in Nashville-Davidson County had initial contact with child welfare services after normal office hours, when no emergency services were available except what the police might offer. As a result, more children were entering the child welfare system than should have been admitted. Once in, the bureaucratic door closed, and they found it difficult to get out. No one wanted to take responsibility for releasing the children back into a possibly dangerous home environment. Bureaucratic inertia asserted itself, and procedures had to be followed, forms filled out, hearings held, interviews conducted. The burden of proof shifted from the agency, which, in its view, had acted correctly in removing the children, to the parents who must now prove why their children should be allowed to return home.

Burt and Blair concluded their study, entitled *Options for Improving the Care of Neglected and Dependent Children,* with a proposal for the development of a comprehensive child welfare emergency services program.

The proposal had two goals: (1) to bring about a successful coordination and reorganization of child services; and (2) to expand existing programs to include a *comprehensive emergency service system.* The aim was to screen out those children who did not need to get in, while providing more comprehensive services for those who did.

With support from federal, state, and local governments, the Comprehensive Emergency Services (CES) reforms were implemented in Nashville-Davidson County, Tennessee, in April 1972 (Burt and Bayleat, 1978). The project provided for 1) a centralized coordination of service delivery and 2) the implementation of an emergency services system encompassing four areas:

1. Coordinated emergency intake services on a 24-hour, seven-days-a-week basis.
2. Emergency caretaker service for children temporarily left without supervision because of an unforeseen circumstance or emergency. Caretakers would stay at the home with the children until the parent could return. When appropriate, every attempt would be made to keep the child at home and out of the service delivery system.
3. Emergency homemaker service for those children or families where extended in-home care was needed.
4. Emergency foster care provided only until children could be returned home or placed elsewhere.

Notice that the focus of CES was to provide services to families in difficulty with the idea of preventing the need for placement. In part, the CES system was viewed as a diversion program designed to ensure retention of children in their own home or, if that was not possible, to return them home at the earliest possible time.

The CES project had several specific objectives that were ideally suited for measurement. The first was to "reduce the number of neglect and dependency petitions filed and the number of children entering into the system by screening out those cases where a petition was not justified" (Burt and Blair, 1971: 25). Figure 3.2 shows that the number of children diverted increased from 770 in 1969–70 before the program started, to 2,156 in 1973–74, two years later. More importantly, the number of children entering foster care decreased from 353 to 174 even though three times as many children came to the attention of child serving agencies.

The second objective of the CES program, reminiscent of current family preservation programs, was to keep children in their own home whenever possible (Forsythe, 1992; McGowan, 1990). Again, the results were substantial. As seen in figure 3.2, the number of children placed in residential facilities was reduced from 262 to 8.

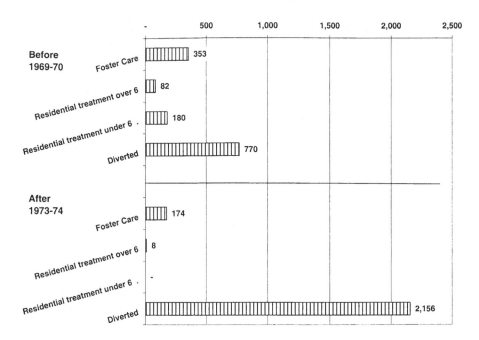

Figure 3.2 Impact of the CES System on Child Placements
Source: Burt and Bayleat (1978).

Clearly, the demonstration program altered both the type and number of services delivered. The use of residential treatment was almost eliminated, while the use of foster care was dramatically reduced. In brief, the program was highly successful in averting placement.

The third objective of the CES program was to ensure that children were placed in safe, stable environments. The aim of diverting children whenever possible from substitute care back to their home would have been pointless if the child had simply shown up again seeking admittance due to continuing abuse or neglect (essentially creating a revolving door of children seeking service). However, this did not happen.

Finally, the CES project sought to be cost-effective. In this regard, despite start-up costs, the program achieved a substantial net savings over previous years' budgets. Further, if one considers that the direct savings reported did not include the amortized savings of foster care payments that would have been required for children kept in long-term foster care, the program achieved substantial long-term savings.

There is little doubt that the coordination of services for families in need brought about by the CES program substantially improved the care of neglected and dependent children in Nashville-Davidson County. The question is why this approach, which proved so effective, was not widely adopted and implemented elsewhere.[1] As Carol Meyer (1984: 499) observed, "The research in child welfare has been prodigious and exemplary. In view of these potential strengths, one might ask why this field, particularly foster care, stays the same no matter what is learned empirically."

The CES program was a precursor to the family preservation services approach,[2] and its success no doubt explains the interest in family preservation, which is essentially an "emergency services" system in which child welfare social work professionals play a central role. In the CES program most direct services were provided to families by persons with no training in social work (paraprofessional homemakers and caretakers). In contrast, orthodox family preservation services are provided by trained social workers with limited caseloads (two or three families receiving intensive services for a two- or three-month period).

What is most remarkable about the CES program is its spectacular results. Before the program's implementation 46 percent of the children who came to the attention of child welfare authorities were placed in foster care. After the CES system was implemented the rate of placement dropped to 8 percent, a more than fivefold decrease in the rate of placement.

A major criticism of CES was that in reducing the number of inappropriate placements, it may have denied services to many children who should have received them—a concern echoed by critics of family preservation (Wald, Carlsmith, and Leiderman, 1988; Gelles, 1996; Epstein, 2000). If this were true, such children, although denied access to services at first approach, would likely show up again, and so would appear in recidivism statistics. However, follow-up studies indicated that the rate of recidivism actually declined after the implementation of the CES system.

From a methodological perspective, a major drawback of the CES study involves the limitation of a before and after quasi-experimental design. Because the study did not use a randomized control group, other factors might

---

[1] In 1976 the General Accounting Office (GAO) conducted a study of the impact of research supported by the Administration for Children, Youth, and Families (ACYF) on public child welfare agencies. The report found that most of the research had not influenced the policy or practice of the public agencies. When contacted, most of the agencies reported not being familiar with the ACYF funded research. Of particular concern to the GAO was the lack of knowledge regarding the CES project that the ACYF had funded. The GAO called for both (1) increased efforts to involve agency personnel in the research process (through participation in the setting of priorities and the selection of projects for funding) and (2) for the ACYF to make greater efforts to disseminate the results of funded research.

[2] Family preservation programs focus on identifying children in imminent need of placement. Generally, these are families in crisis who might have their children removed if they do not receive needed services to help them through their crisis (Wells and Biegel, 1991). (See chapter 2.)

partly explain the changes observed by the researchers. In our view, it would be difficult to suggest that the dramatic reduction was the result of alternative explanations not controlled by the research design. Overall the results of the CES program indicate the potential achievements possible through the provision of services to families in need (Nelson et al., 1988).

The Alameda Project

While the Comprehensive Emergency Services system attempted to modify the intake process in order to prevent inappropriate placement of children in foster care, the Alameda Project focused on the delivery of effective services to the client after entry. The Alameda Project had three major objectives. First, it attempted to ensure continuity of care for children taken in. Of major concern was the apparent lack of vigorous interest among caseworkers in returning children to their biological family. Too many children, after coming into foster care, were cast adrift. According to project investigators Theodore Stein, Eileen Gambrill, and Kermit Wiltse, three social work researchers at the University of California at Berkeley's School of Social Welfare, the caseworker's primary responsibility was to "gather objective data demonstrating that the initial problems requiring placement have been resolved and that a child may be returned to his or her parents or, in the absence of such resolution, that alternative planning for the child occur" (1978: 77). As we learned from the Jenkins and Norman (1972) study of the pain and sadness experienced by mothers who had their children taken from them only to be placed in foster care, too often this was not happening.

The Alameda Project was also concerned with the lack of services offered to the biological parent—the mother who had her child taken away. Research by Fanshel, Jenkins, and their colleagues at Columbia University had shown that services to the biological family were crucial in restoring the child to the family, and that the best predictor of restoration was parental visits (Fanshel and Shinn, 1978: 521–522). Thus, the Alameda Project placed an emphasis on ensuring parental visits to facilitate restoration.

Another goal of the Alameda Project was to compare the effectiveness of a systematic case management procedure, including behavioral intervention methods, with conventional casework methods, which until now had involved limited systematic planning (Gambrill and Stein, 1981). Indeed, many children had failed to have case plans developed. Part of the proposed systematic case management procedure involved using "contracts" with biological parents to encourage visiting. When children came into care, the experimental caseworkers would develop a contract with the biological parent that outlined the expectations, procedures, and responsibilities of the agency. In addition, the contract spelled out the actions the parent must take in order to have their children reunited with them. This included a visitation schedule, as well as other provisions that varied from case to case. In other words, the caseworker would assist the mother who had her child removed so that she could quickly get her child back.

Thus, the strategy of the Alameda Project was to involve the biological parents in the process that would lead to restoration. At the same time, problems in the family that had necessitated the substitute care were identified and became the target of behavioral intervention and change. The primary task of the caseworker was to provide the services the biological parent needed in order to have their child reunited.

Finally, the Alameda Project attempted to assess the value of dividing services among two social workers, one concentrating on problems within the biological family, the other serving the child and the foster family, and of monitoring the success of casework in both areas. The task of casework was to assist the parent in solving the problems that led to the removal of their children. Although the idea seemed obvious, the emphasis of child welfare services too often concentrated on the child while the parent was left to take care of her or himself.

Quasi-experimental Design. The project staff first underwent training in the use of systematic case management procedures, including the use of behavioral intervention methods (Stein and Gambrill, 1976). The project was then implemented in Alameda County, California, using a quasi-experimental design,[3] in which children were assigned to either an experimental group or control group. Children in the experimental group would be served by the experimental staff according to the guidelines developed by the project, while children in the control group would continue to be served in the usual way by workers not associated with the project.

In light of previous studies questioning the effectiveness of casework services, the results of the Alameda Project were impressive. As can be seen in figure 3.3, at the end of the second year 60 percent of the experimental group children had been restored to their families, compared to only 32 percent of those in the control group. Further, 15 percent of those in the experimental group had been adopted, whereas only 9 percent of those in the control group had been adopted. At the end of the experimental period, 57 percent of the children in the control group remained in long-term foster

---

[3] Quasi-experimental designs allow for conducting an experiment without random assignment to experimental and control groups. Although such designs use matched control groups for comparisons, they employ modified statistical tests that account for the lack of random assignment (Campbell and Stanley, 1963; Bawden and Sorenstein, 1992).

care, compared to only 21 percent in the experimental group. Clearly, the Alameda Project staff had greater success in both restoring children to their biological homes and providing them with a sense of permanency through adoption, than did the conventional foster care program.

The casework management and behavioral intervention methods developed by the Alameda Project represented the application of a promising technology for improving the effective delivery of service by trained workers. Working with parents to aid in getting their children back by accomplishing agreed-upon tasks, the caseworker was truly the parents' ally in the finest sense of the social worker tradition.

The Alameda Project was not without critics (Firestone-Seghi, 1979). Probably the most important methodological limitation of the study resulted from its departure from pure random assignment. At the beginning cases were volunteered for the groups, which were then supplemented by new cases randomly assigned to either the experimental or the control group.

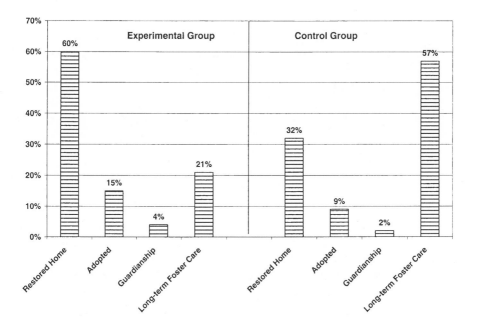

Figure 3.3 Outcomes of the Alameda Project
Source: Stein, Gambrill and Wiltse (1978).

However, the experimental and control group did differ on important dimensions that must be considered in assessing the study.[4] Despite this, the quasi-experimental design methodology of the Alameda Project represented a significant advance over the design used in the CES system. If we are to develop an empirical knowledge base in child welfare, wider use of this approach in research and evaluation is critical.

The Oregon Project

Whereas the Comprehensive Emergency Services project examined reform of the intake system and, like family preservation services, how unnecessary placement could be prevented, and the Alameda Project examined programmatic changes in casework services once children are admitted into foster care, the Oregon Project focused on how children ultimately leave care. The Oregon Project was a collaborative effort between Victor Pike (1976, 1977) of the Oregon Children's Services Division and Arthur Emlen, a social work researcher at Portland State University. The project examined strategies for reducing the backlog of children who had accumulated in foster care due to the lack of just such systematic interventions as those used in the Alameda Project. Studies of the foster care system had consistently found that, despite the best efforts of workers and agencies, some families and parents did not respond, and an unwarranted large number of children accumulated in long-term foster care. No one had yet developed a strategy either to restore them to their families or to place them in a permanent setting. The children too often simply drifted for years in long-term foster care, experiencing multiple placements and being denied the sense of permanency they might otherwise find in their own home. Victor Pike urged a concerted effort to end the plight of these children.

Underlying the desire for permanency was the recognition that long-term foster care was undesirable, even harmful. First, as the work by Bowlby (1958, 1969), and later Harlow (1958, 1961) pointed out, the denial of parental love and compassion can diminish the capacity for these qualities in children raised in foster care. Second, foster care had never been regarded as a therapeutic modality, only a temporary way of getting a child out of harm's way. That the family's problems often remained unresolved was a telling comment upon the effectiveness of the methods used

---

[4] One essential difference between the two groups was that only 6 percent of the experimental group was over twelve years old, while 22 percent of the control group was over twelve. The Oregon Project (Emlen et al., 1977) indicated that children over twelve were more difficult to place and thus did not include them in their demonstration effort to achieve permanency.

by the child welfare system (Knitzer, Allen, and McGowan, 1978). Third, children were not necessarily safer in foster care. In fact, studies suggest that foster care is often more dangerous than the family the child is removed from (Bolton, Laner, and Gai, 1981; Pryor, 1991; Spencer and Knudsen, 1992). Finally, long-term foster care was expensive. Cost to the state of maintaining a child in long-term foster care was approximately $15,000 per year (Fanshel and Shinn, 1972; Forsythe, 1992). In this regard, the Oregon study came to be of particular interest to legislators, who were eager to find ways to reduce costs while also improving the child welfare system.

Faced with more than 4,400 children in foster care in Oregon at the time of the study, the project staff proceeded to develop strategies designed to place the child permanently, either with the biological family or with an adoptive family. An initial study by Emlen in 1976 had found that the absence of an organized and coordinated effort to get children out of care was the major problem to permanent placement: "The foster care system does tend to favor the maintenance of relationships in foster care, and the use of foster care itself as a treatment or care setting, rather than the planning necessary to secure the child's future in a family. . . . Indecisiveness and deeply ingrained attitudes favor the maintenance of placement in foster care. A strong commitment from caseworkers and all levels of the state agency, as well as from other institutions and society at large, is needed to change the character of foster care practice" (Emlen et al., 1977: 44).

Child welfare agencies need to develop institutional mechanisms and incentives to reduce the number of children in foster care. Following this proposition, the Oregon Project staff designed a screening procedure to identify those children currently in care who appeared likely candidates for long-term care. The goal was, by concerted effort, to permanently place these children rather than allow them to drift. The criteria posed four questions that, based upon previous experience, would likely identify such children.

- Had the child been in care more than one year? If so, the child was likely to be headed for long-term foster care unless something was done.[5]
- Was the child unlikely to return home? Did difficult, unresolved problems still remain with the biological family which would indicate that the child was likely to continue in care?

---

[5] Research had indicated that with each subsequent year in foster care, a child's probability of leaving diminished (Fanshel, 1971; Goerge, 1990; Maas and Engler, 1959). Half of the children selected by the screening process had been in foster care for more than two years before the project began, with the average length of time being more than twenty-nine months. As well, multiple placements were common: 33 percent of the children had one placement, 30 percent had two placements, and 37 percent had three or more placements.

- Was the child adoptable? One of the purposes of this project was to identify those children who were adoptable, or who would most likely benefit from permanency planning efforts.
- Was the child less than twelve years old? The project focused on children under twelve because they were considered the most readily adoptable.

Terminating Parental Rights

With some parents the issue of restoring their children culminated in a dead end. Many biological parents received, except in the case of the Alameda Project, few services. However, even when services were provided some parents showed little interest in having their children returned. What could the caseworker do when the parent(s) did not want to cooperate? Was there a limit on the efforts at reunification the caseworker should make?

The Oregon Project developed procedures that would free children for adoption when the parents showed a marked lack of interest in having them restored (Pierce, 1982). One of the most important was the right of the caseworker to petition for termination of parental rights. Historically, this action had been viewed as a last resort to be invoked under only the most extreme circumstances. As Hewitt (1983: 229) observed:

> Termination proceedings are among the most dramatic actions the state can take against its citizens. A termination of parental rights is the ultimate legal infringement on the family. There are few state-imposed deprivations more unyielding and personal than the permanent and irrevocable loss of one's children. Termination of parental rights is even more severe than a criminal sanction. Only the death penalty is a more severe intrusion into personal liberty.

Prior to the Oregon Project, some legislative guidelines for the Termination of Parental Rights (TPR) had been established. These included:

- If a parent who had abandoned the child could not be contacted after searching strenuously for six months, or
- If the parent had deserted the child for more than one year and could not be found, or
- If after deserting a child for more than a year, the parent is found, but it is determined that placement with the parent would be detrimental to the child, or
- If the parent suffers a condition that is seriously detrimental to the child and is not remediable, or

• If a parent with no diagnosable condition continually fails to perform minimally to work toward change that would lead to the restoration of the child.

To put teeth into the warnings that caseworkers would take decisive action on behalf of the child if parent(s) did not demonstrate a sincere commitment, the project staff sought to strengthen and clarify the termination of parental rights statutes. Termination had long been a neglected area of child welfare, and the law surrounding it had been the principle domain of the legal community. Child welfare caseworkers called upon termination proceedings for only the most severe cases of abuse or felony behavior by the parents (i.e., drug trafficking, serious sexual assault, severe physical harm, etc.).

Like the Alameda Project, the Oregon Project staff developed a training program and materials to aid the project social workers, focusing on what rules and procedures might best get children out of long-term care and into permanent placement (Downs and Taylor, 1978; Pike and Downs, 1977; Regional Research Institute for Human Services, 1978). In a way, the project staff represented a special "strike force" whose task was to find permanent placements for the backlog of children in the foster care system. Their major new weapon was the threat of termination of parental rights if the parents did not cooperate (see Smith, 2002).

How successful was the Oregon Project? During a three-year period beginning in November 1973, the staff worked with 509 children selected from the 2,283 children in foster care. By October 31, 1976, permanent plans had been implemented for 72 percent of these children (see table 3.1) Twenty-seven percent had been restored to their biological family, and 52 percent had either been adopted or were in the process of being adopted, an unheard of level of success in freeing children for adoption. Clearly, the backlog of children in the foster care system was being shifted out of temporary care into a permanent setting.

Although the Oregon Project did not have a comparison or control group, it was evident that the progress achieved was greater than would otherwise have been achieved using normal procedures. When compared to children in other nonexperimental counties, the Oregon Project children were more rapidly and frequently placed in permanent settings. In counties where the project was implemented the average daily population of children in foster care dropped by 31 percent, compared to only a 4 percent reduction in nonproject counties.

Table 3.1 Results of the Oregon Project

	Plan Implemented	In Progress	Total	%
Restoration	131	5	136	27
Adoption				
By foster parents	96	63		
By new parents	<u>88</u>	<u>20</u>		
	184	83	267	52
Contractual foster care	37	3	40	8
Relatives	15	1	16	3
Plan not successful	0	0	50	10
	<u>52</u>			
	367	92	508	

Source: Emlin et al. (1977).

In addition to providing children with a sense of permanency, the Oregon Project resulted in considerable financial savings. A cost analysis estimated that the project saved more than a million dollars in foster care payments alone (even without amortizing payments for children over their projected duration in foster care). It is important to note that although initially the project was not cost effective, "the cumulative savings from decreased payments overtook the cumulative expenses of operating the Project in January, 1977" (Emlen et al., 1977: 89).

Conceptual Base for Reform

One has to conclude from the record of the reforms that discrete improvements (permanency planning, FP and so forth) are subverted and swallowed up in a pathological system. It is like dropping touches of color into paints that have run together and turned gray. The increments disappear into the gray.
Alvin Schorr, *The Bleak Prospect for Public Child Welfare*

Overall, the Comprehensive Emergency Services Program (Nashville), the Alameda Project, and the Oregon Project showed that comprehensive improvements to the child welfare services system could be achieved (Lindsey, 1982).[6] Further they provided a clear picture of what kinds of achievable reforms were necessary. Emergency services to parents when

---

[6] Sherman, Neuman, and Shyne (1973) examined efforts to facilitate reunification of children in foster care by providing special services. The results of this demonstration were disappointing (see Epstein, 1999).

acute stress occurs were needed to divert inappropriate cases and to prevent inappropriate placements. For children appropriately placed in foster care, the system had to ensure that they be restored to their homes as soon as possible. This required substantial effort by caseworkers to assist disadvantaged families. Consequently, efforts to achieve restoration had to be the central concern of child welfare caseworkers. And finally, for those children who remained in foster care for more than a year and who seemed likely to continue in foster care for a long period, case workers trained in systematic case management procedures had to take decisive action either to restore the children to their biological family or to find an appropriate permanent alternative.[7]

The demonstration programs had developed a technology that would permit a substantial reduction of the number of children in foster care. The CES system produced a fivefold decrease in the rate of foster care placements. The Alameda Project achieved a rate of restoring children to their biological parents within the first year almost twice as high as that by an equivalent control group (60 percent versus 32 percent). The Oregon Project, working with children who seemed likely to remain in care for years to come, was able to find permanent placements for almost 80 percent within three years. In combination, the reforms might achieve a substantial reduction (perhaps on the order of fivefold) in the number of children entering care. By conservative estimate the cumulative impact of these reforms could likely reduce the number of children in foster care by more than 90 percent. The stage was set for major child welfare reform.

Permanency Planning

> The permanency planning movement is shown to have failed on several counts
> . . . mainly because of its lack of impact on the provision of preventive and
> supportive services and because of its superimposition on a casework system
> with a dysfunctional structure.
>
> Leroy Pelton, *Beyond Permanency Planning*

The single unifying theme among the demonstration projects was the concept of permanency planning, which postulated that foster care be temporary and that children either be returned to their biological family or placed

---

[7] As a result of the success of these three demonstration programs, training materials were developed to facilitate dissemination of these successful strategies to child welfare professionals (National Center for Comprehensive Emergency Service to Children, 1976; Regional Research Institute for Human Services, 1978; Stein and Gambrill, 1976). The National Institute for Advanced Studies assembled a comprehensive syllabus for these programs and other important studies (Children's Bureau, 1980; Cohen and Westhues, 1990).

in adoption as soon as possible. No longer should children enter foster care inappropriately, and then remain in care for years with little effort made to restore them. Systematic case management (scientific casework) should work toward either restoration with the biological family or termination of parental rights, thus freeing the child for adoption.

Further, foster care was not a treatment modality. It did not provide a cure to children. The goal of foster care, as expressed by Jenkins (1974: 4) "is not upward mobility for the lower-class child, but typically the return of the child to the same milieu from which he [or she] came." It was, as the Alameda Project demonstrated, only an adjunct service the caseworker could use while assisting the parents with problems that prevented them from adequately providing for their child. The caseworkers' objective was to achieve reunification. If this could not be achieved, the child should be freed for adoption.

Overall, the demonstration projects had shown that if the objectives of foster care were clear, the system could meet those objectives effectively. The studies demonstrated the potential of child welfare professionals using research-based knowledge to achieve more effective social service programs. Further, substantial advance in science is spurred when measurable utility can be derived. In this regard, child welfare may well be at the forefront in demonstrating the usefulness of empirical knowledge from the social and behavioral sciences. Finally, the projects provided direction for comprehensive program reform of the foster care system at a national level.

The Adoption Assistance and Child Welfare Act (PL 92-272)

Following the success of the demonstration projects, child welfare professionals were for a time in the early 1980s hopeful and expectant that fundamental reform guided by scientific research was not only possible but also imminent. With reform would come decreased numbers of children in foster care. In fact, the demonstration programs ushered in major federal child welfare legislation, particularly the Adoption Assistance and Child Welfare Act (PL 96-272) passed by the U.S. Congress in 1980 (Administration for Children, Youth, and Families, 1984). This act implemented the concept of permanency planning and provided federal funding to the states to support efforts to restore children to their biological parents or to free them for adoption using legal efforts to terminate parental rights. The legislation required that states, through periodic review, demonstrate what efforts were being taken to reduce the number of children lingering in foster care. It allocated additional funding to facilitate these efforts.

The number of children in foster care began declining after nation-wide efforts to implement the findings from the permanency planning research. The Adoption Assistance and Child Welfare Act of 1980 provided federal funding to support permanency planning. However, the funding promised by the legislation was not made available and much of the promise of permanency planning was lost (see Kamerman and Kahn, 1990).[8] Under the Reagan Administration, the 1980s were characterized by broad-scale reductions in federal spending for social programs. Child welfare services saw a virtual end to support for major demonstration programs, even though these represented a proven technology to reduce the number of children in foster care.

Following a brief decline, the number of children in foster care rose again. In 1977 the number of children in foster care was estimated at more than 500,000. Two years after the passage of the Adoption Assistance and Child Welfare Act the number of children in foster care had dropped to 262,000. However, beginning in 1982, the number leveled off and began to increase (see figure 3.4).

The next great federal opportunity for child welfare reform came with the Clinton administration in the early 1990s. Hilary Rodham Clinton, the first lady of the new administration, was deeply committed to children's issues and had worked for the Children's Defense Fund. In 1993, Congress passed legislation providing federal support for family preservation services (intensive casework services) which was at the apex of its popularity. This was unfortunate timing because the opportunity for major child welfare reform was captured by advocates of an unproven and, ultimately, ineffective approach (see chapter 2). The Family Preservation and Family Support Services Program was part of the Omnibus Budget Reconciliation Act and appropriated nearly $1 billion over a five-year period for family preservation services. Despite substantial evidence questioning the effectiveness of this intensive casework services approach to preventing children in "imminent risk" of foster care placement, funding for the program was included in the omnibus legislation that was passed and signed into law. The result was a nationwide effort to develop family preservation

---

[8] With the passage of the Adoption Assistance and Child Welfare Act in 1980, child welfare funding to provide for permanency planning was, according to Kamerman and Kahn (1990: 33), "to increase gradually from approximately $3 billion in fiscal year 1981 to approximately $3.7 billion in fiscal year 1985. Instead, by 1985 the combined funding was less than in 1981—$2.8 billion. In contrast to the expectations for implementing the 1980 reforms, in 1981 Title XX funds were cut from $3 billion to $2.4 billion and so service plans for children and families are not implemented and directives from judicial and other external reviews are not followed." Permanency planning legislation provided "a new philosophy and a service framework. The federal government did not, however, provide the resources on which all else was premised" (Kamerman and Kahn, 1990: 9).

programs. One of the inevitable outcomes of this approach was an increased risk to children. With the emphasis shifted to keeping children with their parents, even when they were reported for abuse, numerous children were exposed to increased risk of harm.

Not long after the passage of Family Preservation funding news stories began appearing of children suffering and dying at the hands of parents who were able to retain their children as a result of family preservation efforts (Gelles, 1996; Murphy, 1997; Quinn, 1996; Roberts, 2002: 105–109; Spake, 1994). The empirical reviews of the intensive casework services offered as "family preservation" reported disappointing results (Heneghan, Horwitz, and Leventhal, 1996; Lindsey, Martin, and Doh, 2002; Rossi, 1995).

Family preservation services were designed, in part, to prevent unnecessary placement of children in foster care. The notion was to provide intensive services to families whose children were in "imminent need" of placement and thus reduce the large number of children ending up in foster care. However, passage of the Family Preservation and Family Support Services Program did not lead to a reduction of the number of children entering foster care. In fact, despite the billion dollar expenditure, there was a dramatic nationwide increase in the number of children removed from their families and placed in foster care (figure 3.4).[9]

The Adoptions and Safe Family Act

Within several years the disappointment with "family preservation" and the concern with the continued rise of the number of children in foster care led to the Adoptions and Safe Family Act (1997). The year prior to this legislation the Clinton administration took efforts to encourage adoption with the goal of doubling the number of children adopted annually. Several years prior to the enactment of the Adoptions and Safe Family Act (ASFA) Congress enacted the Multiethnic Placement Act (1994) which prohibited the delay or denial of foster care or adoption placements based on race. There was considerable debate and disagreement on the issue but the bill was passed and signed into law. The legislation was meant to increase the opportunity for children who linger in the foster care system to find a placement and to make sure that the effort to find a placement was not hindered because of the race of the adoptive parent (Barth, 1997).

---

[9] There is substantial variation in foster care populations by state. Foster care programs are administered by state and county child welfare systems. To examine the state variations in foster care populations see the information displayed by state at www.childwelfare.com. Be sure to examine the foster care report cards for the different states.

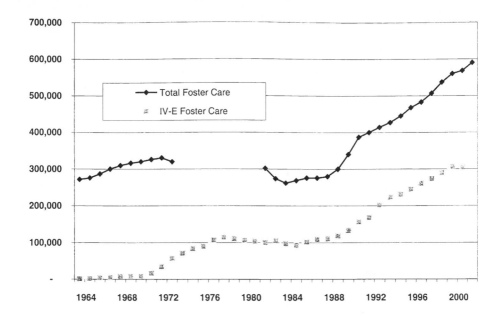

Figure 3.4 Foster Care Population in the United States, 1962–2000

Source: Tatara (1993), Department of Health and Human Services. VCIS Survey Data from 1986, 1987, and 1988. Washington D.C.: Caliber Associates and Maximus Inc. VCIS Survey Data from 1990 through 1997. Washington D.C.: Caliber Associates. 1998–2000 data from the Adoption and Foster Care Analysis and Reporting System.
See: www.acf.dhhs.gov/programs/cb/dis/tables/sec11gb/national.htm#national.

The Adoptions and Safe Family Act represented a major shift in emphasis from keeping the child with his or her biological parent whenever possible and making every effort to reunify children who were removed—family preservation—toward limiting the number of years children could drift in the foster care system without efforts toward finding a permanent placement or adoption.

Children in foster care were to be prepared for reunification and, if that was not possible, were to be freed for adoption. After 15 months in care, where reasonable efforts to return the child home had been made, the child welfare agency was required to file a petition for termination of parental rights (Barth, 1997). Thus, if the child could not be returned home in a reasonable time, the child welfare agency must work toward freeing the child for adoption.

One of the major concerns with this new legislation is that it represented a shift toward more rapid initiation of termination of parental rights proceedings against biological parents whose children were lingering in foster care. What were the rights of these parents?

There was little effort or concern to address the needs of the biological parents who were having their children taken away. Roberts (2002: 112) observes, "Foster parents have a great deal of influence over the children in their care and their visitation schedules. They are instructed to report negative incidents between biological parents and children. When both caseworkers and foster parents team up to pursue adoption, it is easy to sabotage biological parents' efforts to maintain ties with their children."

The Adoptions and Safe Family Act provided funding to support these efforts and facilitate increased adoptions. The impact of this legislation has been a more than doubling of the annual number of adoptions nationwide in the last five years (see figure 3.5).[10] There has also been a sustained increase in federal adoption subsidies which now total more than a billion dollars annually.

One result of the Adoptions and Safe Family Act has been a major increase in foster care cases where the biological parents' rights have been terminated (Stein, 2003).

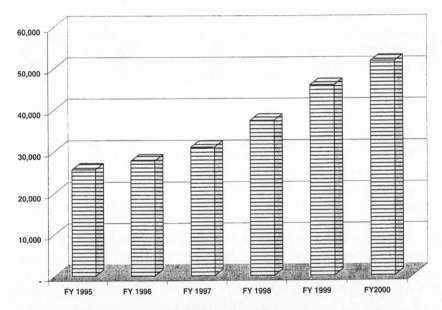

Figure 3.5 Children Adopted through Public Child Welfare Agencies

Source: Administration for Children, Youth and Families (2002). Missing data estimated. See: www.acf.dhhs.gov/programs/cb/dis/adoptbase.htm

---

[10] As with the foster care program, adoption programs are managed at the state level with considerable variation by state. For state data see www.childwelfare.com and select "Information by state."

In some states the success in terminating parental rights has led to a burgeoning of children freed for adoption and, thus, waiting to be adopted. For example, in 1998 there were 4,819 children adopted through public child welfare agencies in New York. During this same year 13,596 children were reported freed for adoption. If this imbalance between children being adopted and children being "freed for adoption" continued, then thousands of children waiting for adoption would accumulate in New York's child welfare system. Consequently, 31 children were freed for adoption in 1991. The drop from 13,596 to 31 reflects the virtual ending of the termination petitions because it didn't make sense to free children for adoption when there were not families ready to adopt them. In fact, for both 1998 and 1999 more than three-quarters of the children experienced a "time to adoption" that exceeded four years.

The good intentions of the Adoptions and Safe Family Act (ASFA) need to be considered against the reality of the public child welfare agency. As Stein (2003:680) observes:

> There is no basis to quarrel with ASFA's timelines for decision making and its emphasis on child safety to the extent that this focus will put a stop to *recurring* efforts to assist severely troubled families, and in so doing, to draw a line beyond which a child's right to stability trumps a parents right to unending efforts to reform their behavior. However, we must keep the following facts in mind. ASFA has shortened the timelines for decision making despite the paucity of substance abuse and related services and without taking into account deficiencies in the judicial and social service systems. In addition, agencies that are responsible for child safety are apt to be risk averse, causing them to remove children from their homes when the media treats as normative the tragedies that no system can fully avert. For these reasons, it is reasonable to suggest that the most severely troubled families will bear the brunt of Congress' good intentions. The need to protect children cannot be justified as fulfilling a moral and legal obligation if such protection is accomplished by terminating the rights of parents who have been denied any service.

Although there is an adoption demand that exceeds supply for white babies, for older children and children of color, there are too few families willing to adopt. Many states and nongovernmental agencies have gone to the Web to solicit adoptive parents. These Web sites display thousands of pictures of wonderful and beautiful children looking for homes. Roberts (2002: 103) observes, "Click onto www.mnadopt.org/search.asp or www.state.il.us/dcfs/adlink.htm.

You will find on these and other state web sites hundreds of photographs of children in foster care who are available for adoption."

The Color of Adoption

In Cook County, Illinois, the state filed 5,990 termination petitions in 1997—
up nearly five times from 1993. . . Remember, Black children make up nearly
95 percent of child welfare cases in Chicago, the main segment of Cook
County.

Dorothy Roberts, *Shattered Bonds*

In Illinois, Black children represent less than one-fifth of the state's child
population but they represent three-quarters of the state's child population
waiting to be adopted (Testa and Slack, 2002). In recent years Illinois has
dramatically increased the number of children adopted (see table 3.6). To
cope with this demand for adoptive families Illinois redefined "adoption"
to include guardianship placements of children with kin (Testa and Slack,
2002). In virtually every state Black children are substantially over represented among the population of children waiting to be adopted. Even with
increases in subsidized adoptions, there still remain many children waiting
to be adopted, particularly children of color.

Why are Black children so over represented in the pool of children
waiting to be adopted? The issue of racial disproportionality is a reoccur-
ring theme in the public child welfare system (Courtney and Skyles, 2003).

Table 3.6 The Color of Children in the Adoption System, 2000

	Black Children		
	Percent of State Population	Percent of Children Waiting to be Adopted	Percent of Children Adopted
California	7	31	22
Delaware	24	68	55
Florida	21	48	35
Georgia	34	60	56
Illinois	19	77	77
Indiana	10	48	43
New Jersey	16	69	66
New York	18	48	47
North Carolina	26	54	45
Ohio	14	48	43
Pennsylvania	13	57	56
Texas	12	31	26
Wisconsin	8	36	39

Source: www.childwelfare.com, Adoption Report Card, Slide 8.
See www.childwelfare.com select state and *Child Welfare Outcomes*

There are variations in the demand for children to be adopted. Brooks and James (2003) examined the willingness of adoptive parents to adopt Black children and found that white parents who want to adopt an infant are highly unlikely to be willing to adopt and to actually adopt a Black foster child. The problem is not that agencies are unwilling to place Black children with white adoptive homes (the Multiethnic Placement Act prohibits this) but that there simply are not enough adoptive homes for these children. The situation of Black children in the foster care system highlights the fine line between permanency planning by way of family reunification and/or adoption (Maluccio, 2002).

The over representation could also be explained by the higher poverty rates of Black children (Hines, Lemon, Wyatt, and Merdinger, forthcoming). William Epstein (2003:2) suggests that the over representation "reflects a certain reality of subcultural damage, that is, embedded cultural poverty that needs far more attention" than simply focusing on income poverty. "The broader issue is ... that economic poverty is not simply the result of a sudden economic catastrophe but rather reflects institutionalized differences in opportunity between groups over many generations. Both the poor and the majority culture adapt to these differences in different ways."[11]

As seen in table 3.6, Black children in New Jersey represented one-sixth of state population but more than 70 percent of the children waiting for adoption. In both Florida and New York Black children represent about one-fifth of the state population but half of the children waiting to be adopted (Smith and Devore, forthcoming).

Conclusion

The decline of federal support for "permanency planning" during the Reagan administration was by itself probably not sufficient to derail reform of the child welfare system. Other forces were emerging that would prove decisive. Beginning as early as the late forties, while social workers were attending to the problems of children in foster care, fundamental societal changes had begun occurring that were to shift the ground upon which the

---

[11] Epstein (2003) believes the economic solutions proposed in Chapters 11 and 12 may be too limited. He writes, "An institutionalized approach to differences will not succeed by simply reassigning limited funds. It will take an immense effort of will and a large commitment of resources over generations to equalize family situations, education, employment, and income." "The problems of cultural poverty—deprivation in the central social structure of socialization—are probably the cause of many of the problems the nation faces, notably expressing themselves as income inequalities" (p. 1).

traditional approach to child welfare services rested. Even as Kadushin was codifying the traditional definition of child welfare as a "helping" institution, indicating how it should function, and what it must strive to accomplish (within a residual framework), and even as the demonstration programs struggled to institute reforms that would allow child welfare to better fit that definition, the traditional approach was being weakened by forces beyond its control. First, the family was being affected in ways that the residual and casework perspectives were unable to address.

Second, the 1980s ushered in a new era in child welfare—the triumph of child protection through mandatory child abuse reporting laws. The agency that used to provide assistance to needy and disadvantaged families was, in a fundamental sense, turned on its head and now became the agency which controlled and monitored the lives of the disadvantaged. Threat of investigation and blame became the central characteristics of the new system. The traditional child welfare system was trampled by the laudable efforts of crusaders concerned with the safety and well-being of children.

In the next chapters we explore these and other changes.

4

The Changing Portrait of the
American Family

The family, though the smallest and seemingly most fragile of institutions, is proving itself to be humankind's bedrock as well as its fault line.

Steven Ozment, *Ancestors*

In this time of crisis it is important to remember that mothers of young children can make no finer contribution to the strength of the Nation and its vitality and effectiveness in the future than to assure their children the security of home, individual care, and affection. Except as a last resort, the Nation should not recruit for industrial production the services of women with such home responsibilities.

Frances Perkins, *The Roosevelt I Knew*

The traditional approach to child welfare which located the problems of clients in the parent/child relationship (Kadushin and Martin, 1988) was developed at a time when the economy was expanding, the divorce rate low, and children born out-of-wedlock rare. Just as the traditional approach was taking hold, broad social changes began impacting families and creating problems that had little to do with the parent/child relationship, and were not amenable to being solved through the traditional child welfare approach.

During the fifties, sixties, and seventies, the typical nuclear family was portrayed in the popular media like a Norman Rockwell portrait: four people—a mother, father, and two children—living comfortably in a modest suburban home (Usdansky, 2003). The father, who headed the household, worked eight to five in a white-collar job, while the mother stayed home to raise the children. The family ate together every evening and went to church on Sundays. Family aspirations included continued promotions for dad, a college education, marriage, and career for the kids, followed by grandchildren and eventual retirement. Family problems centered around which youngster should cut the lawn or use the family car on weekends. The economy appeared to be in a long-term upward trend, in which real wages were rising and opportunity increasing. Society was perceived as moving inevitably through ever more wondrous technological innovations and home improvements toward a kind of utopia. Television, just then emerging as the dominant media, romanticized this ideal in such early shows as *Leave It to Beaver*, *Father Knows Best*, and *The Nelson Family*. But even as America was staring fondly at this image, the everyday reality was undergoing major changes.

In fact, the changes had started during World War II when women had come out of the nurseries, parlors and kitchens to work in the defense plants building the planes, tanks, and munitions to be used by their husbands and sons in a far-off war. Between 1942 and 1945 almost five million American women left the confines of home to work in factories and defense plants. Seventy percent of the new jobs had actually been men's work and the women taking them were paid the same wages that had previously been reserved for men (Polakow, 1993: 38). It was a new experience for women, who became pipe fitters, welders, machinists, painters, carpenters, die cutters, plumbers—working roles that for generations had been held by men.

In 1945, when victory brought the men back to reclaim their former positions, women were thanked for their efforts and sent back into the home to become mothers and housekeepers. The substantial federal government child care subsidies which women had enjoyed during the war ended. As Tobin, Wu, and Davidson (1989: 219) observed, "The full-time mother enjoyed her greatest popularity in America in the 1950s, an era in which large numbers of men returning from the war and needing jobs pressured society to endorse an ideology that would justify the expulsion of women from the work force."

For many women, however, the war experience had shattered the old conventional roles. They had tasted the independence, opportunity, and sense of achievement that working in the labor market afforded, and they liked it (Kessler-Harris, 1982). Many women realized that, given the chance, they could succeed in whatever job they chose as well as or better than a man. In the next decades women began entering the labor market in increasing numbers, many choosing to work even when they had children. Before 1950 it was unusual to find a mother working outside the home only 12 percent of mothers with children under six did so (figure 4.1). By 1960, the numbers had increased to 20 percent, by 1970 to more than 30 percent, and by 1990 to 60 percent. By 1990, more than half of all mothers with infants less than one year old were employed outside the home. By 2000, almost two-thirds of mothers with children under six worked outside the home, a rate more than 5 times greater than five decades earlier.[1]

---

[1] For single mothers the rate of employment is even higher: 73 percent for both mothers with children under three and under six (U.S. Census Bureau, 2001a).

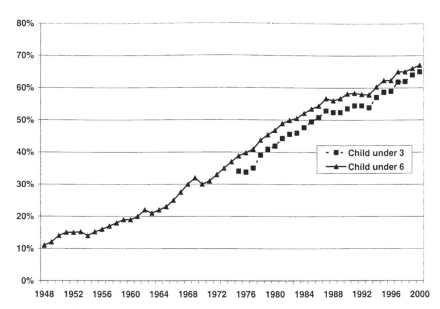

Figure 4.1 Mothers with Young Children Working Outside the Home
Sources: U.S. Bureau of Labor Statistics (1988); Zill and Rogers (1988: 40);
Cherlin (2002: 291).

Mothers with Young Children Enter the Workforce

> Employment of mothers with dependent children . . . is to be deplored, as ex-
> perience shows that unless the mothers' earnings are sufficient to enable them
> to employ competent assistance in the home, the children will be neglected
> and the mothers' health will break under the double burden of serving as
> wage-earners and home makers.
>
> Grace Abbott, *The Child and the State*

The entry of women into the labor force, especially those with children,
raised difficult new questions: What will happen to the family while the
mother is working? Who will cook? Keep house? Wash, dress, and feed
the children? The questions seemed straightforward and innocent at first,
but underneath they addressed broad social developments that were complex, and held disruptive and ultimately decisive implications not only for
family social structure, but for the traditional approach to child welfare
which attempted to safeguard that structure. Fifty years later the questions
are still being asked, despite the fact that many of the answers have already
materialized, producing an American family portrait decidedly different
from earlier years (Casper, Hawkins, and O'Connell, 1994).

Distribution of Household Chores

In the half century since these changes have been taking place, the roles of men and women have changed. Since the 1970s men's contribution to housework has almost doubled. Coltrane (1995) found that in families where both the husband and wife work outside the home, men account for one-third of the time spent shopping, caring for the children, and in meal preparation. However, Coltrane also found that in these same households men do 15 percent of the laundry. This is a substantial increase from the 3 percent of laundry work done by men before 1970. Even though men in dual-earner families share more of the housework, many households have largely failed to establish an equitable equilibrium in their family responsibilities. The issue of who is responsible for what chores remains an area of conflict in many households.

Beginning in 1965 Bianchi, Milkie, Sayer, and Robinson (2000) asked a national sample of men and women (between the ages of 25 and 64) to keep a diary on the amount of time they spent on various household chores during the week (including cooking, laundry, cleaning, outdoor chores, cleanup after meals, paying bills, and repairs). In 1965, men reported spending less than 5 hours a week while women reported 34 hours (see figure 4.2). By 1995, the number of hours for men had increased to 10.4 hours while for women it had decreased to 19.4 hours. Thus, in 1965 the number of hours spent on housework by women was seven times greater than for men. By 1995, the number was less than twice as much. The unequal division of household chores had been reduced. The trends indicate continued and increased sharing of housework (Coltrane, 1995). Nonetheless, these changes in the division of labor in the home did not occur without considerable tension.

The modern family in the mid 1980s still saw women carrying major responsibility for household chores. A survey found that when both husband and wife worked full time, the wife did twice as much housework as the husband and three times as much child care (Conway, 1990: 103). Calasanti and Bailey (1991), examining the division of household tasks among working couples, found that women performed between 73 and 84 percent of all domestic labor. Thus, even when both the husband and wife worked an equal number of hours outside the home, the wife still carried the major burden of household chores.

In 1992, Galinsky, Bond, and Friedman surveyed men and women in dual-earner households regarding their participation in child care. The men reported sharing equally in child care 43 percent of the time, but the women in the survey reported that the men shared equally 19 percent of the time.

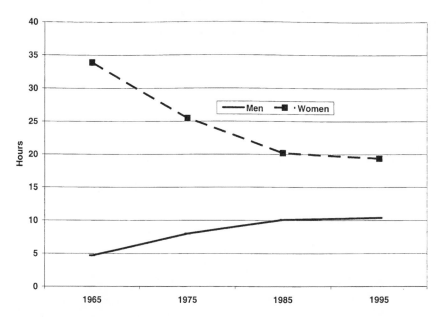

Figure 4.2 Changing Share of Household Chores for Married Men and Women (Ages 25 to 64)

Source: Bianchi, Milkie, Sayer, and Robinson (2000).

In the same survey 81 percent of the women reported they took major responsibility for the cooking, and 78 percent reported they took major responsibility for cleaning even when both men and women worked full time outside the home. According to the men's reports, the women took major responsibility for the cooking 70 percent of the time and responsibility for cleaning 63 percent of the time. Even when women earned more than the men they still carried the greater burden for household chores. Variations in the division of household labor were not a product of social class. Wright, Shire, Hwang, Dolan, and Baxter (1992) found no difference in the proportion of housework done by men and women in different social classes in the United States and Sweden.

Divorce and Unwed Motherhood:
Two Paths to Becoming a Single Parent

Children in families disrupted by divorce and out-of-wedlock birth do worse than children in intact families on several measures of well-being. Children in single-parent families are six times as likely to be poor. They are also likely to stay poor longer. Twenty-two percent of children in one-parent families will

experience poverty during childhood for seven years or more, as compared
with only two percent of children in two parent families.

> Barbara Defoe Whitehead, *Dan Quayle Was Right*

Accompanying the entrance of women into the workforce and the changing division of labor at home have been other social developments that
have further altered the family social equation. The most significant
change has been the rapid rise in the divorce rate that began in the mid-
1960s. Between 1960 and 1975 the number of divorces in the United
States tripled, from approximately 450,000 to more than 1,200,000 a year
(see figure 4.3). Why the sudden increase in divorces during the decade of
the sixties? Numerous explanations have been offered, including the tension rising from more women working outside the home and the resulting
disruption of the traditional roles and responsibilities (Cherlin, 2002). As
women entered the labor force they naturally expected their family roles
and responsibilities to change. There was an increased expectation that
husbands would take on additional household chores and child caring responsibility. Yet, as we have seen, in the modern two-earner family where
mom works full-time outside the home, she continues to carry the primary
responsibility for child care and household chores.

Marriage as a Sacred Institution

What the Supreme Court called a "sacred obligation" in the 19th century
was referred to as "an association of two individuals" in the 20th century.

> Patricia Cohen, *The Marriage Problem*

From the earliest history of the United States marriage had been viewed as
a sacred institution entered into by two persons for a lifetime (Becker,
1981; O'Neill, 1967). Society frowned on divorce and this view was codi-
fied in state laws that required proof of specific wrongs, such as adultery,
desertion, and mental or physical harm, before a divorce was permitted
(Cherlin, 2002; Goldstein, 1999; Phillips, 1991). However, in the seventies
the United States began passing no-fault divorce laws (Glendon, 1987) that
ushered in an "era of unrestricted divorce." Cherlin (2002: 423) observes
that "in most liberal no-fault states and nations, [divorce] had become
something close to an individual right."

The emergence of the sexual revolution and the demand for equal
rights for women also contributed to tensions about the traditional roles
within the family. During the early sixties the introduction and widespread
acceptance of the birth control changed sexual relationships. Akerlof and
Yellin (1996) argue that during this period sexual relationships were fundamentally altered by a "reproductive technology shock."

Table 4.1 Changing Reproductive Behaviors

	1965–69	1970–74	1975–79	1980–84
Unmarried Women Using the Pill at First Intercourse (percent)	5.7%	15.2%	13.4%	NA
Abortions for Unmarried Women 15–44	88,000	561,000	985,000	1,271,000

Source: Akerlof and Yellin (1996).

The historic requirement of marriage before sexual relationships was undermined by two reproductive technologies—the birth control pill and medically safe abortions. As seen in Table 4.1, the number of unmarried women using the birth control pill at first intercourse more than doubled from 5.7 percent in the period from 1965 to 1969 to 15.2 percent a decade later in the period from 1975 to 1979. The rate of abortions increased during this same period by ten fold.

The idyllic model of a two-parent family where the father was employed outside the home and the mother stayed home and took care of the house and raised the children had rapidly given way to households where both parents worked outside the home (Blankenhorn, 1995). In the face of changing demands on the family, including mothers entering the labor force, the loosening of requirements for divorce, the demands for equality for women, and the widespread use of the birth control pill and abortion, there was a cultural shift in attitudes toward divorce, and the historic prohibition against divorce was loosened (O'Neill and O'Neill, 1972).

Following the spike in divorces in the sixties, when the divorce rate more than doubled (from about 8 to more than 22 per 1,000 marriages), the divorce rate stabilized in the early seventies and remained at the new high rate for the next several decades with only a modest decline (Cherlin, 1992 and 2002; Goldstein, 1999). Currently, almost one-half of all marriages end in divorce. In the last quarter of a century, although the overall child population has remained stable, the number of children involved in divorce has tripled (figure 4.3).

Unmarried Mothers

In the old days of the 1960s, 50s, and 40s, pregnant teenagers were pariahs, banished from schools, ostracized by their peers or scurried out of town to give birth in secret. [Today they are] supported and embraced in their decision to give birth, keep their babies, continue their education, and participate in school activities.

New York Times (2002)

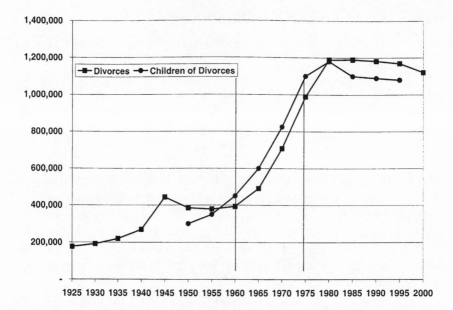

Figure 4.3 Number of Divorces and Children Involved

Source: Norton and Miller (1992); National Center for Health Statistics (1999).

Another change impacting the family structure was the steadily increasing number of children born out of wedlock. From 1950 to 2000 the number of children born out of wedlock in the United States increased from 142,000 per year to more than 1,300,000 per year (see figure 4.4). During this same period, from 1950 to 1998, there was a decline in the percentage of women who were married from 66 percent to 55 percent; for African American women the decline was from 62 percent to 36 percent (Bachrach, 1998).

The Single Parent Family

The consequence of increased divorces and increasing numbers of children born out of wedlock has given rise to a social phenomenon known as the single parent family, usually a woman, who is responsible for raising children by herself. The number of single parent households has increased from 2.8 million in 1960 to more than 12 million in 2000, of which only 16 percent were headed by fathers. In 1940, less than 100,000 children were born out of wedlock. By 1960, the number had more than doubled to 200,000, and by 1970 to 400,000. In 2002, the number of single parent families increased 13 percent to more than 13 million (representing almost 30 percent of families with children).

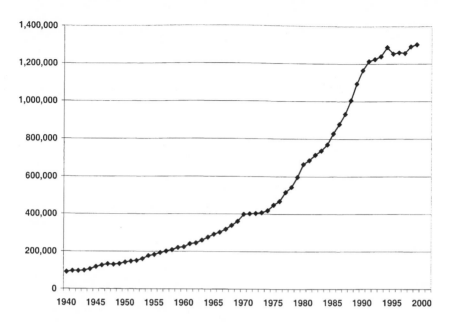

Figure 4.4 Births to Unmarried Women
Source: Ventura and Bachrach (2000, Table 1).

By 2000 more than 1.3 million children were born out of wedlock and represented one-third of all births in the United States (see figure 4.4).

The rise in single mother families has been particularly steep for African Americans, for whom it is now the predominant family arrangement. In 1998, the poverty rate for unmarried African American families with children was almost ten times greater than the poverty rate for married African American families (27 percent versus 3 percent).

Poverty: The Consequence of Being a Single Parent

The increase in divorces and children born out of wedlock spawned a rise in single parent families (see figure 4.5).[2] Single parents, the vast majority

---

[2] In Europe there has been an increase in the number of single parent families to almost 10 percent of all births in Western Europe and as high as 20 percent in the United Kingdom (1.6 million out of 7.5 million households with children in the U.K.). Between 1961 and 1981 births to single mothers increased from 2 to 5 percent in Ireland. By 1996, the births to unmarried mothers represented 25 percent of all births.

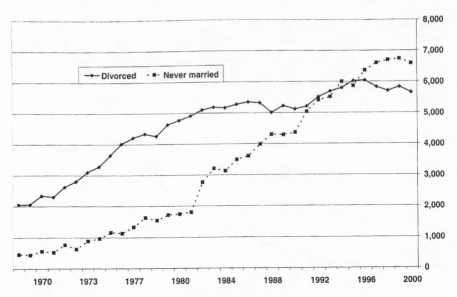

Figure 4.5 Number of Single Mother Households in the United States, 1970–2000.

Source: National Center for Health Statistics (1999).

of whom are women,[3] are obliged to find work outside the home even when they have children under two (especially after the passage of welfare reform in 1996). To support their family, almost three-quarters of all single mothers must shoulder the burden of two full-time jobs—homemaker and employee (U.S. Census Bureau, 2001a). As they have grappled with these almost crippling demands, their economic situation has declined.

The Economics of the Single Parent Family: Divorce

As we have seen, there are two routes to single parenthood; divorce and out of wedlock birth. What have been the consequences of the single family's economic situation for the children? While it might be expected that, after divorce, child support payments and alimony would cushion any threat to economic conditions for both father and mother, the actual consequence has been a downward economic plunge for the mother and children (whose care invariably falls to the mother), often matched with improved economic circumstances for the father.

---

[3] In 2000, there were 10 million single parent mothers and about 2 million single parent fathers (U.S. Census Bureau, 2001a).

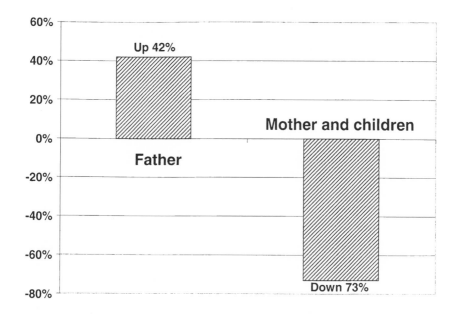

Figure 4.6 Change in the Financial Situation After Divorce
Source: Weitzman (1985).

Examining the economic situation of families after a divorce, Weitzman (1985: xii) found that the mother and children experienced a 73 percent decline in their standard of living, while the father's standard of living increased by 42 percent (see Figure 4.6). Espenshade (1979: 623) has observed that following divorce, "in general, wives are left worse off than their former husbands. Not only are they usually the ones awarded custody of the children without commensurate financial help from fathers, but they generally face other impediments in the labor market to higher pay and adequate employment opportunities."

For women, restoration to predivorce income almost always requires remarriage. Duncan and Hoffman (1985) observed that this occurred even though the percentage of women who worked more than 1,000 hours per year increased from 51 percent before the divorce to more than 73 percent after. Corcoran and Chaudray (1997) report that the average yearly income for women before divorce was $43,600 and declined to $25,300 after divorce (see table 4.2).

Table 4.2 Impact of Divorce on Mother's
Household Income

Before Divorce	$43,600
After Divorce	$25,300

Source: Corcoran and Chaudray (1997).

Divorce often has a devastating impact on both the economic and emotional conditions for children. Seltzer (1994) reports that the household income for children declined by an absolute value of 37 percent for children (and a relative value of 21 percent). Studies of divorce consistently report the emotional harm and hurt suffered by children (Wallerstein, Lewis, and Blakeslee, 2000).[4] McLanahan and Sandefur (1994) found that children in single parent families consistently have a more difficult time in school (also see Fagan, 1999).

Often these children lose contact with their fathers after divorce. Seltzer found that for many fathers once a marriage dissolves so does their relationship with their children. In her study 20 percent of fathers had not seen their child a year after divorce and only half had seen their children more than several times during the year.

Children Born Out of Wedlock

Children born out of wedlock are more likely to live extended periods of their childhood in poverty. Examining data from the *National Longitudinal Survey of Youth,* Rector, Johnson, and Fagan (2001) calculated the average time children spent on welfare by their family type. As seen in table 4.3, children living in never married families are likely to spend close to 50 percent of their childhood on welfare (or 1/20 as much). The children in married families are likely to spend less than 2.5 percent of their childhood on welfare. Clearly, child poverty and welfare are often the outcome of out-of-wedlock births.

The declining support from income transfer programs such as Temporary Assistance for Needy Families (TANF) and social assistance has also exacerbated the problem of single parents (as we shall see in chapter 10). Too often, current income assistance programs have proven a trap for single parents.

---

[4] Wallerstein, Lewis, and Blakeslee (2000) suggest that it is later in life that the child of divorce experiences the greatest emotional struggles.

Table 4.3 Average Time Spent on Welfare for Children by Family Type, 1979-1996.

Family Type	Average Percent of Childhood on Welfare
Never Married	44.5
Subsequent Marriage	20.4
Divorced	10.7
Married	2.5

Source: Rector, Johnson, and Fagan (2001).

Eligibility and levels of support for TANF have been tied not to care and provision of children, but to labor force participation by the single parent outside the home. Consequently, single parents have faced a situation where program eligibility requirements have too often failed to make it cost-effective for them to leave public assistance. McLanahan and Garfinkel (1993: 23) observe that "single mothers with low earnings capacity in the U.S. are forced to choose between working full time, living at the poverty line and having no time for their children, or not working, living below the poverty line, and having time with their children."

The Feminization of Poverty

During the last several decades, while the work load carried by men has been decreasing, the work load for women has increased substantially. Besides greatly increasing their participation in the labor market, women continue to carry primary responsibility for child rearing and household chores. One would expect that as women worked longer their overall economic situation would improve. However, as women have taken on substantial new burdens, their economic situation has, in fact, deteriorated. The median income of first marriage families was $48,000, while the median income for a never married single parent was $15,000, and $18,500 for divorced/separated families (Fagan, 1999).

As seen in figure 4.7, the economic situation of children is largely determined by the structure of their family. Children living in single parent families constitute almost three-quarters of the poorest 20 percent of families and less than 5 percent of the top 20 percent of families based on income. Likewise, children in two parent families are less than a quarter of the poorest families but more than 95% of the top fifth, based on income.

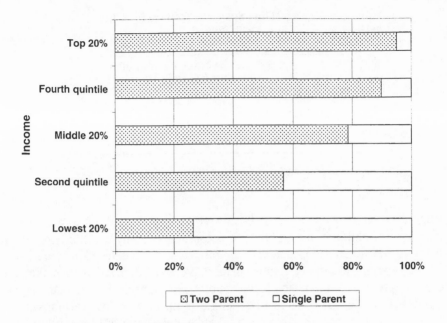

Figure 4.7 Families with Children by Income Quintile and Structure
Source: U.S. Census Bureau (1997).

This economic disadvantage for single parent families is not surprising. In this sense, Dan Quayle's critique of Murphy Brown was on target (White-head, 1993). Most single mothers are not financially self-sufficient. With only one potential wage earner, single mothers with children face major barriers to earning adequate income. Two-thirds of working women are secretaries, waitresses, or sales clerks, traditionally low-paying jobs (Ehrenreich, 2001; Faludi, 1991).[5]

This feminization of poverty has little to do with women's commit-ment to work, since relative to men, as well as overall, women are working more. Rather, the *feminization of poverty* is a product of policies and pro-grams that have failed to provide for child care needs, protect the eco-nomic security of single parents, and ensure equitable treatment in the la-bor market.

The result is that today single mothers and their children constitute the largest social group afflicted by poverty. Currently, almost 60 percent of all households headed by single mothers have income below the poverty line (National Council on Welfare, 1993: 20, table 14). Single mothers in the United States face enormous demands with little of the infrastructure

---

[5] Conversely, less than 0.5 percent of top corporate managers are women (Faludi, 1991).

of programs and policy support found in other industrialized nations (see chapter 11). Single parents in the America receive almost no community or government support. Their economic situation has led to more than one-fifth of all children growing up in poverty.

The Responsibility of Fathers

Where are the fathers in this picture? The primary burden of child care usually falls to the mother (Amato, 1998; Furstenberg and Cherlin, 1991). One would expect that, at the very least, the father should be expected to provide child support? Because child support collection in the United States is a civil matter, responsibility for collecting it has fallen to the single mother. However, the courts have proven an ineffective tool for mothers to use in enforcing child support. Overall fathers have found the court-based collection system, with all of its safeguards and protections, an easy enforcement mechanism to sidestep.[6]

Since child support collection lacks reciprocity (that is, the mothers have nothing to withhold from the nonpaying fathers), the consequences for fathers who avoid payment have too often been insignificant. If the father pays, it is more out of moral obligation than any legal coercion. Consequently, most mothers and their children have ended up going without child support, and either make do with less or work harder to make up the difference. Once in sole charge of the children, most mothers uphold their child care responsibilities, not for fear of being reported for child abuse and neglect, but because they love their children.

The situation for unwed mothers is even more difficult. Those women who elect not to terminate an unplanned pregnancy or not give up the child for adoption assume an eighteen-year responsibility (burden) of raising the child on their own. Although a father has obviously been involved, before he can be compelled to pay child support, paternity must be established. Census studies have indicated that fewer than one in eight unwed fathers pay child support (Hacker, 1992: 88).[7] For an unwed teenage mother, the

---

[6] The U.S. Department of Health and Human Service's Office of Child Support Enforcement (2002) reports that only about half of all child support that is due is collected. Further, of the more than $84 billion in back payments for child support that are due, less than 7 percent is collected annually. The Canadian Advisory Council on the Status of Women reported that 50 to 85 percent of divorced husbands and fathers default on child support payments (Conway, 1990: 125). In 1989, only about 26 percent of court-ordered child support payments in Ontario were complied with.
[7] With the passage of welfare reform there has been a substantial increase in the number of child paternities established, although there are wide variations by state.

task of providing proper child care, maintaining a household, and working full-time is difficult to say the least.

The two-parent family has always been viewed as the ideal setting for children. As two parents they have greater earning capacity, so they are much better situated financially to raise children. The average single parent in the United States earns about one-quarter of what the average two-parent family earns. More importantly, a two-parent family is able to share in the labor-intensive effort required to nurture and discipline children.

Single parents are at an enormous disadvantage. They must carry responsibility for child rearing while maintaining the home and earning an income, responsibilities that most single parents are unable to balance satisfactorily. Further, the children of single parents often become the victims of stereotyped expectations that children from "broken" homes are more troublesome and difficult to manage. As Archard (1993: 120) observes, "If a child is brought up to believe that it is less well-off and abnormal for having only one parent, then that belief can only too easily be self-confirming."

Should public policy aim at assisting single parents who are disadvantaged? To do so could be viewed as either disfavoring the two-parent family or favoring the single parent. Should public policy discourage the formation of single parent families or promote marriages?[8] If so, how can this be accomplished?

The public child welfare system emerged to serve the needs of orphaned or abandoned children. These "leftovers" or residual children were cared for in orphanages and later in foster care. The residual model of the child welfare system continued even as the population served by the public child welfare system changed. By the 1960s, the children served by the public child welfare system were no longer orphaned. The problem of orphaned children had long since ended. Rather, the children entering the child welfare system were removed from mothers who were incapable or unable to properly provide for them. Many poor mothers were provided services so they could keep their children.

The changes in the family which began in the late fifties and erupted in the sixties—birth control, divorce, and out-of-wedlock births—were more than the residual model could bear.

---

[8] Furstenberg (2002) has pointed out that current efforts to promote marriage are untested and likely to be ineffective (cf. Sawhill, 2002).

Limitations of the Residual Model

[The residual approach] is laid on us by a history that may no longer be functional; it is maintained by its own tendency to perpetuate itself; on the whole we have not even known we were making a choice . . . the losers are always the same—children and the poor.

Alvin Schorr, *Children and Decent People*

The major difference between the programs developed by the Children's Bureau in the first half of the twentieth century in the areas of infant mortality, mothers' pensions, and child labor and the programs of today's public child protection system focusing on child abuse, foster care, and adoptions is that the former were primarily "universal" programs while the latter are essentially "residual" programs (see chapter 1). Universal programs provide benefits to all; the constituency is everyone. In contrast, residual programs are subject to "eligibility" or "means testing" to determine those most in need. The problem is that these programs come to rely on mercy and charity for the disadvantaged. While often a reliable source of support, this source can waiver. Over time support for most "means-tested" programs recedes. As the famous British social welfare theorist Richard Titmuss argued, programs for the poor become poor programs. Over time, funding support tends to decline. As the programs fail to end poverty, their funding is continually reduced, making them even more likely to fail.[9] In Europe the social programs for children and seniors tend to be "universal." The broad use of "means-tested" residual social programs to address child poverty is largely limited to the United States (Gauthier, 1999; Rainwater, 1999).

Major Concerns with the Residual Model

The first problem with the residual model is that it waits until the problem occurs before doing anything. This is too often too late. This is particularly true in terms of child welfare. As we have seen, one of the major causes of child poverty is reliance on a single parent, particularly children born to unmarried mothers. In our modern economy these mothers are at a considerable competitive disadvantage. The residual model waits until the young woman has a child she is ill prepared to care for. At this point it is too late.

---

[9] This has been the history of AFDC/TANF in the United States. Over the years the benefit levels for welfare have consistently declined. In 1970 the average monthly AFDC benefit per family was $713; 608 in 1975; 509 in 1980; 467 in 1985; 458 in 1990; and 377 in 1995 (Wilensky, 2002, 299). While the history of AFDC/TANF is well known, the history of the residual model in child welfare has rarely been questioned (Skocpol, 1997; 2000).

Once a child is born to a young mother the new family unit is on a life trajectory that is very likely to lead to poverty. There is very little that can be done to significantly change the life circumstances of this family unit, and it will be very difficult for the mother to achieve financial independence.

Second, the residual model places an unintended premium on failure. Services are not provided *until* the client demonstrates need because of limitations or failure. Because of limited resources there is always a question of "means testing" in order to provide services for those most in need. Thus, the client is served who is most in need, who is most desperate, who is in worst shape. The client understands this. If they want service they need to be most in need. There is almost a perverse pressure to fail in order to benefit from services.

Third, services are ameliorative rather than curative. Powerful interventive technologies have not been developed which can effectively ensure cure or change. Child welfare programs such as foster care do little to substantively change the life trajectory of the young person in difficulty. There is a delicate balance struck between ameliorating the pain and suffering and altering the situation of client. State intervention is too often ratcheted down to the poverty level. The client can be sustained at poverty level but little else.

Finally, the residual model provides services to involuntary clients. It is motivated by charity or concern for protecting the weak and disadvantaged. Clearly in times of acute emergency charity is in order. But charity can also have a corrosive effect on the sense of competence and self-sufficiency of the individual. It encourages passivity and dependence. It takes away from the sense of personal responsibility.

Services provided within a residual model are unable to restore the economic viability and opportunity of the affected individual. The safety net is the vision of the residual model, but, as critics of the modern welfare system have pointed out, too often that safety net traps and entangles all that it catches (Murray, 1984). A different vision based on individual self-determination, empowerment, and entrepreneurial spirit is required (Gilbert and Gilbert, 1991).

The Residual Approach, the Changing Family, and Child Welfare

The traditional (residual) approach to child welfare focuses on the problems in the parent/child relationship and the provision of services to ameliorate those problems (Kadushin and Martin, 1988). However, the broad social changes that affected the families—increasing divorce, out-of-wedlock births, and mothers employed outside the home, as well as serious economic disruption—had little to do with the parent/child relationship. Further, the problems created by these major social changes are not amenable to solution through the residual model.

The main service provided by the residual child welfare system is foster care (Godfrey and Schlesinger, 1965). Yet, the provision of foster care does not address the problems women face as a result of their increased entry into the labor market. The residual approach does not address the problem of the increased divorce rate or the rise in single parent families (Longfellow, 1979). It simply provides a system to respond to the most egregious problems which result from these trends in the form of soft police who monitor, through the use of the child abuse reporting systems, the actions of poor mothers—or as Pelton (1989) calls them, the poorest of the poor—removing children when failure to provide proper child care reaches an unspecified threshold for intervention. The residual approach does not lead to policies and programs that would substantially reduce or prevent these problems from occurring in the first place.

The residual perspective does not speak to issues such as the feminization of poverty, or even child poverty. Nor have social programs been developed that take proper consideration of the circumstances of single mothers. At the federal level, children's programs have suffered from benign neglect.[10] With increasing numbers of married women and single mothers entering the labor force, and thus unable to remain at home and care for their children, it is difficult to understand why so little attention has been given to providing universal child care. It is an obvious policy need that has remained unaddressed since World War II. But of course, women have been largely absent from the halls of legislatures, and family

---

[10] As an example, the provisions of maternity leave programs of European democracies allow mothers to maintain their jobs while bearing children (Conway, 1990; Eichler, 1988; Kamerman and Kahn, 1978). West Germany allows mothers six months at full pay. Sweden has a "parenthood insurance" program that provides twelve months at 90 percent pay (Liljestrom, 1978). Italy provides five months at 80 percent pay. Norway provides every working woman an eighteen-week leave at 90 percent pay (Henriksen and Holter, 1978). In Canada, women are entitled to eighteen weeks unpaid maternity leave. Unemployment insurance (UIC) guarantees women in Canada a compensated maternity leave of fifteen weeks at 60 percent pay (to a maximum of $363 per week in 1989). Until recently, the United States had no government provision for maternity leave. Hewlett (1991: 28) observes that the United States is the "only rich country that fails to provide new mothers with maternity benefits of job-protected leave." Alison Clarke-Stewart (1993: 148) adds, "The United States lags behind almost all other industrialized countries in the supply, quality, and affordability of day care. The United States, alone with South Africa among advanced industrialized nations, has no clear and integrated national policy to provide support and services for children and families." In 1993, the U.S. Congress finally enacted family leave legislation.

policy has relied on predominantly male legislatures that have historically shown little interest in this area.[11]

Although the needs of children are frequently recognized, child welfare policy has been limited to reforms of the residual system, usually after a tragic incident compels public concern. The residual approach retains its hold even though the assumptions about family on which it is based have collapsed (Meissner, 1975). As Polakow (1993: 23) observes, "While families have changed in profound ways, particular myths of the family and consequently of motherhood have endured, myths that have placed mother in a specific domestic and social space in relation to husband, children and the state." The tenacious hold of these mythical views of the family have restricted progress toward solutions, especially in the area of child care.

Who's Watching the Kids?

[Welfare reform] will tell young mothers to be employed, away from their children for much of each week. These children, already fatherless, will now become primarily motherless. They will be raised by somebody else. A grandmother? A neighbor? An overworked day care manager? Or they will be left alone.

James Q. Wilson, *The Marriage Problem*

Raising children is a labor-intensive responsibility (Adams and Schulman, 1998). When mothers are employed outside the home, most on a full-time basis, then someone has to look after the children. Ideally, the person who looks after the children will provide the same type of loving care and training that the mother would provide were she available (Whitebook, Howes, and Phillips, 1998). As we have seen, even when mothers work outside the home on a full-time basis they still carry the primary responsibility for child care when they come home from work.

---

[11] Legislative bodies determine how resources (such as the Gross National Product) will be distributed. In a society where special interest politics shape governmental interests, those groups able to use their financial advantage to fund the campaigns of elected officials will likely see legislation enacted which is favorable to protecting and improving their interests. Likewise, those groups who are unable to make contributions to the campaigns of elected officials will likely see their interests go unprotected. Further, those groups, such as single mothers and the poor, who have historically recorded low voter turnout will be especially ignored. And most of all, those who do not vote—children—are unlikely to have their interests protected, and will likely fare poorly in competition with others in the arena of political decision-making. This contrasts with the political power of seniors and their powerful lobbying groups, such as American Association of Retired Persons (AARP) with 35 million members.

With women increasingly entering the work force, the question became: Who was left to raise the children? As we entered the new millennium more than 60 percent of mothers with children under two worked
outside the home (Green Book, 2000). What child care arrangements did
the mothers use? Using data from the U.S. Census Bureau, the Urban Institute found that most small children were left in low-cost child care facilities (Capizzano, Adams, and Sonenstein, 2000; Capizzano and Adams,
2000a,b). Less than a third were cared for in organized child care facilities
(see table 4.4).

As seen in table 4.4 most children are cared for in informal arrangements in another home (40.1 percent). Relatives play a major role in providing care; grandparents (14.5 percent), fathers (12.8 percent) and siblings (5.6 percent) help out almost a third of the time. Research by Presser
(1999) indicates that one-third of two-earner families with preschool children work different shifts (evening, night, or rotating) in order to provide
child care. Presser (1994) found that many of the husbands in these arrangements do more of the housework, including cooking, cleaning, and
laundry.

The major factor which determines the type of care that children under
six receive is cost. Many working mothers select child care arrangements
which they can afford or which are least costly. The Children's Defense
Fund (Adams and Schulman, 1998) survey of child care centers across the
country found that in almost every state the average annual tuition exceeds
$3,000 per child, but in seventeen states it exceeds $5,000 annually. As
seen in table 4.5, for mothers employed outside the home the cost of child
care is substantial. For low-income mothers (less than $1,500 a month in-
come) or mothers in poverty, the cost of child care is about 30 percent of
their family income. For families with monthly income over $4,500, the
percentage of income spent on child care is about 6 percent.

Marital status also influences the use of child care. Single mothers,
especially divorced and separated mothers, rely on child care. The passage
of welfare reform led to a substantial increase in the percentage of single
mothers with young children who are now working. More than 80 percent
of divorced mothers with children under three are now in the labor force.

Children Unsupervised after School

For child welfare one change of particular concern is that with women
working and child care difficult to find, many children, especially school-
age children, have been left virtually unsupervised.

Table 4.4 Primary Child Care Arrangements for Children Under Five with an Employed Mother

	Full time	Part time
Care in child's home		
By grandparent	5.4	6.5
By sibling age 15 or older	.5	1.1
By sibling under 15	.3	.3
By other relative	2.3	3.1
By nonrelative	<u>4.6</u>	<u>5.4</u>
	13.1	16.4
Care in another home		
By grandparent	9.1	11.1
By sibling age 15 or older	3.0	2.4
By family day care provider	18.9	9.6
By nonrelative	<u>9.0</u>	<u>5.8</u>
	40.1	29.0
Organized child care facility		
Day/group care center	20.2	13.1
Nursery school/preschool	6.3	5.2
Kindergarter/grade school	.6	.7
Head Start Program	<u>1.4</u>	<u>1.6</u>
	28.5	20.8
Parental care		
By father	12.8	22.7
By mother at work	<u>3.6</u>	<u>8.3</u>
Total children involved	6,336,000	3,601,000

Source: Survey of Income and Program Participation, U.S. Census Bureau.

Table 4.5 Average Weekly Child Care Expenditures for Employed Mothers of Children Under 5 and Percent of Income Spent on Child Care (1995) in the United States

	Weekly cost of care	Monthly family income	Hours worked	Percent of monthly income spent on child care
Poverty status				
Below poverty	$66.94	$968	33	30.0 %
Above poverty	99.26	5,176	36	8.3
Monthly family income				
Less than $1,500	66.41	980	35	29.4
$1,500–$2,900	83.51	2,353	36	15.4
$3,000–$4,499	89.90	3,685	37	10.6
$4,500 and over	118.12	8,210	36	6.2

Source: U.S. Census Bureau, Survey of Income and Program Participation (SIPP), Wave 9. Internet release date: October 31, 2000.

The U.S. Census Bureau has estimated that approximately 2.1 million children under thirteen are left without adult supervision both before and after school (the so-called latchkey children). Pryor (1991) has observed that "child left unattended" is the major reason children are reported for child abuse in New York.

Mothers employed outside the home receive substantial child care assistance when their children reach school age. In a sense, mothers of children from six to eighteen receive free child care in the form of public school education. These parents have the added security of knowing their children are in a constructive and educational setting. However, when children get out of school child care needs to be arranged for them if their mother is not there to take care of them. This problem can also occur before school begins if the mother starts work before the child is in school. According to the Census Bureau (2000) almost 2.5 million children ages 5 to 14 have no child care arrangements other than caring for themselves.

Government Inaction on Child Care

Today, nowhere is there a greater need for action and attention by all of us than in the area of child care—responsible, cost-effective care and supervision provided to preschool children so that their mothers can work. Although virtually all industrialized countries provide publicly funded and operated child care for children ages three to six, the United States has developed a patchwork system of child care with many gaping holes (Gauthier, 1999; Los Angeles Times, 2002; Stingle, 2002).

With 60 percent of poor mothers of children under six now in the labor force, an enormous need for child care services has arisen (Kamerman and Kahn, 1988a). However, only a small fraction of children are accommodated by current programs.

The French Model

A number of studies had confirmed that early access to nursery school was an important factor in children's future academic success and social integration, particularly in underprivileged areas.

French Prime Minister's Report

In contrast to the United States, which ended child care after World War II, France developed a comprehensive child care system to protect the children of women who went to work rebuilding and industrializing France after the war. For the 4.5 million children under the age of six in France today there is a vast constellation of child care programs (Greenhouse, 1993). For infants and toddlers, from three months to three years of age, child care is provided in day care centers and day care homes. Day care homes are government-licensed baby sitters who look after young children in their own home. The day care home staff must pass medical and psychological tests and have their facilities regularly inspected.

For children ages two and a half to five years, subsidized preschools are provided. These are normally open from seven in the morning until seven at night. Cost is based on a sliding scale, ranging from $390 for poor families, to $3,200 for middle-class families, $5,300 for upper-income families. The remaining costs are subsidized by the French government at a cost of approximately $7 billion a year. As a result, more than 99 percent of three-, four-, and five-year-old children attend preschool at no or minimal charge. This is sharp contrast to the United States. Stanley Greenhouse (1993: 59) writes, "Comparing the French system with the American system—if that word can be used to describe a jigsaw puzzle missing half its pieces—is like comparing a vintage bottle of Chateau Margaux with a $4 bottle of American wine."

Almost all of the countries in Western Europe provide publicly financed care to children ages 3 to school age (see Table 4.6). In response to the increasing participation of mothers in the labor market, these countries have built and expanded public child care facilities. Germany, France, and most of the countries in Europe provide entitlement to a kindergarten for every child three years of age or older.

In 1971, the U.S. Congress passed the Comprehensive Child Development Act providing universal free child care. President Nixon promptly vetoed the bill, arguing that it would be a serious error to commit "the vast moral authority of national government to the side of communal approaches to child rearing over and against the family-centered approach." Since then child care in the United States has been largely a personal responsibility with only minimal government support. Most public funding for child care today is provided in the form of child care tax credits for middle- and upper-income families. With welfare reform there has been increased pubic funding of child care services for low-income parents.

Ambivalence toward Working Mothers

The lack of affordable child care in the United States is indicative of the ambivalence toward working mothers that few have been able to resolve. Given the choice, should a woman with a preschool-aged child work outside the home or not?

Table 4.6 Percent of Children Age Three to
School Age Enrolled in Publicly Financed
Child Care Facilities

Country	Percent Provided
Austria	75
Belgium	95
Denmark	79
Finland	43
France	99
Germany*	100
Greece	64
Ireland	52
Italy	97
Netherlands	69
Portugal	48
Spain	84
Sweden	79
United Kingdom	53

Source: Gauthier (1999: table 5), updated by author.
*Percentage for Germany represents those eligible
but not necessarily enrolled.

Largely in reaction to the women's rights movement, conservative critics argue that small children need close personal contact with their mother, and that women should be at home with them. At the same time, it is widely felt that mothers, even of young children, should work outside the home, since their additional earnings will help make the family self-sufficient (Kamerman and Kahn, 1988a). For impoverished single mothers caught in an economic vise, the choice is irrelevant. For mothers in two-parent households the choice only becomes possible when both parents are not required to work. Even then, the result for the woman is guilt and confusion. As Tobin, Wu, and Davidson (1989: 182) observe,

> In the midst of this cacophony of discordant, often accusatory voices, mothers cannot help but feel accused and confused. Even if a mother, after some difficulty, manages to locate a good preschool for her child, she invariably feels a sense of guilt and dereliction of duty. Conversely, a woman who chooses to stay home with her child is subject to real or imagined criticism from feminists and other employed women. Fathers are not completely immune to these feelings, but balancing parenting and work remains clearly a woman's problem.

Declining Relevance of the Traditional Approach to Child Welfare

In the changing world of working women, divorce, unwed mothers, impoverished single parent families, and the limitations to the traditional approach to child welfare become obvious. With its focus on the "deficits" of parents in meeting their parental responsibilities and its concern with psychological faults and shortcomings, the traditional approach has been unable to recognize or embrace the new structural realities. However, given the enormous role that poverty has had in bringing children to the attention of the public child welfare system, the realities are becoming increasingly difficult to ignore (Wallerstein and Kelly, 1979). Welfare programs which attempt to ameliorate poverty are inextricably entwined with deeply felt political issues, and in its effort to achieve professional status the public child welfare bureaucracy has had to tread softly. However, by ignoring the issue of poverty the child welfare system has given itself over to treating symptoms and not causes (Pine, 1986).

The result continues to be an ever increasing host of problems which the residual child welfare system is increasingly incapable of dealing with. Without the means of addressing the broad structural problems that produce poverty, the traditional approach has progressively restricted its focus to include only those children experiencing ever more "severe" forms of abuse and neglect. The problem is that the residual orientation provides too narrow a perspective to solve the problems created by current social realities. Although the residual perspective was congruent with the traditional casework method, the problems children and their single parents now face require an *expansion* of perspective before the social and structural dimensions within which family problems arise can be understood.

While the residual perspective may have been appropriate for an earlier time, it no longer represents an effective approach toward the problems that children and families face in the twenty-first century. For decades it allowed society to provide services "on the cheap," targeting only those "most in need." Indeed, it retains its enduring appeal largely because it promises to cost the least by doing the least. However, it has proven itself ineffective in dealing with long-term problems brought about by irrevocable social changes. Somehow a new understanding of the limits and possibilities of child welfare must be developed, one that reflects the enriched knowledge base in the field and an understanding of the social conditions within which public child welfare services operate.

The situation can be compared to business and industry, which routinely look to the government for assistance in developing the capacity to compete in the global economy. To function, the business community *requires* an economic infrastructure that provides assistance in a variety of forms to all businesses, not just those businesses in difficulty. The business community would certainly not accept anything resembling a residual perspective in developing policies and programs that regulate commerce and industry. Likewise, families and children, which represent the country's future, require a broad-based infrastructure to support their development and economic opportunity.

Conclusion

While it may seem that the traditional approach had little opportunity to continue after such sweeping social changes had occurred, it nevertheless has continued to hold sway throughout the field of child welfare, although with very little practical effect. The residual model of the past continues to shape and guide policies and programs despite its apparent deficiencies and inadequacies in the new era. To borrow an analogy from Marshall McLuhan, the child welfare profession continues to drive forward with eyes fixed on the rearview mirror. We drive based on our knowledge of the roads behind, instead of seeing the road in front and the changing conditions of the family and assessing what is required to navigate this road ahead.

The public child welfare system that evolved to assist the families in the 1950s was ill equipped to meet the needs of the changing American family emerging in the 1960s. Divorce and out-of-wedlock births led to a different and larger set of demands on the child welfare system. Unprepared and unable to meet these new and increased demands made the child welfare system the subject of disaffection and critique. The child welfare system was ripe for fundamental reform.

Although few saw it coming, a major transformation of the public child welfare system was on the horizon. In the 1960s another phenomenon would eclipse all efforts for child welfare reform, and would, within a few years, remove any pretense of maintaining the approach to child welfare as delineated by Kadushin (1967). Everywhere the phenomenon would redirect the mandate of child welfare agencies in their delivery of services. The phenomenon was child abuse. Overnight, almost out of nowhere, the beating and killing of infants and children would command headlines, mobilize legislators, and transform child welfare agencies. Within less than a decade child welfare agencies across North America, developed to provide services to needy and disadvantaged children, would be foundering in a flood of child abuse reports. How did it happen?

5

The End of Child Welfare:
The Transformation of Child Welfare
into Child Protective Services

There I was confronted by a startling finding. An examination of the *Reader's Guide to Periodical Literature* and the *Social Science and Humanities Index* showed that absolutely no articles on "child abuse" (regardless of what term one used) had been published before 1962.

Barbara Nelson, *Making an Issue of Child Abuse*

In time . . . we realized that we were creating a system of reporting . . . which could invade and harm the lives of parents and children as easily as help them.

Alan Sussman and Stephan J. Cohen, *Reporting Child Abuse and Neglect*

In 1946, a distinguished radiologist, John Caffey, exploring the use of X-rays with infants and young children, reported puzzling symptoms in children who had been admitted to the hospital for treatment of subdural hematoma (pooling of blood under the skull). Caffey's X-rays revealed that, in addition to the subdural hematoma, the children had multiple long-bone fractures in their arms and legs. Altogether in the six children studied he found twenty-three long-bone fractures and four contusions (injuries to subsurface tissues where the skin is not broken). It was a puzzling phenomenon. What had caused such fractures and tissue injury? By this time, rickets and bone syphilis had become rare diseases. The most likely explanation was trauma of some sort (i.e., an externally caused injury), resulting perhaps from an accident or fall. Caffey knew that trauma did indeed produce such skeletal changes in infants and young children (Caffey and Silverman, 1945). Being a radiologist who did not have direct contact with the patient or the family, Caffey had no reason to suspect trauma from assault. Were the fractures related somehow to the subdural hematoma?

Table 5.1 The Emergence of Medical Evidence of Physical Child Abuse

Year	Author	Title /*Journal*	Summary
1945	Caffey & Silverman	Infantile Cortical Hyperostos. *American Journal of Roentgenology*	Use of X-ray to examine injuries to children
1946	Caffey	Multiple Fractures in Long Bones of Infants Suffering from Chronic Subdural Hematoma. *American Journal of Roentgenology*	Identified 6 children with skull - injuries also had fresh, healing multiple fractures with no adequate explanation
1950	Lis & Frauenberger	Multiple Fractures Associated with Subdural Hematoma in Infancy. *Pediatrics*	Additional case similar to Caffey's findings, no etiology established
1950	Smith	Subdural Hematoma with Multiple Fractures. *American Journal of Roentgenology*	Case report similar to Caffey's but no explanation of origin
1951	Barmeyer, Alderson, & Cox	Traumatic Peristitis in Young Children. *Journal of Pediatrics*	Finding of increased metaphysical fragility in infants, no etiology
1952	Marquezy, Bach, & Blondeau	Hematome sousdural et fractures multiplas des os longs chez un nourrisson de N. mois. *Arch. franc. pediat.*	An additional case similar to Caffey's
1953	Silverman	Roentgen Manifestations of Unrecognized Skeletal Trauma in Infants. *American Journal of Roentgenology*	Reported 3 cases similar to Caffey's & urged histories of patients to understand etiology of injuries
1954	Marie & others	Hematome sousdural du nourrisson associe a des fractures des membres. *Semaine hop. Paris*	An additional case similar to Caffey's
1955	Woolley & Evans	Significance of Skeletal Lesions in Infants Resembling Those of Traumatic Origin. *Journal of the American Medical Association*	Study finds multiple injuries to 12 infants are associated with unstable households
1956	Bakwin	Roentgenographic Changes in Homes following Trauma. *Journal of Pediatrics*	Examines 3 case studies of children with multiple injuries
1958	Fisher	Skeletal Manifestations of Parent Induced Trauma in Infants and Children. *8th Medical Journal*	Indicates importance of parental history in understanding injury to children
1959	Kempe & Silver	The Problem of Parental Criminal Neglect and Severe Abuse in Children. *Journal of Diseases of Children*	Suggests injuries to children need to be brought to the attention of legal authorities
1959	Milter	Fractures among Children - 1, Parental Assault as Causative Agent. *Minnesota Medicine*	Suggests that multiple injuries are often result of parental assault
1961	Adelson	Slaughter of the Innocents: A Study of Forty six Homicides in which the Victims Were Children. *New England Journal of Medicine*	Retrospective study of 46 child homicides; 37 were killed by their parents
1961	Gwinn, Lewin, & Peterson	Roentgenographic Manifestations of Unsuspected Trauma in Infancy: A Problem of Medical, Social, and Legal Importance. *Journal of the American Medical Association*	Examination of 25 cases of children with multiple injuries; stresses need to remove child from else death may occur
1962	Kempe & others	The Battered Child Syndrome. *Journal of the American Medical Association*	Evidence of the "battered child syndrome"

Might the two be symptoms of some new children's disease? Caffey (1946) duly reported the symptoms in the *American Journal of Roentgenology,* the professional journal for research on the medical applications of X-ray technology.

During the decade following Caffey's report, other radiologists and physicians reported similar findings. Lis and Frauenberger (1950) in the United States, Smith (1950) in Canada, and Marquezy, Bach, and Blondeau (1952) and Marie (1954) in France all reported cases similar to that reported by Caffey (see table 5.1). In 1953, Silverman reported three cases of infants with symptoms similar to those observed by Caffey. Silverman, however, concluded that the bone changes observed with X-rays were obviously the result of traumatic injuries accumulated over time. He urged physicians to obtain reliable patient histories so that the etiology of these injuries might be better understood. However, Silverman cautioned that physicians not alarm parents with feelings of guilt by appearing too suspicious about the parents' actions and intentions.[1]

Such cases continued to accumulate. In 1955, Woolley and Evans published a review of reports of infants coming into medical facilities with serious physical injuries that were "unaccompanied by readily volunteered and adequate account of injury." Woolley and Evans identified two syndromes of serious physical injury of unknown origin in infants: (1) subdural hematoma with multiple long-bone fractures, and (2) traumatic periostitis (inflammation of bone tissue). No evidence existed to suggest that these syndromes were due either to a disease process or to an unusual bone fragility in the affected infants. In their search for an explanation, the researchers examined the infants' family backgrounds. Their study of twelve infants "presenting multiple areas of bone damage which appeared to have accrued over an extended period of time and for which no easily elicited story of injury was available" revealed that the infants "came invariably from unstable households with a high incidence of neurotic or frankly psychotic behavior on the part of at least one adult" (Woolley and Evans, 1955: 542–543).

Woolley and Evans published their work in the *Journal of the American Medical Association* where "it reached the radio, television, and press and electrified the public" (Radbill, 1974: 18). The study contributed to the emerging concern of the U.S. Children's Bureau with child abuse reporting legislation. It laid the foundation for the understanding of "battered chil-

---

[1] Scott (1978) suggests that the early reports of the radiologists (Caffey, Lis and Frauenberger, Smith, Silverman, and others) failed to understand the role of parents in the traumatic injury to infants because they had limited contact with parents (Cameron, 1978; Churchill, 1974). Radiologists do most of their work "in a darkened and silent room, far from the crying babies and weeping or sullen parents" (Scott, 1978: 175).

dren" developed by Kempe and his colleagues, six years later. Summarizing the work of the radiologists, Costin (1992: 194) wrote, "The long dormancy of child abuse as a major professional and public issue might have continued had it not been interrupted by new knowledge and the skills of radiologists."

The Battered Child Syndrome

> Attention to child abuse, as distinct from child neglect and poverty, burst forth in the mid-1960s with the identification by doctors of "the battered child syndrome." . . . A new image of child maltreatment seized the public eye: behind the closed doors of their homes, parents from all social classes might brutally beat their children, then escape detection by fabricating accidents and falls.
> Mary Larner, Carol Stevenson, and Richard Behrman, *Future of Children*

In 1962, C. Henry Kempe and his colleagues surveyed eighty-eight hospitals in which they identified 302 children who had been "battered." Kempe sharpened the focus on what was clearly emerging as "child abuse" by defining the "battered child syndrome" as a child or infant less than three years old who presented the physician with unusual injuries, broken bones, or cranial injuries that were inadequately or inconsistently explained. When published, this survey, which graphically catalogued brutality to young children, many of whom suffered multiple injuries, ignited a broad-based national effort to find ways to protect children (Gil, 1970; Nagi, 1977). Specifically, it led to calls for implementation of mandated child abuse reporting systems, to ensure that whenever a "battered child" was even suspected, the case would be reported and measures taken to protect the child. Reporting was viewed as the first step in providing protection to the suspected battered child.

During this period (early 1960s), the Children's Bureau, responding to physicians' concerns, began developing a model reporting law that mandated that physicians report cases of suspected child battering. By 1963, thirteen states had adopted mandatory reporting laws. Bagley and King (1990: 33) report that "by 1966 all fifty American states had passed new legislation regulating child abuse." Shortly after, every state had developed much broader definitions of abuse than the "battered child syndrome," all of which mandated reporting. In 1986, every state but one required reporting of neglect, and forty-one states made explicit reference to reporting of emotional or psychological abuse (Hutchison, 1993).

The early intent had been to limit mandated reporting to physicians only. However, the American Medical Association, which objected to being singled out, urged that mandated reporting be required of other professionals as well. As a result, state mandatory reporting laws were not limited to medical professionals, but included teachers, nurses, counselors, and the general public.

The Avalanche of Child Abuse Reports

The state-mandated reporting laws resulted in an immediate and meteoric rise in child abuse reports across the United States. In 1962, when Kempe and his colleagues published their report, "The Battered Child Syndrome," there had been about 10,000 child abuse reports (see table 5.2). By 1976, the number of child abuse reports had risen to more than 669,000, and by 1978, to 836,000.

Table 5.2 Reports of Child Abuse

	Number of Reports
1975	294,796
1976	669,000
1977	838,000
1978	836,000
1979	988,000
1980	1,154,000
1981	1,211,323
1982	1,262,000
1983	1,477,000
1984	1,727,000
1985	1,919,000
1986	2,086,000
1987	2,157,000
1988	2,265,000
1989	2,435,000
1990	2,557,000
1991	2,684,000
1992	2,909,000
1993	2,967,000
1994	3,062,000
1995	3,105,000
1996	3,120,000
1997	3,232,000
1998	3,193,000
1999	3,244,000
2000	3,500,000*

* Estimate based on trend line derived from child fatality data (see table 5.4).
Source: Peddle and Wang (2001).

By 2000, there were estimated over 3.5 million reports of child abuse nationwide.

Historical Precedents for Protective Services

To understand the impact of child abuse reports on child welfare agencies, it is important to understand the perceived mission of child welfare agencies prior to this time. Public child welfare agencies' responsibility to protect children from harm and cruelty began well before the turn of the century (Antler and Antler, 1979).

In 1874, when eight-year-old Mary Ellen was brought before a New York court wrapped in a blanket, the judge turned his head away rather than view the child's tortured body. The judge removed the child from her guardian and placed her in the custody of the American Society for the Protection of Animals, there being no organization at the time to protect children. The case led to the founding that year of the New York Society for the Prevention of Cruelty to Children. Although child protection in North America began with a narrow focus on cases of physical cruelty, it soon broadened its focus to include neglect, abandonment, and child welfare in general (Antler, 1981; Lynch, 1985). Gradually, child abuse became only one of many concerns of the public child welfare system.

Although cases of severe physical abuse continued to arouse public outrage and so provide substantial support for the efforts of the children's aid societies, the main focus of the societies was, in fact, the thousands of abandoned and orphaned children. By the early twentieth century, severe physical abuse had become a minor concern, because it represented such a small part of the problems that came to the agencies' attention (Costin, 1992). As Kadushin observed, the absorption of protective services into public child welfare resulted in a "decline of interest [in protective services] between 1920 and the 1960s. Child maltreatment as a social concern dropped out of the public agenda" (Kadushin and Martin, 1988: 222-223). Thus, while child abuse was "discovered" in 1874 and the child protective movement spread rapidly, it just as quickly receded. Costin (1992: 177) observed, "By 1910, more than 200 societies [to prevent child cruelty] existed in the United States. Twenty years later, however, the anticruelty movement had lost momentum, changed in purpose, and become much less visible. The social work literature of the early 1900s through the 1950s reflects a sharply diminished discussion of child abuse as a condition requiring intervention by community agents."

Indeed, the child welfare studies by Brace (1880), Theis (1924), and Trotzkey (1930) focused on the relative merits of foster care and institutional care. No major studies on child abuse appeared during this period. As for the calls for research in the 1950s, little mention was made of child abuse (Dybwad, 1949; Kahn, 1956; Norris and Wallace, 1965).

Part of the explanation for this silence had to do with the difficulty of proving that children's injuries had been inflicted by the parents, who often could provide a variety of plausible explanations for an injury. The only person who could contradict them were the children, who were generally regarded as neither credible nor reliable. As well, even in the face of the most severe brutality, the child would often cling to whatever love or bond existed with the parent (Elmer, 1967). Social workers lacked the tools to determine when the bruises and severe injuries were accidental and when they were intentionally inflicted by an angry parent.

Thus, by the time the Social Security Act was passed in 1935, the child welfare system had been defined as being for the "protection and care of homeless, dependent and neglected children and children in danger of becoming delinquent." Concern with the issue of physical child abuse had receded. For the next thirty years child welfare services went about providing foster care along with an assortment of other services (including diminishing institutional care) to needy children and families.

The decades from 1950 to 1970, which saw the rapid growth of the public child welfare system, were characterized by an effort to construct an empirical knowledge base that would guide and inform public policy regarding the child welfare system. Alfred Kadushin synthesized the results of the emerging research into a theoretical framework that firmly established the field (Kadushin, 1967). The child welfare system, according to Kadushin, was to help parents meet their child-rearing responsibilities through the provision of supportive and supplementary services or, when that was not possible, to remove the children from their parents and provide substitute care. Child abuse was not central to the perspective, but was regarded as an "interaction event" that derived from problems in the parent-child relationship (Kadushin and Martin, 1988). Kadushin's definition was illustrative of how psychological theories that had been evolving steadily since the 1920s were being integrated into social welfare practice. With the emergence of mandated child abuse reporting, however, the perspective changed, and the goals of the agencies were abruptly redirected toward a whole new set of problems. The view developed by Kadushin, which may have been appropriate for an earlier time, was swept aside by the tide of child abuse reports. As Besharov reported (1983: 155), "the great bulk of reports now received by child protective agencies would not have been made but for the passage of mandatory child abuse reporting laws and the media campaigns that accompanied them."

Impact of Child Abuse Reporting on the Child Welfare System

In 1990, Kamerman and Kahn reported on their comprehensive study of child welfare programs in a range of localities throughout the United States. Although they found major differences between the locations they studied, one overarching theme emerged: child welfare agencies within the decade of the 80s had been changed from foster care agencies into protective service agencies whose function was to investigate the ever-increasing avalanche of child abuse reports. Kamerman and Kahn (1990: 7–8) wrote:

> Child Protective Services (CPS) (covering physical abuse, sexual abuse, and neglect reports, investigations, assessments, and resultant actions) have emerged as the dominant public child and family service, in effect "driving" the public agency and often taking over child welfare entirely . . . Child protective services today constitute the core public child and family service, the fulcrum and sometimes, in some places, the totality of the system. Depending on the terms used, public social service agency administrators state either that "Child protection is child welfare" or that "The increased demand for child protection has driven out all other child welfare services."
>
> For the most part these protective services are child rather than family-focused. They are organized around investigation and risk assessment rather than treatment, and as a result the large proportion of cases where the allegations are not substantiated receive no help regardless of how troubled the children and families may be . . . Child protective staff fear errors—especially the failure to take endangered children into care—and the subsequent public response to deaths or severe abuse and neglect.

Child welfare resources were, as a result of mandatory reporting laws, redirected from providing services to needy children and families toward investigating and intervening in the increasing number of child abuse reports. For every report received, a child welfare agency worker was sent to investigate. The worker interviewed parents, neighbors, teachers—anyone who might have evidence to substantiate or deny the allegations brought forth in the complaint. The investigation might take a week, two weeks, a month, or longer, before sufficient data was collected that would permit a decision on what action should be taken. The process was difficult and expensive.[2]

Throughout the seventies and eighties, as public awareness campaigns alerted the public to the prevalence of child abuse, the number of reports

---

[2] There have been various concerns with the reporting laws. For example, Besharov has suggested that increased reporting has often led to higher numbers of unfounded reports (Besharov, 1990a; Eckenrode, et al., 1988; Giovannoni, 1989). However, Finkelhor (1990) has criticized this view. See also Daro (1991) and Besharov's response (1991).

escalated, which in turn increased the need for more investigators and resources in child welfare agencies. At the same time the mood in society
and government was turning increasingly skeptical toward social programs.
Throughout the eighties, expenditures for social services were repeatedly
cut. Paradoxically, while the public continued to demand greater efforts be
made to curb child abuse, it was increasingly unwilling to fund those efforts. Thus, child welfare was having to confront a steadily growing problem with steadily diminishing resources (Faller, 1985). Even for a field that
from the beginning had been required to accomplish more with less, the
task was impossible. The result was a continual narrowing of focus regarding who should receive child welfare services (Garbarino, Carson, and
Flood, 1983; Weston, 1974).

The residual approach had always necessitated a "means test"—
poverty, neglect, abandonment, being orphaned—before the child would be
granted services. Child abuse now became the litmus test for conferring
eligibility for services. Moreover, how severe was the abuse? Was the child
being beaten, sexually molested, starved, tortured? Was the situation life-
threatening? The millions of children living in destitute families, whose
hopes and dreams were daily obliterated by poverty, and whom the agencies had previously attempted to aid, now, because they did not qualify,
began dropping through the holes of the protective services safety net. To
make matters worse, family supportive services that might have alleviated
the demand for child welfare services were often cut to finance the new
protective service investigations. In Virginia, for example, "increases in
CPS budgets for investigation . . . were matched by decreases in AFDC
service budgets" (Dattalo, 1991: 13).

The Accused Parents' Perspective

> In hearings to adjudicate parents' rights to get their children back, parents are
> at a significant disadvantage. . . parents must defend themselves against a
> veritable army of opponents seeking to keep them separated from their chil-
> dren. Parents, who are almost always indigent, often stand alone before the
> judge. At best, they are represented by a public defender or pro bono attorney
> assigned by the court. Only rarely can parents threatened with termination af-
> ford to hire a private attorney of their choice.
>
> Dorothy Roberts, *Shattered Bonds*

From the outset, the approach taken by agencies in investigating child
abuse reports was accusatory. That is, the caseworker's responsibility was
to collect information that might eventually be used to build a case against
the accused parent in order to protect the affected child. Whereas previ-

ously the welfare worker might have been viewed as coming forward to help a troubled family, the worker now was unmistakably cast in the role of inquisitor prying into and judging the affairs of the family, with predictably adverse effects on the family. Elizabeth Hutchison (1993: 60) notes:

> Investigation of a report of child maltreatment is not an innocuous intrusion into family life. By the time an investigation is complete, the family has had to cope with anxieties in both their formal and informal support systems alerted to state suspicion of their parenting. Even if the report is expunged from the central registry due to lack of substantiation, it is seldom expunged from the mind of the family—or from the memories of persons in the support system.

Pelton (1989: 123) offers a perspective on the predicament of parents who are reported for alleged child abuse:

> The parent-agency interaction represents a particular type of conflict, one in which—far from the two parties having more or less equal power—one party is vastly more powerful than the other. The agency has on its side the police, the law, and public opinion. The caseworker has emergency legal power to remove a child from his home on the spot. When the agency goes to court, it has an abundance of reports containing interpretations according to its own lights, the product of vast investigatory resources. The case record is embellished with reports in sophisticated language with opinion freely expressed, from school officials, psychologists, and representatives of other agencies. It contains the results of psychological tests and medical examinations, not to mention the allegations of neighbors. Confronted with this array of power, the parent may see little means at her disposal, except to "clam up," become secretive, pull her shades down, avoid the social worker and neighbors, prevent her children from talking with anyone, lie, and "say what the caseworker wants to hear."

While protective services seek to protect the child, the parent, who may be innocent of the charge, is without protection.[3] Pelton (1989: 123) continues:

> No one is advocate for the allegedly abusive or neglectful parent. No one investigates and collects evidence on her behalf, presents her side of the story, presents results of psychological tests commissioned by her rather than the

---

[3] Kendrick (1990:111) observes that in situations where there is disagreement between the child welfare social worker and the parent about an alleged abuse, the cards are stacked against the parent. "In such situations, the [Children's Aid] Society's ability to assemble a case against a parent dwarfs the ability of a parent to mount a defense against the state, especially when the agency has the ability to almost reshape the historical events that form the basis for the termination."

government, nor bears witness on her behalf. Pathologized by psychiatrists and victimized through her interaction with the agency, she stands isolated and alone. As cruel as her actions toward her children might appear, she deserves an advocate. Her hostility, which has often been observed within the context of her interaction with the agency, may stem at least in part from her utter powerlessness within the situation, having no advocate.

While impoverished parents may often experience the situation Pelton describes, the more affluent parents have other options. Attorney Douglas Besharov (1990b: 220) offers the following advice to accused parents having adequate financial resources:

> The problem is knowing whether you need a lawyer during the investigation. Early representation by a lawyer can be crucial to preventing a court action. It is much easier to convince investigators and prosecutors not to seek an indictment than it is to have them dismiss one. Many court actions are filed because of a simple breakdown in communication. A lawyer may be able to convince investigators that you are innocent or that the case is better resolved informally. No jurisdiction, however, will provide a lawyer before the initiation of a court case against you. Hence, if you want legal representation during the investigation, you will have to pay for it yourself. Legal fees are expensive: Expect hourly charges of $75 to $200, with a required retainer of $1,000 to $5,000.
>
> *You should consider hiring a lawyer whenever you are unhappy with the direction the investigation is taking.* (Italics in original)

Besharov and Pelton are not examining different phenomena. They are simply writing to different audiences. Pelton is concerned with understanding the existential condition of the many single mothers accused and investigated for child abuse (who constitute the majority of those who have their children removed) and how they come to perceive the child protection services provided. For Pelton it is not possible to separate child welfare services from an understanding of the poverty and economic despair most clients of public child welfare endure. Besharov, as a lawyer, is providing a practical word on how the system works to affluent parents who can afford legal counsel in the rare instances when they might be accused. These vastly different accounts, with one resembling an image from Kafka's *Trial* and the other a *Better Homes and Gardens* coffee table chat with an expert, point out the inherent injustice of the current system. Those who can afford counsel are less likely to be accused. In the rare instance when they are accused, they are usually able to protect themselves against an unfair or unsubstantiated allegation. Unfortunately, the same cannot be said of the single mother mired in poverty who is accused of abuse or neglect. Unable to afford independent legal counsel, she is at the mercy of the court and, to an ever greater extent, the child welfare caseworker.

Key Issue:
Has Mandated Child Abuse Reporting Reduced Child Abuse?

From the beginning, mandatory reporting was perceived as leading to a decline in child abuse, especially fatalities. Besharov (1998; 1990b: 10–11), the first director of the National Center on Child Abuse and Neglect, argues the case for increased reporting:

> Child protective services still have major problems . . . Nevertheless, one must be impressed with the results of this twenty-year effort to upgrade them. Specialized "child protective agencies" have been established to receive reports (usually via highly publicized hotlines) and then to investigate them. And treatment services for maltreated children and their parents have been expanded substantially.
>
> As a result, many thousands of children have been saved from death and serious injury. The best estimate is that over the past twenty years, *deaths from child abuse and neglect have fallen from over 3,000 a year (and perhaps as many as 5,000) to about 1,000 a year.* In New York State, for example, within five years of the passage of a comprehensive reporting law that also created specialized investigative staffs, there was a 50 percent reduction in child fatalities, from about 200 a year to under 100. Similarly, Drs. Ruth and C. Henry Kempe, well-known leaders in the field, reported that "in Denver, the number of hospitalized abused children who die from their injuries has dropped from 20 a year (between 1960 and 1975) to less than one a year." (Italics added)

According to this assessment, increased reporting not only saved the lives of thousands of children, but probably also spared even larger numbers of children from physical and sexual abuse that did not end in death. This view holds that child abuse fatalities are just the tip of the iceberg. Underneath the fatality counts are thousands of children who suffer severe pain and injury at the hands of their parents.

There is considerable debate about the nature and seriousness of various forms of emotional, sexual, and even physical abuse (Giovannoni and Becerra, 1979; Ringwalt and Caye, 1989; Select Committee on Children, Youth, and Families, 1989a: 225). By selecting child abuse fatalities Besharov has selected the ultimate dependent variable. Death, unlike other forms of abuse, is difficult to cover up. It calls for an involvement of the police and the courts as well as the social worker. Most of the time an autopsy is required, especially if there are any unusual circumstances

(Greenland, 1987; Schloesser, Pierpont, and Poertner, 1992).[4] Although disagreements may arise over whether the fatality was due to child abuse, there is usually agreement that a nonaccidental death occurred. The death might be ruled suspicious or homicide, but the death is recorded. Consequently, if it can be demonstrated that increased reporting has led to a reduction in child abuse fatalities generally, measured as either homicide or homicide plus deaths caused by "injury undetermined whether accidentally or purposefully inflicted," the argument that increased reporting has decreased child abuse overall is significantly strengthened. This, of course, assumes that child abuse fatalities are the most reliable and valid indicator of child abuse currently available. Unfortunately, Besharov's assertion of a decline in child abuse fatalities "from over 3,000 a year (and perhaps as many as 5,000) to about 1,000 a year" after mandatory reporting laws were enacted is either not supported or contradicted by data from several other sources (Sedlak, 1991).[5]

Data from the National Center for Health Statistics

According to the National Center for Health Statistics the homicide rates for both infants (birth to one) and children ages one to four have not declined since the passage of mandatory reporting laws in the mid-sixties, but have increased. In 1970, approximately 7.9 infants and 3.2 children under five per 100,000 have died as a result of homicide or "injury undetermined whether accidentally or purposefully inflicted" (Select Committee on Children, Youth, and Families, 1989b, 174–175).

By 1986, these rates had increased to 9.6 for infants and 2.9 for children under five. Not all of these "undetermined injury" deaths were the result of child abuse. Yet, the rate of infant and child homicides also increased from 1965 to 1991 (see table 5.3). Meanwhile, during this same period the number of official child abuse reports increased several fold. In 2000, the homicide rate for infants was 9.1 (see table 5.3).

---

[4] Citing data from the National Center for Health Statistics, Sharpe and Lundstrom (1991) report that autopsies are performed by states on any child under nine years of age from 30 to 60 percent of the time. However, for children who die of Sudden Infant Death Syndrome (SIDS), autopsies are performed between 70 to 100 percent of the time (with the exception of Arkansas). Approximately 5,000 infants die each year in the United States from SIDS, making it the most common cause of death for infants one week to one year old. Sharpe and Lundstrom (1991: 2) speculate that "while the vast majority of suspected SIDS cases are legitimate, some murders are discovered only by chance."

[5] Howitt (1992: 196) observes, "If accurate, this is a remarkable figure. But, of course, one needs to know precisely what such statistics refer to." To date, Besharov has not provided a source.

Table 5.3 Deaths of Infants and Young Children

| | Homicide Rate[2] | | Rate of Homicide and Undetermined Injury[2] | |
	Infants	Children 1–4	Infants	Children 1–4
1960	4.8	0.7		
1965	5.5	1.1		
1970	4.3	1.9	7.9	3.2
1975	5.8	2.5	8.9	3.6
1980	5.9	2.5	7.8	3.3
1982	6.7	2.7	8.7	3.2
1984	6.5	2.4	8.1	2.8
1985	5.3	2.4	6.7	2.9
1986	7.4	2.7	8.8	3.1
1987	7.2	2.3	8.6	2.9
1988	8.1	2.6	9.6	2.9
1989	8.5	2.7		
1990	8.4	2.6		
1991	9.5	2.8		
1992	8.1	2.8		
1993	8.8	2.9		
1996	8.8	2.7		
1997	8.3	2.4		
1999	8.7	2.3		
2000	9.1	2.5		

[2]Rate per 100,000.

Source: National Center for Health Statistics, *Vital Statistics of the United States*.

Data from Uniform Crime Reports

According to the Federal Bureau of Investigation (FBI) data in figure 5.1, the rate of child homicides per 100,000 reported each year has not declined over the last quarter of a century. Since the implementation of mandated reporting no discernible decline in the number of children murdered each year has been reported by the FBI. In fact, the child homicide rates reported by the FBI are several times higher among juveniles aged fourteen to seventeen compared to children under fourteen. It is the oldest children who are at greatest risk of homicide.

As can be seen in figure 5.1, children become more vulnerable as they grow older. Children ages fourteen to seventeen were particularly vulnerable during the period from 1990 to 1996. There was an epidemic of gang violence which took the lives of many children during this period. If the interest is to reduce homicide for those most vulnerable, efforts should focus on the great risk which young males in this age group face.

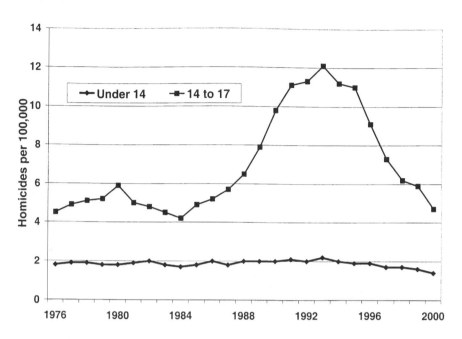

Figure 5.1 Child Homicide Rates, 1977–2000.
Source: FBI, Supplementary Homicide Reports, 1976–2000.

The Color of Homicide Victims

What is particularly striking about the child homicide data from the Federal
Bureau of Investigation (FBI) is the overrepresentation of Black children,
particularly Black males. As seen in figure 5.2, Black males have the highest child homicide rates. Clearly Black children, especially Black males,
are the most vulnerable to child homicide. The data in figure 5.3 examine
the child homicide rate for children by age. Black child homicide rates are
several times higher than for white children. Black children are at the highest risk of homicide. This is true for Black teenagers, especially those involved in gang violence, but is also true for Black infants and preschool
children. Clearly, those children most at risk of homicide are teenagers.
Efforts to reduce child homicide would target children in their teen years.
As seen in figure 5.3, children 15 to 19 are at much greater risk than any
other age group.

Homicide rate per 100,000

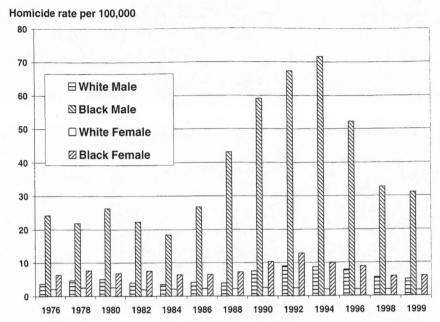

Figure 5.2 Child Homicide Rates by Race and Gender
Source; FBI, Supplementary Homicide Reports, 1976-99.

Homicide rate per 100,000

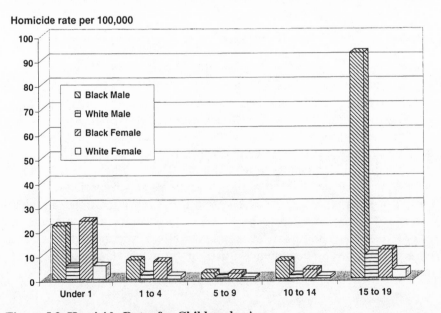

Figure 5.3 Homicide Rates for Children by Age
Source; FBI, Supplementary Homicide Reports.

Efforts to end the danger of child fatalities should focus on protecting these most vulnerable children. During the last quarter of a century there has been essentially no decline in the number of children under five intentionally killed.

Data from the National Committee for the Prevention of Child Abuse

One of the first national organizations to collect and publish data on child abuse and child abuse fatalities was the National Committee for the Prevention of Child Abuse. Until recently, their annual report was the major source of national information. The National Committee for the Prevention of Child Abuse (NCPCA) data corresponds closely with the data reported by the National Center for Health Statistics (see figure 5.4). According to NCPCA data (McCurdy and Daro, 1993), the number of child abuse fatalities reported each year has risen only slightly over the last decade. As seen in table 5.4, since the passage and implementation of mandated reporting laws the NCPCA has observed no decline in child abuse fatalities.

Table 5.4 Child Abuse Fatalities in the United States

	Number of Child Abuse Fatalities	Fatalities per 100,000 Children
1985	798	1.30
1986	1,014	
1987	1,074	
1988	1,093	
1989	1,103	
1990	1,143	
1991	1,255	
1992	1,261	
1993	1,255*	
1994	1,250	1.84
1995	1,209	1.79
1996	1,195	1.73
1997	1,214	1.74
1998	1,277	1.83
1999	1,269	1.81
2000	1,356	1.87

*Estimate derived from trend line.

Source: Wang and Harding (1999); Peddle and Wang (2001); Peddle, Wang, Diaz and Reid (2002).

Clearly, the data reported by the National Center for Health Statistics, the FBI, and the National Committee for the Prevention of Child Abuse fail to confirm Besharov's assertion that mandatory reporting has led to a reduction in child abuse fatalities. As can be seen in figure 5.4, since the passage of the Child Abuse and Prevention Act of 1974, there has been a steady rise in the number of child abuse reports. Yet, there has been no decline in the number of child fatalities as measured by the National Center for Health Statistics, the Federal Bureau of Investigation, and the National Committee for the Prevention of Child Abuse.

Other Discrepancies in Besharov's Data

Besharov (1990b) indicated that child abuse fatalities in New York had declined from about 200 to under 100 within five years of the passage of a comprehensive reporting law. Evidently, the effect of the law was short-lived because about five years later (1986) New York reported 181 child fatalities. In 1988, the state reported 198 child fatalities (Select Committee on Children, Youth, and Families, 1989a: 113–114), and in 1990, 212 child abuse fatalities (Pryor, 1991: table 12).

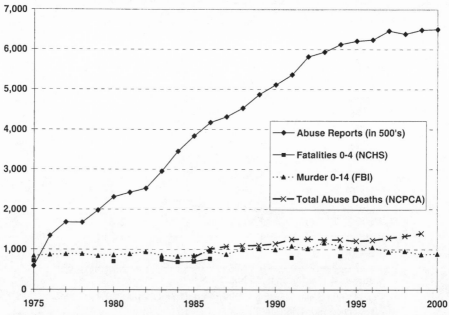

Figure 5.4 Trends in Abuse Reporting and Child Fatalities, 1975–2000.
Source: McCurdy and Daro (1993); Peddle and Wang (2001).

Further, Besharov indicated that in Colorado, after the mandatory reporting laws were implemented, the number of child abuse deaths declined from about twenty a year to only one. In fact, Colorado reported twenty-six child abuse fatalities in 1988, indicating that the decline from about twenty a year reported in Denver hospitals to less than one a year was not sustained by the progress made in child abuse reporting (Select Committee on Children, Youth and Families, 1989a: 113).

Counting child abuse fatalities has always proven a controversial issue. Since child protection advocates are concerned that the full measure of the problem be understood, national estimates are viewed as being unable to detect alleged "hidden" child abuse fatalities that are covered up or made to appear as accidents. Nevertheless, it is surprising to find that four major national studies of the incidence of child abuse fatalities arrive at similar numbers. According to the National Center for Health Statistics, the National Committee for the Prevention of Child Abuse, the National Incidence Studies of Child Abuse and Neglect by the U.S. Department of Health and Human Services (Sedlak, 1989, 1991), and the FBI's *Uniform Crime Reports,* the total number of child abuse fatalities in the United States has remained roughly stable at 1,000 per year for the last thirty years. Given this, we are inclined to conclude that, contrary to Besharov, increased reporting has not reduced the rate of child abuse fatalities.

Comparison of Child Abuse Reports and Fatality Rates Between States

If increased reporting did indeed reduce child abuse fatalities, we would expect to find a relation between rates of child abuse fatalities and rates of child abuse reporting among the states. That is, those states with higher reporting rates would be expected to have had fewer fatalities than those with lower reporting rates. However, the data comparing rates of child abuse reports and fatalities by state do not support this hypothesis (see Lindsey, 1994).[6] States with higher reporting have not had fewer fatalities when compared with states with low reporting rates.

Within states there is also considerable variation in child fatality reports depending on the agency reporting. The California Attorney General's office examined the number of child fatalities reported from three different sources during the period 1992 to 1995. As can be seen in figure 5.5 there is considerable variation.

---

[6] I computed a least squares regression analysis of the rates of child fatalities in 1986 with the rate of child abuse reports (1986) by state (Select Committee on Children, Youth, and Families, 1989a: 111–114). The results indicated no relationship between child abuse reports and fatalities ($R2 = .008$).

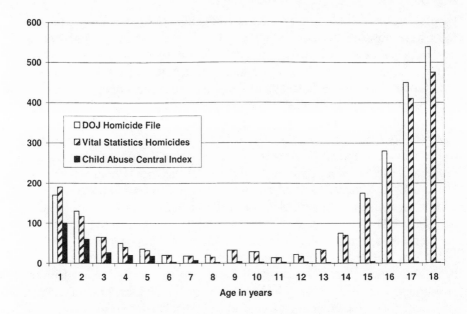

**Figure 5.5 Variations in Child Fatality Reporting by Source
in California (1992 to 1995).**

Source: FBI, Supplementary Homicide Reports, 1976–2000.
Online at www.ojp.usdoj.gov/bjs/homicide

The Child Abuse Central Index, which collects data only on "child abuse
and neglect" fatalities, finds few child fatalities beyond preschool age.
However, data from the Vital Statistics Homicides, as well as from the Department of Justice's Homicide File, report that that most of the child fatalities occur for children older than six.

It may be that without the increase in reporting many more child fatalities would have occurred. We can examine this issue by (1) analyzing data
on nationwide trends in family violence, (2) examining the relative change
in child homicides compared to the rates of homicide for other age groups,
and (3) comparing rates of abuse reports and fatalities between states.

Nationwide Trends in Domestic Violence

Straus, Gelles, and Steinmetz conducted a study of violence in the family,
entitled *Behind Closed Doors* (1980), in which they estimated that between
3.1 million and 4 million children were kicked, bitten, or punched by their
parents at some point during childhood. According to the data they collected, approximately 2 million children were seriously beaten by a parent

or threatened with a gun or knife. Further, they estimated that 46,000 children were actually shot or stabbed by a parent and that more than 1,000 died as a result of these attacks. Straus and Gelles (1986) replicated this study ten years later and found a 47 percent decrease in the level of serious violence against children.[7] They found that about 1 million children were subjected to serious physical child abuse in 1985. The data from these studies suggest that the level of violence in families did not increase during the period 1975 to 1985, but rather declined.

In other words, rather than a nationwide increase in violence toward children, there has been a decline. If the data are correct we would also expect a decline in the number of child abuse reports. However, during the same period, the number of child abuse reports rose sharply, increasing sixfold. Further, there was no decline in the number of child fatalities even though the overall rate of violence had decreased, and surveillance, in the form of mandatory child abuse reporting, had increased.

Explaining the Absence of a Relationship Between Increased Reporting and Fatalities

What explains the absence of a relationship between increased child protection efforts and child homicides? Three possible explanations come to mind: (1) inadequate technology in the areas of risk assessment and child abuse prevention, (2) insufficient funding, and (3) too broad a definition for required reporting.

Inadequate Technology

The transformation of child welfare into protective services has not been the result of scientific breakthroughs in understanding child abuse. While radiologists had identified that severe physical abuse, apparently inflicted by a caretaker, had occurred, advances in developing a technology to treat, cure, or prevent child abuse did not follow. There were no major breakthroughs in research and theory that led to increased protection for children (Baldwin and Oliver, 1975). If a breakthrough had occurred, then there would have been a decline in child abuse fatalities. But, as the data re-

---

[7] Gelles and Straus (1987) provide a number of explanations for the decrease in violence. Both their original study and its replication involved two-parent families and, thus, may not be representative of all children who are abused. They also suggest that the increased public concern with child abuse may have made parents more reluctant to self-report abuse in 1985 (Lindsey and Regehr, 1993).

viewed here indicate, no systematic decline in child fatalities has occurred as a result of the dramatic increase in child abuse intervention (Lindsey and Trocmé, 1994).

Risk Assessment. Presumably, increased reporting allows more families to be identified and screened in order to prevent future child abuse. However, can the child welfare caseworker adequately assess the risk faced by children after they are reported? Further, even if a child's risk of abuse can be assessed, the agency may not have the knowledge, technology, or skills to provide the child adequate protection (Alfaro, 1988; Anderson et al., 1983; Fein, 1979). In 1990, Daro and Mitchel reported that approximately half of all children identified as child abuse fatalities were active cases known to local protective service agencies at the time of their death.

Protection against child abuse is usually attempted by either increasing surveillance on suspected families or by removing the child from the family. Both types of protection have proven difficult to provide. First, although it might be feasible to implement a system of surveillance that would prevent any child from ever being harmed, it is far from clear that, as Dingwall (1989: 49) observes, "a free society would ever tolerate the sort of surveillance that would be necessary to provide such a guarantee. More to the point, we have seen that our tools can never be refined sufficiently to achieve this goal."

Removing a child from the home where abuse has occurred has also proven an illusive goal. Before removing the child the agency must conduct an investigation of the facts and make a determination based on those facts. Studies of children placed in foster care have questioned the reliability of the decision-making process that leads to removal. Further, empirical studies of risk assessment and prevention strategies have consistently reported imprecision and low reliability in predicting abuse (Dingwall, 1989; McDonald and Marks, 1991; R.H. Starr, 1982; Wald and Woolverton, 1990). After reviewing the risk assessment literature, Dingwall (1989: 51) concludes, "this paper must come to a bleak conclusion. The amount of scientifically validated research on child abuse and neglect is vanishingly small. The value of any self-styled predictive checklist is negligible."

Neither have efforts to identify potential child abusers in the general population met with great success (Gambrill and Shlonsky, 2000; Shlonsky and Gambrill, 2001). In 1981, Garbarino and Stocking reported, "The most detailed and fully developed of these profiles [Helfer, 1978] designated 60 percent of the general population at risk for becoming involved in child abuse" (p. 7). When more than half the population is determined to be at risk of abuse, then questions have to be raised about the adequacy, appropriateness, and precision of the risk assessment process. As Besharov (1987: 306–307) observed:

The unvarnished truth is that there is no way of predicting, with any degree of certainty, whether a particular parent will become abusive or neglectful. Despite years of research, there is no psychological profile that accurately identifies parents who will abuse or neglect their child in the future. At the present time, unless the parent is suffering from a severe mental disability, the only reliable basis for predicting future danger is the parent's past behavior.

Child Abuse Prevention. Related to the issue of risk assessment is prevention. If it were possible to identify those children at greatest risk of serious abuse, prevention strategies could be targeted to these "at risk" populations. However, the development of prevention technology has not been sufficiently successful that we can safely rely on the approaches we have (Gibbons, 1997; Hardicker, Exton, and Barker, 1991; Kaplan and Reich, 1976).

Kempe and Kempe (1978) examined a sample of 350 children in which they identified 100 mothers as "high-risk" child abusers. As a comparison group they selected a low-risk group of 50 mothers. However, only 8 of the 100 high-risk families were ever reported to the Central Child Abuse Registry. Using this definition of child abuse, Montgomery (1982) suggested that the Kempe and Kempe screening was only 8 percent accurate—or 92 percent wrong.

Kempe and his colleagues then divided the original group of 100 mothers into two groups. Half of the high-risk mothers received routine follow-up services, while the other half received intervention and prevention services especially designed to prevent abuse. The prevention strategy included close monitoring and care by a pediatrician, detailed observation in the hospital, frequent telephone contact, regular health visitor contact, and, when necessary, referral to medical and mental health facilities. Analysis of the results of these prevention efforts found no statistically significant difference between the two groups on the key measure of Central Child Abuse Registry reports, observed abnormal parenting practices, accidents, or scores on the Denver Development Screening test.

One of the largest screening and prevention program subjected to clinical examination was conducted by Lealman and colleagues (1983) who screened 2,802 maternity cases and identified 511 families as "at risk." These families were divided into three treatment and intervention groups. One group of 103 was treated as "high-risk intervention" and provided contact with a project social worker. A second group of 209 was regarded as a high-risk nonintervention group and given no treatment or intervention. The third group of 199 was assigned to the high-risk social work group where families were already receiving social work support. How successful was intervention in reducing child abuse? The researchers reported that "we have no statistical evidence to support the view that intervention improved parenting practice" (See chapter 2).

After reviewing the research studies on prevention, Parton (1985: 144) observed: "Certainly if there are two populations who suffer from the disease and only one is treated you would anticipate the incidence and prevalence of the disease in the treated population to decrease. However, there are very few studies which attempt to evaluate the success of interventions into child abuse. Those that do, cast serious doubt on the efficacy of such efforts."

In 1994 MacMillan, MacMillan, Offord, Griffith, and MacMillan reported the results of their review of child abuse prevention research. They identified 1,526 child abuse prevention studies and determined that only 30 were methodologically sound. They report that of the 30 methodologically sound studies 11 examined physical abuse and neglect. Of these 11 studies, they report that only two showed a decrease in child abuse as measured by a reduction in hospital admissions, visits to emergency departments or child abuse reports.

Child Abuse Treatment. Children who have been abused need care and treatment for the injuries suffered. Yet, Cohn and Daro (1987) argue that waiting until abuse and neglect occur before providing treatment is to wait too long. They reviewed major evaluation studies of child abuse treatment programs that served more than 3,000 families in ninety different programs. Their findings raised concern about the effectiveness of such treatment. They wrote, "Treatment effects in general are not very successful. Child abuse and neglect continue despite early, thoughtful, and often costly intervention. Treatment programs have been relatively ineffective in initially halting abusive and neglectful behavior or in reducing the future likelihood of maltreatment" (p. 440). Ratiner (2000: 369) observed, "There may be more agreement about the need for treatment research regarding child abuse and neglect than about any other single issue regarding abuse. . . Without a firm commitment to scientific dialogue and a growing body of meaningful investigation, we as child advocates run the risk of losing credibility within the scientific and lay communities while increasing numbers of children are referred."

Inadequate Funding. The second explanation for the failure of mandated reporting to reduce child abuse is that our current child protective services agencies are inadequately funded for the tasks presented them. If sufficient funds were provided to handle the large volume of reports, abuse would decline. Anne Cohn Donnelly (1991: 106), president of the National Committee for the Prevention of Child Abuse, argues the point:

Times have changed a lot for children's protective service agencies in this country [United States]. Once the agency to whom families were referred for help when problems of child abuse were apparent (and from whom help was provided), children's protective services today largely serve only an investigative function. With increased numbers of reports and no increases in funding have come increased caseload sizes and, most regrettably, fewer and fewer services for families. Once families at risk for abuse were helped by CPS; today, even in the most serious of confirmed child abuse cases, help may not be offered. The result—abuse continues. As long as protective service agencies are not offering help to families, efforts to prevent child abuse will be stymied. During the next decade we must work to restore to children's protective service agencies their original function of helping families, largely by ensuring they receive the increased funding required.

Too Broad a Definition of Abuse

The assumption that mandatory reporting leads to accurate and relatively complete identification of endangered children is contradicted by existing data . . . The "battered child syndrome" can be easily identified but this is not true for the more general problem of child maltreatment.

Elizabeth Hutchinson, *Mandatory Reporting Laws*

A major concern about the mandatory reporting laws has been that their definition of abuse is too broad (Besharov, 1990a; Hutchison, 1993). Beginning with a limited concern with the severe physical abuse observed by physicians, the definition of child abuse was expanded to include any act that harms a child. Since the mandatory child abuse reporting laws were not accompanied with additional funding, public child welfare agencies have had to shift their focus and reduce their services, with the result that many children receive nothing more than an "investigation." Recent data in California suggest that approximately 9 percent of children who are reported for child abuse and neglect receive any services (Barth, 1991, verbal communication; see Barth, Berrick, and Courtney, 1990). Thus, for more than 90 percent of children, services are limited to investigation.

Hutchison (1993) has suggested that narrowing the definition of child abuse would allow for greater protection of those children most vulnerable to serious injury or death. She urges that serious physical injury to a child, threats of imminent physical harm, or acts of sexual molestation should be the only forms of abuse included in mandated reporting legislation.

Hutchison is not alone in attempting to narrow the definition of abuse. For nearly two decades, legal theorists have been suggesting that the state should intrude into family life only in cases of severe abuse (Goldstein, Freud, and Solnit, 1979; Mnookin, 1973)—that is, when the children have been "severely assaulted," "systematically tortured," "sexually abused," or have been in a situation "so dangerous that it poses an immediate threat of serious injury." But, of course, it was the medical evidence of serious physical abuse that had led to the mandatory reporting laws in the first place. Still, among the public from whom the reports emerge, the perception of abuse covers a wide range. In 1991, Pryor reported that in New York State, less than 1 percent of child abuse allegations involved "battered children," that is, children presenting serious physical injuries including fractures, subdural hematoma/internal injuries, or death. The most frequent reason for a child abuse allegation was "lack of supervision" (Pryor, 1991).

The broadening of the definition of child abuse has also limited progress in the search for predictors. Dingwall (1989: 42) has indicated that two methodological fallacies have been responsible for the limited scientific advances made in the field of child abuse: "The definitional fallacy is the confusion of social and scientific problems and the failure to construct persuasive operational definitions of abuse or neglect. The statistical fallacy is the failure to recognize that, when one is dealing with a phenomenon which has a low rate of prevalence, even the best predictors yield a high and probably unacceptable level of errors."

Fatalities Are an Outlier. For various reasons then, it appears that increased reporting is not a variable affecting the rate of child abuse as indicated by child fatalities. But are fatalities even a reliable indicator of the rate of abuse? Child abuse fatalities are, in fact, a rare event. In 2000, there was less than one fatality for every 2,500 child abuse reports in the United States. We lack the scientific knowledge that allows finding the one child fatality that will occur for each 2,500 cases of abuse reported (Shlonsky and Gambrill, 2001). Cammasso and Jangathan (2001) observe, "The reliability and predictive validity of risk assessment is questionable, however, and concerns continue about the validity of using lists of explicit criteria in protective services decision-making." After an exhaustive review of risk assessment in child protective services, Gambrill and Shlonsky find little evidence of reliable and valid instruments that would significantly improve the prediction of risk (Gambrill and Shlonsky, 2000; Shlonsky and Gambrill, 2001).

Despite the general lack of precision in predicting child abuse deaths, for the general public fatality data remain the most important indicator of abuse. Few events mobilize public sentiment more than the death of an innocent child at the hands of the parent(s). The American Humane Association examined the coverage of child abuse in the major newspapers in forty-eight states in the same year that the "Battered Child Syndrome" report was published (1962) and identified 662 reports of abuse (DeFrancis,

1966). Of these, 178 led to a child fatality. In other words, one of every four abuse reports covered in the mass media were fatalities, even though fatalities represent only a small segment of abuse reports, less than one per 2,500. Clearly, it is the dramatic horror of a child fatality which attracts media attention. Unfortunately, this disproportionate reporting of cases of child brutality and fatalities leads to popular misconceptions about the nature and extent of the problem of child abuse (cf. Nunnally, 1961).

Do Children, Once Identified, Get Protection?

Fully 48% of the child abuse deaths in 1995 involved children previously known to the authorities. Tens of thousands of other children suffer serious injuries short of death while under child protective agency supervision.
> National Committee to Prevent Child Abuse, *Annual Survey*

It is not clear that, even if precise definitions of abuse were available, those children who are reported would eventually be provided adequate protection (Zigler, 1979). As mentioned, child welfare agencies have found it difficult to determine whether a child should be removed from the home (Franklin, 1975). This has been true even for severe abuse cases (Dingwall, 1989). The literature consistently indicates imprecision and even bias in deciding whether to remove a child from his or her family because of abuse (Lindsey, 1991b; Packman, Randall, and Jacques, 1986).

In 1986, Katz and colleagues examined the records of 185 suspected abused or neglected children admitted to Boston's Children's Hospital. The investigators sought to determine how demographic variables and measures of the severity of injury influenced the decision to remove the child. They developed a four-point scale to assess the injuries of children coming to the hospital. Was the injury:

- Life threatening (death imminent without medical intervention)?
- Serious (death unlikely but further deterioration of function highly probable without medical intervention)?
- Moderate (death or deterioration of function unlikely but the condition serious enough to interfere with the usual function and treatment of some type necessary to hasten reversal of the injurious process)?
- Minimal possibility of slight loss of function (injury can resolve with or without medical intervention)?

Most of the children in the sample were treated either through the hospital emergency room (44 percent) or through the surgical emergency room (39.2 percent). After assessing cases according to this scale three case outcomes were distinguished: the child was returned home without services, the child was returned home with services, or the child was removed from the home.

To what extent did the severity of the child's injury influence removal from the home? Katz and colleagues (1986: 257, 259) report: "Severity of condition was not significantly associated with [a particular] outcome. [In fact] . . . the presence of a physical injury decreased the likelihood of a child being placed outside of the home . . . Specifically, families that were Medicaid-eligible were more likely to have their children removed than were more affluent families in cases of physical injury." Hampton and Newberger (1985) found that social class and race were more important than the degree of severity of abuse. They write: "If the reporting of child abuse is as biased by class and race as these data suggest, there is a need for a critical review of the system as well as the process of reporting. To the extent that we selectively invoke agents of the state to police the lives of the poor and nonwhite families, we may be inappropriately and unfairly condemning these families as evil" (p. 58).

The same weak relationship between severity of abuse and removal of a child from the home has been observed in sexual abuse cases. Using a logistic regression model, Hunter and colleagues (1990) reported "severity of abuse" (i.e., fondling versus penetration) was not predictive of removal of the child in their sample (412, table 1). Thus, severity of abuse, when it can be reliably determined, is no gauge of whether the child will be subsequently protected.

Substantial Variations in Abuse

Although broad changes at the federal level have shaped child welfare in the United States, it is important to keep in mind that the child welfare system is based in the individual states. The public child welfare agencies are operated at the state level by state or county agencies. There is substantial variation among the states in terms of how they structure and operate their public child welfare agencies.[8] The consequences of this variation can be seen in table 5.5, which displays the rate of substantiated child abuse (per 1,000) for the states ranked by those with the lowest and highest rates.

---

[8] The Web site childwelfare.com includes extensive materials and links to the various state agencies. It is useful to visit this site and to explore the material from the various state agencies. In addition, the site includes report cards on the performance of the public child welfare systems in the various states.

Table 5.5 **Comparison of Rates of Substantiated Child Abuse**
(substantiated abuse per 1,000 children)

States with Low Rates	Abuse Rate	States with High Rates	Abuse Rate
Pennsylvania	1.9	Alaska	37.1
New Hampshire	3.9	Florida	23.2
New Jersey	4.9	Kentucky	23.1
Virginia	5.9	Idaho	22.6
Wisconsin	6.0	Connecticut	21.4
Wyoming	6.2	Ohio	20.4
Vermont	6.3	North Carolina	19.5
Colorado	6.7	West Virginia	19.3
Arizona	7.1	Oklahoma	18.9
Texas	7.1	Massachusetts	18.9
Hawaii	7.3	New York	18.6
Tennessee	7.5	California	17.7

Source: Green Book (2000: 708–709).

Why is it that the rate of substantiated child abuse in Pennsylvania is less than ten times the rate found in the bordering state of Ohio? North Carolina and Virginia share a long border and would seem to be similar, yet the rate of substantiated child abuse in North Carolina is more than three times greater than Virginia. Likewise, the rate of abuse in Kentucky is three times greater than the abuse reported in Tennessee.

Why these differences? Since the states seem not to be that dissimilar, it would appear that the result has more to do with the idiosyncratic structure and operation of the public child welfare system in these states than with the underlying prevalence of child abuse actually occurring.

The variation found among the states raises concern about the larger question of the reliability and validity of administrative data on child abuse. Clearly, these data reflect what occurs in terms of the operation of public child welfare agencies. But it needs to be kept in mind that these data reflect the operation of state agencies and are not necessarily congruent with the actual rates of child abuse found in the states.

The Color of Child Abuse

The color of America's child welfare system is the reason Americans have tolerated its destructiveness. It is also the most powerful reason to finally abolish what we now call child protection and replace it with a system that really promotes children's welfare.

Dorothy Roberts, *Shattered Bonds*

Table 5.6 The Color of Substantiated Child Abuse, 2000

| | Black Children | |
	State Population (%)	Substantiated Child Abuse Population (%)
California	7	16
Delaware	24	44
Florida	21	30
Georgia	34	46
Illinois	19	35
Louisiana	41	51
Michigan	17	40
New Jersey	16	44
New York	18	32
North Carolina	26	37
Texas	12	20
Wisconsin	8	19

Source: Child Welfare Outcomes (2003).
See www.childwelfare.com select state and *Child Welfare Outcomes*

As seen in table 5.6, in most states Black children are overrepresented in substantiated reports of child abuse. In New Jersey, almost half of the cases of substantiated cases of child abuse involve Black children, even though they are less than one-sixth of the state's child population.

In Wisconsin, Black children represent less than one tenth of the states child population, but they represent 30 percent of the state's cases of substantiated child abuse. In Michigan, Black children represent 41 percent of the cases of substantiated child abuse even though they are about one sixth of the state's child population. In Illinois and Texas Blacks are overrepresented by more than twice in the substantiated reports than would be expected based on their representation in the population. In these and most other states Black children are substantially overrepresented in substantiated cases of child abuse (Smith and Devore, forthcoming).

Prevalence of Child Abuse in the United States

As part of the Child Abuse and Prevention Act of 1974 the federal government mandated under P.L. 93-247 that every eight years the National Center for Child Abuse and Neglect (NCCAN) conduct an incidence study to estimate how many children in the United States are actually abused—not just those reported for abuse, but all children who are actually abused.

The problem with previous studies is that they rely on agency data. These data do not permit assessment of child abuse that occurs outside the notice of child protective service agencies.

To assess the full extent of child abuse requires an *incidence* study. The advantage of an incidence study is that it includes reports of child abuse to public agencies but also estimates the remaining number of children who are being abused but who do not show up in agency reports. To conduct the incidence study NCCAN designed the largest, most comprehensive study of child abuse ever conducted in the United States. So far the study has been conducted three times.[9]

The National Incidence Studies (NIS) worked with a number of key individuals in each of the selected counties to identify all the children who were being abused. The key individuals included teachers, clergy, police, nurses, mental health care professionals, day care workers, parents, and others who come into contact with the children in the community. The NIS researchers worked with the child protective agencies to identify and provide basic demographic data.

The first National Incidence Study (NIS-1) was conducted in 1979 and 1980. The NIS-1 study estimated that 625,100 children a year were abused in the United States during that period. This was similar to the number of substantiated abuse reports estimated by the National Committee for the Prevention of Child Abuse (Daro and McCurdy, 1991).

The second National Incidence Study was conducted in 1986 and 1987. The NIS-2 estimated that 931,000 children were abused in 1986. This number was greater than the 834,000 substantiated abuse reports estimated by the National Committee for the Prevention of Child Abuse. The NIS-2 study indicated that child abuse increased by almost half between 1980 and 1986. The NIS-3 study reported that child abuse increased to 1,553,000 by 1993. This represents a 67 percent increase from 1986 to 1993 and an almost 150 percent increase between 1980 and 1993 (see table 5.7). Even though there had been a substantial increase in child abuse reports and investigations during this period, there was no decrease in child abuse. Clearly, the transformation of child welfare in child protective services did not reduce the incidence of child abuse in the United States.

The National Incidence Study (NIS) represents the best data available on the extent of actual child abuse in the United States. The data in table 5.7 indicates a continual increase in child abuse in the United States despite the transformation of the public child welfare system into child protective service agencies.

---

[9] To ensure the study sample would be nationally representative the NIS-3 selected forty-two counties from across the United States.

Table 5.7 Incidence of Child Abuse and Neglect in the United States

	Incidence of Child Abuse in the U.S.	Rate per 1,000
National Incidence Study -1 (1980)	625,000	9.8
National Incidence Study -2 (1986)	931,000	14.8
National Incidence Study -3 (1993)	1,553,800	23.1

Source: Sedlak (1988); Sedlak and Broadhurst (1996).

The evidence from the NIS studies indicate that, contrary to the unsupported claims of Besharov, the transformation of the public child welfare system did not lead to protection for children. The best data on the incidence of child abuse indicates that despite the dramatic increase in child abuse reports and investigations, which resulted from mandatory reporting laws, there has not been a reduction in child abuse. Rather, during the quarter of a century since the passage of the Child Abuse and Prevention Act in 1974, which transformed child welfare into child protective services, there has been a steady and substantial increase in child abuse (see tables 5.7 and 5.8).

The data in table 5.2 (earlier in the chapter) demonstrate that child abuse increased steadily during the last two decades as measured by child abuse reports. The data from the incidence studies confirm these findings.

There was a substantial increase in the incidence of child abuse from NIS-2 (1986) to NIS-3 (1993). As seen in table 5.8, the increase has been in all categories of abuse.

Table 5.8 Increase in the Incidence of Child Abuse from NIS-2 (1986) to NIS-3 (1993)

	NIS-2 (1986)	NIS-3 (1993)
Physical neglect	141,700	565,000
Physical abuse	269,700	381,200
Sexual abuse	119,200	217,700
Serious injury	141,700	565,000

Source: National Incidence Study, 1996.

Income and Child Abuse

> Severe poverty, not just poverty, is the lot of most families who end up in the
> child welfare system, and the mediating variable that pushes a small percent
> of poor families into that system is the inability to deal with that poverty.
>
> Malcolm Bush, *Families in Distress*

One of the major criticisms of the data used in previous research on child
abuse is that it is derived from public agencies and therefore reflected the
more extensive patrolling of poor and disadvantaged neighborhoods. Consequently, studies of child abuse using this data have consistently reported
that poor children constitute the majority of children who were abused.

In one of the earliest studies of this issue David Gil (1970) reported
that nearly 60 percent of the families involved in the abuse incidents had
been on welfare. According to the American Humane Association, 42 percent of the families involved in validated reports were receiving public assistance in 1976 (American Humane Association, 1978). During this same
year (1976) two-thirds of reported families with validated abuse reports
had very low incomes (under $7,000). Families involved in neglect reports
had average incomes of $4,250. In 1986, the American Humane Associa-
tion (1988) reported that about half of all families reported for abuse were
receiving public assistance. Finally, child homicide studies have consistently reported the presence of poverty in child abuse and neglect families.
(Adelson, 1961; Kaplan and Reich, 1976; Weston, 1974).

Data from the National Incidence Study-2 (1988) picked up where
these earlier studies of poverty and child abuse left off and provided substantial evidence of the relation between income and child abuse. As can be
seen in table 5.9, the rate of reports of abuse was much higher among low-
income families for all categories of abuse. The data in table 5.9 indicate
that the rate of child abuse is consistently much higher for children in families with income below $15,000 compared with children in families with
income above $15,000. The rate of physical abuse is more than four times
greater. In terms of serious injury, the rate is more than six times greater.

Table 5.9 Family Income and Child Abuse Incidence
(rate per 1,000 children)

	Annual Income Above $15,000	Annual Income Below $15,000
Physical Abuse	2.5	10.2
Sexual Abuse	1.1	4.8
Emotional Abuse	1.2	6.1
Fatal Injury	.01	.03
Serious Injury	.9	6.0
Moderate Injury	5.5	30.9
Probable Injury	.9	5.4
Endangered	.6	11.7
All Abuse	4.4	19.9

Source: National Incidence Study-2, 1988.

The findings relative to physical abuse are similar for children who are neglected (see table 5.10). All categories of neglect are several times greater for families with annual incomes below $15,000 compared to families with incomes above $15,000. The NIS-2 study allowed for examination of the influence of income by comparing rates of abuse for those with incomes above or below $15,000. Clearly the income variable proved vital in understanding variations in rates of abuse.

Table 5.10 Family Income and Child Neglect Incidence
(rate per 1,000 children)

	Annual Income Above $15,000	Annual Income Below $15,000
Physical Neglect	1.9	22.6
Educational Neglect	1.3	10.1
Emotional Neglect	1.5	6.9
All Neglect	4.1	36.8
All Maltreatment	7.9	54.0

Source: National Incidence Study-2, 1988.

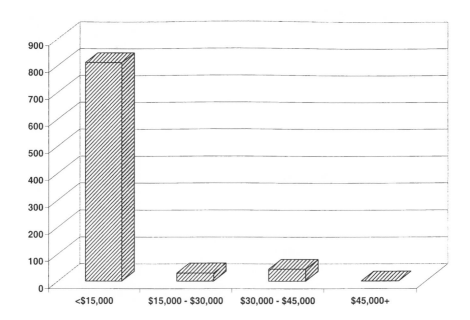

Figure 5.6 Incidence of Child Abuse Fatalities by Income
Source: National Incidence Study-3, 1996.

The NIS-3 research allowed for even more precise analysis of income on abuse rates. The findings from the NIS-3 data provided even stronger evidence of the impact of income and poverty on child abuse rates. As seen in figures 5.6 and 5.7, children in families with annual income less than $15,000 are many times more likely to be abused compared to those in families with incomes above $45,000 in terms of serious injury, moderate injury, and inferred injury. Since the numbers are so small, it is not possible to determine from this figure the variation in rates for fatal child abuse. Thus, the data for fatal child abuse are displayed in figure 5.6. They demonstrate that child abuse fatalities are largely limited to children from low-income families. According to data from the most recent NIS-3 study, the impact of income and poverty on child abuse was overwhelming.

The data in figure 5.7 demonstrate the substantial influence of income on the incidence of child abuse. Most child abuse occurred in families with annual income below $15,000. There was some abuse in families with incomes between $15,000 and $30,000.

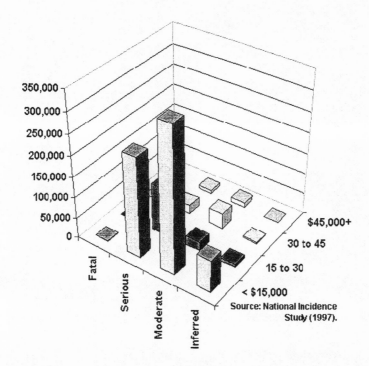

Figure 5.7 Incidence of Child Abuse by Income in the United States

**Table 5.10 Family Income and Incidence of Death
and Serious Injury from Child Abuse**
(Child neglect per 1,000 children from families with
annual income above and below $15,000)

	Below $15,000 :		Above $30,000
Abuse and Neglect			
Neglect	44	to	1
Physical Neglect	40	to	1
Physical Abuse	16	to	1
Sexual Abuse	18	to	1
Injury			
Moderate Injury	18	to	1
Serious Injury	22	to	1
Likely to die from maltreatment	60	to	1

Source: National Incidence Study-3, 1996.

It is useful to note that serious injury was substantially higher for families with income between $15,000 to $30,000 compared with families with income from $30,000 to $45,000. The incidence of maltreatment in all categories of abuse among families with income above $45,000 was relatively rare.

The most startling finding of the NIS-3 study was the dramatic differences in rates of child abuse by income. The data in table 5.10 indicates that neglect is 44 times greater in families with incomes below $15,000 compared to families with incomes above $30,000. Physical abuse is 16 times more frequent and sexual abuse is 18 times more likely.

What is perhaps most disturbing are the higher rates of injury among poor children. Using the same base of comparison—annual income below $15,000 compared to income above $30,000—the incidence of abuse that ends in moderate injury is 18 times greater among poor children. The incidence of abuse that leads to serious injury is 22 times greater. Most disturbing of all, the incidence of abuse that is likely to lead to death is 66 times greater for poor children.

It is important to keep in mind that these numbers are not percentage differences but rather differences of magnitudes. There is a greater than 60-fold difference in the rate of death from child abuse for children from low-income families compared to families with moderate or higher income. It is difficult in the face of these powerful findings not to conclude that child abuse is largely a phenomenon confined to low-income and poor families.

Is This the Right Direction?

The child welfare system predicates its cries for increased funding not on evidence of past success in reducing harm but on the supposed growth of the problems themselves.

Leroy Pelton, *For Reasons of Poverty*

We have reached a point where it is useful to ask: Is the child welfare system going in the right direction by concentrating resources on child protection? Has the narrowing of focus and purpose achieved by the transformation of child welfare into child protective services led to improvement in the welfare of children? Despite the increased reporting of child abuse, child fatalities have not been reduced. Rather, as a result of the increased reporting, agencies are overburdened and underfunded. Child welfare agencies have been forced to abandon fighting child poverty, a goal present since the field's inception. There is little evidence that this shift of direction or resources has achieved the goal of providing safety for children and a reduction in child abuse. If such evidence existed, we could be satisfied that child welfare, in its current manifestation as child protective services, is going in the right direction.

In one sense, mandatory reporting laws have accomplished nothing more than to change the framework of the intake process of the child welfare system. Before the advent of mandatory child abuse reporting laws, services were provided to the family with the aim of restoring the children to their home when the problems that led to their removal had been addressed. The goal was to achieve "permanency planning," in which children were reunited with their families as soon as possible, while providing services to that family (Emlen et al., 1977; Fein et al., 1983; Pike et al., 1977; Stein et al., 1978).[10]

Within the prevailing protective services approach children are removed within a context of accusation and blame (Janko, 1991). Services are allocated not on the basis of a parent failing to adequately provide for the child but from an assessment deriving from alleged abuse, in which the parent is the suspect. The caseworker is not intervening primarily to help the family but to investigate and determine wrongdoing.

The crucial question is whether the caseworker is qualified to adequately conduct such an investigation. Is the resulting assessment of risk accurate and reliable, and does it lead to adequate protection? The limited available data suggest that the answer is "no" on all issues. The protective service caseworker does not seem able to reliably assess risk or provide protection except when the abuse is substantial and extreme.

The question then becomes: Why mandate reporting if correct assessment cannot be made and sufficient protection provided? The only result, as we have seen, is that agencies are forced to shift limited resources to clients who cannot be reliably identified. In the process the child welfare system takes an accusatory tone toward parents, making them a less-than-willing participant in the recovery process. Traditional goals are abandoned, and millions of needy and deserving children go unserved.

Case Finding

The central problem for child welfare narrows to the question: Who should receive services and why? It is a question that highlights the essential drawbacks of a residual system, in which scarce resources cannot be given

---

[10] The term "permanency planning" highlighted the concern that foster care didn't provide children with a permanent home. Instead, children were viewed as drifting in foster care for years. Permanency planning allowed that foster care might not be detrimental to a child, even though it didn't provide the type of permanent home the child would have if reunited with his or her parent or placed for adoption.

to all who need them. Child abuse has shaped the process by saying that only those who have been abused get services, which means that services are not provided until abuse occurs. Further, services are no longer provided within a noncoercive framework of help, but rather within a coercive framework that attempts to shield the child from the accused parent. In some instances parents do severely physically or sexually assault their children, but these are the exception. Most children, as we shall see, are taken into care by the child welfare agencies for other reasons.

The proper foundation for effective child abuse prevention strategies assumes the ability of all parents to provide the basic needs of food, shelter, clothing, housing, and medical care for their children. In 1975, Sussman and Cohen, who were architects of the early mandatory reporting laws, pointed out the need to ensure that parents not be reported for abuse or neglect simply because they lacked the resources to provide for their children. They urged delaying enactment of expanded mandatory reporting laws until programs were in place that would ensure that all affected parents had the resources to provide adequate food, shelter, and housing for their children. Without this, mandated reporting laws would be rendered ineffective—which, essentially, is what has occurred.

Conclusion

During the last quarter of the twentieth century child welfare was transformed into child protection. In virtually every state child welfare system remains, if at all, in name only. State support for disadvantaged and poor children has been restricted to investigating reports of child abuse. After a child abuse investigation is complete the major service provided is child removal and placement in foster care.

Although the child welfare system has been transformed into a child protective service designed to protect children from physical and sexual abuse at the hands of their parents, there is virtually no evidence that the change reduced child abuse fatalities, or even increased safety for children. Since the transformation, child abuse in all forms and child fatalities have increased. We do know that the transformation has increased the number of families being investigated for abuse. In the process, the child welfare agency has changed from being viewed as helping parents to policing parents.

The child protection system that has evolved from mandatory reporting must be assessed against evidence demonstrating that children are safer as a result. Without ensuring that the basic needs of all children are met, the potential effectiveness of mandated reporting may go unrealized, as the drafters of the original reporting laws cautioned.

In the next chapter we examine the research supporting the core activity of child protection: the decision to remove children from their family and place them in foster care.

6

The Decision to Remove a Child

Responding to calls from doctors, police, teachers, and grandparents who believe a child has been mistreated, caseworkers knock on doors, ask personal questions, look inside refrigerators, and check children's bodies for bruises and burn marks. They have the power to take children temporarily from their homes and parents, if the risk of harm appears severe. They also have the discretion to determine that nothing serious happened, or that it is safe for the child to remain home while the parents are urged to change. The stakes are high. Overestimating the degree of danger could needlessly shatter a family and rupture the child's closest relationships. Underestimating the danger could mean suffering or even death. The decisions caseworkers make every day would challenge King Solomon, yet most of them lack Solomon's wisdom, few enjoy his credibility with the public, and none command his resources.
    Mary Larner, Carol Stevenson, and Richard Behrman, *Future of Children*

Upon what evidence do child welfare professionals decide to investigate child abuse or to place children in foster care? What factors influence their decision? Are the decisions reliable, consistent, fair? Insofar as foster care has become the de facto solution to child abuse, which has become the principal concern of child welfare agencies, the answers to such questions are the key to evaluating the direction, fairness, and effectiveness of the child welfare system.

Over time, the residual perspective has tended to narrow the scope of the child welfare system in determining who gets what. In the context of shrinking resources, the function of decision-making has been to allocate increasingly limited services to a narrowing group of children, by determining the child's risk of abuse at the hands of alleged abusing parents. Reliable and valid decisions thus represent the linchpin of the current child welfare system.

Foster Care Decision-making

Removing a child from a parent is neither for amateurs nor the faint of heart. It is complex, major surgery which in most cases will adversely affect the lives of both parents and children.

                                                        Patrick Murphy, *Wasted*

Although research studies have examined the decision-making process that leads to foster care, professionals have never fully understood exactly how such decisions are made. In 1963, Scott Briar observed: "Perhaps no decisions in social casework practice pose more awesome responsibilities for the caseworker and are more far-reaching in their potential consequences for the client than those involved in the placement of children in foster care . . . Systematically, we know next to nothing about how the child-placement worker makes these decisions" (p. 161).

More than twenty years later, Schwab, Bruce, and McRoy (1986), while attempting to build a computer model to assist in the child placement decision-making process, noted that research had found "no consensus among social workers about which placements were best for which children" (p. 360; cf. Schuerman and Vogel, 1986; Allan, 1978). In 1989, Howling and colleagues summarized:

> The extensive body of research on the etiology and effects of child maltreatment is characterized by flawed methodology, marked by inadequate definitions, lack of sound theoretical foundation, cross-sectional design limitations, sampling gaps, inadequate or missing control groups, and unidimensional measures. As a result, far reaching decisions in the field of child welfare have been based on questionable findings. (p. 3)

Deborah Daro (1988) provides a similar assessment. She writes, "The scholarly and popular literature on child maltreatment since 1962 is, to say the least, abundant. . . . Unfortunately, the results of these research efforts have not been as accessible or as useful to the decision-making process as their authors had hoped. Barriers to effective utilization have included methodological problems such as small, nonrepresentative samples, an uncertainty over which variables to explore and monitor, a very narrow range of intervention strategies to assess, and the absence of control groups" (pp. 2–3).

In 1993, a report from the National Research Council concluded that empirical research on child maltreatment was "in its infancy" and, in particular, that research on decision-making was minimal. Assessing progress in developing knowledge for child protective services (CPS), Larner, Stevenson, and Behrman (1998) concluded, "the distance separating CPS agencies from the goal of "research-based child welfare practice" remains great.

In a secular society, any decision to remove a child from his or her parents must have a scientific basis to ensure that it is not biased or prejudicial. As Stein, Gambrill and Wiltse (1978: 5) observe,

> Children have been removed because the court disapproved of the parents' life style or child rearing practices. Removal has occurred, for example, because the parents were not married, because the mother frequented taverns or had male visitors overnight, because the parents adhered to extreme religious beliefs or lived in a communal setting, because the parent was a lesbian or male homosexual, because the parents' home was filthy or because the woman was the mother of an illegitimate child. In none of these cases was there evidence of harm to the children. In such instances, socially unacceptable behavior of the parents is condemned on the pretext of acting in the child's best interest.

When a moralistic approach takes precedence over a scientific approach, personal and subjective value judgments and opinions are greatly encouraged. Such a nonscientific process undermines the whole purpose of state intervention to protect children, making it difficult to establish accountability for services provided.

Diagnostic Assessment and Placement:
The Emerging Medical Model

> The disease model of child abuse, with its emphasis on individualized treatment, cure and prediction, is the dominant paradigm in research policy, and practice. Child abuse is conceptualized as a pathological phenomenon with roots in personality or psychodynamics of abusing parents.
>
> Nigel Parton, *The Politics of Child Abuse*

Over the years attempts have been made to develop guidelines and diagnostic criteria that would aid the caseworker in deciding for or against placement. The first major contributions emphasized the use of the casework method (Charnley, 1955; Gordon, 1956). In 1957, Glickman proposed the psychodynamic theory which emphasized two psychological factors: first, was the level of emotional disturbance severe enough to upset the family balance? And did sufficient compensations exist within the family to offset the imbalance? Second, what was the location of the disturbance (i.e., child, mother, father, siblings, mother's boyfriend?), and did it intrude upon the parent-child relationship?

In 1972, Kline and Overstreet, building on the work of Glickman, developed a similar psychodynamic approach in which they delineated four clinical areas where the diagnostic judgments for decision-making should focus:

- The nature of the crisis and the presenting problems of the child and family.
- The ego functioning of the parents in their major life roles and their capacity to cope with the current family crisis.
- The family's situation, organizational level, and resources.
- The developmental status and condition of the children.

Within this framework the placement decision was based on a quasi-psychiatric diagnosis of both the type and degree of emotional pathology experienced by the parent. For Kadushin (1965: 28–29) the need for placement was seen as resulting from such factors as:

- Parental incapacity to love because the parent himself was not adequately loved.
- Parental incapacity in meeting dependency needs since the parent himself is still childishly dependent.
- Reactivation by the child of unresolved conflicts relating to the Oedipal situation, sibling rivalry, sexual identification—a reactivation which threatens the precarious emotional equilibrium of the parents.
- Parental narcissism manifested in neglect of the child's needs.
- A superego which is not sufficiently controlling to help the parent consistently meet the demands of parenthood, with this superego deficiency a consequence of a lack of stable, affectionate opportunities for identification.

Kadushin adds:

The shorthand characterization of such parents is that they are immature and in their immaturity neglect their children. Personality disturbance, if not the sole cause for separation, is regarded as the principal cause. The practitioner, while recognizing that ego faces id, superego, and the world of outer reality, tends to the ego's relationship to id and the superego in assessing the factors which have resulted in failure to perform adequately.

Thus, early work on the child placement decision focused on the clinical dimensions of the child and the family, gradually narrowing to the psychological problems of the parent (Specht, 1990). The approaches were based on a deficit model, in which lack of personality development and psychological growth in the parent prevented the parent from adequately caring for the child (Stein et al., 1978: 9–11). The social or structural issues that affected these families—such as inadequate income, unemployment, discrimination, lack of decent employment opportunities, deteriorating neighborhood conditions (including such factors as widespread drug addiction and crime)—were outside the concern and intervention of the child welfare caseworker. As Kadushin (1965: 29) explained: "Although the social situation is recognized as a contributing factor, it is given secondary consideration and is always somewhat suspect as the 'true' cause of the problem. Reality stresses tend to be regarded as convenient parental rationalization which permit the parent to defend himself against a recognition of his true rejection of the child."

However, clinical approaches that helped workers in deciding whether to remove a child from the family had limitations (Mech, 1970). First, as Mahoney and Mahoney (1974) pointed out, they provided no empirical support for the diagnostic criteria they identified. The psychodynamic model could not be subjected to scientific examination. Rather, the views were derived from clinical case analysis and judgment.[1] Second and more important, one could not assume that child welfare caseworkers had the professional training in clinical diagnosis that the models required. Overall, the psychodynamic models that the clinicians developed went unused, largely because few child welfare caseworkers ever became familiar with them. Early studies of the decision-making process revealed little consensus among caseworkers regarding criteria to use in deciding the future of children and families.

The Decision-making Process: The Foundation Studies

First Study. In 1963, Briar, in one of the earliest studies on the reliability of foster care placement decision-making, examined the judgment of caseworkers using hypothetical case material. Each worker in the study was asked to prepare diagnostic and prognostic judgments about two hypothetical cases involving either a mildly or severely disturbed child. One group of twenty-one caseworkers received cases involving a mildly disturbed child, while a second group of twenty-two caseworkers received cases involving a severely disturbed child.

Briar wanted to know whether the child's problem (i.e., mild or severe disturbance) determined the type of placement the child would receive.

---

[1] The one exception was the research by Boehm (1962), which examined the criteria used to decide when a child should be removed. Boehm asked child welfare caseworkers to rate 100 placement and 100 nonplacement families on a checklist of behavioral items. The major difference between the two groups was on the dimension of maternal behavior. Boehm concluded that the decision to remove a child was dependent on the worker's view of the relationship between the parent and child.

The study revealed only a limited association between the two. Although Briar found a relationship between the child's problem and type of placement, it was variable and unpredictable. While some agreement on diagnosis existed, predictions regarding the child's probable future varied substantially from caseworker to caseworker. Given that accurate prognosis is the critical factor in determining removal of the child, the study raised doubts about the reliability of the decision-making process. Briar reported that, in fact, the mother's preference largely determined the type of placement the caseworker ultimately selected. In cases where the mother opposed foster care placement, 77 percent of the workers recommended institutional placement. Similarly, when the mother opposed institutional placement, fewer than half of the workers recommended it.[2]

Second Study. In 1972, Phillips, Haring, and Shyne sought to develop an interview guide that would explicitly define the factors leading to in-home or out-of-home service. They asked workers to develop case plans detailing what services were intended for children in foster care and what efforts would be made to restore the children to their families. The caseworkers developed plans for 309 children in need of service, 71 for whom placement had been recommended. The researchers compared the placement and nonplacement groups on the nature of the service request, socioeconomic characteristics, behavioral and attitudinal evaluations of mother, father and child, and adequacy of parental care.

Fifty variables were associated with the decision to remove a child from the home. This was so many that it was difficult to understand which factors influenced placement. Although the research sought to group the variables into meaningful components, considerable overlap between the groups existed. The researchers therefore sorted the variables into seven groups to improve their predictive capacity. For both two-parent and single mother households, background factors and child traits differentiated between children who were removed and children who were not. For single mother households, mother traits also differentiated between the two groups, while for two-parent families father traits became the differentiating characteristics. The study found that background factors were by far the best predictors of placement, with socioeconomic status being the major determinant (see Garbarino and Stocking, 1981; Page, 1987).

---

[2] Local environmental conditions also influenced the caseworkers' recommendations more strongly than did the child's problem. The study revealed a significant association between the workers' placement recommendations and placement patterns of their agencies. For example, foster care was recommended by 63 percent of workers employed in agencies where this form of care predominated. In contrast, institutional placement was recommended by 75 percent of the workers employed in agencies where institutional care predominated. Workers commented that practical realities, such as the availability of resources, strongly influenced their placement decisions.

Table 6.1 Recommended Dispositions of 127
Foster Care Placement Cases

	Remove Child (%)	Keep at Home (%)
Judge A	53	47
Judge B	17	93
Judge C	72	28
Judge D	43	57
Judge E	34	66
Judge F	49	51
Caseworkers	38	62

Source: Phillips, Harding, and Shyne (1971).

In developing and refining the interview schedule, the researchers also assessed the *reliability* of experienced child welfare workers and judges in recommending for or against removal. In the disposition decisions made for 127 child placement cases the researchers found considerable disagreement between the judges and caseworkers (see table 6.1). The overall agreement of the six judges was less than 25 percent (p. 24). The contrast between two judges (B and C) was particularly remarkable: Judge C was four times more likely to recommend in-home services than was Judge B. Moreover, even when judges agreed to remove a child, which was rare, they varied substantially on the type of plan and services to be provided.

Third Study. In 1980, Donnelly examined foster care placement decisions by asking experienced caseworkers in four California counties to make recommendations on fifteen hypothetical cases. As in the previous studies, the decision to remove a child from the home varied substantially between the caseworkers. Those in Riverside and Alameda counties were more likely to remove a child than were caseworkers in San Bernadino and San Francisco counties, despite the geographic proximity (see table 6.2).

Part of the low reliability of decision-making found in these studies may be related to the validity of the stimulus materials used. That is, in all three studies the caseworkers used written case materials instead of actually meeting and interviewing the families. Nevertheless, in the absence of reliability studies with actual cases, the studies represent the best current indicator of reliability in foster care placement. The studies suggest that limited consensus exists on what criteria should be used in removing a child from the home.

Table 6.2 Recommended Dispositions of 45 Foster Care Placement Cases in
California

	Percent Child Removed (%)	Percent Child Keep at Home (%)
San Bernadino	29	71
Riverside	51	49
Alameda	58	42
San Francisco	36	64

Source: Donnelly (1980).

Further, the reliability of the decision-making process is either not statistically significant (Donnelley, 1980; Gart, 1971; Philips, Haring, and Shyne, 1971) or low (Briar, 1963).

Decision-Making as a Random Process

What are the consequences of such a low rate of reliability in selecting children for placement in foster care? To answer this question, we examined this low rate within the context of a hypothetical model that viewed decision-making as a stochastic (random) process (Groenveld and Giovannoni, 1977; Tyler and Brassard, 1984).

I considered a hypothetical system involving 100 children serviced by an "ideal" decision-making child welfare system in which the reliability rate was 1.0 (see Lindsey, 1994: 167, table 6.3). That is, every placement decision made by the system was correct. In this system 31 children would possess "true need for placement" and be placed in foster care, while the 69 who possessed lesser "true need for placement" would be retained with their families. When an assumption of a reliability of .25 was applied to the system (a level of reliability greater than was found in previous studies), the model clearly demonstrated the limitations of the current decision-making process. Only 16 of the 31 children who should have been placed in foster care were properly selected, while 15 children who did not need placement were improperly taken from their biological parent(s)—displacing 15 children who actually needed placement. In short, low reliability leads to a system that is unable to discern which child should be removed and which child should be left at home.

The most salient feature of the stochastic model is that it does not require assumptions of bias or prejudice on the part of the caseworker to account for the removal of many children not in need of placement or the returning home of large numbers in true need of placement. Caseworkers in doubt about a child's situation usually make the safe decision to remove a child. As Stein, Gambrill, and Wiltse (1978) point out, the caseworker is often in doubt, and thus, too often places the child in foster care. Kamerman and Kahn (1990: 8) observe, "Child protective staff fear errors, especially the failure to take endangered children into care, and the subsequent public response to deaths or severe abuse and neglect."

It is hard to imagine how the results of the stochastic model could be more distressful, in terms of what it suggests for the outcome of children considered for removal. If the level of reliability were to slip much further than .25, all children, except in the most extreme cases, would have an equal likelihood of being placed in foster homes, meaning that the decision-making process would be roughly equivalent to a lottery!

Explaining Low Reliability

Why is the level of reliability in assessing need for placement so low? Stein and Rzepnicki (1984: 8) offer an explanation:

> While worker's decision-making behavior is constrained by resource deficits, by the fact that some decisions are made by others before a worker receives a case, and by practices within a given agency, failure to identify practice principles that govern the selection of options is distressing. . . . It is not surprising, therefore, that reliability in decision-making is poor and that individual discretion and personal bias have been found to exert a strong influence on the decision-making behavior of child welfare staff.

The studies of the psychodynamic model, which focused on the parent-child relationship, assumed a supporting body of scientific knowledge that, in fact, did not exist. A review of these studies reveals idiosyncratic decision-making within a context of limited scientific knowledge. Caseworkers, even had they known of these models and had been following them, would likely have achieved little better than random success. But even within an ideal scientific context, limits exist on the ability of skilled practitioners to successfully predict client behavior. As Besharov (1987: 307) has observed: "Expecting child protective workers and judges to predict future child maltreatment is completely unrealistic and ultimately counter-productive. Overstating their ability to predict future maltreatment puts them under enormous pressure to remove children from their parents lest they be blamed if a child subsequently suffers serious harm."

The Scientific Basis for Child Removal

There is no penalty for the wrongful taking of a child. And the pressures to remove are intense. I was trained to do removals in cases that did not necessarily qualify as abuse or neglect because, as one of my supervisors reminded me, "prevention is better than a cure." When I was resistant to doing a removal on a case, that same supervisor's advice was, "It's better to be safe than sorry." And at moments of uncertainty, the mantra was "Cover your ass"—a phrase heard often around the office.

Dorothy Roberts, *Shattered Bonds*

Two points must be underscored. First, the child welfare field does not possess an adequate scientific knowledge base for determining which cases are best served in-home and which need out-of-home care (see Karski, Gilbert and Frame, 1997; Stein et al., 1978; Shlonsky and Gambrill, 2001; Stein and Rzepnicki, 1984). The limited research in this area has often only categorized and documented current casework procedure, forsaking systematic investigation that might identify which indicators in fact do lead to the desired outcome for children. To date, we still do not know with any precision when foster care is appropriate, for how long it should be administered, or what services should be combined with it. Second, environmental factors, funding patterns, and organizational characteristics of social service bureaucracies (i.e., variables external to children and their family) may be more instrumental in influencing the worker's decision about placement (Amacher and Maas, 1985; Hutchison, 1989; Proch and Howard, 1986; Roberts, 2002).

Factors Affecting the Foster Care Placement Decision

Foster children tend to come largely out of the ghettos and poverty areas of our country in what seems to be almost a random process. There is no research in the literature to indicate that entrance into foster care can be predicted.

David Fanshel and Eugene Shinn, *Children in Foster Care*

Since hundreds of children across the country are daily being removed from their families and placed in foster care, the question we are compelled to ask is: In practice, how do case workers make their decision?

Adequacy of Income

While a lack of agreement might have existed within the traditional model on why a child should or shouldn't be removed, when we examined the children who actually had been removed, we found that it was adequacy of family income which best differentiated those who had been removed from those who had not (Lindsey, 1994). The analysis indicated that children were being removed from their parents and placed in foster care because their parents did not possess adequate income. We can only recall what Fanshel and Shinn (1978: 506) had observed: "that foster children tend to come largely out of the ghettos and poverty areas of our country in what seems to be almost a random process."

Child welfare workers can only use the intervention services available to them. Increasingly, they are limited to foster care as the only available method of intervention. If social workers could provide preventive or income support services to families, the number of children placed in foster care would likely decline (Stein, Gambrill, and Wiltse, 1978).[3]

To account for the emphasis on income, we must look to other factors linked to income. What, for example, is the link between education and income? In this sample, the parents, by and large, lacked education. Emlen (1977: 19) found in his sample of families whose children were in foster care in Oregon that 83 percent of the mothers and 85 percent of the fathers had not gone past the eighth grade, a condition that certainly affected their ability to gain and hold employment.[4] Emlen reported that 92 percent of the mothers and 69 percent of the biological fathers were unable to report having steady employment. Some 76 percent of the mothers and 46 percent of the fathers had always or usually been on public assistance.

Single Parenthood

> Only one variable other than single motherhood was a better predictor of child removal: poverty. . . . The Society [protective services] was sensitive to allegations that it kidnapped poor people's children, and its stated policy was that it never removed children from their homes for poverty alone. But poverty was never alone. The characteristic signs of child neglect in this period [1880–1920]—dirty clothing, soiled linen, lice and worms, crowded sleeping conditions, lack of attention and supervision, untreated infections and running sores, rickets and other malformations, truancy, malnutrition, overwork—were often the results of poverty.
>
> Linda Gordon, *Heroes of Their Own Lives*

---

[3] In part, this is the argument of advocates of family preservation services. Their argument is that provision of preventive and support services would alleviate the need to remove a child and allow preservation of the family (compare with the approach developed in the Comprehensive Emergency Services program discussed in chapter 3).

[4] Several of the children in the sample lived with their mother and a legal father who was not their biological father (i.e., stepfather). In those cases where it was applicable, 56 percent of the legal fathers were unable to report steady employment.

A connection can also be made to the predicament of single parents. Most of the children in foster care come from impoverished single parent households. In 2000, the poverty rate for children in single mother households was over 50 percent for Blacks, 45 percent for Hispanics, and 37 percent for whites (Census Bureau, 2001). One of the major reasons many of these families are poor stems from the departure of the income producing parent who seldom contributes to the support of the children left behind (Colon, 1981). Numerous studies have documented that child support payments from the income-earning spouse to the child-caring spouse are erratic and often nonexistent, especially for low-income households (Chambers, 1979; Kamerman and Kahn, 1988a; Stuart, 1986).

Research has consistently demonstrated that adequacy of income is the crucial determinant in the decision to remove a child (Lindsey, 1994). Even though the normative and psychodynamic theories that focus on the parent/child relationship may not consider income source variables, these variables nevertheless have the greatest discriminative accuracy in differentiating children who are removed and placed in foster care, from those who are not. This direct measurable influence has yet to be demonstrated by the other clinical variables.

In 1975, Jenkins and Norman conducted a follow-up study of children in foster care. Five years after the sample entered care, 73 percent had been discharged to the care of their biological mothers. The researchers noted that "the chronic conditions that underlay their placement still persisted. Most families were living on the borderline of self-management, in terms of income, health and stability" (pp. 131–132). In fact, the financial situations of the mothers had deteriorated.[5] Turner (1984) reported that child protective service (CPS) social workers returned children from foster care without ever addressing the problems identified as the reasons for removal, particularly if the problems were economic.

Services to the Biological Family

It seems Orwellian to call what the child welfare agency does "serving" families, when the vast majority of its clients are "served" against their will. The agency's service plan usually has little to do with services for the family. It is typically a list of requirements parents must fulfill in order to keep their children or get them back. Rarely are parents asked what services they need. The

---

[5] At the time of the original placement 48 percent of the mothers were on AFDC, while five years later 71 percent were on AFDC. Little had changed for these families except the return of the child from foster care (Jenkins and Norman, 1972; Jenkins and Sauber, 1966). The return of the child to the biological family did not appear to be related to improvements made in the biological family situation.

plans remind me of probation orders that list requirements and restrictions judges impose on criminals. Violation of a single provision lands the offender back in jail. In the child welfare system, parents who fail to comply risk never seeing their children again.

Dorothy Roberts, *Shattered Bonds*

One would expect that services would be provided to address the problems that led to placement (Gambrill, 1990; Karski, Gilbert. and Frame, 1977). If a child is removed because of a parent's drug and alcohol problem, clinical services would be forthcoming to address this problem. However, examining national data, I found that once the child was removed from the home, the biological parent was less likely to receive services than if the child was kept at home (Lindsey, 1994).

That large numbers of parents receive no services once their children are removed challenges fundamental premises on which removal is based, implying essentially that little effort is being made to restore the child. Fanshel and Shinn (1978: 486) observed, "This is another indication that service to parents of children in placement is the most manifest and blatant area of failure in service delivery that one can find as one reviews the foster care phenomenon."

Instead of assisting the biological mothers with the immediate demands of child care, the placement worker may actually be increasing their problems and reducing the likelihood of their ever regaining custody and care of their children. Besharov (1988b: 198) has observed:

Treatment services for the parents of children in foster care are largely nonexistent. In fact, the child's placement usually results in a reduction in the level of services parents receive. For example, the parent's public assistance grant will be reduced by the amount attributable to the child, often requiring the parent to move into a smaller, less attractive apartment—from which she will have to move again (to a larger apartment) before she can regain custody of the child. In today's housing market, this is no easy task. In addition, food stamps, homemaker services, and even the intermittent caseworker visits may be suspended during the time the child is in foster care. Only parents who wish to be relieved of the obligations of parenthood gain anything from their child's placement.

As can be seen, the vulnerable child was the one whose family received income from neither government nor self-support (cf. table 6.6 earlier). Presumably their income derived from other sources: family, friends, and alimony, all of which have the potential of being less stable and predictable than government or self-support. Such a child was more than 120 times more likely to be removed and placed in foster care than the child whose family income derived from self-support.

Clearly, an unstable income source represented the highest predictor of removal. This finding, which is consistent with previous research on the impact of income on placement (Fanshel and Shinn, 1978; Lindsey, 1991d; Testa and Goerge, 1988), suggests that programs providing direct income support to the parent would likely prove effective in preventing placement. In 1978, reflecting on the foster care children in their longitudinal sample, Fanshel and Shinn wrote:

> We have no faith in the ability to predict or prevent the entrance of children into foster care. True prevention would require strong support for all families in their child-rearing efforts, particularly the most impoverished. If such support is not forthcoming in our country, more children will inevitably wind up in foster care. Cutting public assistance budgets, ending support for public housing, terminating mental health facilities—all grim phenomena of this recent period—are sure ways to increase the number of families where parental breakdown will occur and children will require foster care. (p. 507)

Decision-making in the Current Child Protection System

At the heart of the child protection enterprise is the removal of children who have been abused or neglected from their families and placement of the children in foster care. As we have seen in previous chapters, the primary marker in identifying rates of abuse is child poverty. What is perplexing, however, is when we examine the actual rates of child removal (and foster care) by state there are vast differences that seem to have little explanation. The differences are not explained by either the actual incidence of child abuse or child poverty within the various states. Rather, these major differences occur without a credible explanation. The differences point out the arbitrary and unfair nature of the child protection system. They underscore the lack of a scientific foundation.

As seen in table 6.3, California has the highest rate of child removal, while Alabama has the lowest. The rate of removal of children who are victims of child abuse is sixteen times greater in California compared to Alabama. Children are removed at a rate ten times greater in California compared to New Jersey. What is the explanation? There is no credible reason to explain how child abuse can be substantiated at a rate ten times greater in California in comparison to New Jersey.

Table 6.3 Variations in Rates of Child Removal and Placement in Foster Care by State

	Child Population	Child Victim Removed	Rate per 1,000		Child Population	Child Victims Removed	Rate per 1,000
Alabama	1,060,177	310	.29	California	8,923,423	42,670	4.78
New Jersey	2,003,204	894	.45	Oregon	827,501	3,924	4.74
Colorado	1,065,510	652	.61	Oklahoma	882,062	4,019	4.56
Iowa	719,685	550	.46	New Mexico	495,612	2,225	4.49
Virginia	1,664,810	1,317	.79	North Carolina	1,940,947	7,654	3.94
Arkansas	660,224	553	.84	Nevada	491,476	1,705	3.47
Indiana	1,258,991	1,667	1.09	Kentucky	965,528	3,169	3.28
Pennsylvania	2,852,520	3,121	1.09	New York	4,440,924	13,257	2.99
Texas	5,719,234	6,487	1.13	Florida	3,569,878	10,579	2.96
Missouri	1,399,492	1,620	1.16	Ohio	2,844,071	8,305	2.92
Arizona	1,334,564	1,905	1.43	West Virginia	403,481	1,081	2.68
Mississippi	752,866	1,133	1.50	Michigan	2,561,139	6,684	2.61
Wisconsin	1,348,268	2,062	1.53	Georgia	2,056,885	5,003	2.43
Illinois	3,181,338	5,016	1.58				

Source: www.childwelfare.com

The administrative data do not conform with the real differences between the states. Victims of child abuse in Oregon are removed from their family at a rate seven times greater than in Colorado. These are all children who have been victimized. It is just that in some states the decision to remove is far more frequent—by several fold—than in others.

No other data are more representative of the outcome of the child protective system decision-making process than the decision to remove the child. It is the most fundamental decision the child protection system makes. Further, no other data more clearly illustrates the capricious and idiosyncratic nature of the decision-making process of the child protection system. Removal of a child from his or her family is the most intrusive and potentially harmful act of the state. The decision to remove a child should only be done with the greatest of caution. The data in table 6.3 suggests that the current state-run child protection systems lack both reliability and validity in their core decision-making process and fail to provide adequate legal protection to affected families.

Summary

Over time, the residual model has erected a child welfare bureaucracy whose function is to develop and maintain selected residual categories. The model assumes that we can ultimately resolve the problems children face by precisely identifying those categories. Unfortunately, the central tenant is flawed. The research has consistently demonstrated that only a very limited consensus exists on what children fit what categories. More and more, the variables we thought had some bearing in deciding the issue appears to be a smoke screen masking the real issue, which is poverty.

Mnookin (1973) suggested that two principles should govern the decision to remove a child:

- Removal should be a last resort, used only when the child cannot be protected within the home.
- The decision should be based on legal standards applied in a consistent and even-handed way, and not influenced by the values of the deciding judge.

As the analysis presented here suggests, Mnookin's principles have not been widely implemented. Currently child welfare caseworkers may simply be relabeling "inadequate income" as "abuse," "neglect," "child behavior"—all socially and legally acceptable reasons for child removal. A single parent without adequate income apparently has little chance of keeping her child once she has come to the attention of the public child protection system. Removing a child from his or her parent is a severe form of state intervention, even if the removal is only temporary. As Fanshel and Shinn (1978) have written: "People should not be penalized because they are poor, because they are mentally ill, or because they are afflicted with drug addiction or alcoholism. They should not be penalized because it is less expensive for society to terminate their (parental) rights and allow others, endowed with better economic means, to replace them as the parents of their children."

How often is removal the last resort? How often might not services designed to retain the child in the home be more effective? At what economic cost—and what human anguish over the loss of one's children and the stigma that attaches to both parent and child—are alternatives ignored?

Conclusion

In this chapter we have examined the decision-making process from several angles. In every case the results have been discouraging. First, the stochastic model, assuming an optimistic reliability factor of .25, revealed that current decision-making practices possessed little predictive value in accurately assessing who should receive foster care and who should not.

The data examined in this and other studies corroborate the findings from the National Incidence Studies that suggest that poverty is the major factor influencing child abuse and the decision to remove a child from his or her parents. Inadequacy of income, more than any other factor, constitutes the reason that children are removed—a conclusion that strikes at the very heart of the child protection system.

The data on the wide variations in rate of child removal among the states further demonstrates the imprecision and capricious nature of the child protection system as it operates within the various states. Apparently some states are reluctant to remove children when abuse occurs while others are far more willing to remove children when they are the victims of abuse.

Reliable decision-making is the linchpin of the child protection system. If decision making is unreliable then the system is doomed to fail its purpose of protecting children.

7

Dealing with Child Abuse,
the Red Herring* of Child Welfare

"This system has been sued and sued and orders have been issued and people have just continued on their merry way" (Committee on Ways and Means, 1988). These efforts at reform have all failed because the core tasks of the child protection system—investigation of families and child removal—remain unchanged.

Emerich Thoma, Lifting the Vail

From the outset, the current system is fueled by an inclination to investigate parents to find evidence that they are to blame for the harms and dangers befalling their children, and the balance in the dual role is tipped toward the investigative/coercive/child removal role to the detriment of the helping role. Attention is deflected from the context of poverty in which most families live who are reported to the agency.

Leroy Pelton, Beyond Permanency Planning

Although not originally a concern of the residual model, child abuse is today the principle focus of child welfare agencies, to the exclusion of nearly all other issues. How and why this happened is no mystery, since child abuse represents the extreme, logical focus of the residual approach. If the residual model seeks to help the socially excluded—the outcasts, the abandoned, the less fortunate—the abused child is the perfect client, since he or she is excluded in a way that no one else can be. While others may suffer poverty, neglect, prejudice, racism, the abused child is denied the most precious and necessary qualities human beings require when they awaken upon the earth—love and nurture from the parent. Child abuse that ends in death becomes the ultimate exclusion.

---

* A red herring is a highly charged issue that draws attention away from the real and more difficult problem.

It should come as no surprise that in adhering to the residual perspective the child welfare profession has narrowed its focus almost exclusively to child abuse. Child abuse, especially severe physical and sexual assault, are high-valence issues which draw the public's attention. All other concerns are set aside while focus is riveted on these horrific incidents. The irony is that the more effort, attention, and resources we devote to the problem, the less we seem to achieve.

In untangling the problem of child abuse, we encounter a number of important and interrelated issues. Child abuse is not just a social phenomenon in and of itself but an issue that has affected child welfare practice as nothing else has ever done, transforming child welfare policy in a way that obscures the traditional focus of what child welfare is all about. Further, it has detrimentally affected the justice system, corroding and impeding the rights of families and individuals (Murphy, 1997; Roberts, 2002). Preoccupation with child abuse wastes valuable human and monetary resources, and daily deprives agencies of the ability to deliver services to others more appropriately in need of their services. By handing responsibility for dealing with severe physical and sexual assault over to the child welfare system, we deny children the protection the police would otherwise provide and, consequently, expose them to greater harm. By sidestepping the police we allow perpetrators to escape criminal sanction and prosecution, leaving them free to repeat their offense.

Scope of the Problem

The highly charged nature of criminal child abuse makes it difficult to find rational agreement on just how prevalent child abuse fatalities are. Large-scale studies all indicate that child abuse fatalities are relatively rare. The estimate of the National Incidence Study (Sedlak, 1991) that approximately 1,000 children a year die from child abuse corresponds with data reported from the National Center for Health Statistics (Select Committee on Children, Youth, and Families, 1989b) on deaths to children from homicide or "undetermined injury." The figures from these studies closely match data reported by the American Humane Association, the Federal Bureau of Investigation, and the National Committee for the Prevention of Child Abuse (see figure 5.2).

One of the most comprehensive in-depth reviews of child abuse fatalities was conducted by Cyril Greenland (1987). Working with extensive data from a study of 100 child abuse fatalities in Ontario, Canada, Greenland (1987: 19) observed, "With the passing of the rhetoric about the virtual epidemic of child-abuse deaths, it is reassuring to discover that abuse and neglect severe enough to maim or destroy young children is comparatively rare. However, due to the moral panic associated with child abuse, this conclusion may not be welcomed by the professional community."

Greenland's conclusion is supported by other statistics. Pryor (1991) reported that in 1990 in New York state less than 1 percent of all reports to child welfare agencies involved severe physical abuse. The state of New York used a Central Register to record all child abuse and neglect reports and classified them as either "abuse" or "maltreatment." For the decade 1981 to 1990 abuse reports accounted for about 10 percent of all reports registered (Pryor, 1991: table 3). In 1990, abuse reports accounted for 8.7 percent of all reports, while maltreatment accounted for 91.3 percent. The child abuse allegations are displayed by category in figure 7.1. The major reason in the "other" category was leaving the child unsupervised. Many parents are not aware of the age limits or laws governing the leaving a child unsupervised.

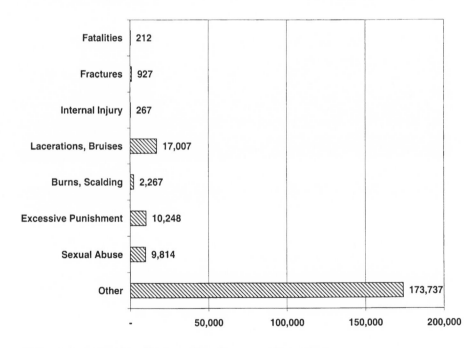

Figure 7.1 Allegations Reported by Category, New York
Source: Pryor (1991).

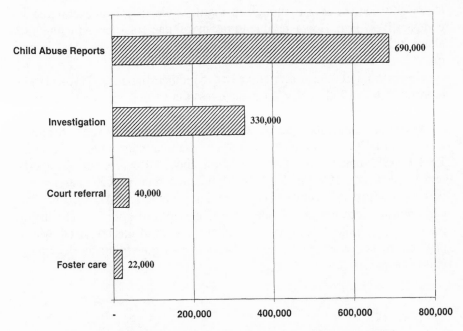

Figure 7.2 The Processing of Child Abuse Reports in California, 1995
Source: Karski, Gilbert, and Frame (1997).

In California in 1995 most child abuse reports were not investigated (see figure 7.2).[1] Out of almost 700,000 reports, about 40,000 received court referral (6 percent), which led to 22,000 children being removed and placed in foster care (3 percent). Thus, only a small percentage of child abuse reports resulted in major state intervention.

Even after a child abuse case is investigated and abuse is substantiated, most of these confirmed cases are not prosecuted. Karski (1999) examined a sample of cases in California and found that cooperation with the child protection agency and poverty were important factors in the court referral decision. Only a small percentage of cases where abuse was confirmed, irrespective of seriousness, were referred to the court. Finally, less than 5 percent of abuse reports led to court referral and removal of the child for placement in foster care.

---

[1] Van Voorhis and Gilbert (1998: 214) report that "in 1994, there were 664,294 official child abuse reports registered in California (Children Now, 1995). However, the 1994 data collected through the National Child Abuse and Neglect Data System (NCANDS) reveal only 352,059 official reports. The reason for this discrepancy is that California does not include reports closed at intake in the calculation of child abuse reports for the data provided to NCANDS."

When viewed within the larger scope of child welfare problems, serious physical and sexual assault affects a relatively small portion of children. Reece estimates the number of children who suffer severe physical and life threatening abuse is about 160,000 children, while approximately 1,300 children die from severe physical child abuse. When measured against the total number of children living in poverty (13,000,000) and extreme poverty (5,000,000), severe child abuse represents a small segment (see figure 7.3). Thoburn, Brandon and Lewis (1997: 190) observe, "All the evidence from this and other studies points to the conclusion that children coming into the child protection systems are the 'tip of the iceberg', and representative of many more families struggling with children who have serious problems and whose health is being significantly impaired because needed services are not provided."

It is important to remember from the most recent National Incidence Study (NIS-3) that the likelihood of fatalities and severe injury was highly correlated with poverty. In fact, the rate of severe injury for families with annual income below $15,000 was twenty-two times greater than for families with income above $30,000. The rate for fatalities was 60 times greater for poor families (see table 5.10).

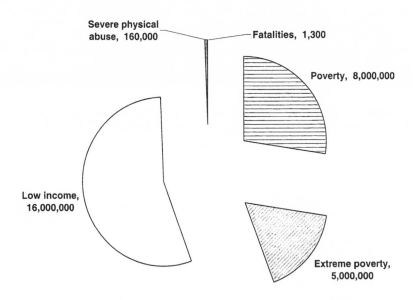

Figure 7.3 Circumstances of Children in the United States, 2000
Source Peddle and Wang (2001); Reece (2000: xv); Song and Lu (2002).

Table 7.1 Causes of Child Deaths in California, 1992-1995

Natural Deaths	
Perinatal conditions	6,643
Congenital anomalies	4,611
Sudden Infant Death Syndrome (SIDS)	2,096
Malignant neoplasms	1,123
Infectious and parasitic diseases	774
Pneumonia and influenza	550
Heart disease	538
Unintentional Injuries	
Motor vehicle	2,317
Drownings	642
Suffocations	188
Firearms	140
Poisonings	79
Intentional Injuries	
Homicides by firearms/explosives	1,482
Suicides	464
Other homicides	372
Child abuse homicides	218

Source: California Department of Health Services, Vital Statistics Death Records.

This data does not mean that criminal child abuse is not a severe and compelling problem, but it does compel us to ask: Are our efforts for the care and protection of children being channeled in the right direction? Is our definition of child abuse broad enough? Should child abuse be confined to the 1,300 children killed each year by their parents, or should it include the more than 13 million children living in homes of poverty and despair? More than 16 million children come from families eligible for subsidized free lunch (less than 130 percent of poverty line).

Child abuse fatalities are a small part of all child deaths. As seen in table 7.1, child abuse fatalities occur several times less often than child homicides from handguns. Concerted effort to improve handgun safety would likely save more lives but receives substantially less attention. As serious and often horrible as child abuse is, and especially child abuse fatalities, does it warrant the complete transformation of public child welfare from a system serving a broad range of disadvantaged children into one designed primarily to protect children from battering and sexual assault? Most children who come to the attention of child welfare agencies and who are the victims of neglect or inadequate care, but have not been battered or sexually assaulted, are, given the new priorities, virtually excluded from receiving assistance.

The abuse reporting laws enacted in the late 1960s and early 1970s did not include additional resources to meet the increased demand for services these laws produced.[2] To fund the new demand for services, child welfare agencies changed the definition of whom they serve. They now rarely respond to requests for service unless an allegation of abuse is involved, and even then the cases are screened over the phone to reduce investigative requirements (Karski, 1999). Requests for service or aid to families in distress or chronic crisis receive low priority and, in some instances, no response at all (Kamerman and Kahn, 1990; Maluccio and Anderson, 2000).

Commenting on the almost exclusive focus on physical and sexual abuse, Greenland (1987: xiii) observed that "many child-protection agencies have little or no interest in the equally pernicious mischief caused to children by poverty and neglect. The challenge for the child welfare field in the next decade must surely be to deploy its resources, moral as well as economic and political, to promote the welfare of all children. Treating emotionally, physically, and sexually abused children who come to public attention is most important—but it is not enough."

Popular Misconceptions About Threatened Children

Why agencies have a preoccupation with child abuse to the exclusion of almost everything else is not difficult to understand. Public outrage and fear, fanned by media coverage of horrifying incidents, have tended to grossly misrepresent the dimensions of the child abuse problem (Nelson, 1984; Spector and Kitsuse, 1977). In 1978, then Congressman Paul Simon stated that "50,000 young people disappear each year, because of 'stranger kidnapping.' That is the most conservative estimate you will get anywhere" (U.S. House of Representatives, 1981: 10). This statement was later embellished by others with such phrases as "there is general agreement among professionals" that 50,000 children a year are kidnapped by strangers. Although it was never clear where this figure came from, few questioned it. The more it was quoted, the more alarmed the public became. Pictures of missing children began appearing on milk cartons and grocery bags. In school, public education programs warned children of the perils of talking to strangers. The media, alert for a story that would sell (and often irrespective of its veracity), highlighted the most tragic cases of

---

[2] Only Illinois passed an appropriation with its first reporting law (Nelson, 1984: 132). Also see Datallo (1991).

abducted children.[3] Testifying to Congress (U.S. Senate, 1983: 33), the father of one missing child reported, "This country is littered with mutilated, decapitated, raped, and strangled children." When runaways and children abducted in child custody disputes were included, the number of missing children swelled to 1.5 million. The emotional uproar made it difficult to objectively assess the problem of missing children.[4] Anyone who questioned the facts or figures was suspected of lacking compassion for the plight of threatened children (Best, 1990).

---

[3] In 1973, U.S. Congressman Mario Biaggi testified at a U.S. Senate hearing on the Child Abuse and Neglect Prevention and Treatment Act that child abuse was the "number one killer of children in America today" (cited in Pelton, 1989: 30). *The New York Times* reported in November 30, 1975, that "more than a million American children suffer physical abuse or neglect each year, and at least one in five of the young victims die from their mistreatment, the Government announced today" (cited in Pelton, 1989, 29). This meant that 200,000 children were dying each year from child abuse, an exaggeration that more accurately describes the number of fatalities that would have occurred over two centuries. As we have seen, the number of child abuse fatalities in 1975 was approximately 1,000. Pelton reported that this exaggerated number continued to gain nationwide publicity through the news media for several weeks. The number of fatalities was based on an interview with Douglas Besharov, then director of the National Center on Child Abuse. Besharov claims he said 2,000.

[4] Media has a central role in mediating information and forming public opinion. The media casts an eye on events that few of us directly experience and renders otherwise remote happenings observable and meaningful. Consequently, if an issue is to be established in modern society as a social problem requiring state intervention, the role of the media is crucial (Best, 1991). In this regard, press coverage of an issue that produces such public outrage at the brutal death of a child can be angry and critical of a system that is seen as responsible for preventing the senseless death, yet somehow unable and unwilling to act. Newspaper headlines in Britain in 1973 are illustrative (Parton, 1985: 89–99): "The *Times* headlines include: 'Social Worker Made Error of Judgement' (3 November); 'Social Worker Booed at Brighton Enquiry' (6 November); 'Social Workers Wrong, QC Tells Inquiry Into the Death of Maria Colwell' (8 November); 'Social Worker Accepted Bruises' (13 November); 'Social Worker's Job "Not at Risk" After Took Little Interest in the Child's Death' (14 November). The front page report is head-lined 'Two-Babies Are Battered to Death Each Day.' A study of 29 men imprisoned at Brixton for killing their children was reported in the press: "One of the most disturbing findings…is the lack of guaranteed security for abused children once their plight has come to light…Eight men in the Brixton cases were being visited by social agencies because of child abuse when they killed their children" (Scott, 1973). Golding and Middletown (1982) quote additional headlines from 1980, "Malcolm Died As He Lived, Freezing Cold, Starving And Surrounded by Social Workers' (*Daily Mirror*, 16 January 1980); 'Early Victim of Do-Nothing Welfare Team' (*Daily Mail*, 21 February); 'Welfare Woman in Row Over a Dead Baby' (*Daily Mail*, 4 November)." Reviewing these press reports Golding and Middleton (1982,90) argue "hat such children suffer from ineffectual intervention by incompetent social workers is a common theme in these cases…Social workers represent in human form the excessive intervention of the state in people's lives, and also the naivete of the bureaucratic mind…Thus social workers are too numerous, do not act when they should, and are largely unnecessary."

In 1985, a Pulitzer Prize–winning story in the *Denver Post* finally debunked the issue, suggesting that the problem of missing children had been blown completely out of proportion (Best, 1990). Using FBI statistics, the newspaper reported that in 1984 the number of child abductions by strangers was not 1.5 million but 67. Commenting on these numbers, Gelles suggested, "The odds of a child being abducted by a stranger are about the same as his chances of being struck by lightning" (cited in Best, 1990). As suddenly as they had begun waving it, the media now dropped and furled the banner of missing children. As Best (1991) reports: "*US News and World Report* called the concern with missing children a 'faddish hysteria,' *Harper's* referred to it as a 'national myth' (Schneider, 1987: 50); Nicholas von Hoffman in *The New Republic* mocked claims that there ever had been 1.5 million abductions a year: 'In a decade, that means that 15 million children have gone through the doughnut hole into the antiworld.'"

Looking back now, we smile that such inflated statistics received public acceptance. Yet, child abuse represents a nearly identical situation. When even one child dies from abuse, the child welfare system comes under immediate scrutiny. How is this allowed to happen, the public demands? How many other children are being clubbed to death in their cribs? Are we wasting our money on these bungling child welfare bureaucrats? Over the last two decades, such questions have transformed child welfare agencies from benevolent, helping organizations into a quasi-legal, investigative, accusatory, protective service systems (Frost and Stein, 1989; Howells, 1975).

Investigation and Prevention of Child Abuse

The shift of responsibilities for investigating child abuse from the police to child welfare agencies has changed the practice of the courts (Donzelot, 1979). During the last decade the discretionary power of child welfare agencies has increased, as has court involvement in child welfare cases. With the courts and legal system behind them, child welfare caseworkers now exercise considerable authority to remove children from their biological parents. Goldstein, Solnit, and Freud (1998) suggest that existing legislation gives courts and social workers "almost limitless discretion to act in accord with their own child-rearing preferences in areas generally under the exclusive control of parents." This power often intimidates the mother whose child is the subject of an abuse allegation, since she knows that the caseworker can call on the courts to enforce any requests the caseworker makes.

The removal of children from parents can occur in two ways. First, the parent may voluntarily release the child to the care of the child welfare social worker and agency, or second, if the parent refuses to cooperate voluntarily, the caseworker may petition the court to order placement.[5] When a court becomes involved it makes both a jurisdictional and a dispositional judgment, decisions that may occur in varying time frames. The court assumes jurisdiction based not on specific harms to the child but on such descriptive criteria as observed parental behavior, apparent neglect or abuse to the child, and so on. Once jurisdiction is established, investigation of specifics commences. The dispositional judgment that follows an investigation, and which rests upon a standard known as "in the child's best interest" (Wald, 1976: 629), decides upon a remedy based upon the specific harms to the child revealed by the investigation.

It is no exaggeration to say that caseworkers often establish jurisdiction through a subtle masquerade of benevolent intent. Knocking on a family's door, they ask to "assess" the family situation, the implication being that services and aid may be forthcoming. It is an innocent request that once granted often backfires on parents who cooperate, for, if accepted, it establishes the caseworker's legal jurisdiction. At any point thereafter "assessment" can turn into "investigation" and benevolent "inquiry" into "accusation."[6] As Giovannoni and Becerra (1979: 69–70) have observed:

> The social workers have brought with them their special orientation to and definitions of the problems and modes of managing them. The nature of the ideal social work intervention is one of therapy and rehabilitation, not one of social control. Social workers' authority rests on professional competence rather than legal authority. Justification for use of the authority is thus not customarily sought on legal grounds but rather on the grounds of the benefits to the clientele.

Given that most children are removed from their families not for abuse, or even severe abuse, but for reasons related to poverty, the upshot may be

---

[5] Court involvement is sometimes mandatory as a matter of agency policy, regardless of whether the parent voluntarily relinquishes the child.

[6] Theodore Stein (1991b) has observed that "the courts are beginning to rule that if a social worker is conducting an investigation and has as her/his purpose the possible criminal prosecution of a parent [which due to all the criminal prosecutions of sex abuse reports happens with increasing frequency] she or he may well be responsible for providing a *Miranda* warning as do police conducting similar investigations." Other attorneys have suggested they would advise clients not to permit "assessments" or investigations without a court order. Further, they would recommend that clients not discuss their situation with a social worker in an abuse investigation without the presence of counsel (a lawyer).

a dispositional judgment recommended by the caseworker and acceded to by the court, which the family neither expects nor deserves.

The relationship between the child welfare agency and the court should be understood. In many jurisdictions, the court and agency work hand-in-glove in the disposition of abuse and neglect cases. What the agency recommends, the court approves with minimal review, becoming, in essence, little more than a rubber stamp to the policies of the child welfare agency. It is not so much cynical indifference or corrupt collusion that promotes this but simple expediency. Because their dockets are full to bursting, the courts find it convenient to relinquish more and more decision-making authority to the child welfare professional. As the National Commission on Children (1991) reported, "Most judges have 35 to 40 cases on their individual calendars [every day], and they have an average of 10 minutes to spend on each case. Five years from now, with double the caseloads, the judges will have not 10 minutes, but five minutes to determine each child's fate and each family's future" (p. 283, citing Paul Blond, Presiding Judge at Los Angeles County Juvenile Court).

The muted objections of impoverished parents, too intimidated by the court process to vociferously defend their rights, are swept aside. "In acting symbiotically with the child welfare agencies, the courts have assumed the 'coloration' of social agencies" (Levine, 1973: 34, citing Eastman). By allowing child welfare agencies to intrude into the lives of families where no "criminal" wrongdoing exists, and to act on recommendations based on that intrusion, the courts have empowered the child welfare agency to act as their agent. In this regard, they have abandoned their duty to make independent and perhaps conflicting judgments apart from the agency. By invoking the courts in neglect and maltreatment situations, child welfare agencies have used the court to sanctify their actions. In the context of expediency, the court has failed to provide conventional safeguards. As a result, court involvement has become a corrosion of the legal system that is slowly undermining the rights of poor families and threatening traditional due process.

The Court as Independent Agent

> These laws set no limits on intervention and provide no guidance for decision making. They are a prime reason for the system's inability to protect obviously endangered children even as it intervenes in family life on a massive scale.
> Douglas Besharov

The value of the court rests in its role as an independent and impartial party to determine if "criminal abuse" has occurred. The decision to remove a child from the home is not a technical question subject to the expertise of the child welfare social worker but rather a moral and legal determination belonging to the court, with the child welfare social worker providing expert testimony and advice. The proper role of the court is to protect the rights of children and parents, in which expert testimony in defense of the parents is also provided. With the involvement of child welfare caseworkers, whose primary efforts have been in the "best interests of the child," the courts have too often proven more responsive to the recommendations of the caseworker than to the rights of the parent.[7]

Because the combination of benevolent and intrusive power held by the caseworker so confounds the caseworker's relationship to the parents in abuse and neglect situations, Levine (1973) has argued that the worker should intervene only without application of legal authority, that is, only without the authority to take any jurisdictional or dispositional action. Although due process safeguards have been implemented at the hearing level in abuse and neglect cases, this still leaves open what may occur prior to entering the courtroom. Levine (1973: 37) argues that withholding procedural safeguards for families until the dispositional hearing occurs is too late (cf. Besharov, 1990b). In establishing jurisdiction should caseworkers follow strict procedures that safeguard the parent? Until such procedures and safeguards are recognized, some legal theorists argue that the parent should not answer the door when the caseworker comes knocking.[8]

Blurring Abuse and Neglect

One of the most serious problems in the decision-making process is the merging of child abuse with child neglect. Child abuse and child neglect

---

[7] An additional explanation of the rubber-stamp behavior of the court has been that child welfare caseworkers and other professionals shape their recommendations to conform to what they think a particular judge will want to decide (Mnookin, 1973: 628). For example, child welfare caseworkers seeking to terminate parental rights in the Oregon Project assumed an active role in obtaining evidence and researching statutes, yet upon entering the court the caseworker had to conform to the district attorney's recommendations based on available legal resources (Burt, 1971; Regional Research Institute for Human Services, 1978: 35).

[8] The same concern with legal safeguards applies to the police. In some communities in Florida, for instance, the sheriff's office has primary responsibility for investigating child abuse reports (Yanez, 2003). Child abuse can be treated as a criminal and civil matter (St. Onge and Elam, 2000). As long as the police treat the investigation as a civil, rather than a criminal matter—and most abuse cases have been treated as *civil*—the procedural safeguards provided in criminal investigations do not apply (Stein, 1991b). In order to provide these safeguards legislation is needed to ensure that child abuse investigations are treated as criminal investigations.

are two qualitatively different issues that should be treated in fundamentally different ways. Too often the boundary between child abuse, for which there should be clear legal grounds for criminal investigation and intervention, is blurred with child neglect, where issues of poverty and public policy arise. As a result, fuzzy decision-making often characterizes the actions of child protective services workers in child abuse cases.

Child abuse involves the intentional physical harm a parent inflicts upon a child.[9] According to the residual view, the etiology of child abuse is found in the psychodynamic relationship between parent and child (Kadushin and Martin, 1981). Central issues include such things as family stress, inadequate understanding of child rearing approaches, an inability to properly manage the child, a proclivity toward or tolerance of violence, and so on.

Neglect involves improper care of children, which derives for the most part from the parent's inability to provide properly for the child. The parents do not have sufficient economic means to furnish adequate food, medical care, clothing, shelter, and the like. In the United States, de facto neglect exists for at least 5 million children whose families have income less than one-half the poverty line.

Historically, child welfare agencies have operated from the principle that no child should be removed "for reasons of poverty,"[10] which means that if at all possible children suffering neglect should be aided in their homes. The approach is not only less expensive but may be less harmful to the child than removal, since the psychological damage that may occur when a child is removed from his or her biological parents is potentially great.[11] When a child is being severely physically or sexually abused, however, the question of removal is fundamentally different. Although it may be less expensive to retain the child in the home, the potential danger to the child is the greater issue, and removal is not only warranted but required.

In the last two decades child abuse and child neglect problems have converged into a combined category of "child abuse and neglect" or "child

---

[9] The "battered child syndrome" discovered by C. Henry Kempe and colleagues (1962) was defined as a child under three years old who suffered severe physical abuse.

[10] Since 1909 there has been a historic principle that children should not be removed from their home for "reasons of poverty" (Bremner, 1971; Pelton, 1989). To remove a child from his or her parent(s) for reasons of poverty would be "cruel and unusual punishment" or severely harsh punishment for conditions which the parent(s) may be unable, at least temporarily, to change. Instead, the child welfare social worker has been mandated to provide services and resources to the family so that removal of the child for reasons of poverty would not be necessary (Barth and Berry,1987).

[11] The study of filial deprivation by Jenkins and Norman (1972) indicates an intensive and long-lasting pain and anguish associated with removal.

maltreatment." This approach has led to conceptual confusion. By blending these two fundamentally different problems, we have diminished our ability to deal effectively with either. As seen in the previous chapter, determinations on identical cases vary from caseworker to caseworker, from judge to judge. What predominates is not agreement but lack of consensus. In some cases children are removed from their families for poverty and neglect, while in others they are left in obviously abusive situations to face increasing violence and danger to their lives. As a result, abuse deaths continue unabated, while neglected, deprived, and dependent children are left without services.

If current approaches had proven successful in reducing child fatalities, we might have reason to be satisfied with the transformation of the child welfare system. However, as we have seen, the rate of child fatalities has continued to rise. Further, approximately half of the deaths from child abuse involve children known to the child protective service system. The failure to make progress in reducing harm to children requires us to question the current approach of reporting child abuse, especially severe child abuse, to public child welfare agencies.

What is required is a separation and clarification of the two issues of criminal abuse and neglect, accompanied by interventions tailored to the unique requirements of each (Pelton, 1992). Severe child abuse, which is a criminal act, should be reported to the police and prosecuted in the courts. It demands strict legal efforts to punish the abuser and provide protection to the abused (Wexler, 1995). In contrast, child neglect requires the compassionate ear and helpful hand of the social worker, with the court playing only a minor role to resolve concerns about cases of abandonment or endangerment of the child, and then only after the parents' rights have been safeguarded.

Currently, the decision to remove a child from the home remains a loosely negotiated one between the parent(s), the caseworker, and the court, in which the decision-making criteria is altogether too fuzzy. A more formalized and rule-oriented procedure is required, preceded by conceptual clarification, from which more reliable judgments and greater consensus between parties can emerge. Further, before we can begin to deal effectively with severe physical and sexual child abuse, we should begin regarding it for what it is. It is not overzealous discipline, nor uncontrolled aggressiveness, nor careless rough housing, nor impatience, nor hot-temperedness, nor inappropriate sexual attention, nor any of the other psychological labels that are used to excuse it. Child abuse, in whatever degree, is *criminal assault and needs to be recognized as such. It requires firm investigation and prosecution by the police, backed by the courts.*

Wife Battering

Assault by a male social partner accounts for more injury to women than auto accidents, mugging, and rape combined. Even more far reaching than injury and death are the psychosocial consequences of abuse. We also found that woman abuse is a factor in almost half of all child abuse and in more than a third of all divorces and is a major cause of attempted suicide, alcoholism, and mental illness among women.

Evan Stark, *Framing and Reframing Battered Women*

Until two decades ago, a woman entering a police station seeking protection from a battering husband received little more than sympathy. Hers was a "domestic" or "marital" problem not within police jurisdiction. The police would take action only if the man severely hurt or killed the woman. After she was treated at the hospital, and if it was a slow night, an officer might escort her home and attempt to negotiate a reconciliation. If this could not be achieved, the woman was advised to stay with a relative or friend, later to see a counselor, or perhaps a minister. Now, of course, we would think it foolish that a woman being assaulted by her husband would call a social worker for help. Rather, the advice is "Call the police!" They will intervene immediately, using force if necessary to subdue the assailant, who will be led away in handcuffs, the details to be sorted out later by a judge.

What has changed? Wife battering is no longer regarded as a private domestic affair. Instead it is *criminal assault,* plain and simple, requiring decisive police intervention. In some jurisdictions in the United States, if there is evidence the woman has been battered, police are mandated to make an arrest, even if the victim does not wish to press charges. In cases of wife battering the responsibilities of the police and social worker are clear. The role of the police is to investigate and prosecute criminal wrongdoing, while the social worker's role is to provide the battered woman with support and other casework services (Mills, 2000; Peters, Shackelford, Buss, 2002). The social worker is not expected to conduct a criminal investigation.

Studies of wife abuse have suggested the variable that has the greatest impact on reducing subsequent abuse is police involvement (Apsler, Cummins, Carl, 2002; Berk et al., 1992; Pate and Hamilton, 1992; Sherman and Berk, 1984). Unfortunately, even with police involvement, the assailant is still likely to continue with some level of abuse. This underscores the importance of police involvement to provide the best available protection (Gelles, 2000). Even though police involvement will not assure an end to abuse, it provides the best approach to protection from future abuse.

How Physical Abuse of Children Differs

Currently, if a child is beaten senseless by a parent, with multiple broken limbs, perhaps a concussion, there is no guarantee that the child will be removed and provided any protection whatsoever from the abusive parent. Indeed, the child is more likely to be removed from the home for reasons of poverty than abuse. Nor is the parent likely to be arrested, unless, of course, the child dies. Instead, if the residual perspective is followed, which emphasizes the psychodynamic child-parent relationship and the parent's personal and psychological "deficits," the parent will likely receive nothing more than "therapy," or "counseling," with the caseworker stopping by from time to time to monitor progress.

The whole routine would be laughably ridiculous were it not so tragic. While counseling and therapy may eventually constitute a partial solution to whatever psychological malfunction has led the parent to abuse the child, the fact remains that another human being has been assaulted, and the assailant is subject to prosecution under the law, which should be applied vigorously and equally to everyone irrespective of race, income, or sex. While the perpetrator should be afforded full legal safeguards, he or she must realize that physical or sexual assault against a child is illegal and will be prosecuted to the full extent of the law.

The question becomes: At what age does striking an individual with a fist or club, with the intent to inflict bodily harm, change from child abuse (treatable by counseling or therapy) to criminal assault (punishable by imprisonment, fine, or both)? Presumably, a person twenty-one years of age could legally press charges against a parent for assault. Why then cannot a teenager, a child, an infant do the same? At what age does a child cease to be the ward of quasi-legal protective service workers and gain the full protection of the law? In fact, the teenager, child, or infant should not have to press charges. Rather, arrest should be *mandated* if there is evidence of severe physical abuse.

Child abuse, like other physical assault, is not an action that should fall within the purview of child welfare agencies. Child abuse is not a clinical syndrome or a psychological disorder requiring specialized therapeutic intervention, support, and care. Child abuse is, first and foremost, a *criminal act,* requiring decisive coercive control, and is, therefore, a police matter. The sooner it is treated as such, the sooner children will be protected to the fullest extent possible. This does not mean that the perpetrator shouldn't be provided with treatment and counseling. Rather, it means that the child abuse needs first to be prosecuted as a criminal act and then, when advisable, to provide treatment to the perpetrator with the best available therapeutic services.

There are significant advantages to adopting this view, aside from the improved protection it will afford children. First, redefining child abuse as criminal assault would clarify the roles of all parties—parent, police, courts, and social worker. Currently, child abuse allegations are resolved in a shifting and ambiguous jurisdiction where almost no one is arrested unless a child dies or is permanently and severely injured; where the law bends to fit bureaucratic rules and regulations, and where defendants' rights may not always apply; where the prosecutor and the judge too often form a darkly suspicious alliance that serves expedience more than justice; and where the charge itself (abuse) is only vaguely defined, ranging from homicide to leaving children unattended, with the penalty often not fitting the crime.

With child abuse recognized as criminal assault, the police would have clear jurisdiction and responsibility to act decisively, whereas now, out of uncertainty, often they do not. Any allegation would be clearly stated, and the parent assured proper defense. Civil rights, due process, and other legal procedures and safeguards would be clarified and upheld. The court, disentangled at last from its partnership with child protective service agencies, would be able to make a just and independent determination.

Second, with abuse properly defined, and the roles of the participants clarified, the ability to prevent child abuse and provide police protection for abused children would increase. Even an angry parent, knowing that he or she is breaking the law and subject to arrest, prosecution, and conviction, might think twice before bruising their child, who might subsequently be observed and reported to the police by a neighbor or teacher.

Finally, child welfare social workers would be freed to return to the duties for which they are most qualified—providing effective and needful services to impoverished and disadvantaged families. Child welfare caseworkers are not police, nor were they intended to be. If they find themselves acting as investigators now, it is only because the role has been mandated for them to investigate the avalanche of child abuse and neglect reports. They have neither the training, the authority, nor perhaps the disposition to effectively investigate criminal activities. Since child abuse, like all other acts of assault, is a criminal act, its investigation and prosecution should be transferred to the police, who have the training and resources to appropriately respond.

Deficiencies in the Child Welfare System

An inadequate knowledge base undergirds the actions of its staff. But, because children's lives are at stake, CPS cannot stop its work while the public debates its mission, or while researchers discover which interventions might help which families. This plane must be fixed while it flies through the air.

Mary Larner, Carol Stevenson, and Richard Behrman, *Future of Children*

The current child protective service system staffed by child welfare social workers too often fails to protect children because it does not possess the investigative technology, training, and resources that are available to the police. It does not have crime laboratories, fingerprint identification equipment, highly trained and skilled criminal investigators who are familiar with the latest advances in forensic science (St. Onge and Elam, 2000: 109-115). Schools of social work do not offer courses in criminal law, court procedures, rules of evidence and other special areas that would enable them to effectively investigate and prosecute criminal behavior.

The emphasis in social work education is on helping. When responsibility for investigating child abuse is shifted to child welfare agencies, or even child protection units within these agencies, the affected children are denied adequate protection. Child abuse comes to be seen as something amenable to therapeutic and professional help rather than criminal investigation.

The Skills of the Social Worker

Social workers do have interviewing and assessment skills that are useful in determining whether abuse has occurred (Cooper, 1993). The child welfare social worker may be able to establish a rapport with the abused child and even the abusing parent, a perspective that is often denied the police. In this role, the child welfare worker may best be able to determine if abuse has occurred. Thus, they could be hired by police departments to function much as they do in hospitals or schools, by providing particular services to assist the agency in achieving its objectives. The child welfare social worker might be "deputized" to investigate and thus would provide the child with the strongest possible protection and the "alleged" abusive parent with legal safeguards (that is, by providing proper *Miranda* warning to the parent).

Realizing that they are strictly an accessory to the legal apparatus that prosecutes child abuse, child welfare workers would be more likely to identify for police those families in which criminal child abuse is occurring. Currently, caseworkers are often reluctant to accuse parents of abuse, preferring to view it in terms that match their therapeutic interventions (Dingwall, Eekelaar, and Murray, 1983).[12] The child's broken arm, bruised face, or scalded leg are due to the parent's "impulsivity," "alienation," "depression," "egocentricity," "overaggressiveness," "lack of self-esteem," and the like, all of which are regarded as treatable through therapy or counseling (Margolin, 1992). Yet, there is precious little evidence to support the effectiveness of these optimistic interpretations of severe abuse. Sadly, on the hope of such unproven optimism for rehabilitation of criminal child abusers are sacrificed the lives of countless children.

Too, caseworkers sense their lack of experience and authority to investigate and prove allegations of abuse. Even if they could prove abuse, they have no technology to correct it. Like most people, they want to get along, to promote harmony and cooperation with the parent, whose goodwill they view as essential to restoring the family to health. The result is that too many severe abuse situations are politely swept under the rug, leaving the endangered child virtually defenseless.

With abuse cases being investigated and prosecuted by police and justice departments, the child welfare agency's principal responsibility would become one of providing a "place of safety" for the assaulted child. Although the agency might also assist in the investigation, the responsibility of pursuing the assailant would properly belong with the police. At most, the child welfare social workers become soft police unable to effect an arrest or conduct a thorough criminal investigation. When children have been criminally assaulted and abused they are entitled to the same protection afforded all citizens—full police protection.

Establishing Rule-Oriented Standards

Concomitant with a new understanding of child abuse should come revised rule-oriented standards for the removal of children in abuse and neglect cases. The wide discretion currently permitted enforcers of child abuse

---

[12] One of the unique qualities of the child welfare social worker, derived from professional training, is that he or she often focuses on the strengths of the parents even in severe abuse cases. Dingwall, Eekelaar, and Murray (1983) found that caseworkers operate under a "rule of optimism." They suggest that at each stage of the decision-making process caseworkers tend to favor the least stigmatizing interpretation of available information and the least coercive disposition. Their research indicated that the only situation that provoked coercive intervention involved "parental incorrigibility" (when parents failed to cooperate and appreciate the contribution of the child welfare caseworker) and a "failure of containment" (when the case appeared to be moving beyond the caseworker's sphere of influence or control to involve other family members or other agencies).

laws has failed to protect children, and left both parents and the public unclear regarding what the rules governing abuse and neglect are.

Professionals have long wrestled with the problem of developing a
rule-oriented standard for child removal. Mnookin (1973), Wald (1976),
Goldstein (1999), and others have argued for a standard that would retain
the child at home unless a clear and present danger exists to the child's
well-being. Mnookin holds that before removal occurs, evidence of physical harm must be demonstrated by an explanation of why intervention
would not be possible with the child remaining at home (Mnookin, 1973:
631). Wald (1976: 642) has proposed that state intervention is legitimate in
cases where the child has suffered serious physical harm, serious and specifically defined emotional damage, or sexual abuse, or where the child is
in imminent physical danger. He would require the level of proof to vary
depending upon the harm in question (i.e., physical abuse would require
less proof than emotional damage).

Goldstein, Freud, and Solnit (1979) advocate limiting the coercive arm
of the state to those cases where the child faces an "imminent risk of death
or serious bodily harm." Advocates of strict legal standards suggest that
removal is justified only if the parents' past behavior was itself sufficiently
harmful—that is, if it caused or was capable of causing "serious harm."
Legal scholars have proposed specific guidelines to determine if a child
should be removed (Besharov, 1987: 312–313). The framework shown in
appendix I in the first edition of this book (Lindsey, 1994) is illustrative of
the "rule-oriented" approach.

When possible, the length of placement should be specified before
placement occurs. Placement decisions should be based on a common set
of principles with the same criteria applied equally to all. Even if the par-
ent(s) desire placement, they should know that the child will return home
after a specific time—either that or the state will arrange for another permanent home, including, if necessary, court action to terminate parental
rights (Mnookin, 1973: 637). The Oregon Project's effort to terminate parental rights in certain cases of long-term foster care "drift" provides examples of how the court can take decisive action in this regard (Hewitt,
1983; Mlyniec, 1983). Of course, before placements occur, the state should
offer, when appropriate, alternative services that would enable a child to
remain at home.

Wide Discretion and Poverty

The disproportionate number of Black children in America's child welfare
system is staggering. Black families are overrepresented in child maltreat-

ment reports, case openings, and the foster care population. Spend a day at dependency court in any major city and you will see the unmistakable color of the child welfare system.   Dorothy Roberts, *Shattered Bonds*

The most disturbing aspect of the wide discretionary power that child welfare authorities currently wield in removing children is that the results are unfair and discriminatory. Too often, child removal is limited to poor families. National studies have found that less than one-fourth of the children removed from their families and placed in foster care are from financially self-supporting families (Lindsey, 1991). In Los Angeles County, with a population of more than 9 million people, there were more than 40,000 children in foster care. More than 95 percent of those in foster care lived in poverty before placement. Rein, Nutt, and Weiss (1974) point out that while many children are in out-of-home placements such as boarding schools, military schools, and living with friends and relatives, it is poor children, by and large, who are placed in foster care.

Developing a Child Abuse Legislation Model

In addition to rule-oriented standards for removal, child abuse legislation is needed that would outline specific guidelines to regulate the investigation and decision-making process in abuse and neglect cases (Duquette, 1980; Falconer and Swift, 1983). Such legislation would provide criteria to follow at each stage of an investigation (see Lindsey, 1994: 179–183).

For example, if a child was abused severely enough to require medical treatment, the criteria might specify that the child be placed in a "safe house" for seventy-two hours during which the police investigated the alleged or suspected abuse. If abuse was substantiated, the police would file charges against the perpetrator while seeking protective service supervision (e.g., foster care arranged by a child welfare worker) for a specified period of time (e.g., three months). If the physical abuse was repeated severely enough to require medical attention, the police would seek "termination of parental rights."

Likewise, if a child was sexually abused, the police would remove the child from the home environment where the abuse occurred, and then investigate, and, if the allegations were substantiated, prosecute the perpetrator (Myers, 2000). If the abuse was repeated, further prosecution would follow, along with an effort to terminate parental rights. A parent would not be held harmless solely because he or she did not actually engage in the abuse. The only permissible excuse would be that the parent was unaware of the sexual abuse and exercised reasonable care to protect the child from it.

In such a way, legislation would articulate the specifics of criminal physical and sexual assault, detailing the steps to be taken and penalties to be imposed, should the specific allegations be substantiated (Turner and Shields, 1985). The law would be applied as firmly and consistently as feasible. If parents knew that child abuse law was clearly defined, and violations prosecuted vigorously, physical and sexual assault of children would likely decline.

Again, we note that the investigating officer would not be a child welfare caseworker but a law enforcement official specifically trained to investigate such criminal matters. The child welfare worker would provide appropriate casework services, such as counseling the abusing parent if the court so ordered it, and arranging foster care services for the child. Beyond this, the child welfare agency might assist in public relations efforts to prevent and combat child abuse.

Conclusion

The transformation of the child welfare system into a child protection system has led to a preoccupation with child abuse that has displaced the system's original obligation to a much larger population of children. By defining child abuse in a proper social and legal framework, by clarifying the roles that the courts, the police, the social worker, and the parent play in the phenomenon of child abuse, progress can be made in stemming the growing tide of abuse while freeing the child welfare system to return to its original and more appropriate mandate.

In 2002, more than 12 million children lived in poverty in the United States. More than 5 million children lived in households with income less than "half the poverty line"—a phrase that does not adequately reveal the depths of hopelessness these children daily experience. They are the poorest of the poor, subject to hunger, disease, despair, and death. The mission of the child welfare system should not be limited to protecting children from criminal assault by loved ones. Rather the goal should be to aid impoverished children. The child welfare system must shift responsibility for protecting criminally abused children back to the police and the courts, where it is best handled. Only then can the child welfare system concentrate on providing an infrastructure of social programs that will ensure the economic security and well-being of disadvantaged and impoverished children.

The child welfare system should be judged by its success in reducing poverty among children, in providing them the means to break the cycle of poverty and become productive citizens, not by its effectiveness in controlling the incidence of criminal physical and sexual assaults, in which it has and will likely continue to fail.

The child welfare system has been transformed into a child protection system. The transformed child welfare agency has failed to improve the safety and security of children. On virtually every major measure children are less safe today than they have ever been. The agency assigned responsibility to provide protection has proven ineffective. It is time to reconsider the assignment of child abuse reports to child welfare agencies.

If we truly want to protect children we will ask the agency which has proven most effective to carry this responsibility. We will need to assign the protection of children to those with the training and resources best suited to investigate and prosecute criminal assault. Seniors, wives, and others are protected from assault by the police. We should provide no less for children.

Part II

Ending Child Poverty

The Great Depression stimulated the development of income support policy in the 1930s. The Social Security Act, unemployment compensation, and welfare programs were passed in response to massive unemployment, bread lines, and families being evicted from their homes. They established the principle that the resources of the government are required to deal with those aspects of poverty and insecurity that are not due to personal inadequacies or indolence.

Robert Haveman, *Starting Even*

One by one, with astonishing rapidity, the Communist regimes of Eastern Europe and the Soviet Union crumbled before the assertion of people's power, whose common watchword was the realization of a genuinely representative and responsible democratic form of government. In the last decade of the twentieth century democracy rediscovered its optimism and universality.

Neil Harding, "The Marxist-Leninist Detour"

Instead of understanding the broad social problems of the poor as the product of the dysfunctional behaviors of individuals, social reformers during the Great Depression struggled to alter dysfunctional social arrangements. The great strength of the free market economic system was found in its link to the democratic political system. When broad economic problems arose, the democratic political system provided the flexibility needed for adjustments and reform. The collapse of the Soviet bloc socialist economies was as much a failure of political structure as it was the crumbling of stale economic ideas.

When economic calamity struck in the 1930s a deep and wide despair spread across North America. Faith in fundamental social, political, and economic institutions began to give way. Bold and imaginative leadership was called for. In the United States Franklin Delano Roosevelt initiated sweeping social programs and policies that helped, along with the advent of World War II, to lead the country to economic recovery. Following

World War II, the United States emerged as the most powerful economy in the world.

Once again, calamity has struck, only this time it is confined to a narrow segment of society—single parents and their children. In 2002 more than 12 million children live in poverty in the United States and another 1 million in Canada. Current programs that deal with child poverty were developed decades ago and have proven hopelessly ineffective. What are needed are innovative and imaginative solutions that will address the problems poor children face in a postindustrial economy.

The major barrier to progress against child poverty has been the limited view of our collective responsibility toward poor children. Social policies and programs have been guided by a perspective that requires we wait until a problem is severe before we act—the residual approach. However, when 12 million children live in poverty, with no end in sight, we must begin looking to structural explanations and solutions that will prevent chronic child poverty.

To the extent that the problems which children in poverty face are structural (i.e., induced by external socioeconomic forces and circumstances), they must be approached at that level. Until now the approach in child welfare has predominantly been a residual one in which limited resources are allocated to society's less fortunate when they can be identified and classified. While the residual approach may have been sufficient in the nineteenth and early twentieth centuries, it is not suited to the social and economic conditions to which our society has evolved.

The child welfare system must confront the problem of child poverty head on. If there is to be any hope of developing workable solutions to child poverty, the child welfare system must begin looking to the wider social and economic problems which families face. The child welfare system must be well matched to the capitalist free enterprise system. The child welfare system needs to take advantage of the strengths of the free enterprise market economy.

The child welfare system is the set of public institutions that represent our collective interest in assuring that needy and disadvantaged children have opportunity. The role of child welfare is to provide the institutions required to combat child poverty; the great public universities are an example of this kind of an institution. They provide access to a higher education at a cost that is affordable for the needy and disadvantaged young person and assure opportunity.

In the following chapters, I attempt to identify those child welfare problems that are best treated through a structural approach, while redefining and clarifying those services that must continue to be addressed through a residual approach. I begin in chapter 8 by examining the distribution of economic resources in the United States and other modern market economies. What economic and social assumptions drive our free-market system? How much wealth and income is produced and distributed? How is wealth and income allocated? How much goes to children, especially children in poverty? With what consequences? Poverty has two dimensions—income and wealth. Both dimensions of child poverty are examined in detail. This chapter aims at providing a perspective on the scope of the problem and how it must be addressed through public programs and policies.

Chapter 9 examines the root causes of many child welfare problems. When young people start a family before they have the resources and maturity to be self-supporting they are forced to rely on public assistance. For most of these young people the consequence will be a life of poverty and despair. For many this is part of a larger cycle of poverty stemming from the lack of opportunity for poor children. In this chapter I examine the debate surrounding the welfare system. In this regard, chapter 9 examines the issues which preceded the historic welfare reform legislation enacted in 1996.

Since 1936 the major federal program to reduce child poverty has been the welfare entitlement program contained within the Social Security Act—Aid to Families with Dependent Children (AFDC). This welfare program protected children against the grimmest consequences of poverty. In the 1960s the proportion of children in poverty covered by the program increased, leading to a major rise in the welfare caseload. For sixty years the welfare program provided a minimal level of income protection for the poorest children in the United States. During the last two decades there has been a recurring assault on the welfare program, with calls to end it.

In 1996, after several decades of often acrimonious debate, major welfare reform legislation was enacted that has led to the selective dismantling of "welfare as we knew it." The selective and disproportionate dismantling of welfare raises the question of what income protection programs remain for children. In chapter 10 I focus on the impact of welfare reform on child poverty. The chapter also explores innovative approaches that would lead us out of the woods of the stale welfare debate.[1]

---

[1] On a personal note I should add that I am disheartened by much of the current welfare debate. Too often it fails to recognize the plight of the children involved. I share these concerns not to stifle criticism or proffer some form of a "politically correct" debate. Rather, it is to suggest that during the debate we need to respect the dignity and humanity of the subjects of our inquiry, lest we further exacerbate the problems we wish to redress. Those who are suspicious of the morals and values of single mothers who struggle to raise their children might do well to spend time with these mothers who endure poverty with fortitude and sacrifice against insurmountable odds to provide and care for their children in the face of a frequently mean-spirited and dehumanizing welfare system (Berrick, 1993; Ehrenreich, 2001; Polakow, 1993).

Chapter 11 examines social policy and program initiatives designed to alter the current structural arrangements responsible for the condition of poor children. If the families served by child welfare agencies suffer from severe economic hardship, and this hardship is a factor that contributes to the problems child welfare is attempting to solve, social and economic policy changes to address this hardship need to be pursued. Further, solutions to these problems do not necessarily require more money as much as a rethinking and redesign of policies and programs that have proven ineffective and out of date. Children suffer because of an ineffective and obsolete court-administered child support collection system. They also suffer because of inequities and inefficiencies in the publicly funded income support programs for children. I review these programs and suggest needed reforms.

Chapter 12 offers a "social savings" approach that would break the continuing "cycle of poverty" among children. This is the same approach that was used to effectively end poverty among the elderly. No doubt the proposal has limitations, but it suggests the kinds of approaches and strategies, within a broader structural understanding of child welfare, that might solve the problems poor children face. Child poverty is a phenomenon that can be eradicated. Not all developed countries have child poverty, certainly not to the extent it is found in the United States. To end child poverty will take more than programs that provide income assistance for immediate relief of hardship. Long-term solutions designed to break the cycle of poverty are required.

The closing chapter brings the arguments together and presents a summary of the analysis and a discussion of future directions.

8

Wealth and Poverty in America:
The Economic Condition of Children

In the game that determines how our national income is distributed, there are winners, there are losers, and there are those who aren't even in the game.

Robert Haveman, *Starting Even*

The social welfare system enacted in this century has all but eliminated poverty among the aged, but has had much less effect on children, leaving high rates of poverty at any one time, and horrendous rates over time.

Daniel Patrick Moynihan, "Towards a Post-Industrial Social Policy"

During the 1950s and 1960s, not only was the United States the showcase of democracy and the standard of egalitarian achievement for the world, it was also the wealthiest nation, producing an extraordinary 40 percent of the world's wealth (Hewlett, 1991: 271). The U.S. free enterprise market economy produced such affluence that its citizens were enjoying a level of material abundance unparalleled in the history of civilization. Disease was receding, hunger and want were disappearing, and thanks to technology and free enterprise, which appeared capable of accomplishing almost anything, life was getting better (Keynes, 1964; Kindleberger, 1996). The overall expectation was that, except for a few nagging social problems which would within a few years probably work themselves out, society was approaching what looked like utopia (Bruchey, 1988; Phillips, 2002).

Of course, in the decades that followed, things did not work out quite the way we envisioned. While many things did indeed improve, many others got worse. Despite our nation's fabulous wealth, poverty continued and even increased, especially among single parent families, among people of color, and of particular concern, among children (Bush, 1987; Sarri and Finn, 1992a, b).

The residual view of child welfare assumes that child abuse can only happen within the family, centered on the parent/child relationship. This may be true of severe child abuse involving physical or sexual assault, but child abuse and neglect can also happen at a broader societal level (Gil, 1970, 1975). Children living in poverty in a nation of great material abundance suffer a chronic abuse that is corrosive and destructive in the worst way (Duncan and Brooks-Gunn, 1997). While the brutality and horror of physical and sexual assault of children are easily recognized, too often we ignore the inequity and unfairness of a situation where children, because of the circumstances into which they are born, are denied the basic economic resources for a decent life. Today, the broad and pervasive condition of child poverty is the fundamental problem confronting child welfare, which to understand, requires a broader economic perspective. In this regard, it is useful to pull back and examine how a free enterprise market economy such as the United States creates and distributes income and wealth.

The Distribution of Wealth in Free Market Economies

> Wealth inequality is still an unresolved issue in America. Levels of wealth inequality are so extreme that most people hardly register any wealth at all, yet wealth is one of the central indicators of financial well-being and security. Wealth inequality was not always as extreme as it was in the early 1990s; indeed, it got considerably worse during the 1980s and 1990s than it had been in the preceding decades.
>
> Lisa A. Keister, *Wealth in America*

Economic growth in modern market economies requires the development and continual nourishment of an affluent middle class (Phillips, 1990, 2002). Advanced free market economies like the United States routinely provide the infrastructure for the development of such a middle class by ensuring all citizens equality of opportunity.[1] Most nations with advanced market economies have been able to produce substantial material affluence for most of their citizens by generating modest wealth for a broad middle class, along with substantial and even enormous wealth for a small number of upper-income families (Keister, 2000; Kolko, 1972). Those market economies that have achieved the broadest social participation in the wealth of the nation are viewed as the most stable and successful.

During the last several decades the United States has developed a large underclass characterized by severe poverty and diminished opportunity

---

[1] In this regard, child welfare programs are responsible for both providing avenues of opportunity for all children and ensuring that children from the least successful families also have fair opportunities. Ensuring fair opportunity, as we shall see later, is a difficult balance between assisting children from low-income families and encouraging independence and personal responsibility among the parents which income support for children might undermine.

(Jargowski, 1997; Wilson, 1987). It is, of course, a situation that threatens our society, for in the coming years it may be difficult for the United States to compete in the global economy while carrying the burden of a large impoverished underclass. Other nations who have, in the words of Polakow (1993: 173), "succeeded in alleviating the 'social asphyxia' of poverty" and who do not have to carry a similar burden may be at a substantial economic advantage. The economic expense of providing support for a large portion of the population who are outside the economic mainstream places too great a marginal strain on the productive work force through higher taxes and reduced internal markets.

An important point to be understood is that in a regulated economy such as the United States, poverty among a large portion of the population cannot be an accidental or unavoidable phenomenon, but rather is the result of economic or political policies that for whatever reason skew the distribution of the nation's wealth. As Michael Katz (1989: 7) observes, when we talk about poverty

> some things remain unsaid. Mainstream discourse about poverty, whether liberal or conservative, largely stays silent about politics, power and equality. But poverty, after all, is about distribution; it results because some people receive a great deal less than others. Poverty no longer is natural; it is a social product. As nations emerge from the tyranny of subsistence, gain control over the production of wealth, develop the ability to feed their citizens and generate surpluses, poverty becomes not the product of scarcity, but of political economy.

The issue is essential, for when the distribution of wealth and income leaves millions of children in poverty, obviously through no action of their own, then the rules, policies, and programs governing the distribution need to be reexamined. We are compelled to ask: How has this come about? How can it be ended? Our nation's collective economic and social future is shaped by the manner in which we provide for our children. If many of them are despairing, suffering from poverty and disease, especially in the midst of plenty, not only are we as guardians called to question, but a warning is sounded for our society as well.

Wealth in the United States: Who Has It and Who Doesn't?

> Americans smugly assumed that European societies were more stratified than their own, but it now appears that the United States has surpassed all industrial societies in the extent of its family wealth inequality.
>
> Lisa A. Keister, *Wealth in America*

In 2000, total privately owned assets (defined as household net worth) in the United States were estimated to exceed $40 trillion (Phillips, 1990, 118; Thurow, 1992, 235; USA Today, 2003; Wolff, 2001), which, if it were divided equally among the country's roughly 290 million population, would amount to about $125,000 for each man, woman, and child, or, for a typical family of four, more than $500,000.

It is difficult to argue against an economic system that has produced such great wealth. The free enterprise system with its commitment to market mechanisms and individual ownership of "the means of production" has released enormous productive energies. The imagination of the entrepreneur combined with the efficient regulation of the free market has proven an optimal economic arrangement (Gilder, 1984).

A closer examination, however, reveals great and increasing inequality. If the $40 trillion worth of household new worth were viewed as a giant pie, most families in the United States would be seen to have a very small slice, much smaller than an equal share. Analyzing data from several sources, Wolff (2001) reported that in 1998 the bottom 40 percent of the U.S. population owned less than half a percent of the wealth in the United States. This was an improvement since 1989 when this same group—the bottom 40 percent of the population—had a negative net worth. According to Wolff (2001), the bottom 80 percent, as a group, owns a total of 16.6 percent of the nation's wealth. In contrast, the top 1 percent of the population own 40 percent of the wealth (see figure 8.1).

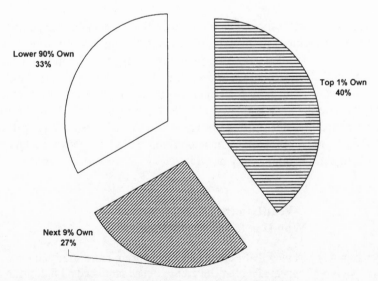

Figure 8.1 Distribution of Wealth in the United States
Source: Wolff (2001)

Table 8.1 Household Net Worth by Wealth Class, 1998

Wealth Class	Average Net Worth	Threshold
Top 1%	$10,204,00	$3,352,100
Next 4%	$1,441,000	
Next 5%	$623,500	$475,600
Next 10%	$344,900	$257,700
Fourth 20%	$161,300	
Middle 20%	$61,000	
Bottom 40%	$1,900	(Negative)

Source: Wolff (2000: table 3 and note to table 5).
Online at www.levy.org/docs/wrkpap/papers/300.html

The average net worth of the top 1 percent of households is greater than $10 million. In contrast, the average net worth of the bottom 40 percent is negative (see table 8.1).

The concentration of wealth in the United States can be discerned by examining the ownership of corporate assets—stocks and bonds. As table 8.2 shows, the top 10 percent of the families in the United States own several times as much of this wealth as the bottom 90 percent. How did this come about? The market economy is designed to reward effort and encourage risk-taking. Yet few would hope for an outcome that produced such extreme inequality as is observed in the United States.

Stocks. Virtually all businesses and corporations in the free enterprise economies, which are responsible for the country's industrial production, are privately owned. Among the available corporate assets (stocks, corporate bonds, and tax-free bonds) stocks are the most widely held and represent the "title" of corporate ownership. The value of all stock traded on the stock exchanges exceeds several trillion dollars (approximately 17.25 trillion dollars in 2000). This stock represents the ownership of our economic system.

When we examine who owns this stock, and therefore "title" to the economic system, we find that about 50 percent of all families in the United States directly own stock. Of these, fewer than 15 percent are active shareholders trading regularly (Avery et al., 1984a, b). As seen in table 8.2, almost half of all corporate stock in the United States is owned by the top 1 percent of the families (Phillips, 1993, 2002; Wolff, 2001). The bottom 90 percent own less than 15 percent.

Table 8.2 Ownership of Corporate and Business Assets, 1998

Families	Business Equity	Stocks	Financial Securities
Top 1 percent	67.7%	49.4%	50.8%
Next 9 percent	24.0	35.7	33.2
Bottom 90%	8.3	14.9	15.9

Source: Wolff (2000).

Bonds. Besides stocks, corporate bonds are the other major way of participating in the productive capacity of the nation. Whereas stocks represent outright ownership of a company, bonds represent money owed to an individual by the company. In 2000, businesses owed several trillion (*Wall Street Journal*, May 9, 1985: 1; Phillips, 2002), most of which took the form of corporate bonds. Again, the top 1 percent of families own more than 50 percent of all bonds. The wealthiest 10 percent of families own more than 80 percent of all bonds and other financial securities (see table 8.2).

Impact of Economic Policy on the Accumulation of Wealth

The findings suggested that between 1962 and 1995 there was extreme inequality in household wealth ownership in the United States and that inequality increased over that period.

Lisa A. Keister, *Wealth in America*

During the last two decades federal economic and social policies in the United States were aimed at stimulating the accumulation of wealth needed for capital investment and economic expansion. While there is some question whether these goals were accomplished (Thurow, 1991), the policies did significantly enhance the economic position of the upper-income groups (Phillips, 1990, 2002; Sherraden, 1990; Wolff, 2001), so that there is now an increased concentration of wealth.

One indicator of this is the increased number of millionaires in the United States. In 1964, fewer than 100,000 millionaires were recorded in the United States. By 1988, this figure had grown to more than 1.3 million. Even after adjusting for inflation, the number of millionaires grew at an extraordinarily high rate. According to Stanley (1988) the population of millionaires has increased at a rate almost 15 times faster than the rest of the population.

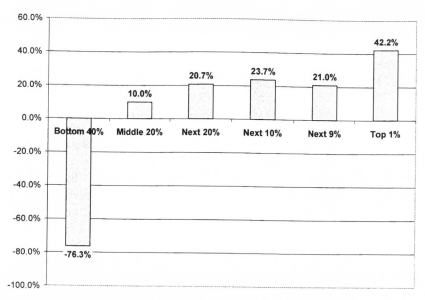

Figure 8.2 Change in Average Household Net Worth, 1983–1998
Source: Wolff (2000: table 3).
Online at www.levy.org/docs/wrkpap/papers/300.html

Along with the number of millionaires, there was also a dramatic increase in the number of individuals with million-dollar annual incomes.
From 1978 to 1988 the number increased from 2,041 to 65,303. Phillips
(2002: 120) estimated that by 1997 there were more than 142,000 households with annual income of more than $1 million (data derived from the
Internal Revenue Service). Thus, we are observing a trend, already quite
advanced, in which a relatively small percentage of families have been
able to acquire ownership of the vast majority of wealth in North America
(Keister, 2000).

While the average household net worth of the wealthiest families increased as much as 40 percent, the net worth of the bottom 40 percent of
families experienced an average drop of more than 75 percent from 1983
to 1998 (see figure 8.3). The material economic situation of the bottom 40
percent of families has experienced a substantial decline during the last
fifteen years.

Distribution of Income

This year the richest 2.7 million Americans, comprising the top 1 percent, will
have as many after-tax dollars to spend as the bottom 100 million put together,

and they'll have 40 percent of the nation's wealth. The top fifth of earners will have over half the nation's income and almost all its wealth.

                                                        Robert Reich, "The Great Divide"

A family's income normally derives from a variety of sources: employment (wages), stocks and bonds (dividends, interest, and capital gain), private businesses, and real estate holdings (rent). Not all families receive an equal share of income, in large part because not all families have equal assets. According to the U.S. Census Bureau, in 2000 the median annual household income in the United States was $42,148, which is to say that half of all households reported an income greater than this amount and half reported less. While this median figure gives a general idea of where the typical family is financially, a more revealing picture is gained by examining the distribution of income across society.

Figure 8.3 divides all people in the United States in 2000 into five equal groups ranging from lowest income to highest income. The top 20 percent received almost half of all recorded income (49.6 percent), while the bottom 20 percent received less than one-twelfth of that (4 percent). It is, of course, the bottom fifth (the poor) who make up the client base served by the public child welfare system. The distribution of wealth is also included in figure 8.3. The top fifth own almost four-fifths of all privately held wealth. The bottom fifth have a negative net worth.

Narrowed further, the wealthiest 1 percent of the population in the United States received an average annual income of $515,600 in 1999, while the bottom 20 percent received an average annual income of less than $8,800, or less than 2 percent as much. Viewed another way, the combined income of the wealthiest 1 percent of the American population nearly equals the combined income of the poorest 40 percent of all Americans (Labor Trends, August 1990; Nasar, 1992).

The shape of the distribution of wealth, where a few have so much and so many have so little, is not a naturally occurring phenomenon in wealthy, highly developed industrial democracies. Rather, it is shaped by tax policies and social programs that shift wealth upward and withdraw the floor of social support for the poor (Braun, 1997; Children's Defense Fund, 2002; Katz, 1989).

There is also a major difference in income by race (Conley, 1999; Oliver and Shapiro, 1995). The poorest of the poor are more often Black. The Census Bureau reported that in 2000 more than 15 percent of African American families lived in households with income less than $10,000 per year. More than 40 percent of African American families lived in households with incomes below $25,000. This is less than half the median household income for white families. In 1998 Wolff estimated that the median household net worth varied substantially by race (see table 8.3).

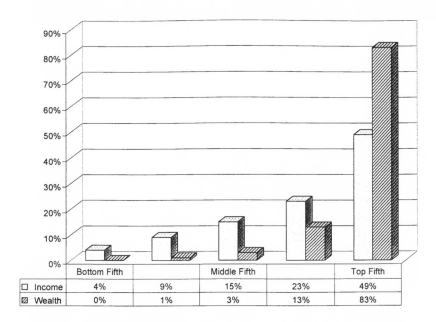

	Bottom Fifth		Middle Fifth		Top Fifth
☐ Income	4%	9%	15%	23%	49%
▨ Wealth	0%	1%	3%	13%	83%

Figure 8.3 Distribution of Household Income and Wealth in the United States, by Quintile, 2000

Source: Census Bureau (2001); Wilhelm (1998); Wolff (2001).

Table 8.3 Median Household Net Worth by Race/Ethnicity, 1998

	Median Net Worth	Median Financial Wealth
White	$ 81,700	$ 37,600
Black	10,000	1,200
Hispanic	3,000	0

Source: Wolff (2001).

Comparison with Other Countries

Although most industrialized market economies are characterized by an unequal distribution of wealth and income, the discrepancy between rich and poor is substantially greater in the United States than anywhere else (Braun, 1997). Of all the industrial nations, Japan has achieved the most egalitarian distribution of income (see figure 8.4).

Ratio between the top fifth to the bottom fifth on household income

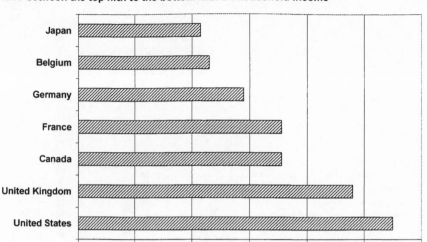

Figure 8.4 International Comparison of Income Inequality
Source: Public Agenda (1996); Shapiro, Greenstein, and Primus (2001).

As can be seen, the difference between the portions of income going to the top fifth of the population and to the bottom fifth varies sharply by country. Those countries with the most egalitarian distribution have also proven effective in producing the greatest amount of overall income per person. The standard indicator of the economic productivity of a society is the gross domestic product (GDP). The countries with the most equitable distribution of wealth also have the highest levels of GDP.[2] Recent economic research suggests, in fact, that there is a positive correlation between equitable distribution of wealth and rates of economic growth (Nasar, 1994).

When and How Changes in Income Occurred

The average annual salary in America, expressed in 1998 dollars, went from $32,522 in 1970 to $35,864 in 1999. In the same period, according to Fortune magazine, the average annual compensation of the top 100 C.E.O.'s went from $1.3 million—40 times the pay of an average worker—to $37.5 million, or over 1,000 times the average worker's pay.

Felicia Lee, *Does Class Count in Today's Land of Opportunity?*

---

[2] Among developing countries the disparity between the top and bottom 20 percent can be even greater. For Brazil, for example, the ratio is 26 to 1.

Galbraith (1967) argued that in the new industrial order knowledge and technology emerge as the primary ingredients for economic growth and success. Poverty in the new industrial order is not the result of the exploitation of the lower classes. Rather, most of those who live in poverty are outside the economic mainstream. They lack productive roles in the new high technology and global economies, and are attached only through an increasingly reluctant welfare system. The poor are not exploited for their surplus labor as was argued in early socialist writings (Marx, 1862, 1867). Because of modern technology and offshore manufacturing much of the unskilled and low-skilled labor the poor can provide is not required. Yet, not all societies have dealt with these economic changes in the same way. In the United States unskilled and low-skilled workers have received different treatment than they have in Japan and Western Europe (Thurow, 1992).

Research by Paul Krugman (1992) of the Massachusetts Institute of Technology indicates that the decade of the 1980s produced substantial gains for high-income groups. During the 1980s the top 1 percent of families in the United States got 60 percent of the after-tax income gain achieved during the decade. Overall, the portion of the income gain going to the top 10 percent of the population was 94 percent, while the other 90 percent of the population shared the remaining 6 percent of the gain. As the economy grew from 1977 to 2000, the income of the top 1 percent grew by 115 percent, while the income of the bottom fifth of families actually fell by 9 percent. Economic policies of the last two decades produced substantial gains for the wealthy, while the poor were left out (LaRoe and Pool, 1988; Phillips, 2002).

Although poverty has always existed in the United States, it was during the 1980s and 1990s that the poorest families experienced the most precipitous decline in their economic situation. From 1977 to 1999 income of the poorest 20 percent of families declined 9 percent (from $14,620 to $13,650) while the income of the top 5 percent increased from $87,780 to $150,200 during this same period (Center on Budget and Policy Priorities, 2002). Clearly, the last two decades produced substantial gains for the wealthiest families in America, while the situation of the poor deteriorated.

Even before the 1980s, the wealthy had made substantial income gains. From 1947 to 1979 the income share of the top one fifth of wealthy Americans increased 94% (see table 8.4). But during this same period, the income of the bottom one fifth also increased by 120 percent. In other words, during the almost three decades after World War II the expanding American economy brought substantial income gains to all income categories.

216   **Ending Child Poverty**

Table 8.4 Change in Family Income from 1947 to 2001

Percentage Change in Income from 1947 to 1979 by Quintile

Bottom one-fifth	116%	
Middle one-fifth	111%	**all income groups participated**
Top one-fifth	99%	

Percentage Change in Income from 1977 to 2001 by Quintile

Bottom one-fifth	3%	
Middle one-fifth	17%	**growth concentrated at the top**
Top one-fifth	53%	

Source: Center on Budget and Policy Priorities (2001); Darity, Myers, and Elgar (1998).

Online at www.census.gov/hhes/income/histinc/f03.html
and www.census.gov/hhes/income/histinc/f01.html

But this changed during the last two decades. Most of the income gains were concentrated in the top income group. In fact, the bottom income category actually lost ground. As Reich (1997: 3) observed:

Now in the first few decades after the Second World War, the rising tide really did lift all boats. When John F. Kennedy talked about the rising tide lifting all boats, it really was a growing economy, wherever you were in the income spectrum—if you were in the bottom fifth, if you were top fifth, wherever you were, you saw your income double between 1950 and 1978 in real inflation adjusted terms. But since 1979, we have had a very different kind of economic structure. Instead of the rising tide lifting all boats since 1979, the rising tide has been lifting the yachts, but a lot of the rowboats in the middle, where most people are, have been taking on water. And the little rafts and dinghies at the other end have been sinking.

The data in figure 8.5 display the change in income during the last decade for various income groups. Using data from the Internal Revenue Service (IRS), the Center on Budget Policy Priorities computed the average after tax income for the top 1 percent of tax filers from 1989 to 1998 (Shapiro, 2001). They then compared this with the change in after tax income of other groups including the bottom 90 percent. They found that most of the income gains achieved during this period went to the top income groups. This same pattern continued with the tax reductions of the Bush administration in 2001 (Children's Defense Fund, 2002).

The Economic Condition of Children

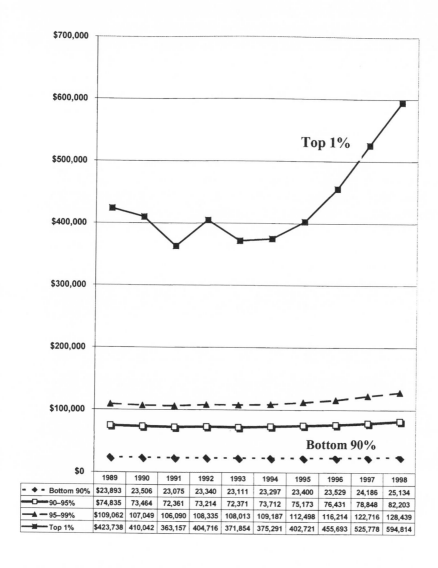

	1989	1990	1991	1992	1993	1994	1995	1996	1997	1998
Bottom 90%	$23,893	23,506	23,075	23,340	23,111	23,297	23,400	23,529	24,186	25,134
90–95%	$74,835	73,464	72,361	73,214	72,371	73,712	75,173	76,431	78,848	82,203
95–99%	$109,062	107,049	106,090	108,335	108,013	109,187	112,498	116,214	122,716	128,439
Top 1%	$423,738	410,042	363,157	404,716	371,854	375,291	402,721	455,693	525,778	594,814

Figure 8.5 Average After-tax Income Gains by Various Income Groups
Note: Income figures adjusted for inflation (1998 dollars).
Source: Shapiro, Greenstein, and Primus (2001: appendix table 1).

During the decade between 1989 and 1998 the top 1 percent of house-holds increased their income by 40 percent, while the bottom 90 percent increased their income by 5 percent.[3]

---

[3] Ackerman and Alstott (1999) report that the top 1 percent hold 38.5 percent of the wealth. Using a different measure that included pensions and the amortized value of Social Security

The tax policies of the recent decades have resulted in a shift of wealth from the middle and upper class to the very top one percent of families. As the United States entered the new millennium President George W. Bush accelerated the shift of wealth upward through tax policies that favor asset holders. The Institute on Taxation and Economic Policy working with the Children's Defense Fund (2002) calculated the benefit which various income groups would receive as a result of the Bush tax cut. As seen in Figure 8.6, the top 1 percent receives the greatest benefit. The top 1 percent of families will receive more in tax cuts than the remaining 99 percent combined. Families with an annual income over $1 million per year will average $342,000 in tax cuts over the decade. Commenting on the tax cut Edelman (2002) observes that "something is out of kilter when just three of our wealthiest Americans possess greater wealth than the incomes of seven million American families." This is more than the income of the ten million children living in poverty in the United States.

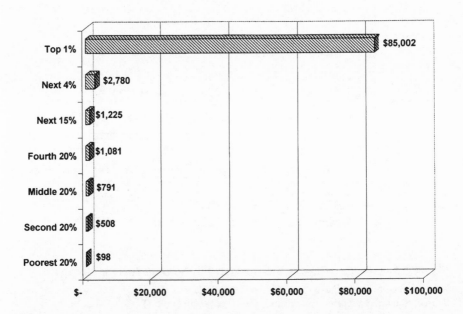

Figure 8.6 Impact of the Bush Tax Cut in 2010 by Income Group
Source: Institute on Taxation and Economic Policy and Children's Defense Fund (2002).

estimated that the top 1 percent owned 21.2 percent of all wealth (Wolff, 1996). Other studies have questioned these findings (see Kennickell and Woodburn, 1997; Weicher, 1997).

The Gini Coefficient

The Gini coefficient,[4] a measure of inequality between income groups, actually declined after the end of World War II (1947) relative to 1968. As can be seen in figure 8.7, beginning in the decade of the seventies, economic inequality in the United States began increasing and then rose sharply in the 1980s and 1990s.

The consequence of inequality is that the majority of families have been left out of the great economic growth of the last several decades. The data in Table 8.5 display the change in disposable income in the United States between 1969 and 1996.

Figure 8.7 Change in Family Income Inequality, 1947 to 2000

Percent Change in Gini Index vs. 1968

Source: www.census.gov/hhes/income/histinc/f04.html

[4] The Gini coefficient is a measure of inequality that ranges from 0 to 1, with 1 representing complete inequality. The data in figure 8.5 examine the percentage change in the Gini index from 1947 to 2000.

Table 8.5 The Growth of Disposable Income in the United States and Its Distribution, 1969 and 1996[†]

	1969	1996	Change
Disposable income (in billions)	$2,626	$5,608	+ 114%
Per capita money income	11,975	18,136	+51%
Median income	33,072	35,172	+ 6%
Median income if all income groups had participated equally in income growth	33,072	50,087	+51%

Source: U.S. Census Bureau (1998) P23-196.
[†]In constant 1996 dollars.

Although there was a 114 percent increase in disposable income, this income was not shared by all families, but as demonstrated earlier, benefited primarily the top income group—the wealthy. Yet, while disposable income more than doubled during this period, the median income has increased only 6 percent, increasing from $33,072 in 1969 to $35,172 in 1996. If inequality did not exist and all income groups had roughly the same increase in income, as was the case between 1947 and 1979 (see table 8.5), then the median income would have been substantially higher. Instead of a median income of $35,126 in 1996, the median income might have been greater than $50,000 (see table 8.5). The social and economic situation of the average American family would have been very different.

The result of the increased inequality has been felt most by middle-income families. It is reasonable to suggest that the result of economic policy in the last several decades has been to shift wealth and income from the middle class to the wealthy.

After World War II the United States experienced a long period of sustained economic growth. From 1947 to 1979 individuals in all income groups benefited from the expanding economy. There was a broad rise in the standard of living as seen in table 8.4. During the 1950s many ex-servicemen supported by the GI Bill decided to go to college who would otherwise never have thought to go. As a result the educational level of the American workforce was greatly improved (Ackerman and Alstott, 2002).

But beginning in 1980 the broad participation in economic gain ended. As Robert Reich (1998: 3) noted, "median wealth (the wealth of the household in the middle of the distribution) was about 10 percent lower in 1995 than in 1983. By contrast, the top 1 percent of families became much wealthier: by 1995 they owned almost 39 percent of the total household wealth of the nation. Excluding the value of homes, they owned 47 percent. The top fifth owned 93 percent." It is vital to reward effort in a free enterprise economy. However, when the bottom 80 percent shares in just 3 percent of the total gain, something is fundamentally wrong. The gains which have been made in family income have primarily been the result of the increase in two-earner families. Ackerman and Alstott (1999: 2) observe, "Since the early 1970s the average family income has grown little, and the typical male worker has seen his real wages decline. Only the entry of vast numbers of women into the labor force has produced meager gains in median family income." Perucci and Wysong (2002) observe that the "new reality is a society in which one-fifth of Americans are privileged, with job security, high wages and strong skills. The other 80 percent belong to a 'new working class' that despite great variability within the group lacks the same security and high wages" (reported by Lee, 2003).

The Impact of Tax Policy

The shift of wealth upward during the decade of the eighties was largely the product of conservative economic policies that led to a quiet but massive redistribution of wealth through tax cuts (see figure 8.8). Through a program of substantial tax reductions for high-income earners, it was argued that more wealth would be accumulated and concentrated and thus made available for the nation through capital reinvestment, with the result that everyone in society would eventually benefit. As figure 8.8 shows, the tax rate on the wealthiest families has declined during the last five decades from about 90 percent to about 39 percent.

Of course, when taxes on the wealthy were cut, the top 1 percent of families was able to accumulate a much greater share of the wealth. This came about not only through the production of *new* wealth but also through a redistribution and shift upward of *existing* wealth.

Moreover, the tax cuts were not financed through a reduction in federal spending, since during the eighties reduced federal spending on domestic programs was more than matched by increased spending on military defense. As seen in table 8.6, the source of taxation was shifted from a reliance on corporate income tax, and excise and estate taxes, which primarily affect the wealthy, to increased borrowing and reliance on payroll taxes, which affect the poor and middle class. While the portion of federal revenue collected from personal income taxes remained relatively stable over the last several decades, the corporate income tax rate has been cut sharply, so that today the United States has one of the lowest corporate income tax rates in the world. By comparison, the corporate income tax rate in Japan is roughly equivalent to the rate that existed in the United States in the fifties.

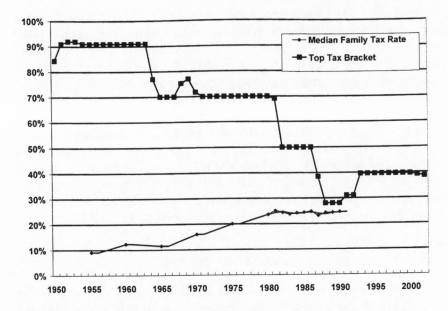

Figure 8.8 Tax Rate for the Average Family Compared to the Top Tax Bracket, 1950 to 2002
Source: Internal Revenue Service (2002a); Phillips (1993: 110).

Payroll taxes collected to pay for Social Security and Medicare, which have risen steadily over the last five decades, are regressive, which means they weigh most heavily on those least able to pay them. While these taxes are used to fund a "social insurance" program (Social Security), they allow wealthy individuals to stop paying Social Security tax on all income exceeding $84,900 (as of 2002).

Table 8.6 The Changing Source of Tax Revenue in the United States from 1950 to 2001

	Corporate Taxes as a Percent of Total Receipts	Payroll Taxes/ Social Security and Medicare	Individual
1950	26.5%	6.9%	
1960	23.2	11.8	
1969	20.4	17.6	51.9
1980	13.9	24.7	55.4
1990	10.4	34.8	51.1
2001	8.8	32.0	55.3

Source: Internal Revenue Service (2002b); Phillips (2002: chart 3.19).

In other words, all families pay about 15 percent of their income to Social Security (combined employee and employer contribution) up to $84,900, after which the income is no longer taxed. Along with this inequity, taxes that were once carried primarily by the wealthy, such as estate taxes, have also been cut over the last decades. Observing the net result of these tax policies in the 1980s and early 1990s, Phillips (1993: 123) concluded, "the progressivity of the U.S. income tax system had been largely lost."

In the eighties and late nineties it was argued that tax cuts on the wealthy would stimulate them to accumulate capital which they would then use for investments that would produce economic growth and, in the end, produce even more taxes than temporarily lost through the tax cuts (Buchanan and Lee, 1982). The tax cuts enacted on this argument were substantial. Cuts resulting from the Tax Reform Act of 1986 alone amounted to more than $18 billion a year for the wealthiest 65,000 families (less than one-thirtieth of 1 percent of all families). For the top 10 percent, the tax cuts were close to $100 billion a year (in 1989).

One of the major sources of revenue tapped to offset the large tax cuts, and that has primarily benefited high-income and wealthy families, has been increased federal borrowing. This has resulted in an even greater shift of wealth upward. After all, it is the wealthy that purchase the government bonds that finance the debt. Thus, for many wealthy families the tax cuts, rather than producing substantial investment capital, instead produced funds to finance the debt. The net result was that the unequal distribution of wealth was further increased. As Phillips (1993: xxiii) pointed out, "In the United States, merely to service the $4 trillion national debt of 1992— up fourfold from $1 trillion in 1980—required some $235 billion a year in net interest payments, most of which went to high-income bondholders (and some went abroad) while the money to make the payments was raised from broad-based taxes."[5] However, Phillips argues, since the poor have so little, the tax burden is primarily shouldered by a shrinking and increasingly overburdened middle class.

---

[5] To pay the interest on the accumulated federal debt requires half of all personal income taxes collected. The accumulation of this federal debt thus further compounds the shift of wealth upward. Columnist George Will (1988) observed, "This represents, as Senator Pat Moynihan has said, a transfer of wealth from labor to capital unprecedented in American history. Tax revenues are being collected from average Americans and given to the buyers of U.S. government bonds—buyers in Beverly Hills, Lake Forest, Shaker Heights, and Grosse Pointe, and Tokyo and Riyadh."

The Growing Abyss of Poverty: Creating Poor Families
Through Social and Economic Policy

The growth of wealth in the United States during the last three decades, along with the growth of poverty, has largely been the product of economic and taxation policies. Although conservative economic theorists have developed arguments that blame poverty on the poor because of indolence and avoidance of work, the facts point elsewhere. Kevin Phillips (1993: xx) observed:

> The victories of Thatcher and Reagan in 1979-80 in the West's two leading financial centers launched what conservatives excitedly called "revolutions"—transformations that were supposed to unleash capitalist energies and market economies on a grand scale. By 1986-87 the Group of Seven leading economic nations had undergone startling political alignments: aggressive free-market conservatism was in style, more so than at any other time since World War I. The ensuing policy changes, ranging from tax reductions to financial deregulation, regulatory permissiveness, strict treatment of labor and glorification of the rich, proved to be an elixir for global stock markets, property values and business opportunities, just as supply-side economists had predicted. The drawback in the United States, however, was that as the 1980s boom crested, rising taxes and other costs were gobbling up much of the nominal income gain of the middle class, while public services and the government safety net were starting to deteriorate.

In the absence of policies and programs to improve opportunities for the middle class, their relative economic situation has continued to decline. The shift of income and wealth from the middle class to the wealthy has created in the United States what Phillips (1990: 14) termed an extraordinary pyramid of affluence:

> A record number of billionaires, three thousand to four thousand families each worth over $50 million, almost one hundred thousand with assets over $10 million, and at least one and a quarter million households with a net worth exceeding $1 million. . . . The caveat was that if two to three million Americans were in clover—and another thirty to thirty-five million were justifiably pleased with their circumstances in the late 1980s—a larger number were facing deteriorating personal or family incomes or a vague but troubling sense of harder times ahead.

Throughout this period the middle class has been left out of the economic growth. In most families two persons are now required to work where only one worked two decades earlier. Yet even this often fails to produce an improved standard of living. While the middle class are being squeezed by higher taxes and declining opportunity, the poor are being battered. The struggles of the middle class have given rise to a new climate of hostility and bitterness toward the poor. Somehow the poor are today seen to be the cause of declining opportunities for the middle class.

The sixties saw an effort to eliminate poverty. Programs were developed to assure opportunity to those who had historically been denied opportunity. These programs would grow during periods of broad economic growth, but when circumstances changed and the middle class began having to struggle for opportunity, the stage was set for a broad assault on programs aimed to assist the poor and assure affirmative action for those who had historically been denied opportunity.

As seen in table 8.7, the United States has provided opportunity for fabulous wealth creation. These individuals have made significant contributions to the wealth of the nation. Each of the persons on this list individually has more money than is spent annually on cash assistance for the millions of poor children on welfare. In a sense, the concern with welfare, even though it represents very little money, took the focus off the declining participation of the broad middle class in the economic gains of the eighties and nineties. There was a dramatic increase in the number of millionaires during this period (Phillips, 2002). The "number of households worth at least one million dollars almost doubled from the early 1980s to the late 1990s, even after accounting for inflation" (Leonhardt, 2003). In the last decade there has also been a sharp increase in the number of billionaires.

Table 8.7 The 30 Richest Persons (in Billions)

Gates, William H. III	43.0	Anthony, Barbara Cox	9.5
Buffett, Warren Edward	36.0	Chambers, Anne Cox	9.5
Allen, Paul Gardner	21.0	Redstone, Sumner M.	9.0
Walton, Alice L.	18.8	Johnson, Abigail	8.2
Walton, Helen R.	18.8	Newhouse, Donald E.	7.7
Walton, Jim C.	18.8	Newhouse, Samuel I. Jr.	7.7
Walton, John T.	18.8	Pritzker, Robert Alan	7.7
Walton, S. Robson	18.8	Pritzker, Thomas J.	7.7
Ellison, Lawrence J.	15.2	Johnson, Samuel Curtis	7.0
Ballmer, Steven A.	11.9	Soros, George	7.0
Dell, Michael	11.2	Warner, H. Ty	6.0
Kluge, John Werner	10.5	Icahn, Carl	5.8
Mars, Forrest E. Jr.	10.0	Murdoch, Keith Rupert	5.0
Mars, Jacqueline	10.0	Bloomberg, Michael R.	4.8
Mars, John Franklyn	10.0	Broad, Eli	4.8

Source: Forbes List (2002). Online at www.forbes.com/lists/.

The Measure of Poverty

To measure the number of persons lacking sufficient economic resources to meet basic needs (food, clothing, and shelter), the federal government uses an index of poverty developed by Mollie Orshansky for the Social Security Administration in 1964 and revised in 1969 (Orshansky, 1965, 1967). According to this formula, the poverty line is calculated at three times what the Department of Agriculture estimates a given family spends on food.[6] Thus, if a family of four needs $300 a month for food, a monthly income of less than $900 means the family is living below the poverty line. In this calculation, income includes cash payments from Aid to Families with Dependent Children (AFDC), Supplemental Security Income (SSI), General Assistance, and other income assistance programs.[7] In 2001, the poverty line was $14,269 annually for a three-person family and $18,022 for a family of four. Thus a single mother and two children with annual income below $14,629 would be defined as "poor."

While the government's measure of poverty is a function of a family's ability to purchase the necessities of life, poverty can also be measured relative to the income of others (Frank, 1985). But even here the relative position of the poor has declined over the years. In 1960, the poverty line was roughly equivalent to half the median income for a family of four, but by 2001 it had declined to about 43 percent of the median family income (Levitan, 1990). This change reflects the substantial shift in the distribution of wealth upward. If poverty were defined in relative terms, such as one-half the median family income proposed by some economists and widely used by European economists (UNICEF, 2000), a much greater number of families would have slipped into poverty than the currently defined poverty line suggests.

The Poor—Past and Present
The Elderly

In the middle of the last century, the poor consisted primarily of the elderly. Fortunate was the man or woman who, in his or her seventies and eighties, was sheltered in the family of a child now grown. It was only with the enactment of the Social Security Act in 1935 that the elderly be-

---

[6] Although the poverty line is adjusted for family size, there is no adjustment for regional differences. With the great variation in the cost of housing among the different regions, this is a major limitation. The poverty line measure takes into account such variables as family size, commissions, tips, other cash benefits before deductions for taxes, and pensions.
[7] Income does not include the cash value of medical assistance, social services, food stamps, subsidized housing, child care, and other in-kind benefits.

gan emerging from poverty. Adopted during the New Deal, the Social Security Act provided (1) a federal "social savings" program to make sure people had income in their later years (Old Age and Survivors Insurance) and (2) federal welfare programs for the elderly (Old Age Assistance), for widows and orphans (Aid to Dependent Children), and for the disabled (Aid to the Permanently and Totally Disabled) (Bell, 1965). The "social savings"[8] provision for the elderly has emerged as the major program of the Social Security Act.

As a mandatory "social savings" program, Social Security requires employees (and their employers) to make provision for the employee's retirement by paying premiums to a Social Security fund through automatic payroll tax deductions during the employee's working years. When the individuals retire, or are no longer able to work, they are entitled to receive benefits from the fund based, in part, on the amount of their contribution. With only a few exceptions for government workers, Social Security is mandatory and provides universal coverage for all U.S. citizens.

As the main program of aid to the elderly, Social Security can only be regarded as a resounding success. As Pechman (1989: 160) observes, "There is no question that the Social Security system has successfully redistributed a large and growing amount of income from younger to older people, so that their spending power (relative to their needs) is now equal to or greater than that for most other groups in the society—including families with children."

Despite Social Security, the economic situation of the elderly continued to be characterized by high rates of poverty well into mid-century. By 1959, more than one-third of the elderly in the United States still lived in households with income below the poverty line. The War on Poverty and the Great Society programs of the 1960s and early 1970s, which were targeted at the problems of racial discrimination and unskilled and untrained workers who were unemployable, were not the main factor that led to the decline of poverty among the elderly.

With the passage of the Supplemental Security Income (the Social Security program that replaced Old Age Assistance) in 1972, the economic situation of the elderly poor changed substantially (Lindsey and Ozawa,

---

[8] Social Security is often referred to as a "social insurance" program because it collectively sets aside money to "insure" that the elderly have a basic income during their retirement years. However, the term "insurance" usually refers to the pooling of funds by the collective to protect individuals from personal peril. Thus, unemployment insurance is a form of social insurance that protects workers when, through misfortune, they are unemployed. Crop insurance is another example. However, Social Security is more concerned with "saving" funds for an event that all will experience. The term "social savings" thus highlights the savings aspect of Social Security.

1979). SSI provided a means-tested benefit to the remaining seniors who were not covered by Social Security.

Although passed in 1936, it took many years for Social Security to begin reducing poverty among the elderly. As seen in figure 8.9, the inflection point for Social Security was the fifties. By 1960, more than 60 percent of the elderly were provided retirement coverage. By 1970, more than 80 percent of the elderly were covered. The impact of this coverage was to reduce the percentage of the elderly living in poverty.

In 1966, 40 percent of persons sixty-five or older lived in households below the poverty line (Orshansky, 1967). By 1979, this had been reduced to 16 percent—a more than 60 percent decline in poverty among the elderly. From 1979 to 1989 the number had dropped to 9 percent. Moreover, this decline occurred at a time when the elderly population increased 50 percent. Haveman (1988: 82–83) observes, "One of the biggest success stories chalked up to the nation's redistribution system is its role in pulling up the average standard of living of the nation's older population. As a group, the elderly are no longer poor—no longer a source of equity or fairness concerns."

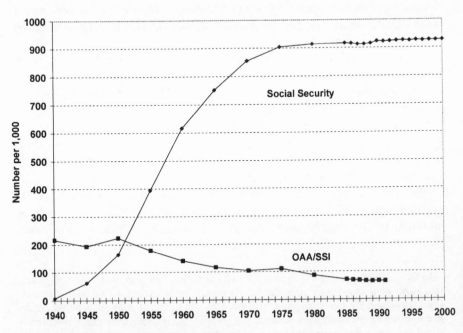

Figure 8.9 Increasing Social Security Coverage of Seniors
Source: Social Security Administration (2001).

The virtual elimination of poverty among the elderly is largely the result of government programs—Social Security and SSI. Taking inflation into account, the average cash transfer received by the elderly poor between 1967 and 1984 increased from less than $5,000 a year to more than $7,000 (Danziger and Gottschalk, 1986). Combined spending for the elderly has steadily risen during the last three decades (Ozawa, 1991, 1993; Green Book, 2000). From 1960 to 1990 total federal spending on Social Security and Medicare increased 150 percent, after controlling for inflation. Without question, the federal government has played a major role in providing income support of the elderly.

As seen in table 8.8, without government programs, 15.6 million elderly would live in poverty. Government programs changed this and lifted more than 12.7 million of the elderly out of poverty—more than 82 percent. Government programs did not provide similar assistance to children. Roughly the same number of children and elderly were in poverty in 1998 before the application of government programs. Whereas more than four-fifths of elderly were lifted out of poverty by government programs, the same was true for less than one-third of children.

In 1990, the federal government spent $11,350 per aged person compared to $1,020 per child under 18 (Ozawa, 1993: 521–522). In other words, on a per person basis the federal government spent ten times more on seniors than on children, a differential in spending that is perplexing.

Table 8.8 Reduction of Poverty from Government Programs for Children and Elderly, 1998

	Children	Elderly
Population	71,338,000	32,394,000
In Poverty	15,365,000	15,604,000
Removed from Poverty by Federal Benefits		
Social Security	1,234,000	11,836,000
Means tested cash benefit	664,000	382,000
Means tested noncash benefit	1,718,000	525,000
Federal taxes	1,519,000	-4,000
Total Removed from poverty	5,135,000	12,739,000
Percent removed from poverty	**33%**	**82%**

Source: Green Book (2000: 1320–1325), derived from tables H-19 and H-20.

In 1998, federal government programs were responsible for lifting out of poverty more than 80 percent of seniors who would otherwise be poor. Not only has the poverty gap for the elderly fallen substantially, while increasing for others, the incidence of poverty for the elderly has dropped.

Ross and Shillington (1989: 43) point out, "By age, the highest incidence [of poverty] among families was registered by the under-25 age group. Its rate almost doubled between 1973 and 1986. On the other hand, the rate of poverty among elderly families in 1986 was less than a third of what it had been in 1973."

During the presidential election of 2000 both major party candidates jostled over who was more committed to protecting Social Security and securing its financial integrity. The debate over a prescription drug benefit two years later illustrates the political clout of seniors. Writing in the *Los Angeles Times* Ronald Brownstein (2002) observes:

> The overall drug cost to government: $500 billion over the next seven years. That's daunting enough when Washington is already looking at big deficits in its operating budget. But the near-term cost ... is only the tip of the iceberg. As the baby boom retires, the number of seniors will explode from 40 million to 70 million just from 2010 to 2030. ... any prescription drug plan will cost nearly three times as much in its second decade as its first.
> The debate is obscuring a trade-off. ...Expanding access to preschool, rebuilding crumbling schools and providing health insurance for some of the roughly 40 million Americans without it—should subsidizing prescription drugs for seniors crowd out those other needs?
> ...And the percentage of seniors in poverty (10%) is still much smaller than the share of children (16%). Yet no one is talking about throwing half a trillion dollars at kids.

Children

> But things look different at the bottom, where an increasing proportion of children live out their early years. In 1996 children represented 40 percent of all Americans living below the poverty line—but only one quarter of the total population.
>   B. Ackerman and A. Alstott, *The Stakeholder Society*

The largest group of poor is, and has been for some time, children. In 1959, almost two-thirds of all nonwhite children in the United States were living in families with incomes below the poverty line. At the same time almost one-fifth of all white children were living in families with incomes below the poverty line.

Table 8.9 Children and Elderly in Poverty, 1959–2000

Children	1959	1970	1980	1990	2000
Population	64,315,000	69,159,000	62,914,000	65,049,000	71,932,000
% in poverty	27.3	15.1	18.3	20.6	16.2
In poverty	17,552,000	10,440,000	11,542,000	13,431,000	11,633,000
Elderly					
Population	15,557,000	19,470,000	24,686,000	30,093,000	32,979,000
% in poverty	35.2	24.6	15.7	12.2	10.2
In poverty	5,481,000	4,793,000	3,871,000	3,658,000	3,360,000

Source: U.S. Census Bureau (2001: table A-2).

As table 8.9 indicates, from 1959 to 1969, during the years of the War on Poverty and a period of economic growth, the number of children in poverty declined from more than 17.5 million to 9.7 million, even though the child population was increasing. Clearly, the War on Poverty had an impact on reducing poverty among children.

Since 1969, however, the economic situation of children has been deteriorating. From 1970 to 1980 the percentage of children living below the poverty line increased 15.1 percent to 18.3 percent. In contrast, the situation for the elderly continued to improve. From 1970 to 1980 the percentage of elderly living in poverty declined from 24.6 percent to 15.7 percent. The decade of the seventies saw substantial progress against poverty for the elderly but no progress for children.

By the eighties children had replaced the elderly as the poorest age group in the United States (O'Higgins, 1988). During the last three decades poverty among children increased one-fifth, from 15.1 percent to 16.2 percent, while the percentage of elderly living in poverty continued to decline, falling from 24.6 percent in 1970 to 10.2 percent in 2000. Thus, while the elderly in the United States were lifted out of poverty through Social Security (see table 8.8), children continued a steady slide into poverty which has only recently began to reverse.

Children in Single Parent Families

Beginning in the 1960s, the traditional two-parent family began to experience increasing social and economic pressures. More mothers began working outside the home (see figure 4.1) and the divorce rate rose sharply (see figure 4.2). As a consequence, the number of single parent families began increasing dramatically. Since 1980 the proportion of children under the age of eighteen not living in two parent families almost doubled, increasing from 10 percent in 1970 to 19 percent in 1985 to more than 20 percent in 1990 and 30 percent in 2000 (Annie E. Casey Foundation, 2002). Not surprisingly, children of single parent families have become the focus of poverty. Frank Levy (1987: vi) observes:

> Some of the disparity [in income between rich and poor households] was the inequity between investment bankers and high school dropouts. But a more direct cause was the increasing division of American families into two extremes: female-headed families on the one hand and two-paycheck families on the other. The division has implications for the future because the poorest twenty percent of families (many headed by single women) now contain almost one-quarter of all the nation's children.

The single parent raising a child is confronted by a social and economic situation that has proven difficult, and often impossible to change. Polakow (1993) has argued that women have been relegated to the secondary labor market (Ehrenreich, 2001). The primary labor market offers higher wages, steady employment, substantial fringe benefits, and unemployment compensation. For women trying to raise children on their own, opportunities for employment in the primary labor market has been severely restricted. Polakow (1993) observes, "Women often become casual, secondary-sector workers, ineligible for unemployment and health insurance benefits by virtue of their low wages and part-time work." Pearce (1990) indicates that 87 percent of recipients of primary health insurance benefits are in white families headed by men or married couples; only 3 percent are headed by black single mothers.

With reduced economic resources, increased child-rearing responsibilities and limited earning power, the single parent is severely restricted in choices and opportunities. The odds are high that such a parent will remain in poverty for an extended period of time. Children of such single parents have virtually no way of altering or escaping the economic circumstances in which they find themselves. The fate of children is entwined with that of their mothers. Through no fault of their own children are deprived of a host of developmental opportunities available to children of wealthier, two-parent families.

Duncan and Brooks-Gunn (1997) examined the duration of poverty for children. Citing extensive child development literature, they demonstrate that children who spend their formative years in poverty suffer negative effects that have long-term consequences. Duncan and Brooks-Gunn examined over a ten-year period (1982-1991) a cohort of children who were less than six in 1982. They found that 15 percent of these children spent three or more years in poverty. Seven percent spent six or more years in poverty, while 4 percent spent nine or more years in poverty. These latter children had essentially spent their entire childhood in poverty.

The situation was particularly bleak for African American children. Looking at African American children under six in this same period, they observed that 43 percent spent three or more years (out of ten) in poverty. Twenty-eight percent of these children spent six or more years in poverty, while 17 percent spent nine or more years living in poverty.[9]

Minorities and Single Parents

The economic situation of children being raised by single mothers, particularly African American and Hispanic children, is substantially worse than their counterparts in married couple families (see table 8.10). In 1996, the median income of female-headed families was less than one-third of married couple families. The situation was exacerbated for African American and Hispanic children.

As the data in table 8.10 demonstrate, single mothers and their children represent the most vulnerable group in the United States. Much of their economic circumstances results from the inability to manage the labor-intensive task of child rearing with the demands for labor force participation. Because they earn substantially less than men and because they carry enormous child care demands, neither they nor their children are ever likely to escape poverty. Women with a college education and professional training may be able to establish a viable independent economic household, but most unskilled and semiskilled women will not.

Poverty continues to be viewed as a private affair. When single mothers are unable to adequately provide for their children they are too often blamed for circumstances that are beyond their control. Because of their poverty they find their values and judgment questioned. Consequently, single mothers are only reluctantly provided with income assistance, the suspicion being that there is no guarantee the funds will be spent on the children. Will the mothers spend it on nutritious food or just on cigarettes, drugs, or alcohol? The behavior of single mothers is scrutinized in a manner others, like the elderly, would find objectionable—an insult to their integrity and dignity. "This discourse," argues Polakow (1993: 47) "serves to conceal the continuing mean-spirited treatment of poor people and legitimates the minimalist and degrading support policies for single mothers and their children, who suffer the snowball effects of class and race as well as gender discrimination."

---

[9] Examining the duration of child poverty from an international perspective, Bradbury, Jenkins, and Micklewright (2001) found that children in the United States endure the longest periods of poverty. They found that children in the United States are the least likely to move out of poverty.

Table 8.10 Median Income of Female-Headed and Married Couple Families, 1996

	Married Couple	Female Headed
All families	$ 51,768	$ 16,389
White	52,353	18,139
Black	42,697	13,647
Hispanic	31,612	11,241

Source: McNeil (1998).

Children Under Age Six

We can narrow the focus of poverty even further. The economic situation of children under six, of single parents, especially single mothers, is among the most severe of any group (Norman and Glick, 1986). According to the National Center for Children in Poverty (1990) at Columbia University, the number of poor children under six increased by 35 percent between 1968 and 1987, even though the population of children under six remained relatively stable. In contrast, the poverty rate of the elderly fell substantially, even as that elderly population was increasing from 18.5 million to more than 27 million. The data in figure 8.10 indicates the poverty rate for children under three by various racial and ethnic groups. Clearly the highest rates of poverty in the United States are to be found among children, with children under three having the highest rate.

As figure 8.10 shows, minority children under three are especially vulnerable to poverty. When single parenthood is combined with minority status, the probability of the child living in poverty in the United States greatly increases. Thus, African American children under three living with only their mother have a greater than 50 percent chance of being in poverty. For similar Hispanic children the poverty rate is 45 percent. For similar white children the rate is 37 percent.

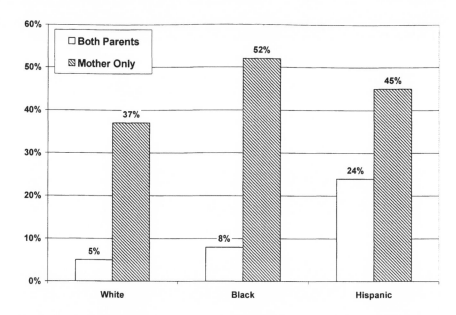

Figure 8.10 Poverty Rates for U.S. Children Under Three by Race/Ethnicity and Family Type, 2000
Source: Census Bureau (2001).

International Comparisons

Rates of poverty among children in other developed countries are often less than half the rate observed in the United States (see figure 8.11). Most developed nations in Western Europe and Asia have essentially ended poverty among children and single parent families (Polakow, 1993). Vleminckx and Smeeding (2001) examined child poverty in the major industrial nations and found it highest in the United States. They observed (2001: 1) that "the relative child poverty rate in New York is considerably higher than in any European country, including Russia."

Worldwide, the situation of single mothers is characterized by higher rates of poverty than is found in two-parent families. As the data in figure 8.12 indicate, the poverty rate for single families is greatest in the United States, the United Kingdom, Germany, and Canada (Lefaucher and Martin, 1993; O'Higgins, Schmaus, and Stephenson, 1985; UNICEF, 2000).

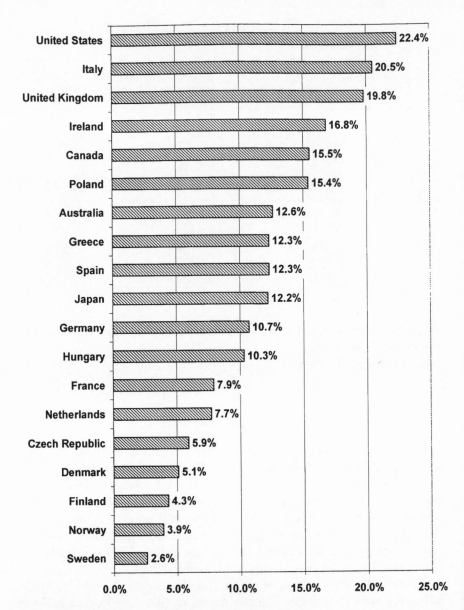

Figure 8.11 International Child Poverty Rates
(Percentage of children living in "relative"[10] poverty)
Source: UNICEF (2000).

---

[10] UNICEF defines relative poverty as half the median income for the particular country (see UNICEF, 2000: 25 for calculations).

What distinguishes the United States, however, is the large percentage of children living in single parent families (which is substantially larger than most countries) and the high rate of poverty among children in these families (see figure 8.12).

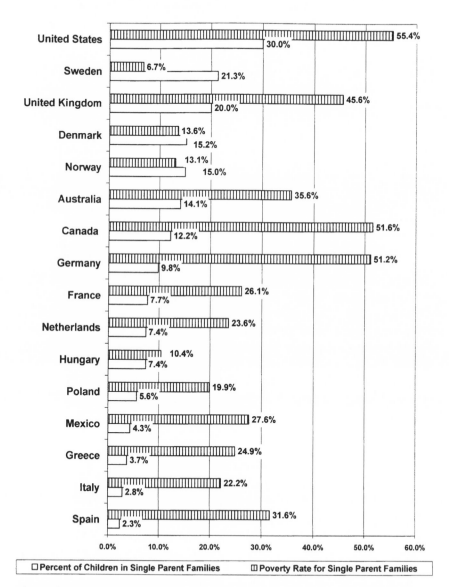

Figure 8.12 Economic Conditions of Children in Single and Two-Parent Families in Developed Countries

Source: UNICEF (2000).

Table 8.11 International Comparisons of Children Lifted Out of Poverty (in percentages)

	Child Poverty Rate before Taxes and Transfers	Child Poverty Rate after Govt. Programs and Transfers	Percent Reduction in Poverty
Norway	15.9	3.9	75.5
Netherlands	16.0	7.7	51.9
Finland	16.4	4.3	73.8
Germany	16.8	10.7	36.3
Denmark	17.4	5.1	70.7
Spain	21.4	12.3	42.5
Sweden	23.4	2.6	88.9
Canada	24.6	15.5	37.0
Italy	24.6	20.5	16.7
United States	**26.7**	**22.4**	**16.1**
Australia	28.1	12.6	55.2
France	28.7	7.9	72.5
UK	36.1	19.8	45.2

Source: UNICEF (2000).

Compared to other developed countries, the children who live in poverty in single parent families in the United States find little assistance from government programs designed to reduce poverty. As seen in table 8.11, the percentage of children lifted out of poverty in the United States as a result of government programs is the lowest in the world and substantially less than found in most countries. Rainwater and Smeeding (1995: table A2) report similar findings from their analyses, which indicate the United States has the highest percent of children living in poverty among industrialized nations.

Implications of Inequality

During the last several decades major public policies and programs in the United States have greatly reduced poverty among the elderly. In the early 1960s close to 40 percent of the elderly in the United States were living in households below the poverty line, restricted from materially altering their condition by physical constraints (old age) and labor market constraints. This has changed. As a result of the Social Security program, today less than 10 percent of the elderly live in households below the poverty line.

Children have not been so fortunate. While the period after World War II began with great hope and expectation of ending poverty among children, this hope has not been realized. During the War on Poverty in the 1960s, the percentage of children in poverty in the United States began dropping, indicating that federal social programs could have an impact. During the seventies, however, the trend reversed. During the last three decades children have replaced the elderly as the group having the greatest percentage of poor. Today children represent 40 percent of all Americans living below the poverty line (Ackerman and Alstott, 1999).

The current scale of poverty among children prompts several conclusions. First, to permit the continuance of such poverty among the most helpless and innocent of our population without taking any action is unwise social policy. No child should be abandoned to poverty.

Second, child welfare must recognize that impoverished children represent their client base. In confronting such increasing levels of poverty the child welfare social worker is constrained by the broad poverty and inequality which these children endure. At some point the extent of child poverty becomes too great and threatens to overtake the best efforts of the child welfare social worker. With more than 500,000 children in foster care, most for reasons of poverty, we have reached the point where the system is overwhelmed. In Florida, New Jersey, New York, Illinois, and elsewhere, the child welfare system is faltering. All of the counseling, the casework, and the means testing—all the tools of the "residual" approach—which have been the major tools thus far, have proven ineffective and are no longer sufficient. Something qualitatively different is required.

Third, our understanding of poverty has focused on the personal deficits of the poor. As a consequence, we have seen poverty as a private affair. Doing so has allowed us to collectively avoid responsibility for the impact of poverty on children.

Yet poverty *is* a public responsibility (Mills, 1959). In affluent societies poverty is a result of policies that govern the distribution of wealth and income and that preserve the continuation of poverty among single mothers and their children. Our usual understanding of the boundary of child welfare must extend to policies that address structural inequality, discrimination in housing (Massey and Denton, 1993), a lack of publicly subsidized child care, inadequate health care coverage, public assistance, and more. As Polakow (1993: 172) observes, "all these changes and reforms have been proposed by leading critics and social and public policy analysts. But until private interests give way to public responsibility and to a notion of civic entitlements rather than undeserving poor benefits, poor children will remain poor in a land of affluence."

Finally, from a larger sociopolitical perspective, the continuation of poverty among large segments of our child population imperils the future of the United States. Since 1776, when Adam Smith wrote his treatise, *The Wealth of Nations,* outlining the "natural laws" that govern a democratic free enterprise system, economists have recognized the need for the accumulation and concentration of wealth among the people, wealth that is reinvested as capital in the economic machinery of society. Whereas Adam Smith saw this accumulation accruing largely through profits to a few industrialists, it is now recognized that such accumulation must occur within the broadest base of the population.

In the United States during the last several decades a small percentage of families have accumulated ownership of the vast majority of the country's wealth. Why this has happened is subject to debate. Some argue that selective laws of nature are at work. They suggest that those in poverty simply do not have the skill, intelligence, enterprise, or "gumption" to effectively engage the economic system for their financial benefit. Others feel that the poor are denied opportunity to fully participate through discriminatory social practices. Still others argue that such unequal distribution of wealth reflects a social order which results when powerful political groups, aided by the collective approbation (or acquiescence) of citizens, have, through legislative processes vulnerable to leveraged financial contributions, shaped and controlled economic opportunities to the advantage of the wealthy at the expense of the poor.

It is not our intent to argue one view over another but to emphasize that, regardless of the reason for the unequal and inequitable distribution of wealth, to permit its continued massive negative impact on large numbers of poor children within a country is unwise in the extreme. What has distinguished the democratic free-enterprise market economy of the United States and other modern industrial nations has been their ability to promote the development of a prosperous middle class, in which populations of extremely poor and extremely rich are minimized. A financially healthy middle class not only provides the purchasing power needed to sustain economic growth, it ensures a socially stable population (Phillips, 2002).

When large segments of society are excluded from the economic mainstream to the extent that we have seen in this chapter, increasingly they begin to affect the society in negative ways—the growth of crime, racial and ethnic hatred, gang violence, child abuse, homicides among children, drug abuse and dependency. Instead of adding to the wealth of the nation through their productivity and consumption, the impoverished children become an ever increasing social burden. In the child welfare field, with a half million children removed from their parents and placed in foster care, we deal only with the most critical cases of child neglect and maltreatment.

But beneath these cases is a subterranean mountain of child poverty and inequality that erodes hope and destroys opportunity.

If poverty among large segments of children continues unabated, the spirit, the soul, and the wealth of the nation, as it is embodied in the aspirations of disadvantaged children, will certainly be depleted and destroyed. As we have provided substantial income protection for the elderly, we must not leave children to suffer in poverty. To make children endure poverty during the crucial years when their character and outlook are being formed is not sound social policy. For the sake of the nation as well as these children, we must begin developing policies and programs that promote wider participation in the benefits of our free enterprise market economy. Welfare programs that only provide income assistance to the poor are not sufficient. What is needed is a means of investing in children, of providing opportunity, thereby ensuring a broader participation in the nation's economic enterprise. This will require economic and social policies that fit with and benefit from the distinctive features of the free market economy.

Conclusion

America is a rich and bountiful country with enough resources to provide for all its citizens. Its free market capitalist system has produced enormous wealth. Yet, in spite of this great wealth there is also great poverty. One of the key reasons for this poverty is the vast political and economic inequality which creates a condition, in which the least powerful are the ones most vulnerable— in this instance, the children of single parents.

In the first two decades after World War II the American economic and political system generated substantial wealth which was distributed to all income categories—the poor, the low income, the working class, the middle class, the upper class, and the wealthy (see table 8.4). However, in the last several decades, despite continued economic growth, the poor and the middle class have failed to benefit. Whereas creative and successful social and tax policies have benefited the wealthy, there has been limited similar effort on behalf of the poor, low-income, and working classes. It is as though frustration with the failings of the War on Poverty have crippled our faith in the ability of social and tax policies to reduce poverty.

Child poverty in an incredibly wealthy society is not an accident, but a product of the inequality which our social and economic system has generated. The problem can be traced to reform of a tax system that demands substantial payroll taxes from the poor and middle class while significantly reducing taxes for the wealthy. High payroll taxes have reduced the ability of the working and middle classes to participate in the economic growth of the last several decades. A single mother working at minimum wage will pay an effective tax rate that is among the highest in the nation. Such a tax rate is not required by our economic system, but rather is likely due to the very limited political influence of single mothers and their children.

Despite being the wealthiest nation in the world, the United States has the highest child poverty rates. During the last half of the twentieth century the United States made great progress in ending poverty among seniors. This same progress can be achieved for children. The United Kingdom, as a society, has made a collective commitment to cut child poverty by half during the next decade. They have developed and begun implementing policies which will allow them to make progress toward this goal. The United Kingdom has declared that it will end child poverty within the next two decades. Child poverty could also be ended in the United States.

Ending child poverty will require fundamental reform of the social and economic policies which produced it. It will include reform of social policies that have worked to the detriment of single parent families with children. It is easy to be pessimistic because such reforms require political clout which poor and disadvantaged children lack. Yet, America is a generous and good society, and when the problem is clear and the opportunity right, change will likely occur.

The vast inequality and resulting poverty doesn't have to be. It hasn't always been this way in America. The vast inequality is what produces the extensive child poverty and leads to the United States—the richest country in the world—also having the highest rate of child poverty. In recent years, public policies and programs have broadened the inequality and deepened the child poverty. The tax policy reforms have led to a shift of wealth upward. Moreover, the social programs designed to protect the poor—especially children—have been the subject of criticism and rebuke. What have we done collectively to alleviate and reduce child poverty? These are the questions we examine in the next chapter.

9

The Rise and Fall of Welfare for Disadvantaged Children in America

Freedom is not enough. You do not wipe away the scars of centuries by saying: Now you are free to go where you want, do as you desire, choose the leaders you please.

You do not take a person who for years has been hobbled by chains and liberate him, bring him up to the starting line of a race and then say, "You are free to compete with all the others," and still justly believe that you have been completely fair.

Thus it is not enough just to open the gates of opportunity. All our citizens must have the ability to walk through the gates.

Former President Lyndon B. Johnson

[The current policy of welfare] subsidizes births among poor women, who are disproportionately at the low end of the intelligence distribution. . . . We urge generally that these policies, represented by the extensive network of cash and services for low-income women who have babies, be ended.

Richard J. Herrnstein and Charles Murray, *The Bell Curve*

The modern welfare program had its roots in the Great Depression, when, to alleviate poverty, the United States developed a welfare program that would provide a safety net for children in poor families. As part of Roosevelt's New Deal this welfare program (Aid to Dependent Children) provided income assistance to poor single mothers and their children. By virtue of citizenship in America, poor children were entitled to means-tested income assistance. For the first twenty-five years the program was used by less than 2.5 million children, many of whom were children of widows. Beginning in the sixties, welfare caseloads began increasing at much higher rates than ever before. Within the twelve-year period from 1960 to 1972 welfare caseloads increased from 2.5 million to more than 10 million children. During the next two decades the number of recipients remained relatively stable, fluctuating between 10 and 11.5 million (figure 9.1).

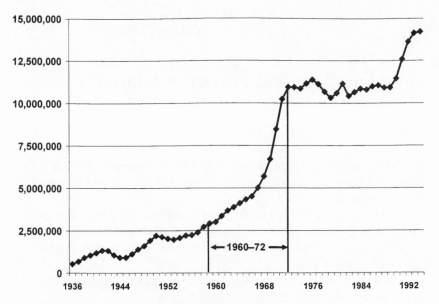

Figure 9.1 Number of Welfare Recipients, 1936–1992[1]
Source: HHS Administration for Children and Families (2002).
Online at www.acf.dhhs.gov/news/stats/3697.htm

This dramatic increase in welfare recipients, most of whom were children, can be explained by several social factors of the period. As we saw in chapter 4, the 1960s were a time of social upheaval, when traditional values were being questioned and new family arrangements adopted. The traditional two-parent family, which for so long had been the bulwark of social equilibrium, was being challenged on several fronts—and was rapidly changing as a result. Women were leaving the home to pursue careers of their own. Sexual experimentation was unleashed with the advent of the birth control pill. The traditional division of household chores was being challenged. Divorce dramatically increased.

African Americans, although making giant strides to achieve equal opportunity and treatment through the passage of civil rights legislation, were nevertheless impacted by powerful social and economic forces that changed their families and communities substantially. Overall, society would never again be as it was.

---

[1] Prior to enactment of the Personal Responsibility and Work Opportunity Reconciliation Act of 1996 and Temporary Assistance for Needy Families(TANF), cash assistance for needy families was provided through Aid to Dependent Children (1936-1962), later called Aid to Families with Dependent Children (1962-1997).

In this chapter we trace the rise of the modern welfare system in the United States, and the causes that led to the continued high rates of welfare up to the end of the twentieth century. We examine the conservative arguments against welfare which led ultimately to its reform and, some say, its essential end. Many of the changes we detail began in the late 1960s but continue even today. As we will see, although the welfare program designed to provide income assistance to poor children has been reformed and largely dismantled, the social and economic conditions it was designed to address are still present.

Raising children is a labor-intensive activity, and two parents have a far easier time meeting the demands of child rearing than does one. The historic family structure in the United States has been two parents, and for most of the last century more than 85 percent of children lived with two parents (see figure 9.2). However, as a result of divorce and out-of-wedlock births an increasing percentage of children have grown up in single parent families. The significant decline in two-parent families that began around 1970 coincides with the dramatic rise in welfare. Why did two-parent families decline and what caused the rise in welfare?

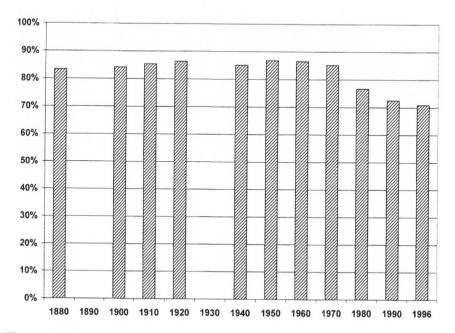

Figure 9.2 Historic Living Arrangement of Children in the United States: Percent Living with Two Parents

Increase in Divorces

The revolution in reproductive technology—the birth control pill and legalization of abortion (see table 4.1)—combined with the increased involvement of women in the labor force outside the home increasingly led
to strains on family life. These strains were reflected in an increased divorce rate, which is the main reason for the dramatic increase in welfare
recipients from 1960 to 1972.

Examining the number of divorces and the number of welfare recipients during the period in question—1960 to 1972—one is struck by the
parallel movement of the two[2] (figure 9.3). The change in the number of
children on welfare closely mirrors the change in the number of children
involved in divorce but is relatively independent of other changes such as
the number of children born out of wedlock. A regression analysis examining the relative impact of divorce and out-of-wedlock births on the number
of children on welfare over the period from 1954 to 1992 revealed that it
was the increase in "children involved in divorce" that most influenced the
increase in welfare usage, accounting for more than 94 percent of the variation (see Lindsey, 1994: 269).[3] Further, as Patterson (1994) demonstrates
in his study of the increase in the welfare caseload, the proportion of eligible families who were receiving welfare increased from one-third in the
early sixties to nine-tenths in 1971. Divorced mothers were viewed as "deserving" welfare recipients and made full use of the program (Katz, 1989;
Handler and Hansenfeld, 1991).

---

[2] Other explanations for the sharp rise in welfare recipients between 1965 and 1972 have
been offered (see Kristol, 1971; Piven and Cloward, 1970; Kayx, 1989; Rector and
Youssef, 2001). Jay Hein (2001) points out that the National Welfare Rights Organization
(NWRO) was founded by George Wiley in 1966 just when the number of recipients began
its rapid increase. The NWRO brought together concern with civil rights and poverty and
suggested that the poor were *entitled* to welfare assistance. Hein writes, "It was this effort,
more than any other, that infused black women, who comprised over 90 percent of
NWRO's membership, with the belief that welfare was an entitlement rather than an act of
generosity ... It succeeded in swelling the [New York] city's welfare rolls from 250,000
recipients in 1960 to more than one million adults by the time Giuliani became mayor thirty
years later."
[3] Elsewhere we have examined the relation between the number of (1) children receiving
welfare benefits, (2) children involved in divorce, (3) children born out of wedlock, and (4)
children living in poverty. The data for figure 9.3 derive from figures 4.2, 4.3, 10.3 and
table 8.3. In order to permit a comparison across time for these variables taking into account the different scale measures (that is, "children in poverty" ranging from 10 million to
20 million and "children born out of wedlock" ranging from 200,000 to less than 1.5 million), I used a log scale.

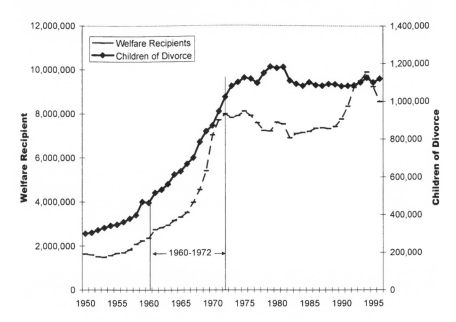

Figure 9.3 Increasing Divorce and Rise in AFDC Recipients

Evidently, the increasing number of divorced women during the period from 1960 to 1972 looked to welfare for income assistance. Applying a content analysis to a sample of welfare mothers from this period, Rein and Rainwater (1978) found that more than half were using welfare to cushion the transition following divorce. The majority of women participated only for a short transitional period after separating from a spouse. In this sense, welfare represented for women what unemployment insurance represented for men in similar income disruption situations. For the majority of women in their study, Rein and Rainwater (1978) found that emancipation from welfare was achieved through remarriage and only rarely through employment.

Sexual Experimentation and Children Born Out of Wedlock

The 1960s were a decade of changing social values, shaped in large part by the revolution in reproductive technology caused by the development of an effective birth control pill and the legalization of abortion (*Roe v. Wade*).[4] Before the sixties sexual revolution young women who became pregnant

---

[4] Roe v. Wade, 410 US 113 (1973).

would likely marry the father (the fabled shotgun marriage).[5] Between 1960 and 1972 both the number of women using the birth control pill and the number of abortions increased several fold (see table 4.1). This period was characterized by a transformation of attitudes and values about sex. Many young people began to experiment with sex before marriage, a trend that has continued to the present day (Becker, Rankin, and Rickel, 1998; Moore, Nord, and Peterson, 1989). Today, almost half of all girls experience sex during their teenage years (U.S. National Center for Health Statistics, 1997). This increased sexual activity has naturally resulted in an increase in the number of teen pregnancies (Forrest and Singh, 1990; Henshaw and Van Vort, 1989). Indeed, the teen pregnancy rate in the United States is today among the highest in the postindustrial world (Child Trends, 2001).

In 2000, there were 479,067 births to teenagers (National Center for Health Statistics, 2001). This translates into almost one in ten white teenagers and one of five African American teenagers between the ages of fifteen and seventeen becoming pregnant each year.[6] Compared to other developed nations, this pregnancy rate is very high. In Canada the rate is less than one in twenty, in the Netherlands less than one in fifty, and in Japan less than one in a hundred (Council of Europe, 1999; Kiernan, 2000; Smith and Poertner, 1993; Vital Statistics of Japan, 1998).

Contrary to popular perception there has been a decline in the *rate* of births to teenagers during the last several decades. In 1950, the rate was 90 births per 1,000 teens (young women ages 15 to 19). By 1990, this rate had declined to 62. What has changed is the percentage of these teenage mothers who are unmarried. In 1960, less than 14 percent of all teenage mothers were unmarried. By 2000, this percentage had increased to almost 80 percent (Allen Guttmacher Institute, 1995; National Center for Health Statistics, 2001: figure 1). The percentage of all teenage births that were to unmarried teenagers increased steadily from about 12 percent in 1950 to 80 percent in 2000 (Ventura, Mathews, and Hamilton, 2001).

---

[5] Over the last several decades the cultural stigma associated with out-of-wedlock childbearing has receded (Goldstein, 1999; Wilson, 2002). In addition, the mechanisms to require responsibility and child support among fathers have been largely ineffective.

[6] Once a woman becomes pregnant out of wedlock she is faced with deciding what to do. In 1995, 40 percent of pregnancies for unmarried women ended in abortion, compared to 7 percent for married women (National Center for Health Statistics, 2001).

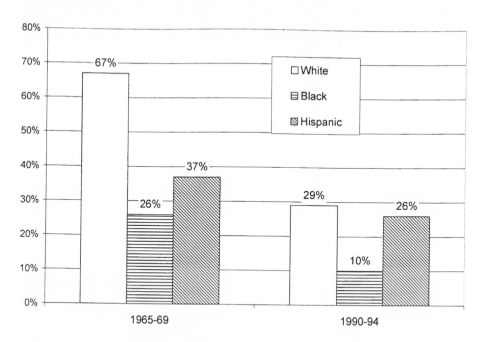

Figure 9.4 Declining Shotgun Marriages.
Among First Births Conceived Before Marriage, Percent Marrying Before Birth of
Child by Race and Ethnicity, 1965–69, and 1990–94
Source: Akerlof (1996).

One of the concerns that critics of welfare have is that many young women
who did not get married were influenced by the availability of welfare,
which provided a secure and reliable income source that may not have been
available through marriage. This was exacerbated by the welfare program's
requirement against a man in the house.

In the last several decades, however, young women have increasingly
given birth to a child conceived out of wedlock without getting married
(see figure 9.4). Akerlof (1996) has studied the increase in children born
out of wedlock and suggested that it is mostly explained by the declining
rate of marriages among the women who conceive outside of marriage.
Akerlof and his colleagues suggest that the increase in out-of-wedlock
births for African American women, for example, would have been two-
fifths of what it was had the "shotgun" marriage rates remained the same
between 1965 and 1985.[7]

---

[7] For White women the rate would have been approximately one-quarter what it was (Akerlof, 1996).

Teenage Child Bearing and Welfare

Within one year after the birth of their first child, half of all teen mothers are receiving welfare benefits (Green Book, 2000).[8] Within five years, the percentage grows to more than 75 percent (Besharov, 1993: 51). Of all mothers under thirty who receive public assistance, about 70 percent began their child bearing as teenagers. Once a teenager has a child, the mother, child, and society embark on an eighteen-year odyssey that is both difficult in itself and difficult to conclude. These mothers and their children will likely be poor (see figure 9.5).

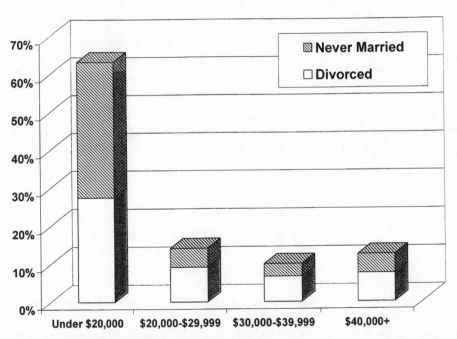

Figure 9.5 Income and Poverty Among Single Mothers
Source: U.S. Census Bureau (2001a).

---

[8] Teenage mothers have been a small part of the welfare caseload. In 1992, they comprised 8.2 percent of the caseload. Most mothers were in their twenties (47.2 percent) or thirties (32.6 percent), while mothers in their forties comprised about 12 percent (Clinton Administration, 1994, 49).

Welfare provides, at best, meager assistance to the young mother and child confronted by difficult economic and personal circumstances. Today, the major program available is Temporary Assistance for Needy Families (TANF). However, the amount of financial support provided by TANF is minimal, roughly one-seventh of the average family income in the United States (Hacker, 1992: 86) and even less than 10 percent in 2001.

Mixed Messages

Young women who get pregnant out of wedlock receive mixed messages (Matthews-Green, 1996; Wilson, 2002). Advocates for the unborn argue on moral grounds that abortion, even for unwed teenagers, is tantamount to taking of a life. Once the child is born, they say, solutions will be forthcoming. The unwed mother, however, quickly learns that the society which so strongly discouraged an abortion has little interest in supporting her and her child after the birth (Crump, Hynie, Aarons, Adair, Woodward, and Simons-Morton, 1999; Sawhill, 1998). Many would like to see the unwed mother give the child up for adoption, which would not only free the mother to enter the work force but provide the child a likely escape from poverty. Adoption, however, is the least-selected option.

Although more than 40 percent of unwed teens have abortions, having an abortion is, in many quarters, discouraged (National Center for Health Statistics, 2001).[9] Between 1965 and 1969 there were 88,000 abortions in the United States. From 1970 to 1974 the number of abortions increased to 561,000. In the next five years this increased to 985,000, and from 1980 to 1984 the number of abortions had increased to 1,271,000. Despite the availability of welfare many young women terminated their pregnancies. During the last several decades the percentage of pregnancies ending in abortion among unmarried women has declined (from 59 percent in 1980 to 41 percent in 1995; see Henshaw, 1998; Ventura and Bachrach, 2000: 11).[10]

Baker (1985) interviewed a sample of adolescent girls across Canada and asked them how they would handle an unplanned pregnancy. Almost half indicated they would keep their baby and raise it as best they could, with or without the help of the father. About a third said they would seek an abortion. Less than 5 percent said they would give their babies up for

---

[9] The abortion rate for young women ages 15 to 19 declined from 41 per thousand in 1990 to 30 per thousand in 1995.

[10] The fact that abortions increased as a percentage of pregnancies reflects the fact that many unmarried women kept children from unplanned pregnancies rather than seeking an abortion and did not subsequently marry the father.

adoption. Ventura and Bachrach (2000: figure 22) reported that about 20 percent of white unmarried mothers released their babies for adoption before 1973. Yet, between 1989 and 1995 this percentage dropped to less than 2 percent of white unmarried women and less than one-half of 1 percent of African American women relinquishing their babies for adoption.[11] That so many young women refuse to give their baby up for adoption is often viewed as evidence of their wish to continue in a state of dependency. Yet, for most women, young or old, surrendering an infant is almost impossible: the maternal bond is too strong.

The Condition of Teenage Mothers

Empirical studies have indicated that teenage mothers quickly descend into deep and abject poverty and suffer from "quashed hopes" and profound disillusionment (Edelman, 1987; Ellwood, 1988; Miller-Johnson et al., 1999). Frederica Mathewes-Green (1996: 2) describes the situation of these young unmarried mothers:

> A story like this begins perhaps a thousand times every day: A woman's hand trembles as she scans the big-city Yellow Pages. The ads for abortion clinics have flowers and birds and slogans about caring, and one shows a pretty couple grinning at each other at the seashore. That makes her start crying again. Her boyfriend never looked at her like that.
>
> But elsewhere on the page she sees an ad showing a woman curled around a baby. The phone number ends with the letters H-O-P-E. She hadn't thought about hope, but she feels like she really needs to talk to someone who has some, right now. She dials the number.
>
> Half a year later, she is stepping out of the Hope Pregnancy Center. It's her first visit since the birth. Her little boy fusses while everyone hugs her. She stands for a moment in the spring sunshine. She's made it through these months after all. It's taken courage, and it's been tough, but this precious child has been brought through safely and given the gift of life. Without the love of the women at the center, this child would have died. She looks down at his wizened face. He is all she has now. Tears prick her eyes again, as she turns and walks to the bus stop.

---

[11] See Ventura and Bachrach (2000: 9) and Bachrach (1986: 250–251). These data need to be viewed with caution. The data used by Bachrach came from the National Survey of Family Growth conducted by the National Center for Health Statistics in 1982. Interviews were completed with 7,969 women between 15 and 44 years of age. Only 60 women in the sample had placed one or more babies for adoption (p. 244). Thus, the rates of placement may not be reliable estimates of national rates. In Ontario, a Provincial government report indicated that 30.1 percent of unwed mothers kept their children in 1968, but that ten years later the number had increased to 88.3 percent (Ontario, 1979: 19, table 2).

What happens to mother and child next?

"It horrifies me sometimes," says Pat Evans, the unpaid director of Birthright, a crisis-pregnancy center in Annapolis, Maryland. "She's on the list for public housing, but that housing is invariably in bad sections. But if she turns it down, she's off the list, or put back on at the bottom to wait all over again." And how does she support herself? "She probably gets $225 a month on welfare, and there's food stamps, WIC [nutrition aid to women, infants, and children], and medical assistance," says Evans, who has counseled thousands of women in her 16 years there. "In all these years, I've seen less than a half-dozen find a way to work. Once they have that baby, how can they find a job that pays enough to buy a car to get to the job, and cover day care as well?" Evans's center, which assists about 1,200 women a year, can help some with housing for a year after the birth, but can't offer permanent housing or employment. "I don't see any answer to that; it's almost impossible. When she has a child, everything gets very hard."

With limited education, few job skills, and the enormous demands of a new infant, most mothers are unable to obtain and hold gainful employment (Maynard, 1996). Further, even when they are able to secure child care and obtain employment, their income is low (Wertheimer, 1998). Given average annual incomes of less than $7,000 a year, the single teen mothers confront a depressing economic plight, with their children suffering as much as they (Levy, 1987: 151).[12] Most of the children in these families will live in poverty.[13]

Children in single parent families have less provision and opportunity in virtually all areas of life (Boyle et al., 1987; Offord et al., 1987; Fagan, 1999; U.S. Bureau of the Census, 1997). Butler (1992: 5) observes, "Children born to teenage mothers have been found to be at greater risk for health problems, poor cognitive functioning, and poverty." They have a significantly higher likelihood of dropping out of school and will themselves be more likely to give birth out of wedlock (Hotz, McElroy, and Sanders, 1997; Manlove, 1998; McLanahan and Sandefur, 1994).

The labor-intensive demands of child rearing severely limited the choices available to a young woman raising a child by herself. To cope

---

[12] Given that unwed teenage mothers have an average annual income of less than $7,000 a year, an unintended consequence of current social and economic policy is to impose severe economic hardship on those who *elect* to keep their children and try to raise them as best they can. Those who are opposed to abortion would be wise to focus on improving the circumstances of the single mothers who elect to keep their child. For many who carry their child to term, the consequence is a life in poverty for both the mother and the child extending for many years.

[13] The poverty rate for female-headed families was 54.7 percent for African American children, 59.6 percent for Hispanic children, and 40 percent for white children (U.S. Census Bureau, Current Population Reports, Series P-60, 1999).

with the difficulties of trying to raise a child born out of wedlock, unmarried teen mothers often turned to welfare. Although welfare provided limited support and had social approbation associated with it, the young single mothers saw it as their only choice.

Not surprisingly, they soon found themselves, in a sense, trapped in dependency. Although welfare was difficult, degrading, and in many ways inadequate, the single mother somehow adapted to the minimal support provided (Segalman and Basu, 1981; Handler and Hasenfeld, 1991). In doing so she became a victim of the very program designed to assist her. Over time, she lost her pride and sense of self-worth and was viewed with disrespect by the larger society that was now burdened with providing for her and her children (Marin, Hill, and Welsh, 1998). Without child care and adequate income support, she rarely gained the opportunity to achieve self-sufficiency.

African American Families

A 1992 Orlando Sentinel study of police videotapes discovered that although Black and Latinos represented only 5 percent of drivers on the Florida interstate highway, they made up nearly 70 percent of drivers stopped by police and more than 80 percent of drivers whose cars were searched.

Dorothy Robertson, *Shattered Bonds*

The African American community and family is a major part of the puzzle of welfare rise in the late 1960s. Certainly, when the history of the second half of the twentieth century is written, one of the most troubling events in U.S. domestic affairs will be the dissolution of the two-parent African American family. The change happened slowly and perhaps imperceptibly at first, but by the turn of the century the consequences were unmistakable. In 1960, more than 70 percent of all African American children lived in two parent families (Moynihan, 1965: 11; U.S. Census Bureau, 1998). When we entered the new millennium close to 70 percent of all African American children were born to unwed mothers. In 1960, less than 10 percent of African American children in single parent families lived with a never married parent. By 1998, this arrangement accounted for 62 percent of all African American children (Green Book, 2000: 1234). How did this situation come about?

To a large extent the roots of severe child poverty in the United States stem from the historical circumstances of African American families, a situation that still continues (Clark, 1965; Myrdal, 1944; Wilson, 2002). For many years African American families lived under the brutal conditions of slavery. After the Civil War and Emancipation, African Americans faced the difficult task of trying to repair decades of damage caused by slavery. In 1896, W.E. B. DuBois wrote in *The Philadelphia Negro*:

> It must be remembered that the Negro home and the stable marriage state is for the mass of the colored people . . . a new social institution. The strictly guarded savage home life of Africa, which with all its shortcomings protected womanhood, was broken up completely by the slave ship, and the promiscuous herding of the West Indian plantation. . . . With emancipation the Negro family was first made independent and with the migration to cities we see for the first time the thoroughly independent Negro family. On the whole it is a more successful institution than we had a right to expect.

Slavery, points out James Q. Wilson (2002), "that vast, cruel system of organized repression that denied to slaves the right to marry, vote, sue or take an oath" and "allowed their children to be sold on the slave block" grievously injured the African America family. The historic and long-term harm of the legacy of slavery didn't end with the passage of Civil Rights legislation in the early sixties.

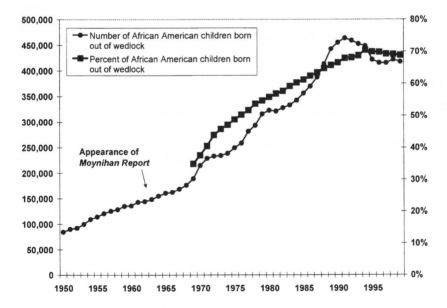

Figure 9.6 Black Children Born Out-of-Wedlock
Source: Bachu (1999); Blank (1997: 34, figure 1.9).

Shortly after passage of the Civil Rights Act of 1964, concerns about the conditions of the African American family were raised in a publication entitled, *The Negro Family: The Case for National Action* (Moynihan, 1965). Written by former Harvard sociologist and then Assistant Secretary of Labor Daniel Patrick Moynihan, the prophetic *Moynihan Report* detailed the increase in male unemployment and the rise of fatherless families in the African American community resulting in widespread poverty. Moynihan argued that the key to the deterioration of the African American community was to be found in the demise of the African American family. "At the center of the tangle of pathology is the weakness of the family structure. Once or twice removed, it will be found to be the principal source of most of the aberrant, inadequate or antisocial behavior that did not establish, but now serves to perpetuate the cycle of poverty." Moynihan suggested that a growing proportion of welfare recipients were African American children growing up in single parent homes and that this family structure had gathered a momentum all its own that was impervious to improving surrounding economic circumstances.

Moynihan pointed out that unemployment and discrimination combined to produce disastrous consequences for African American families and led to high rates of out-of-wedlock births and welfare dependency. Moynihan argued that a concerted national effort was required to strengthen the African American family—a Marshall Plan of sorts. Unfortunately, no such effort ever materialized. Although the *Moynihan Report* was sponsored by President Lyndon Johnson and included contributions by such distinguished social scientists as James Wilson, Kenneth Clark, Erik Erikson, Robert Coles, and Talcott Parsons, there were some who challenged the findings as being prejudicial and contributing to a negative view of the African American family (Rainwater and Yancey, 1967).

In October 1965, Reverend Martin Luther King, Jr. endorsed the *Moynihan Report*'s disturbing findings. However, he expressed concern that the report might be misinterpreted. He observed (1968: 109), "As public awareness of the predicament of the Negro family increases, there will be danger and opportunity. The opportunity will be to deal fully rather than haphazardly with the problem as a whole—to see it as a social catastrophe . . . . brought on by long years of brutality and oppression—and to meet it as other disasters are met, with an adequacy of resources. The danger will be that the problem will be attributed to innate Negro weaknesses and used to justify further neglect and to rationalize continued oppression."

Declining Job Opportunities for Black Males

William Julius Wilson (1987) and others suggest that the decline in two-parent African American families was primarily due to the steady erosion of economic opportunities open to young African American and Hispanic men and women (Hacker, 1992; Blank, 1997). Butler (1992: 12) observes:

> The structure of the urban economy has shifted from manufacturing to service industries, and this has particularly hurt low-skilled workers. Cities have lost thousands of manufacturing and blue-collar service jobs over the last several decades, while gaining jobs in white-collar service occupations (e.g., information processing), which generally require higher education. The proportion of young men who work in manufacturing dropped by one-quarter between 1974 and 1984 and dropped by almost one-half for young men who had not graduated from high school as companies curtailed their hiring and laid off workers with the least seniority. This change has had a particularly devastating effect on the earnings of young men with low education because blue-collar work in manufacturing industries pays considerably better than most other jobs available to low-skilled workers.

In an earlier generation the breakthroughs and advances in agriculture revolutionized farming and vastly reduced the number of employees needed in the agricultural sector. Likewise, in recent decades the global economy and offshore assembly has systematically reduced the demand for unskilled and semiskilled manufacturing employment. As a result, individuals and communities that have relied on these manufacturing jobs have experienced increased unemployment with little hope of new opportunities.

"The weight of existing evidence," writes Wilson, "suggests that the problem of male joblessness could be the single most important factor underlying the rise in unwed mothers among poor black women" (Wilson, 1987: 73). Wilson demonstrated that there had been a structural transformation of the urban inner-city communities, where uneducated black men were often unable to earn more than minimum wage. At this wage, even if they worked full-time the entire year, they would be unable to earn more than poverty-line income for a family of four. Further, many were unable to find full-time work. As a consequence, there occurred a decline in the pool of "marriageable" men (Wilson, 1987; Wilson and Neckerman, 1987). Young women, it was argued, found they could obtain more reliable support from public assistance.

A High School Education

Traditionally, the best assurance of earning an income that would support a family above poverty was a high school education (Furstenberg, Brooks-

Gunn, and Morgan, 1987). However, with the decline and departure of jobs in the manufacturing sector and growth of high technology and knowledge-based industries, even a high school education provided little assurance that a young black man would be able to earn an income above the poverty line.

Among the college educated, almost 90 percent of young white men and 75 percent of young black men have been able to earn an income above the poverty line for a family of four. Yet, attending college was an expensive proposition beyond the reach of many young black men from low-income families.[14]

During the last several decades the marriage rates for African Americans without a high school education have declined substantially. Since 1960 the percentage of African American men who were married has fallen steadily, even after taking account of employment status. In fact, the marriage rate for employed Black men is more than double that for the unemployed.

In recent years the sense of responsibility that comes with employment has been accompanied with an increase in the likelihood of marriage. Since a major concern has been the increasing proportion of children born to unmarried African American women, these data would suggest that strategies designed to improve their employment prospects would have a major influence on increasing the likelihood of marriage.

The responsibility that employment demands has proven a stabilizing affect on families. Women who are employed are more likely to be married and less likely to have children they cannot support. Fathers who are employed are more likely to assume their responsibility to their children and to their female partners.[15] Policies and programs intended to reduce the rise of children born out of wedlock or to reverse these trends will need to include efforts to decrease discrimination in employment for both young men and women.

---

[14] Public higher education represents a form of public investment in young people that averages more than $17,000 per student (Thurow, 1992). The benefit has gone mostly to children from higher-income families. Historically, the prevailing ideology suggested that access to higher education should be assured to all irrespective of income. Recently, however, substantial tuition increases at public higher education institutions have resulted in further restriction of access for children from low-income families. This trend restricts access, converting higher education into a regressive welfare program that accelerates the advantages of children from high-income families at the public expense of all families.

[15] See the *Fragile Families and Welfare Reform* studies (Garfinkel, McLanahan, Tienda, and Brooks-Gunn, 2001) published in *Children and Youth Services Review* 23, (4/5 and 6/7).

Two-Parent African American Families

Altering the situation for African American families is vital to any effort to change poverty trends among children in the United States. Today, less than 40 percent of African American children are living with two married parents (see figure 9.3). If substantial progress against child poverty is ever to be achieved, an essential first step must be to find ways of preventing young people, particularly young women, from starting families that are not economically self-supporting (Fagan, 1999: 9; Galtson, 1986; Hotz, McElroy, and Sanders, 1997; Sawhill, 2002; Wilson, 2002). To do this we must examine why so many young, unwed women have children to begin with. It is a contested issue on which people hold strongly opposing views (Furstenberg, 1991; Whitehead, 1994; Wilson, 2002).

Ellwood and Crane (1990: 81) report that "a long and potent literature in social psychology and sociology, strongly supported by various intervention programs, suggests that out-of-wedlock childbearing is lowest among women with the best 'options,' including good employment prospects." Unwed motherhood is a reflection of helplessness and despair. Duncan and Hoffman (1989) report that even though welfare has had little influence on birth rates, the economic "options" among African American teenagers are the crucial determinants.

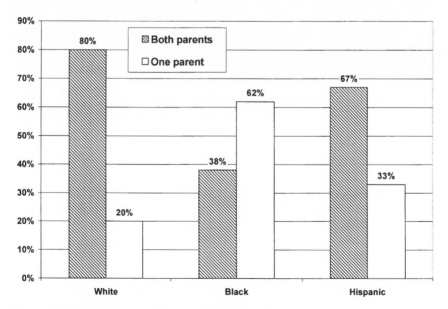

Figure 9.3 Family Composition by Race/Ethnicity
Source: U.S. Census Bureau (2001).

Golden (1992: 5) observes "girls who were persistently poor were 10 times as likely to bear a child before age 18 as girls who were never poor—34 percent of persistently poor young women, compared to 3.5 percent of those who were never poor." Mayer (1997) reports that 40 percent of teen girls in the bottom income quintile become teen mothers, while this happens to less than 5 percent of those in the top income quintile.

What is most important is that young women believe they have real opportunity that would be threatened by an out-of-wedlock birth. However, many poor young women have few realistic prospects of making it into the middle class and they know it. As Furstenberg (1991: 136) observes:

> Persistent inequality and growing isolation among the poor, blacks especially, set the terms for calculating the costs of an ill-timed birth. As I have said, relatively few teenagers set out to become pregnant when they do. However, I have also noted that while the timing of parenthood is inopportune, having a child confers certain immediate benefits for women whose future prospects are bleak. If this is true for a substantial number of those who enter parenthood prematurely, it suggests that many will not take extraordinary measures to prevent pregnancy from occurring. Given the difficulty of using contraception and the moral dilemmas of abortion, many women will drift into parenthood before they are ready.

Programs designed to promote contraception have produced relatively modest effects in reducing out-of-wedlock births (Kirby and Coyle, 1997a). The problem is that providing contraception is not enough. Young people have to believe they have opportunity to achieve a good life (Kirby and Coyle, 1997b). Without a sense of hope and opportunity young people will continue to drift in parenthood even when contraception is provided at no cost. Furstenberg (1991: 136) continues:

> I am not assuming, however, that any one couple makes these calculations when they have sex. It is probably more accurate to see these calculations as embedded in a social and cultural context that is familiar to the teens. In part, then, the task of policymakers involves not only widening opportunities for young adults in disadvantaged communities and the institutions which shape the views of children and youth: neighborhoods, schools, churches, volunteer organizations, and, of course, the family. Cultural redefinitions are likely to take root only when communities and local institutions are remoralized— when they come to see that there is more justice and opportunity for themselves and their children. The current pattern of disintegration of marriage and parenthood probably will not be reversed, if it can be reversed at all, without revising the reality of life at the bottom of American society.

The Assault on Welfare

Throughout the seventies and eighties as the welfare rolls grew and maintained historically high levels, conservative reaction to the program grew. It manifested initially as a broad-based inchoate public resentment toward those receiving something for nothing, while others worked. Nothing aggravated a conservative citizen more than seeing an able-bodied young woman, with one or more small children trailing after her, paying for groceries with food stamps. Gradually such public resentment was stoked, then taken up and trumpeted by political elements, who probably realized that criticism of welfare recipients would effectively distract middle- and lower-income voters—whose economic status was being undermined through historic tax cuts that shifted wealth to a few and placed an increasing economic burden on the bottom 90 percent income group (see chapter 8). What else could explain such a sustained, vitriolic campaign against an otherwise harmless group whose yearly needs amounted to less that one-tenth of 1 percent of the national budget? Indeed, the arguments against welfare became so pervasive and influential that during the 1992 presidential election, Bill Clinton, a liberal Democrat who was particularly adept at stealing conservative issues for his own ends, realized the advantage of campaigning on the promise to "end welfare as we know it."

Charles Murray

Charles Murray of the conservative American Enterprise Institute became one of the principal proponents of the view that while welfare was designed to alleviate child poverty, it had become, in fact, the primary cause of poverty. The result of providing income support through welfare had led, Murray (1984: 166) argued, to a dramatic increase in the percentage of single mothers and their children relying on welfare.

Child bearing had become a relative advantage for poor and low income women, Murray argued, in that by having a child the women became eligible to receive public assistance that would otherwise be unavailable. Thus, it was argued that many young women intentionally had children in order to receive welfare benefits (Gilder, 1981: 123; Hazlitt, 1973; Rector and Fagan, 2001). Conservative theorists were not alone in this view. Rather, they were tapping into a suspicion held by almost half of all Americans who believed that poor women had children in order to get welfare (Goodwin, 1972; Lewis and Schneider, 1985).[16] The view was held even among

---

[16] In April 1994 a CNN/Gallup poll found that 68 percent of respondents "say welfare recipients are taking advantage of the system" (Welch, 1994: 7A).

the poor who benefited from welfare (Ellwood, 1988: 22). Murray (1984: 204) argued that:

> It is impossible to examine the statistics on a topic such as single teenage mothers without admitting that we are witnessing a tragedy. If it had been inevitable, if there had been nothing we could have done to avoid it, then we could retain the same policies, trying to do more of the same and hoping for improvement. But once we must entertain the possibility that we are bringing it on ourselves, as I am arguing that both the logic and evidence compel us to do, then it is time to reconsider a social policy that salves our consciences ("Look how compassionate I am") at the expense of those whom we wished to help.

The problem of single parents and their children was the core problem Murray addressed. His views became central to the public discussion in the United States, Western Europe, and Canada, and were echoed by other conservative theorists including Robert Rector, Patrick Fagan, James Q. Wilson, Douglas Besharov, and others whose views contributed to the demand for welfare reform. Essentially, Murray argued that the consequence of the growth in single parent families was child poverty and social decay. Although public compassion for impoverished children had prompted the development of the welfare system to address child poverty, it was this very system that exacerbated and largely contributed to the severity of the problem. The more that help was provided through welfare, the worse the problem seemed to get. As a consequence, Murray concluded that we would do better doing nothing.

Because of the prominence achieved by his views and the role they played in shaping welfare reform, it is important to examine Murray's arguments in detail (Skopcol, 1997).

Murray's Views on Poverty and Welfare

Although Murray suggested that welfare and other antipoverty efforts had led to greater poverty, the fact was that the number of children living in households with income below the poverty line had *decreased* substantially during the years of the Kennedy and Johnson administrations when the first steps to expand welfare were taken (Blank, 1997; Schram and Wilken, 1989; Wilson, 1987). In 1959, more than two-thirds of children in African American families lived in households with income below the poverty line (see figure 9.7). Most of these poor African American children lived in two-parent families. During the next decade (1960 to 1970), which witnessed the War on Poverty, the number of African American children living in poverty was *reduced* by more than one-third (from 65 percent to 41 percent).

Table 9.4 Children Living in Poverty

	All Children	African American Children
1960	17,634,000	
1970	10,440,000	3,922,000
1980	11,543,000	3,906,000
1990	13,431,000	4,412,000

Source: U.S. Census Bureau (2001: Table A-2).

Thus, the sixties was a period of great progress in reducing child poverty. At no other time in history has there been so sharp a reduction in child poverty. By 1970, the reduction of poverty among children begun in the 1960s had ended. For the next several decades there was almost no reduction in child poverty (see table 9.4). The data on historical poverty rates, rather than supporting Murray's thesis regarding the effect of the War on Poverty, can be, in fact, interpreted as providing evidence contradicting it.[17] Welfare cushioned children, primarily affected by divorce, from economic despair.

Under conservative federal government administrations, which pursued more restrictive welfare policies, reliance on welfare actually increased slightly. Figure 9.10 displays the same data used by Murray but leads to a much different conclusion. The number of welfare recipients increased most dramatically after the election of President Nixon in 1968 and the end of the War on Poverty. It is a stretch to suggest that this growth in welfare recipients was a result of the War on Poverty, which was over, and the fact that a new administration with different priorities was in power. While the number of children in families receiving welfare payments did increase during the War on Poverty (by 30 percent), the largest rise in the number of children in families receiving welfare occurred during the first term of the Nixon Administration when the number of welfare recipients increased by almost 43 percent.[18] Later, during the Carter administration (1976–80), the number of children in welfare families declined more than 4 percent.

---

[17] Murray's view regarding the success of the War on Poverty is reflected by other conservatives (Kristol, 1971; Rector, 2002). In the famous words of former President Ronald Reagan, "We conducted on a war on poverty and poverty won."

[18] Murray (1984) chooses to place the War on Poverty in the period 1965 to 1970. Yet, the presidential administration responsible for the War on Poverty was defeated in 1968 by Nixon. The greatest increase in the number of AFDC recipients occurred between 1968 and 1972 (see figure 9.10). When the data are examined by federal leadership they fail to support the view that the War on Poverty was the cause of the increase in welfare recipients (see Lindsey, 1994: figure 10.2).

The Cause of Out-of-Wedlock Births: Was It Welfare?

Murray suggested that welfare encouraged out-of-wedlock births and that once mothers were eligible they continued to have additional children to get more benefits (Gilder, 1981; Hazlitt, 1973). He wrote (1984: 18), "Many of them had not even been married. Worst of all, they didn't stop having babies after the first lapse. They kept having more . . . The most flagrantly unrepentant seemed to be mostly black, too." Yet, historical data fail to support his thesis.

As seen in figure 9.10, there is little relation between the number of children born out of wedlock and the number of welfare recipients. The slow steady increase in out-of-wedlock births was not the explanation of the rapid increase of children receiving welfare, especially from 1960 to 1972 when the number of children on welfare spiked. During that period (1960 to 1972), 4.6 million children were added to the welfare caseload. During this twelve year period less than three-quarters of a million children were born out of wedlock.

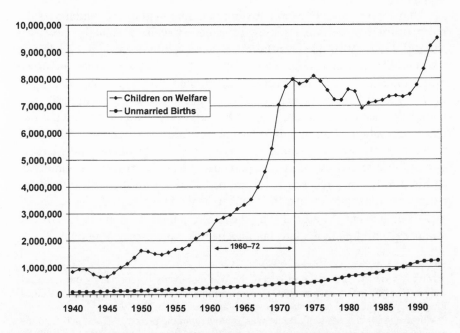

Figure 9.10 Children Born Out of Wedlock and on Welfare, 1940–93
Source: National Center for Health Statistics (1999).

If all these children born out of wedlock were added to the welfare caseload, which of course they were not, they would have accounted for less than 17 percent of the increase in this period.[19]

This variance can be seen even more clearly in figure 9.11 which compares the annual increase in out-of-wedlock births to the increase of children on welfare. As is apparent from figure 9.11, there was no consistent relationship between the changes in the number of children on welfare and the number of children born out of wedlock.

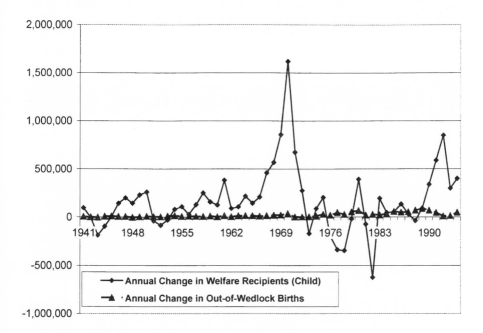

Figure 9.11 The Annual Increase in Welfare Recipients and Out-of-Wedlock Births, 1941–1994

Source: National Center for Health Statistics (1999); Administration for Children and Families (2002).

---

[19] This number is calculated by summing the increase of children born out of wedlock since 1960 using 1960 as the base rate. Thus, the sum of all children born out of wedlock above the base rate in 1960 would account for 16 percent of the *increase* in children added to welfare during the twelve year period from 1960 to 1972 (again using 1960 as the base rate for children on welfare).

From 1980, the average size of the welfare family actually decreased (Butler, 1992; DeParle, 1992).[20] Further, little evidence exists that women had children simply to gain welfare benefits (Ellwood and Bane, 1985; Ellwood, 1988: 58-62). Edelman (1987: 64) pointed out that teenage "pregnancy rates are higher in states with the lowest welfare benefits and lowest in the states with the higher welfare benefits."

The major increase in the welfare caseload occurred during the same decade when divorces more than doubled. In fact, the two increases coincided, indicating that the increase in the welfare caseload was primarily the result of stresses on the family resulting from changing roles for women deriving from the "revolution in reproductive technologies" along with increased labor force participation. The changing roles of women in the family put stress on the traditional family. Who would prepare the dinner, wash the dishes and the clothes, care for the children and the number of household chores now that mother was working outside the home? Paradoxically, it was the increased labor force participation of women which, at least in part, led to stress on families that often resulted in divorce and, thus, the increased welfare caseloads.

The Conservative Explanation for the Dissolution of the African American Two-Parent Family

The declining number of African American children born to married mothers meant that the children born to unmarried mothers made up an ever increasing proportion of all African American children. Murray (1994) suggested that the relationship between out-of-wedlock births and welfare could be properly understood as follows:

> Black behavior toward both marriage and out-of-wedlock childbearing during the period in which welfare benefits rose so swiftly behaved exactly as one would predict if one expected welfare to discourage women from getting married and induced single women to have babies.

If, as Murray implies, welfare was the lure that prompted the rise in out-of-wedlock births, we would expect to see a concomitant rise in the numbers

---

[20] Butler (1992: 14) reports that between 1968 and 1987 the average AFDC payment per family declined from $676 to $470 per month (in 1988 dollars). There is limited evidence that declining AFDC payments reduced program participation. It is clear, however, that the children, who are the majority of recipients, experienced the pain of the reductions. As Jencks (1993: 266) observed, "An unskilled single mother cannot expect to support herself and her children in today's labor market *either* by working *or* by collecting welfare" (italics in original).

of African American families enrolling in welfare. However, during this period, the percentage of African American children on the welfare caseload actually declined, from 34 percent in 1970 to 30 percent in 1988—even though the percentage of children born out of wedlock increased. The failure to build two-parent families did not lead to a concomitant rise in welfare recipients (see also Darity and Myers, 1983; Levy, 1987; Schram, Turbett, and Wilken, 1988; Schram and Wilken, 1989). From 1972 to 1992 the number of African American children living in single parent families increased from 3 million to 5 million. Yet, the number of African American children on welfare remained about the same during this period. In fact, during this period the number of African American women entering the labor force increased, from 56.3 percent to 61.2 percent (Ellwood and Crane, 1990). Thus, even as the number of two-parent African American families was declining, more African American women were entering the labor force and fewer were enrolling on welfare (see table 9.5).

Welfare Benefits and the Rise in Single Parent Families

Murray contended that the improvement in Food Stamps and welfare benefits also had a negative impact on work incentives and family formation for African American families. Although the benefits of these two programs increased between 1960 and 1970, since that period more than three decades ago, the real value of the combined benefits has declined (see table 9.5).

Table 9.5 AFDC Benefits and the Changing Family Situation for African American Children, 1960–1990

	Value of AFDC and Food Stamps for a Family of Four	Percent of African American Children Not Living with Two Parents	Percent of African American Children in AFDC Families
1960	$7,324	33.0%	10.4%
1970	9,900	41.5	33.6
1980	8,325	57.8	34.9
1990	7,741	61.4	30.1

Source: Elwood and Crane (1990)

268

Ending Child Poverty

While the average welfare benefit declined, the percentage of African American children in single parent families increased. Ellwood (1988: 60) observed:

> If AFDC was allowing women to become single parents, the number of recipients would have grown along with the number of single parents. But the number did not increase; it fell. The pattern holds for black children as well as white children. The number of black children in female-headed families grew by over 25 percent between 1972 and 1984 while the number on AFDC fell by 15 percent.

In short, although the percentage of children in single parent families increased, the percentage of these children receiving welfare decreased. Welfare could hardly be viewed as being the cause of an increase in welfare use when its use actually declined.

The number of children receiving welfare benefits reached 8 million in 1971 and remained at about that level for the next two decades. It was not beneficial in the long term to reform welfare solely by adjusting benefit amounts, because *it insulated* poor mothers and their children from the requirements of self-supporting labor force participation. The concern of welfare reform advocates from both the left and the right was that poor mothers may have learned to *depend* on welfare benefits, a situation that led to the view that long-term reliance on welfare was acceptable in a free market economy, even though such acceptance ran counter to deep-seated values toward parental responsibility and work.[21] What was needed during the War on Poverty was reform that embraced strategies designed to integrate and involve poor mothers and their children into *self-sufficient roles* and participation in the market economy. The antipoverty efforts of the sixties focused on income transfer programs to the poor but failed to promote greater self-sufficiency by addressing problems of structural unemployment and declining opportunities (Danziger and Weinberg, 1986). The major welfare reform efforts of the period were not successful (Weaver and Armacost, 2000). In 1969, the Nixon administration proposed a Family Assistance Plan that would have provided a guaranteed family income for the poor. The plan also included support for job training. In 1977, the Carter administration proposed a similar program, called Better Jobs and Income. Neither program was brought to a vote. Instead, welfare was primarily limited to the means-tested cash assistance program—Aid to Families with Dependent Children—enacted in 1935.

---

[21] Piven and Cloward (1970) argued that welfare recipients were essentially outside the modern industrial economy and not needed. The poor were no longer necessarily exploited by the economic structure but were outside and provided for because to do otherwise would lead to social disruption and disorder.

Simply providing cash assistance has often been the least costly approach to child poverty. Proven cost-effective job creation or welfare-to-work strategies had yet to be developed, even though considerable effort and research has been extended in this area. But there was a third approach; and it was this third approach which was followed by most other modern industrial democracies (Gilbert, 2002; Gilbert and Gilbert, 1991).

Strategies for Welfare Reform

Murray's Radical Proposal: Shut Down the Welfare Program

The primary motive supporting public welfare for poor mothers and their children, as Murray (1984) argued, was not any empirical evidence of its effectiveness in reducing dependence on pubic assistance and encouraging self-reliance but rather a notion of charity and compassion (Titmuss, 1968). It was, according to Murray (1984: 236), this charitable impulse that prevented the necessary bitter medicine of terminating welfare assistance: "A solution that would have us pay less and acknowledge that some would go unhelped is unacceptable. To this extent, the barrier to radical reform of social policy is not the pain it would cause the intended beneficiaries of the present system, but the pain it would cause the donors."

To Murray, continuing to provide assistance to single mothers simply compounded the problem, and he recommended (1993: A24) "the AFDC payment should go to zero. Single mothers are not eligible for subsidized housing or for food stamps. From society's perspective, to have a baby that you cannot care for yourself is profoundly irresponsible, and the government will no longer subsidize it." He urged that "the state stop interfering with the natural forces that have done the job quite effectively for millennia." Murray proposed that the naive program of charity—that is, welfare—be revoked in order to restore economic hardship: "Restoring economic penalties translates into the first and central policy prescription: to end all economic support for single mothers."

Murray advised that if a single parent was unable to adequately care for her child when welfare was revoked, the child should be removed and placed in an orphanage. He observed (1993: A24) that "there are laws already on the books about the right of the state to take a child from a neglectful parent. We have some 360,000 children in foster care because of them." We may, he says, need to consider building orphanages for the many children that will be removed from mothers who are unable to properly care for them—not the cold stark orphanages of the past, but new modern facilities that would provide first-rate care.[22]

Murray's prescription of allowing severe economic penalties to befall those unable to provide for themselves in the current economy might provide the "stick" required to discourage out-of-wedlock births. However, it was a solution that compassionate and civilized society was, for a long time, unwilling to consider. Were we to assume that the "natural forces" Murray suggested would take care of the problem included the same as those described by the late British economist Thomas Malthus, who argued that mass death from war, pestilence, and starvation were nature's way of controlling population growth? In a sense, Murray's approach represented a modern-day version of the Malthusian approach with a twist which said that trying to solve the problem merely aggravated it.[23] He argued that while sympathy and compassion motivated helping, they prevented the necessary reform of ending relief. However, the suffering, hunger, fear, stress, and despair that mothers and children on welfare would experience upon the termination of welfare calls forth deep roots of compassion—both secular and nonsecular—which have been central to the definition of a civilized society.

Murray's solution was attractive to many because it suggested that the problem of poverty could be solved at little or no public expense by simply pulling the plug, as it were, on the economic life support system that sustained most of the mothers and children living in poverty. This action would, Murray argued, be so personally devastating to those affected that it would end the behavior which caused the problem—children born out of wedlock. But such a "tough love" approach might drive people to even more extreme and desperate measures in their scramble for survival. Anderson (1994: F1) observed, "The nihilism that you now see among inner-city people would only increase and spread further beyond the bounds of ghetto communities. Cities would become almost unlivable. African Americans would continue to be the primary victims, though; illegitimacy rates would rise, not diminish."

---

[22] This is a violation of the fundamental principle of child welfare that the best place to raise a child is with his or her family (Pelton, 1989). Children growing up in foster care or orphanages miss the essential ingredients of love and attachment which are the foundation of healthy child development.

[23] Murray (1984: 218) writes, "My conclusion is that social programs in a democratic society tend to produce net harm in dealing with the most difficult problems. They will inherently tend to have enough of an inducement to produce bad behavior and not enough of a solution to stimulate good behavior; and the more difficult the problem, the more likely it is that this relationship will prevail."

Table 9.6 Population Growth Rate and GDP

	Population Growth Rate (%)	GDP per Capita
Japan	1.1	39,640
United States	1.0	26,980
West Germany	0.0	27,510
France	0.4	17,829
Argentina	1.4	2,160
Pakistan	3.2	370
Kenya	3.9	360
India	2.2	340

In a sense, a variant of Murray's recommendation for ending welfare had already been tried. The highest birth rates are found in the poorest countries (see table 9.6). Moreover, in a number of the southern states low welfare payment levels have been in effect for decades (Ellwood and Crane, 1990) (see table 9.7). The approach has not led to lower rates of children born out of wedlock in these states. Nor has it led to reduced poverty, especially among children. The opposite has, in fact, been the case. The most severe poverty is found in those states which came closest to meeting the reforms urged by Murray.

Table 9.7 Average Monthly TANF Amount for a Single Mother and Two Children, 2002

Low-Paying States	TANF Amount	High-Paying States	TANF Amount
Mississippi	$140	Massachusetts	$518
Alabama	142	California	491
Wyoming	142	Washington	468
West Virginia	142	New York	457
South Carolina	155	Wisconsin	447
Texas	162	Iowa	350
Tennessee	180	Ohio	320
Louisiana	180	Kansas	304
Oklahoma	219	Florida	250
Illinois	233	Georgia	239

Source: www.childwelfare.com (state Welfare Report Cards, slide 8).

Cash Assistance Is Not Enough

> A mother was offered a combined welfare package worth about $15,000 per
> year (in today's dollars). In order to "earn" this welfare paycheck, the mother
> had to fulfill two conditions: She could not work, and she could not marry an
> employed man. It is difficult to imagine a more destructive system.
>
>   Robert Rector, *Implementing Welfare Reform and Restoring Marriage*

Social theorists consistently point out the limitations of a welfare system
that provides only cash assistance to the impoverished while ignoring the
broader context of available opportunities and possibilities. As Franklin
Roosevelt emphasized during development of welfare and the New Deal
work relief programs seventy years ago, providing the poor with cash assistance alone can be a "dangerous narcotic" (Garfinkel, 1992: 21). It is not
sufficient for welfare to provide only a safety net of minimal or subsistence
income. Efforts must be made to allow young mothers to assume productive and self-reliant roles in a free enterprise economy—even though such
efforts are expensive. Without such efforts welfare too often only sustains
those in poverty and does not allow them to exit their plight.

Essentially Murray's view failed to take into account how the economic policies of the 1970s and 1980s shifted wealth upward while further
disconnecting those at the bottom (Gramlich and Long, 1996; Krugman,
2001; Shapiro, Greenstein, and Primus, 2000). Virtually no social policies
or programs of significance, with the exception of the Earned Income Tax
Credit (EITC), were developed in the last two decades to bring those living
in poverty into the economic mainstream (Epstein, 2002; Haveman, 1988;
Lemov, 1989; Weaver and Armacost, 2000). Rather, imaginative economic
and social policies were directed toward improving the situation of asset
holders possessing substantial wealth, with the view that their success
would seep down to those below (Gilder, 1981, 1984; Phillips, 2002).

Murray's Approach: Science or Ideology?

When examining social policy it is important to take note of views that
lack empirical support but that influence understanding of the issues and
that are sustained primarily by powerful political interest groups. The interest of social science is to examine theoretical problems with objective
research methods in order to empirically test their validity (Cournand and
Meyer, 1976). What is the theory which guides Murray's research? In *Losing Ground* and later in *The Bell Curve*, which Murray authored with
Herrnstein, the argument is made that the poor are characterized by limited
intellectual capacity and that social programs which aim to alter this fact

are doomed to failure. There is no fundamental theory which provides a comprehensive understanding and connects essential concepts together. However, there is the hypothesis that the welfare program aggravated the problem of child poverty and only made it worse. Murray did not take an objective approach to testing the validity of this hypothesis. Rather, he and other partisan analysts too often systematically collected data which supported their hypothesis and argued passionately for its correctness.

Missing from Murray's analysis was a discussion of the limitation of his hypothesis. Why is it, for instance, that Murray failed to discuss the higher poverty rates for African American and Hispanic children? A decade following his influential study on the problems of welfare—*Losing Ground*—Murray undertook a new approach to explain the circumstances of the poor, especially African Americans.[24] In *The Bell Curve*, Murray argued that there was a substantial genetic explanation for the limited success and poverty of children of color—they simply are born with limited genetic abilities that no amount of social programs will be able to overcome. Although his view has been widely discredited by scholars and scientists, it still influences public understanding (Fraser, 1995; Gould, 1994).

In 2000, almost a third of African American and Hispanic children live in poverty, compared to less than 10 percent for white children. What explanation does Murray's view offer to explain this? The *Bell Curve* suggests it is an inevitable consequence of genetic inheritance. Yet the book contains little credible scientific research to support this view. However, the decline in child poverty did not result from those factors identified in the *Bell Curve*. From 1950 to 1970 child poverty among African American children declined because of broad economic improvement. Since 1970 the poverty rate for African American children stopped declining.[25]

Welfare Is At Last Reformed

Even though the arguments against welfare made by Murray, Rector, and other conservative critics did not necessarily conform to the facts, their views eventually forced, in 1996, the legislative reformation of welfare.

In his campaign for the presidency Bill Clinton proposed "ending welfare as we know it." When the Republicans took control of the Congress in 1994 they also urged changing welfare. Not as generous with services to

---

[24] Skocpol (1997) points out that "Charles Murray's factually sloppy 1984 manifesto, *Losing Ground*, became the veritable bible of the Reaganite assault on welfare."

[25] In the former Soviet Union vast numbers of Caucasians with high intelligence live in poverty. Their poverty is more the result of failed social and economic institutions than genetic characteristics.

the single mother as the reforms Clinton argued for, the Republicans sought to end the program which they argued was leading to a large dependent class and increasing numbers of children being born out of wedlock. The combined disaffection of many Democrats with the welfare program and the forceful leadership of Newt Gingrich in the Republican Congress all but assured that fundamental welfare reform would take place.

The debate was contentious and reflected deep-rooted political views (Asen, 2002). Liberals and child advocates asserted that the proposed reform would lead to undesirable dramatic changes for those on welfare, especially children. Supporters of reform suggested that welfare had been most harmful to those it was intended to serve and had, in fact, consigned them to a dependent class.

Excerpts from the Congressional Welfare Debate

Speaking on the House floor in front of a large sign that, "Don't feed the alligators," Congressman John Mica of Florida pointed out that signs such as this were posted around game preserves to warn people that giving food to the alligators, rather than being an act of kindness, would make the alligators dependent on handouts, and thus they would no longer hunt for food. Mica argued that "unnatural feeding and artificial care creates dependency. When dependency sets in, these otherwise able-bodied alligators can no longer survive on their own." Acknowledging that humans were not alligators, Mica argued that the present welfare system "upset the natural order."

Building on Congressman Mica's example, Congresswoman Barbara Cubin of Wyoming used the example of reintroducing wolves back into national parks. Hoping to prepare wolves to live in their natural habitat, park rangers placed them in cages where they were fed elk and venison. But when the wolves were released they did not want to leave their cages. Cubin called this program the "wolf welfare program." She pointed out that the federal government "provided everything that the wolves needed for their existence . . . Just like any animal in the species, any mammal, when you take away their freedom and their dignity and their ability, they cannot provide for themselves."

The examples given by Mica and Cubin angered others who pointed out that the debate was about a program meant to feed poor children, not alligators and wolves. Congressman Sam Gibbons asserted, "Mr. Chairman, in my 34 years here I thought I had heard it all, but we have a millionaire from Florida comparing children to alligators and we have a gentlewoman in red over here comparing children to wolves. That tops it all."

The contentious debate continued outside Congress. In an open letter to President Clinton, Marian Wright Edelman (1995), president of the Children's Defense Fund, cautioned: "It would be a great moral and practical wrong for you to sign any welfare 'reform' bill that will push millions of already poor children and families deeper into poverty . . . Longer-term and perhaps irreparable damage will be inflicted on children if you permit to be destroyed the fundamental moral principle that an American child, regardless of the state or parents the child chanced to draw, is entitled to protection of last resort by his or her national government." She continued: "[The proposed welfare reform] is the domestic equivalent of bombing Vietnamese villages in order to save them. It is moral hypocrisy for our nation to slash income, health and nutrition assistance for poor children while leaving untouched hundreds of billions in corporate welfare, giving new tax breaks of over $200 billion for non-needy citizens."

In an editorial the *Washington Post* (1995) stated: "Now here is the part you need to know: *Mr. Clinton's own advisors have told him that it would likely consign as many as a million more children to poverty, and it would provide several billions less for child care than his own proposal of a year ago*" (italics in original).

Senator Daniel Moynihan (1995) warned, "If in 10 years time we find children sleeping on grates, picked up in the morning frozen, and ask, Why are they here scavenging, awful to themselves, awful to one another . . . it will have begun on the House floor this spring and the Senate chamber this autumn." He went on to describe the welfare reform bill as "the most brutal act of social policy since reconstruction" and predicted "those involved will take this disgrace to their graves."[26]

President Clinton vetoed the first version of welfare reform passed in the Republican-controlled House complaining that it did not provide sufficient services to those on welfare who were trying to find work. The second version, however, passed the Congress against major opposition within his own party and among his own staff. Nevertheless, the president was determined to "end welfare as we know it," and he signed the welfare reform legislation into law in August 1996.[27]

No legislation since the original welfare bill contained in the Social Security Act of 1936 had more impact on poor children. As pointed out by Marian Edelman, all children in the United States had been entitled to live in a household with sufficient income. In other words, welfare had been viewed as an economic safety net for all children and was guaranteed to them by right of citizenship—it was an entitlement. The welfare reform

---

[26] Cited in Ariana Huffington, "Where Liberals Fear to Tread," August 26, 1996.

[27] The House of Representatives passed the welfare reform bill (H.R. 3734) by a vote of 328 to 101 on July 31, 1996. The Senate passed H.R. 3734 by vote of 78 to 21 on August 1.

legislation ended the entitlement status of welfare. Now, children were no longer guaranteed a national standard of income protection. Instead, block grants were granted to the states, outlining certain mandates and parameters but, by and large, allowing the states to develop their own welfare programs to administer as they saw fit.

Conclusion

The landmark Social Security Act of 1936 was built on the premise that government had a responsibility to provide income protection for society's most vulnerable. The Social Security Act provided a federal income support program for the elderly, the blind and disabled, and lone mothers and their children. The Social Security Act represented a new social contract between the federal government and its citizens. It established the government as responsible for the economic well being of its citizens.

For seniors Social Security provided a program of social insurance that required citizens to pay into a government-administered retirement program. Although it took several decades before Social Security began to provide wide coverage to seniors, when it did begin to provide coverage it did so on a universal basis. Seniors who paid into Social Security felt entitled to the benefits they received because they had paid for them. The result of Social Security has been the end of poverty for most seniors.

In contrast to the social insurance program for seniors, the Social Security Act provided poor children and their mothers with a means-tested entitlement program called Aid to Dependent Children (ADC). ADC was a residual program designed to provide a minimal base of income support to the poorest children in the nation. As we have seen, in the last several decades the program was the target of increasing criticism as encouraging dependency and promoting out-of-wedlock births. The dissatisfaction led to fundamental reform in 1996. The passage of the Personal Responsibility and Work Opportunity Reconciliation Act (PRWORA) ended the historic social contract between the federal government and poor children.

With the end of welfare to protect children in poverty the question arises: Does the federal government have any responsibility to protect children living in poverty? Further, what efforts will we collectively take to protect the futures of poor children and to ensure that all children, but particularly poor children, have an opportunity to succeed in America and to take advantage of their potential?

This chapter ends with the end of welfare as we knew it. Welfare reform has presented a new set of hopes and expectations for poor children. Just what have been the results of welfare reform for poor children? We explore this in the next chapter.

10

The Fading Promise of Welfare Reform to End Child Poverty

In the almost seven years since the welfare reform law was enacted, economic conditions have improved dramatically for America's poorest families. Welfare rolls have plummeted, employment of single mothers has increased dramatically, and child hunger has declined substantially. Most striking, however, has been the effect of welfare reform on child poverty, particularly among black children.

> Melissa Pardue, "Sharp Reduction in Black Child Poverty
> Due to Welfare Reform"

[Welfare reform] will tell young mothers to be employed, away from their children for much of each week. These children, already fatherless, will now become primarily motherless. They will be raised by somebody else. A grandmother? A neighbor? An overworked day care manager? Or they will be left alone?

> James Q. Wilson, *The Marriage Problem*

With the passage of welfare reform legislation in 1996 the major program of income support for poor children changed fundamentally. Aid to Families with Dependent Children (AFDC) had been a federally administered entitlement program that assured every child, regardless of his or her parents, a minimal level of income protection since the passage of the Social Security Act, of which it was a part, in 1936. Welfare was intended to provide a safety net of income support for single mothers and their children. Welfare was, in a sense, the social contract that guaranteed economic security for poor children who were concentrated in single parent families.

The Personal Responsibility and Work Opportunity Reconciliation Act (PRWORA), which President Clinton signed into law in August 1996, required that women with dependent children work in order to receive benefits. To promote the search for and acceptance of work the legislation replaced AFDC with a program called Temporary Assistance to Needy Families (TANF) that was, as the name implies, temporary and time limited. The culture of the old welfare office was transformed to emphasize job search, job readiness, and job training. The full effort of the new "employment offices" was directed toward placing the mothers, who had been collecting welfare benefits while not working, into jobs (Blank, 1997; U.S. General Accounting Office, 2001).

The new TANF program was designed to push mothers into jobs and sanction mothers who did not find work. Mothers were advised that there were time limits on the receipt of welfare benefits and warned that after receiving welfare for two years they would need to be employed or in a job program to continue receiving benefits. Further, recipients were advised that they had a lifetime limit of five years—after which they would no longer receive welfare, no matter what. This was a new social contract with the poor mother but one that apparently represented the consensus of the nation. The public had come to the view that it was not acceptable for able bodied adults to receive income assistance without working. Thus, single mothers with dependent children, even preschool children and infants, were expected to find work and earn income.

The Consequences of Welfare Reform:
Substantial Reduction of the Welfare Caseload

It is now possible to assess the results of the 1996 welfare reform legislation. Without question, welfare reform resulted in a dramatic reduction in the number of welfare recipients (figure 10.1).

Figure 10.1 Welfare Recipients, 1936–2002

Source: Administration for Children and Families (2002).

The national picture displayed in figure 10.1 suggests a broad decline in the welfare caseload. But this is a misleading picture. The decline was uneven among the states, varying from 6 to 94 percent between 1996 to 2002 (see table 10.1).[1] Thus, it is misleading to use national welfare data. Welfare reform led to the states having primary authority and control over the welfare program. Each state developed its own version of welfare reform which led to substantial variation among the states. Consequently, to understand welfare reform requires examination of state-level data.

Table 10.1 Percentage Reduction in the Number of Children and Adults Receiving Welfare, 1996–2002

	Children Receiving Welfare	Total Recipients		Children Receiving Welfare	Total Recipients
Wyoming	-93.7%	-93.6%	Kentucky	-54.5%	-55.6%
Idaho	-89.9%	-89.6%	Maine	-54.1%	-53.4%
Florida	-77.0%	-78.0%	Texas	-53.2%	-51.6%
Illinois	-76.5%	-79.6%	Arkansas	-52.1%	-52.3%
Wisconsin	-76.1%	-73.4%	Alaska	-51.7%	-51.3%
Louisiana	-73.1%	-74.2%	New Mexico	-51.5%	-53.2%
Colorado	-69.0%	-68.0%	Utah	-51.2%	-50.5%
Mississippi	-68.3%	-68.7%	Montana	-50.5%	-47.3%
Oklahoma	-66.7%	-64.8%	Hawaii	-50.3%	-54.2%
N. Carolina	-66.2%	-67.2%	Washington	-47.7%	-49.8%
Maryland	-65.7%	-67.9%	Missouri	-47.5%	-48.8%
Ohio	-65.6%	-65.0%	Kansas	-47.0%	-47.7%
Connecticut	-65.2%	-67.2%	Vermont	-47.0%	-47.0%
Georgia	-64.0%	-63.6%	Delaware	-46.7%	-47.1%
New Jersey	-63.7%	-64.4%	Minnesota	-44.7%	-44.7%
New York	-62.8%	-65.2%	New Hampshire	-41.1%	-40.1%
Pennsylvania	-60.5%	-61.3%	Iowa	-39.9%	-40.1%
S. Carolina	-60.2%	-57.3%	Arizona	-38.8%	-45.0%
Michigan	-59.6%	-61.7%	Tennessee	-38.4%	-36.7%
Virginia	-59.2%	-58.5%	Dist. of Col.	-37.8%	-39.9%
South Dakota	-59.2%	-59.4%	North Dakota	-37.5%	-37.7%
Massachusetts	-56.5%	-54.4%	Nebraska	-35.2%	-35.5%
West Virginia	-56.5%	-56.2%	Rhode Island	-33.3%	-33.3%
Oregon	-55.8%	-52.9%	Nevada	-32.5%	-26.4%
Alabama	-55.6%	-59.4%	Indiana	-3.7%	-6.2%
California	-55.3%	-55.8%			

Source: Administration for Children and Families (2002)

---

[1] Several states that have been in the forefront of welfare reform, such as Wisconsin, Florida, and Illinois, have reduced their welfare caseloads by close to 75 percent from 1996 to 2002. However, these states had embarked on welfare reform earlier using waivers and thus achieved even greater caseload reductions than indicated in table 10.1.

During the early debate, proponents of reform, including then President Clinton, suggested that welfare reform would lead to as many as 1 million fewer recipients by the year 2000. In fact, the targets have been far exceeded—more than 7 million taken off the rolls. In most states the number of welfare recipients has been reduced by at least half (Lindsey and Martin, 2003). Several states have seen reductions of greater than three-quarters.

It is difficult to summarize the results in all fifty states because of considerable variation. In presenting the decline in welfare caseloads I ranked the states according to their reduction of welfare rolls from 1993 to December 2001 (which I have treated as 2002) and then selected among them with respect to the size of caseload reduction—the top five, the middle five, and the bottom five. I then graphed the changes. Figures 10.2 and 10.3 depict the small to medium-size states and the large states respectively.

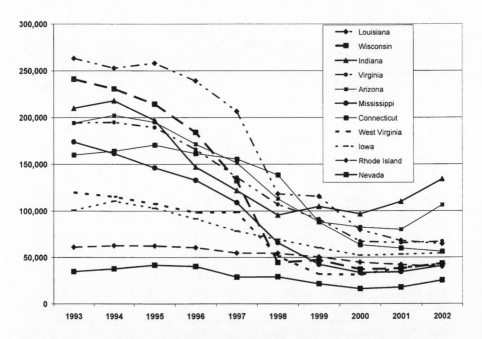

Figure 10.2 Changes in Welfare Recipients in Small and Medium-Size States
Source: Administration for Children and Families (2002).

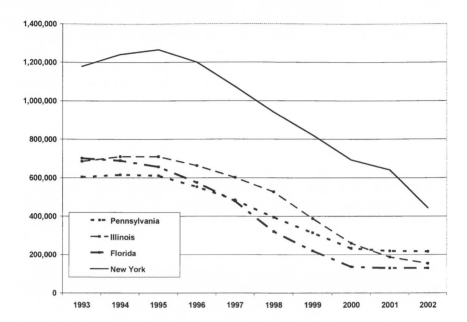

Figure 10.3 Changes in Welfare Recipients in Large States

Source: Administration for Children and Families (2002).

What is apparent from these figures is that the dramatic reduction in the welfare caseload was concentrated in the period immediately following the passage of welfare reform. The consequence of welfare reform legislation has been the rapid removal of single mothers and their children from the welfare caseload. Instead of terming the welfare legislation as "reform," it might more accurately have been termed the selective ending of income protection for poor children.

As seen in figure 10.2, the number of welfare recipients has declined precipitously.[2] In Louisiana, the number of recipients declined from more than 260,000 in 1993 to fewer than 64,000 in 2002. In Wisconsin, the number of welfare recipients declined from more than 240,000 in 1993 to

---

[2] Wyoming and Idaho would be included among the top five states in terms of the percentage decline in their welfare caseload (Lindsey and Martin, 2003). However, they were not included here since they were such small states. The welfare caseload in Wyoming declined from 18,271 in 1993 to 13,531 in 1996 and 856 in 2002. In Idaho the welfare caseload declined from 23,547 in 1996 to 2,360 in 2002. Discussing welfare reform, Sen. Daniel Patrick Moynihan argued, "This is not reform. This is repeal of Aid to Families with Dependent Children." For these two small states Moynihan's words seem prophetic. See PBS Online, *Reforming Welfare*, December 26, 1995.

about 44,000 in 2002. In a few states, like Indiana and Nevada, the decline was negligible.

Figure 10.3 shows the decline of welfare recipients in the large states. In Florida, the number of recipients declined from more than 700,000 in 1993 to about 130,000 in 2002. In Illinois, the number has declined from more than 680,000 in 1993 to about 155,000 in 2002.

Welfare Reform Hailed as Success

Rector and Fagan (2001: 1) report, "Overall poverty, child poverty and black child poverty have all dropped substantially. . . . there are 4.2 million fewer people living in poverty today than there were in 1996, according to the most common Census Bureau figures. Some 2.3 million fewer children live in poverty today than in 1996."

Rector and Fagan (2001) continue, "Decreases in poverty have been greatest among black children. In fact, today the poverty rate for black children is at the lowest point in U.S. history. There are 1.1 million fewer black children in poverty today than there were in the mid-1990s. Hunger among children has been almost cut in half. According to the U.S. Department of Agriculture, there are nearly 2 million fewer hungry children today than at the time welfare reform was enacted. Welfare caseloads have been cut nearly in half and employment of the most disadvantaged single mothers has increased from 50 percent to 100 percent" (p. 1).

Jay Hein (2001) of the Hudson Institute exults, "Indeed, the success of TANF has exceeded even the brightest of reform's optimists. All the important social indicators are pointing in the right direction: welfare rolls are down; employment is up; teen pregnancy is down; and wages are up. And while overall welfare spending is down, the spending per hard-to-serve family is up."

The Evidence of Change

In 1996, there were 8,671,000 children receiving welfare. By 2002 the number of children receiving welfare had been reduced to 3,916,000.[3] Did these children exit welfare because the situation of their mothers had im-

---

[3] The 2001 fiscal year welfare caseload for all recipients was 5,471,863, of which 4,054,672 were children. I multiplied the ratio of children to all recipients in 2001 (.741) by the average of all recipients in 2002 (5,284,711) to estimate the number of children in 2002 (U.S. Department of Health and Human Services, 2002). See www.acf.dhhs.gov/programs/opre/ar2001/chapter02.xls.

proved to the point where they no longer required income assistance? It is instructive to examine the indicators of success cited by those who have proclaimed the achievements of welfare reform.

Besides the reduced number of poor children receiving welfare, probably the most cited indicator of success of reform is the decline in child poverty (Pardue, 2003). According to the Census Bureau child poverty has declined since the enactment of welfare reform in 1996 (figure 10.4). The Census Bureau (2001) reported that in 1996 the overall child poverty rate in the United States was 20.5 percent which declined to 15.9 percent by the year 2000. Specifically, as shown in figure 10.4, child poverty rates for African American children began declining in 1993 and continued to decline after the passage of welfare reform in 1996.

Child poverty for Hispanic children also began a decline in 1996 which continued through 2000 (Census Bureau, 2001). As cited by Rector and Fagan (2001), the child poverty rate for African American children is at a historic low. Is this historic reduction in child poverty largely the result of welfare reform, as Rector and Fagan assert? If so, we would expect to see the greatest declines in child poverty in the states with the largest reductions in welfare caseloads. The most instructive data is the state variations that take into account the differential impact of welfare reform.

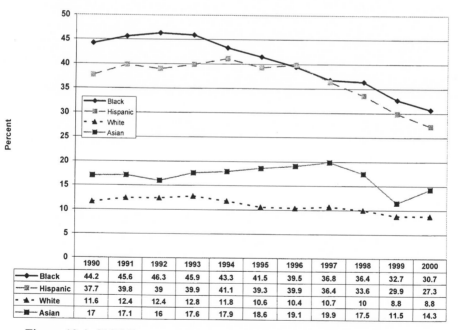

	1990	1991	1992	1993	1994	1995	1996	1997	1998	1999	2000
Black	44.2	45.6	46.3	45.9	43.3	41.5	39.5	36.8	36.4	32.7	30.7
Hispanic	37.7	39.8	39	39.9	41.1	39.3	39.9	36.4	33.6	29.9	27.3
White	11.6	12.4	12.4	12.8	11.8	10.6	10.4	10.7	10	8.8	8.8
Asian	17	17.1	16	17.6	17.9	18.6	19.1	19.9	17.5	11.5	14.3

Figure 10.4 Child Poverty Rates in the United States, 1990 to 2000
Source: U.S. Census Bureau (2002).

Figure 10.5 displays the changes in child poverty in the five states with the greatest reductions in their welfare caseloads. Two of the states with the greatest decreases in child poverty are Mississippi and Louisiana, which have a large percentage of Black children living in poverty.

Although the poverty rate initially declined for these two states, in recent years it appears to have turned up again, even though the number of welfare recipients has continued to decline. For Florida and Wisconsin, the two states with the greatest reductions in welfare caseloads, the poverty rate has fluctuated and headed down.

If children were being removed from the welfare caseload because of declining poverty we would expect that the number of children removed from poverty in each state would correspond to the decline in the number of children removed from welfare. Figure 10.6 displays the percentage of children removed from poverty (Census estimates) and the welfare caseload from 1996 to 2001. In states with the greatest reduction in the percentage of children receiving welfare there is a decrease in child poverty, but it does not correspond with the decline that would have been expected based on the decline in child poverty rates. Between two-thirds and four-fifths of the children removed from the welfare caseload are estimated to remain in poverty.

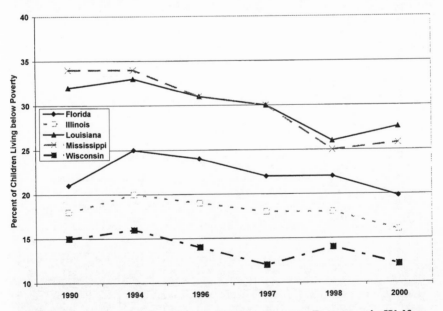

Figure 10.5 Child Poverty in States with the Greatest Decreases in Welfare Recipients

Source: Census Bureau (2001).

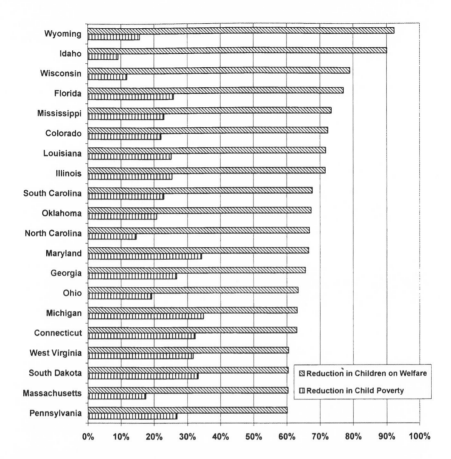

Figure 10.6 The Number of Children Removed from Welfare Compared to the Number of Children Removed from Poverty, from 1996 to 2001

Source: U.S. Census Bureau (2001).

Wyoming and Idaho reduced the number of children on welfare by more than 90 percent. Yet, the child poverty rate in these two states was reduced by less than 15 percent. These are small western states that might be considered exceptional. Examining child poverty in 2001 Edelman (2002) reports "Mississippi had the worst showing (with 27 percent of its children in poverty), followed by Louisiana (26.6 percent)."

In Florida more than 75 percent of children were removed from welfare even though less than 25 percent were removed from poverty. Wisconsin removed many children who remain living in poverty. Mississippi and Louisiana were among the top states in terms of reducing the percentage of children receiving welfare. Yet both these states are also among the top fifty states in terms of child poverty.

A Spearman rank order correlation between the reduction of children receiving welfare and the reduction in child poverty in the fifty states between 1996 and 2001 resulted in a rank order correlation of .03, which was not statistically significant, which means that for the fifty states there is no measurable relation between reductions in child poverty and reductions in welfare caseloads. In short, any reduction in child poverty is independent, and thus not likely the result, of reductions in welfare caseloads.

Foster Care and Reduction in the Welfare Caseload

As we observed in chapter six, there has been a long term relation between poverty and foster care. One would expect that with the decline in poverty (and welfare) that there would be a decline in the number of children removed from their mothers and placed in foster care. Historically welfare has been viewed as a "family preservation" strategy. Providing single mothers with supplemental income (welfare) prevented the removal of children from their custody and placement in foster care. In Florida, after moving hundreds of thousands of children off of the welfare caseload there was a rapid rise in the number of children in foster care (see figure 10.7).

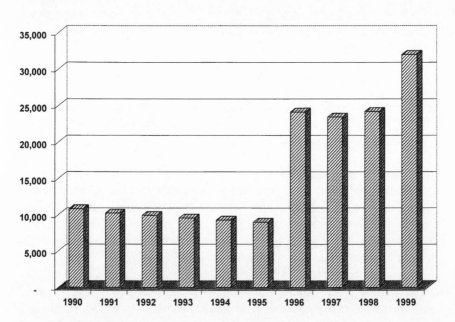

Figure 10.7 Children in Foster Care in Florida
Source: Green Book (2000).
Online at: www.childwelfare.com/kids/States/Profiles/Florida/FosterCareRC/0foster.htm.

Instead of a decline in the foster care caseload, which might be expected to accompany a decline in the welfare caseload, Florida experienced an unprecedented increase in the number of children removed from their families and placed in foster care (see figure 10.7). Kids Count of Florida (2002) reported that "child poverty rates reflect a sad reality for young parents who, despite working full-time, may not earn enough to provide basic health, housing and care for their children. While Florida ranks 36th in child poverty, we rank 20th in overall state per capita income. More than one-of-five Florida children—over 730,000—live in poverty households. There's no greater gap in America between the wealth of a state and the poverty of its children." Botsko, Snyder, and Leos-Urbel (2001: 17) of the Urban Institute reported that, "Many families receiving services from child welfare agencies also receive welfare assistance. These dual-system families may face competing demands. They must meet the new requirements imposed on welfare recipients in order to receive assistance, and at the same time they must meet case plan goals developed by child welfare agencies in order to keep their children or have their children returned to them. Despite the overlap in populations, historically there has been little formal collaboration between child welfare and welfare agencies in Florida."[4]

Wisconsin also experienced a sharp increase in the number of children placed in foster care. In Milwaukee, the state's largest urban center, foster care rose rapidly during the period of welfare reform. The number of children in foster care increased from 3,065 in 1990 to 5,712 in 1999 (Courtney and Dworsky, 2001).[5]

The foster care data in Florida, Wisconsin and Illinois (see table 10.2) suggest that many single mothers in these states that achieved the greatest reductions in the welfare caseload had an increasingly difficult time after welfare reform which led to their children being removed and placed in foster care. Although there was a nationwide increase in the foster care population, it was not as large as the increase in Wisconsin, Florida and Illinois (see table 10.2).[6]

---

[4] Botsko, Snyder, and Leos-Urbel (2001: 16–17) also write that, "Although child welfare caseloads have gone up at the same time welfare caseloads overall have gone down . . . administrators attributed the increase to widely publicized child deaths, especially that of Kayla McKean, which led to legislation in 1999 bearing her name."

[5] The problems of the county-run child welfare system in Milwaukee became so severe that it prompted a state takeover of the system in 1997.

[6] It should be noted that the rates of child abuse reports did not apparently increase as rapidly as the foster care populations. This is surprising because the major entry point into the foster care system is through the child protection system (U.S. Department of Health and Human Services, 2001).

Table 10.2 Changes in the Foster Care Population, 1990–1998

	1990	1992	1994	1996	1998
Florida	10,813	9,928	9,284	24,129	24,202
Illinois	20,753	29,542	41,161	54,540	48,943
Wisconsin	6,316	6,812	8,185	8,424	9,232
Nationwide	400,000	427,000	468,000	507,000	560,000

Source: http://www.acf.dhhs.gov/programs/cb/dis/tables/sec11gb/national.htm#national

Decline of Poverty for Single Working Mothers

The target of welfare reform was single mothers who had come to rely on welfare rather than work to support themselves and their children (Chase-Lansdale, Coley, Lohman, and Pittman, 2003). In this regard, the success of welfare reform can be assessed by the extent to which it led to a reduction in poverty among single working mothers. Porter and Dupree (2001) examined the poverty rate of single working mothers as a result of welfare reform. As seen in table 10.3, there has been a small decline in poverty among this group most directly affected by welfare reform.

Porter and Dupree observe that the decline in poverty rates for these mothers during a period of economic expansion was less than experienced by comparable groups. Most children living in poverty reside in households that are not affected by welfare reform—they are minimum or low-wage working families with children that have incomes below the poverty line. During the period of economic expansion from 1996 to 2000, these "people in other working families with children" who were poor declined from 6.97 to 6.22 million, while "people in working single mother families" increased from 4.13 to 4.2 million.[7] It was the latter group that was most impacted by welfare reform and whose numbers did not decline.

The Fate of Those Who Left Welfare

Data from the Administration for Children and Families (2001) suggest that as a result of welfare reform an increasing percentage of single mothers, especially those with young children (under six), have entered the labor market (see Table 10.3). Studies of those who left welfare suggest that about half left because they found work (Acs and Loprest, 2001).

[7] Although Rector and Fagan (2001) found an estimate—*national* child poverty from the Census Bureau—that supports their view, they fail to identify the limitations of this measure to assess what happened to children as a result of welfare reform at the *state* level.

Table 10.3 Poverty Among Working Single Mother Families

	1996	1997	1998	1999
People in working single mother families				
Number of poor (in millions)	4.13	4.3	4.21	4.2
Poverty rate (percent)	20.4%	21.1%	19.6%	19.4%
People in other working families with children				
Number of poor (in millions)	6.97	6.49	6.29	6.22
Poverty rate (percent)	6.1%	5.6%	5.5%	5.3%

Source: Porter and Dupree (2001).

In fiscal year 2000, employment accounted for 19.7 percent of the reasons for those leaving welfare (Administration for Children and Families, 2002b).[8] Moffett and Winder (2003) suggest "the income gain from leaving is modest, on the order of 11 to 18 percent," in part because of the loss of benefits "cancel out earning gains."

The data in table 10.4 indicate the changing employment status of married and single mothers with income under 200 percent of the poverty line. This is the group of lower income women who would be most likely impacted by the welfare reform legislation (Mincy and Dupree, 2001). Note that between 1996 and 2000, the percentage of single mothers with children under six who were employed increased from 44.4 to 58.5 percent, the largest increase for any group. Many of these single mothers who became employed were likely in earlier times to have relied on welfare.

If we look at the percentage change column of this table, we see that while the percentage of employed single mothers with older children (under eighteen) has not changed as much as for mothers with the youngest children (under six), it has increased substantially. As highlighted by James Q. Wilson (2002), the results of welfare reform have been to separate poor single mothers from their young children so that they could work in low paying jobs. In contrast, married mothers with children do not seem to have been impacted as much as single mothers, although even among this group there has been an increase.

---

[8] According to the Administration for Children and Families (2002) employment was the reason for closure in 19.7 percent of TANF closed-case families for 2000, 23 percent in 1999, 21.7 percent in 1998, and 16.2 percent in 1997.

Table 10.4 Employment Status of Single and Married Mothers, 1990–2000

	1990	1994	1996	1998	1999	2000	Change
Married Mothers							
Under 200% of Poverty							96-00
-with children under 6							
employed	38.36	38.5	39.0	41.2	39.3	42.3	**3.2**
unemployed	4.24	5.9	4.2	5.2	3.9	3.9	0.3
not in labor force	57.23	55.4	56.7	53.5	56.6	53.7	3.2
-with children under 18							
employed	42.6	43.7	44.4	44.5	43.4	46.2	**1.8**
unemployed	4.6	5.6	4.3	5.4	3.9	4.1	-0.2
not in labor force	52.7	50.5	51.3	50.0	52.6	49.6	-1.7
Single Mothers							
Under 200% of Poverty							
-with children under 6							
employed	38.34	39.4	**44.4**	51.1	54.6	**58.5**	**14.0**
unemployed	9.53	10.6	9.6	11.0	9.5	8.0	-1.5
not in labor force	52.11	50.0	46.0	37.8	35.9	33.5	-12.5
-with children under 18							
employed	46.3	46.1	51.1	56.6	59.0	60.8	9.7
unemployed	9.5	10.0	8.6	9.3	7.9	7.4	-1.1
not in labor force	44.3	43.8	40.4	34.1	33.1	31.8	-8.5

Source: Administration for Children and Families (2001).
Online at www.acf.dhhs.gov/programs/opre/ar2001/chap4.xls

In analyzing census data, the Brookings Institution (2002) found that the incomes of female heads of households with children have increased slightly since welfare reform, yet many still remain well below the poverty line (figure 10.8a). The data in figure 10.8a indicates that children in the bottom fifth (in income) of female-headed families remain in poverty despite an increase in earnings for the mothers between 1995 and 2000. The overall income of these families improved slightly during this period.

The largest income gains occurred for the second fifth (in income) of female-headed families. In 2000, earnings for these mothers increased from $6,898 in 1995 to $11,710 (figure 10.8b). As a result means-tested income declined from $5,678 to $2,636 during the same period. Although average earnings increased $4,812 during the period, the net income gain for these mothers was $2,155 as a result of losing welfare benefits (a net effective tax rate over 55 percent).

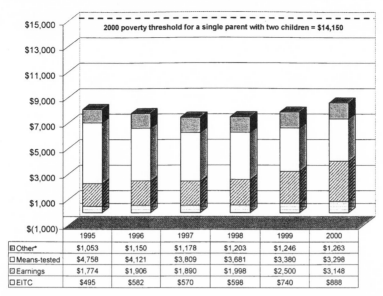

	1995	1996	1997	1998	1999	2000
Other*	$1,053	$1,150	$1,178	$1,203	$1,246	$1,263
Means-tested	$4,758	$4,121	$3,809	$3,681	$3,380	$3,298
Earnings	$1,774	$1,906	$1,890	$1,998	$2,500	$3,148
EITC	$495	$582	$570	$598	$740	$888

Figure 10.8a Family Income for Female Heads of Households with Children (Bottom Fifth), 1995-2000 (In constant 2000 dollars)

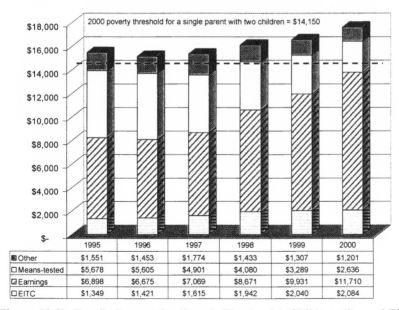

	1995	1996	1997	1998	1999	2000
Other	$1,551	$1,453	$1,774	$1,433	$1,307	$1,201
Means-tested	$5,678	$5,605	$4,901	$4,080	$3,289	$2,636
Earnings	$6,898	$6,675	$7,069	$8,671	$9,931	$11,710
EITC	$1,349	$1,421	$1,615	$1,942	$2,040	$2,084

Figure 10.8b Family Income for Female Heads with Children (Second Fifth), 1995–2000 (In constant 2000 dollars)

Source: The Brookings Welfare Reform and Beyond Initiative (2002).
*Other includes taxes that were not shown in original.
Available online at www.brook.edu/wrb/resources/facts/pres_200207.htm

Many of the mothers and their children, who left welfare without work, have continued to receive government assistance, including Food Stamps and Medicaid. Moffitt (2000) found that "while incomes of single mothers as a whole have risen, incomes of women leaving welfare are only slightly above what they were when the women were on welfare."

Overall, there are several difficulties in assessing the economic impact of welfare reform on children. Once a family leaves welfare, systematic data is no longer collected by the agency. Program data indicate that at the time they left welfare, less than a quarter did so as a result of a job (see footnote 8, this chapter). There have been a number of "leaver" studies that indicate what happens to former welfare recipients after they leave welfare (Acs and Loprest, 2002; Cancian et al., 2002). The results of these studies indicate that about half (54 percent) worked in the fourth quarter after leaving welfare (Acs and Loprest, 2002: table 14.2). The studies report median monthly income of former recipients ranging between $800 and $1,400 for those working. The eleven studies reviewed by Acs and Loprest report a wide range of results that make assessment difficult. In particular, these studies focus on the employment characteristics of leavers but provide limited information on the situation of the children in these families.

Precision of State Child Poverty Rates

One of the major limitations of state child poverty rates is the imprecision of such measures, which are based on samples derived from the Census Bureau's Current Population Survey (CPS). Although such data are useful as a rough measure of the economic condition of children in a state, they are less useful in measuring the change of child poverty within a state. As a result, the *error terms* for these estimates of child poverty are quite high. The estimates of child poverty at the state level derived from census data need to be understood as, at best, rough estimates. For example, the data in table 10.5 estimates 791,789 children in Florida live below the poverty line. However, this is an estimate that could range between 725,207 and 867,770.[9] Yet even this wide range is an estimate with a 90 percent confidence level.

The 90 percent confidence interval for the "rate of child poverty" in Florida is estimated to be between 20 and 23.7 percent.

---

[9] That is, 90 percent of the time the estimate will range between 725,207 and 867,770. Ten percent of the time the estimate will fall outside this range. In short, the Census Bureau is providing an estimate of child poverty based on a relatively small sample of data that include poverty measures as only a small part of the larger interview data collected.

Table 10.5 State Estimates for Children Under 18 in Poverty for, 1998

	90 % Number	Confidence Interval	90 % Rate	Confidence Interval
Florida	791,489	725,207 to 857,770	21.9	20.0 to 23.7
Illinois	498,804	436,158 to 561,449	15.4	13.5 to 17.4
Louisiana	312,008	280,811 to 343,204	25.7	23.2 to 28.3
Mississippi	184,010	163,118 to 204,902	23.9	21.2 to 26.6
Wisconsin	188,461	154,689 to 222,233	13.6	11.1 to 16.0

Source: Census Bureau (2000). Online at www.census.gov/hhes/www/poverty.html.
Note: The 1998 estimates are based on the March 1999 Current Population Survey.

Even for Wisconsin, which is a smaller state, the estimate of the "rate of child poverty" ranges between 11.1 and 16 percent.[10] In Wisconsin the *change* in the estimate of the "rate of child poverty" between 1996 and 2000 is about 3 percent. However, this estimate of the "rate of child poverty" varies by almost five percent. In other words, because of the imprecision of the Census data, it is not possible to use it to determine if there has been a statistically significant change in child poverty in Wisconsin.[11]

In summary, efforts to assess the impact of welfare reform on child poverty require state-level data. However, the available state-level census data are too imprecise to determine if there has been a change in child poverty at the state level. *None* of the observed changes in child poverty within the states examined here are large enough to be *statistically* significant. To assess changes in child poverty will require larger sample sizes at the state level. As we will see later, this data is available, at least indirectly, and will allow us to examine the question about declines in child poverty more reliably.

Current Population Surveys conducted by the Census Bureau collect information on a broad array of topics, of which child poverty is only one. Usually the surveys gather limited information related to child poverty. In this regard, administrative data collected by other federal agencies may provide more accurate data on child poverty, especially if the information

---

[10] This estimate is at the 90 percent confidence interval, which means that the "rate of child poverty" is estimated to range between roughly 11 to 16 percent nine out of ten times. One time in ten in will be outside this estimate.

[11] Census data permit estimating the "rate of child poverty" but is imprecise. The level of imprecision is greater than the amount of change detected during the period of interest. It is like trying to determine the change in the weather with a thermometer which could be off by 5 degrees when we want to know when the temperature goes up 3 degrees.

is primarily focused on income. Taking into account the limitations of available administrative data and census data, the question then arises, where might we find more reliable data on the situation of children who have left welfare?

Are There Better Measures to Assess the Impact of Welfare Reform?

Food Stamp Data

Historically there has been considerable overlap between recipients who receive welfare and those who receive food stamps. Most individuals who receive welfare have, historically, also received food stamps. Both programs are "means tested" and provided to individuals who demonstrate need. Food stamp officials collect extensive income data on clients to determine eligibility. Although some states administer food stamps and welfare from the same welfare office, eligibility for food stamps is independent of welfare eligibility and conforms to a uniform national standard.

Although the welfare reform legislation ended the entitlement to welfare, it did not alter the entitlement status of food stamps.[12] For an able-bodied adult without children, food stamps were awarded with a three month time limit, within which the recipient was required to have found work. Other than this provision, the fundamental components of the Food Stamp program were not altered by welfare reform.

Determination of food stamp eligibility is made at the state level by state agencies operating within the uniform guidelines established by the federal government. The amount of assistance is determined by federal regulations. If a mother with two children has a net monthly income, as defined by the food stamp program rules, of less than $1,220 (in 2002), then the family will be eligible for food stamps. The amount of the food stamp benefit will be determined by the net income below this amount, with a maximum amount of $356 a month. This rule applies in each state.

Changes in the food stamp caseload should, to a large degree, mirror change in the welfare caseload. That is, as welfare caseloads decline, we would expect to see a parallel decline in the number of food stamp recipients, keeping in mind that food stamps might still be provided to some welfare recipients even after they exit the welfare program. The decline should not necessarily be matched and equivalent. Many recipients who

---

[12] The welfare reform legislation did include provisions that reduced or eliminated food stamp assistance for legal immigrants (although some of this was later restored) and established time limits for able-bodied adults without children.

leave welfare because of work are often employed at low paying jobs that leave them eligible for continued food stamp assistance. The data in figure 10.9 display the number of children receiving food stamps and welfare in the United States.

Note that the receipt of food stamps and welfare paralleled each other up until the passage of welfare reform. After passage there was a decline in the number of children receiving food stamps until 2000, when the number turned up. However, the decline has been much steeper for those receiving welfare. Moreover, from 1994 to 2000 the percentage of children in poverty receiving food stamps declined from 94 percent to 75 percent (a roughly one-quarter drop), while the decline for children in poverty receiving welfare has declined from 63 percent to 34 percent (a roughly one-half drop) (see Lindsey and Martin, 2003).

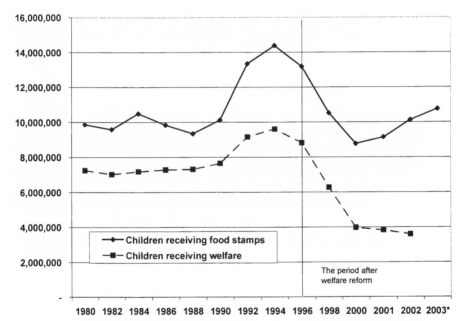

	1980	1984	1988	1992	1996	2000
Percent of children in poverty receiving food stamps	86%	78%	75%	87%	91%	75%
Percent of children in poverty receiving welfare	63%	54%	59%	60%	61%	34%

Figure 10.9 Children Receiving Food Stamps and Welfare
Source: aspe.hhs.gov/hsp/indicators02/appa-fsp.htm#Food.
Online at aspe.hhs.gov/hsp/indicators02/appa-FS.pdf.
*Estimate.

In 2003 less than a third of children living in poverty received welfare benefits. For most poor children in 1996 welfare reform did not lead to an end in poverty, rather, it led to the termination of welfare benefits.

In brief, until welfare reform participation rates in the welfare and food stamp caseload paralleled each other. After welfare reform both the welfare and food stamp caseloads declined, but they no longer paralleled each other. The food stamp program continued to provide for most poor children, while the welfare program systematically terminated services to poor children. Why did poor children continue to receive food stamps while they were taken off welfare? There is little evidence that an improved economic circumstance for poor children provides the explanation.

Food Stamp Benefits

It may be that many of those who left welfare were caught in the narrow band of low-wage workers who have enough earnings so that they no longer qualify for welfare but not enough so that they lost their eligibility for food stamps. To study this issue it is instructive to examine the average food stamp benefit. If the families who left welfare improved their income situation but not enough to lose eligibility for food stamps then we would expect that the "average food stamp benefit" to reflect this improved income by *declining*.[13]

The data in table 10.6 display the average food stamp benefit since 1997 (the figures are not adjusted for inflation). The data indicate that rather than declining, the "average food stamp benefit" has increased, indicating that the overall economic situation of beneficiaries has not improved.

Table 10.6 Average Monthly Benefit per Person for the Food Stamp Program

	FY 1997	FY 1998	FY 1999	FY 2000	FY 2001	FY 2002
Florida	74.21	71.12	72.59	73.00	72.39	74.31
Illinois	76.28	76.22	77.95	83.08	81.80	86.81
Louisiana	74.19	72.49	74.68	74.71	77.59	83.14
Mississippi	65.41	64.41	67.04	68.30	71.18	76.43
Wisconsin	56.88	56.21	56.62	55.61	58.88	62.69
U.S. Average	**71.27**	**71.12**	**72.21**	**72.78**	**74.76**	**79.62**

Source: U.S. Department of Agriculture, Food and Nutrition Service (2003).

[13] The food stamp benefit increases as income for the eligible client decreases. Thus, an increasing average benefit suggests that the income of the average recipient has decreased.

Decline in Food Stamps Varies by State

Although welfare reform put states in charge of designing and administering their welfare program, food stamps remained a federal program that was administered by the states. The result has been considerable variation in the change in caseloads for both welfare and food stamps at the state level. Just as welfare caseloads have fallen in the states, so has the food stamp caseload declined, but far less dramatically. To understand what happened to Food Stamp recipients requires examining the change in caseloads at the state level. In fact, by examining the change in food stamps and welfare caseloads at the state level provides the clearest picture of the impact of welfare reform.[14]

For example, in Wisconsin, the number of welfare recipients was reduced by more than 80 percent, from 241,098 in 1993 to 45,231 in 2002. During the same period, the number of food stamp recipients was reduced by less than 25 percent, from 337,317 to 263,310 (figure 10.10).[15] In 1993, roughly 70 percent of food stamp recipients in that state received welfare (AFDC). By 2002, about 17 percent of food stamp recipients also received welfare (TANF). Why such a dramatic difference? By 2003, the number of food stamp recipients exceeded the number before welfare reform in 1996. While the numbers of food stamp recipients were exceeding their pre-welfare reform levels, the welfare caseload has remained at less than half their pre 1996 levels.

The data suggest the possibility that children have been taken off the welfare caseload, while remaining on food stamps because states have been able to remove impoverished children with impunity since the welfare program is no longer an entitlement.

Why the sharp reductions in the proportion of food stamp recipients receiving welfare? This divergence in assistance programs used by the poor was not replicated in every state. However, a similar divergence was found in most of the states, especially those with the largest declines in their welfare caseloads.

In 2000, Florida had the highest percentage of food stamp recipients who were elderly (18.5 percent). Children represented 46.4 percent of Florida's food stamp recipients.

---

[14] Food stamp data at the state level are based on sample sizes designed to provide reliable estimates at the state level.

[15] Figures 10.10 through 10.11 can be found at the childwelfare.com website. The website provides state information which includes a "Welfare Report Card." Slide 6 of the welfare report card is entitled, "Food Stamps and Welfare Recipients." Consequently, this graph is available for all 50 states.

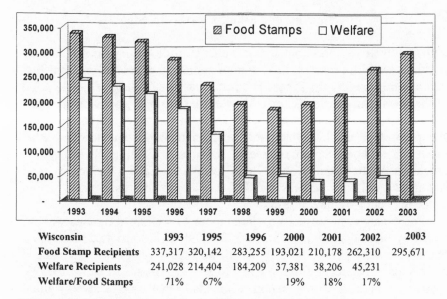

Wisconsin	1993	1995	1996	2000	2001	2002	2003
Food Stamp Recipients	337,317	320,142	283,255	193,021	210,178	262,310	295,671
Welfare Recipients	241,028	214,404	184,209	37,381	38,206	45,231	
Welfare/Food Stamps	71%	67%		19%	18%	17%	

Figure 10.10 Comparison of Food Stamp and Welfare Recipient Declines in Wisconsin

Source: www.childwelfare.com (state Welfare Report Card, slide 6).

Following reform, the welfare caseload was reduced by more than 80 percent, from more than 700,000 in 1993 to less than 130,000 in 2002 (see figure 10.11). Yet, during this same period food stamp recipients fell only about 35 percent, from about 1.5 million to about 950,000 in 2002. In 1993, almost half (47 percent) of food stamp recipients in Florida also received welfare (AFDC) benefits. By 2002, about 13 percent of food stamp recipients in Florida also received welfare (TANF). Again, why the divergence in decline for these overlapping programs?

In Illinois, the divergence between declines in welfare (AFDC/TANF) and food stamps was again repeated. The number of welfare recipients was reduced by 80 percent, from 663,212 in 1996 to 133,708 in 2002, while the number of food stamp recipients was reduced by 20 percent, from 1.11 million to .89 million (and .96 million in April of 2003). During the last two years (2001 and 2002) the number of food stamp recipients began to turn up, while the number of welfare recipients continued to decline (figure 10.11).

The divergence between welfare recipients and food stamp recipients was also mirrored in Louisiana and Mississippi (figure 10.11).

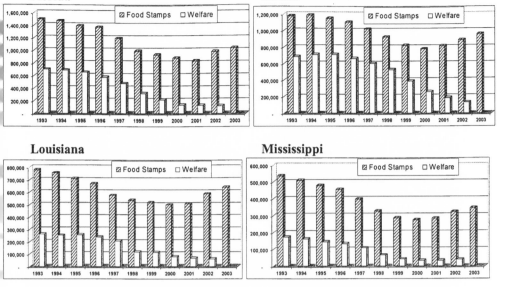

Figure 10.11 Comparison of Food Stamp and Welfare Recipient Declines
Source: www.childwelfare.com (state Welfare Report Card, slide 6).

Overall, in the five states with the largest welfare declines there was a consistent divergence in the decline in welfare caseloads relative to the decline in Food Stamp recipients. Why did this happen, since both programs address the problem of child poverty?

Children as Recipients

While the previous figures have considered all welfare and food stamp recipients, our focus now turns to the child recipients in these programs. We would expect that as the number of children receiving welfare declined, there would be a similar decline in the number of child food stamp recipients. Food stamp data on household income suggests that the overall income of recipients has not increased but has remained about the same (see table 10.6). This is reflected in the fact that the average benefit amount has gone up slightly more than would be expected by inflation, indicating that the income of recipients has remained about the same or declined (see table 10.6). Since the amount of the food stamp benefit is determined based on the recipient's income, as income declines, the amount of the benefit is increased.

As we have mentioned, administrative data from the food stamp program provide an independent measure of the economic situation of poor children. Eligibility for the food stamp program is strictly enforced and has been developed and tested over several decades. Although state agencies administer the food stamp program and monitor eligibility, the criteria used for determining eligibility are established at the federal level. Further, the food stamp program has remained an entitlement. In a sense, the food stamp program provides an independent measure of the economic condition of recipients.

The advantage of the food stamp administrative data is that they are based on a national standard that is consistently applied across the different states. Food stamp eligibility is subject to federal audits to ensure reliability and are therefore likely to be the more reliable indicators of economic change than the welfare caseload counts from the states.

The data in table 10.7 indicates that the states with dramatic reductions of children receiving welfare did not have similar declines in the number of children receiving food stamps.

Table 10.7 Child Recipients of Welfare and Food Stamps, 1993 and 2002

	1993	2002 Actual	2002 Predicted	Difference
Florida				
Children on welfare	481,314	101,431	316,135	214,704
Children on food stamps	695,933	457,100	457,100	
Welfare / FSP	69%	22%	69%	
Illinois				
Children on welfare	469,971	142,934	354,538	211,604
Children on food stamps	589,744	443,172	443,172	
Welfare / FSP	80%	32%	80%	
Louisiana				
Children on welfare	188,110	51,914	141,407	89,493
Children on food stamps	415,848	314,237	314,237	
Welfare / FSP	45%	17%	45%	
Mississippi				
Children on welfare	125,558	27,736	75,327	47,591
Children on food stamps	282,944	171,197	171,197	
Welfare / FSP	44%	16%	44%	
Wisconsin				
Children on welfare	139,216	33,817	108,463	74,646
Children on food stamps	182,826	142,714	142,714	
Welfare / FSP	76%	24%	76%	
US Average				
Children on welfare	9,382,234	3,916,000	6,615,638	2,699,638
Children on food stamps	13,871,937	9,728,879	9,728,879	
Welfare / FSP	68%	40%	68%	

Source: www.childwelfare.com (state Welfare Report Card, slide 6).

To the degree that receiving food stamps provides a measure of the number of children whose income situation would otherwise make them eligible for income assistance (TANF), we can provide an alternative estimate of the number of children who would be removed from the welfare caseload because of their income situation based on food stamp data. In other words, data on the number of children receiving food stamps should allow us to estimate the number of children receiving welfare. Remember, the percentage of children in poverty receiving food stamps has paralleled the percentage of children receiving welfare over the last two decades (figure 10.9). It has only been since the passage of welfare reform that there has been a divergence.

Estimating the Number of Children on Welfare

Historically impoverished children have been provided a package of "means-tested" benefits that served as a safety net. The major benefits in this package included both food stamps and welfare. Most poor single mothers who qualified for food stamps were also eligible for welfare. As a result, it has been possible to make a rough estimate the number of children receiving welfare based on the number of children receiving food stamps. Since the economic situation of children receiving food stamps has not materially changed during the last several years (see table 10.6), we should be able to estimate the number of children who should have received welfare in 2002 using data from the Food Stamp program. To compute this estimate I multiplied the ratio of the number of children receiving welfare over the number of children receiving food stamps for 1993 by the number of children receiving food stamps in 2002. The data in table 10.7 estimates that almost 2.7 million more children should have received welfare benefits than actually did. Since eligibility for foods stamps should predict eligibility for welfare, *these data suggest that close to 2.7 million children may have lost welfare benefits even though their income situation, as measured by receipt of food stamps, has not materially changed.*

The data from children receiving food stamps suggest the economic situation of poor children has not substantially improved since the passage of welfare reform—which calls into question the putative achievement represented by the dramatic state welfare caseload declines, especially with respect to child recipients.

It should be noted that the discrepancy in food stamp caseload decline and welfare caseload decline varies substantially among the states. Those states with the greatest welfare caseload declines record the greatest discrepancy. This suggests that many children have been removed from the welfare program even though their poverty has remained.

Perhaps there is some other explanation for this discrepancy unique to the food stamp program. We can also look at the economic situation of the children removed from welfare by examining another data source that allows assessing the change in the economic situation of poor children during the last six years—school lunches. As with food stamps, children from welfare families have also received a government-subsidized free lunch through the National School Lunch Program.

Child Poverty Measured in the School Lunch Line

The National School Lunch Program (NSLP) provides lunches to children at school.[16] Part of the program includes a federally subsidized free lunch for poor children. To qualify for the program the child's parent must complete an income verification application. A child qualifies for a free lunch if the parent's income is below 130 percent of the poverty line.[17] The advantage of administrative data from this program is that it derives from an income verification application completed and signed by the parent and independent of TANF and the food stamp program.[18] It should be noted that the number of children receiving free lunch through the NSLP does not include infants and young children in poor families who are not enrolled in school. Thus, it is not a complete measure of child poverty, but only a proxy measure of child poverty among school-age children.

As with food stamp data, we would expect that as the number of children receiving welfare declines, there would be a concurrent decline in the number of children receiving free lunches (see figure 10.12).

---

[16] U.S. Department of Agriculture (USDA), Food and Nutrition Service (FNS), National School Lunch Program. National Level Annual Summary Tables: Fiscal Years 1969–2001. See www.fns.usda.gov/pd/slsummar.htm. State information is also available in the Food Research and Action Center's *State of the State: A Profile of Food and Nutrition Programs Across the Nation.* Washington, D.C.: FRAC, 2002. Online at www.frac.org.

[17] The National School Lunch Program (NSLP) is a federal entitlement program. Income eligibility guidelines for the NSLP are derived from the federal poverty guidelines and are updated annually. To participate in the NSLP, schools and institutions must agree to operate food service for all students and to provide free and reduced price lunches to students unable to pay the full price based on income eligibility criteria.

[18] Alberta Frost, *Free and Reduced Price Certification: An Update.* Washington, D.C.: U.S. Department of Agriculture. March 2002. This report suggests that reductions and terminations have increased from 11 percent in 1986–87 to 18 percent in 2000–01.

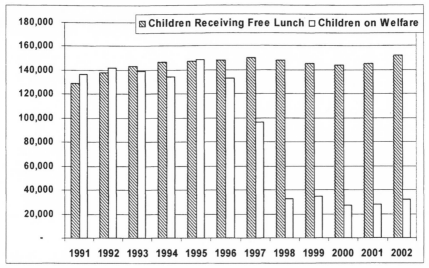

Figure 10.12 Children Receiving Welfare and Subsidized Lunch in Wisconsin
Source: www.childwelfare.com (state Welfare Report Cards, slide 4).

Reports from the National School Lunch Program indicate that the overall income characteristics of those eligible and receiving free lunch has not changed since the passage of welfare reform. Figure 10.12 displays a comparison of the number of children receiving free lunches with the decline in the number of children receiving welfare in Wisconsin.[19]

In 1995, the number of children receiving welfare in Wisconsin was roughly equivalent to the number of children receiving free lunch provided by the NSLP. Shortly after the passage of welfare reform the number of children receiving welfare declined from over 120,000 to less than 35,000. Yet, the number of children eligible and receiving subsidized free lunch continued to increase.

In Florida also, there was a similar divergence in the number of children receiving welfare and the number of children receiving free lunch since welfare reform (Figure 10.13). What is striking with the data from Florida is the dramatically large number of children receiving free lunch relative to the small number now receiving welfare.

---

[19] U.S. Department of Agriculture (USDA), Food and Nutrition Service (FNS), National School Lunch Program. National Level Annual Summary Tables: Fiscal Years 1969–2002. See www.fns.usda.gov/pd/slsummar.htm. State information is also available in the Food Research and Action Center's *State of the State: A Profile of Food and Nutrition Programs Across the Nation.* Washington, D.C.: FRAC Publications, 2002. Available online at www.frac.org.

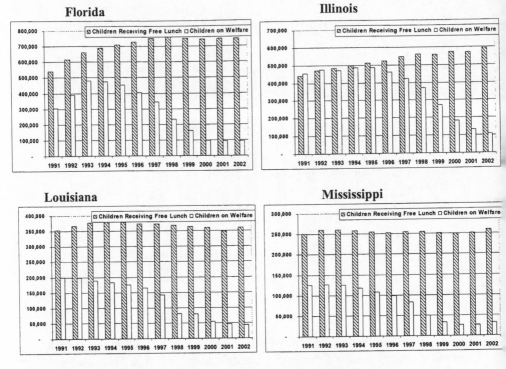

Figure 10.13 Children Receiving Welfare and Subsidized Lunch
Source: www.childwelfare.com (state Welfare Report Cards, slide 4).

The same story can be said for Illinois, where the number of children living in poverty and receiving free lunches has increased, while welfare distributions to them have fallen (figure 10.13). In both Louisiana and Mississippi the number of children receiving free lunch was almost twice the number of children receiving welfare. Since the passage of welfare reform, the number of children receiving welfare benefits has been sharply reduced while the number of children receiving free lunch has remained about the same (figure 10.13).

National Trend

Figure 10.14 displays the national trend in terms of the number of children receiving welfare and the number of children receiving a subsidized free lunch throughout the United States. From 1977 to 1995 the difference between the number of children eligible for the free lunch program at school and the number of children on welfare was about 2 million.

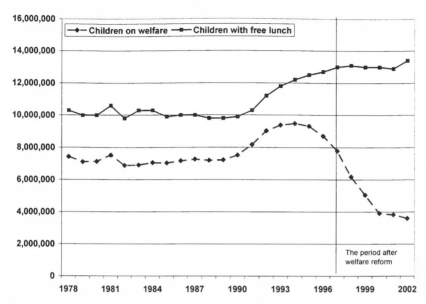

Figure 10.14 Children Receiving Welfare and Free Lunch

After the passage of welfare reform and the resultant reduction in welfare caseloads, the difference has exceeded 8 million. This suggests that many poor children are without welfare benefits even though their economic situation has not improved. In brief, the net result of welfare reform seems to be that many children who received income assistance prior to reform are no longer receiving that assistance after reform.

A Summation

Using administrative data from the National School Lunch Programs's free lunch benefit, it is possible to develop an estimate of the number of children who have lost welfare benefits since the passage of welfare reform, even though their economic situation has not changed (table 10.8). The estimate of the number of children removed from welfare is built on the assumption that the ratio of the number of children receiving welfare to the number of children receiving a subsidized free lunch would remain the same between 1996 and 2002.[20]

---

[20] The eligibility standards for the subsidized free lunch did not change during this period, and the studies of the characteristics of NSLP subsidized free lunch recipients indicate no major change in the recipient population during this period (Wemmerus, Forkosh, and Almond, 1996; Food Research and Action Center, 2002).

Table 10.8 Child Recipients of Welfare and Free Lunch, 1996 and 2002

	1996	2002 Actual	2002 Predicted*	Difference[§]
Florida				
Children on welfare	394,797	101,431	*405,815*	304,384
Free lunch	727,851	748,164	748,164	
Welfare / Free lunch	54%	14%	54%	
Illinois				
Children on welfare	455,591	142,934	*497,351*	354,417
Free lunch	524,111	571,668	571,668	
Welfare / Free lunch	87%	25%	87%	
Louisiana				
Children on welfare	161,763	51,914	*151,397*	99,483
Free lunch	373,101	349,192	349,192	
Welfare / Free lunch	43%	15%	43%	
Mississippi				
Children on welfare	95,992	27,736	*95,798*	68,062
Free lunch	252,395	251,886	251,886	
Welfare / Free lunch	38%	11%	38%	
Wisconsin				
Children on welfare	122,864	33,817	*120,718*	86,901
Free lunch	148,204	145,616	145,616	
Welfare / Free lunch	83%	23%	83%	
U.S. Average				
Children on welfare	8,577,084	3,916,000	*8,778,534*	4,862,534
Free lunch	12,291,578	12,580,270	12,580,270	
Welfare / Free lunch	70%	31%	70%	

*Predicted children on welfare in 2002 (italicized) is calculated by multiplying (the ratio of children on welfare in 1996 divided by children receiving free lunch in 1996) by free lunch recipients in 2002.
[§] Difference between the predicted and actual number of child recipients of welfare in 2002.

As seen in table 10.8, more than 8.7 million children were estimated eligible for welfare based on the school lunch data in 2002. Yet, less than 4 million children received welfare benefits. Thus, this data suggests that welfare reform may, indeed, have resulted in the dropping of millions of poor children from the welfare program.

The data on the subsidized lunch program correspond with the findings from the Food Stamp program, namely, that children have been removed from the welfare program for reasons other than their improving economic situation. The free school lunch data suggest that the children removed from welfare remain poor and need to rely on the subsidized free lunch program.

When welfare reform was being debated researchers from the Urban Institute warned that as many as a million poor children might be removed from the program. The data in table 10.8 suggest that this was an underestimate. The data in this table suggests that as many as 4.8 million poor children lost their welfare benefit even though they remain in poverty as assessed by enrollment in the subsidized free lunch program.

The Color of Welfare

Either I do the housework or Mrs. Long does the housework, or we get somebody to come in and help us, but someone has to do it, and it does seem to me
that if we can qualify these people to accept any employment doing something
constructive, that is better than simply having them sitting at home drawing
welfare.   Senator Russell Long

The dismantling of income support programs through "welfare reform"
raises the question of who suffers as a result of this change. As seen in table 10.9, Black children are the major victims of the dismantling of the
welfare program. In the top five leading states, in terms of caseload reduction, Black children make up the majority of welfare recipients. In Illinois,
the most populous state, almost three quarters of the TANF child population are Black even though Black children are less than one-fifth of the
state's child population. In Wisconsin, Black children represent less than
one-tenth of the state's child population but they represent half of the
state's welfare (TANF) population.

Table 10.9 The Color of Children Receiving Welfare (TANF)

	Black Children		White Children	
	State Population (%)	TANF Population (%)	State Population (%)	TANF Population (%)
Wisconsin	8	50	82	18
Florida	21	55	57	23
Illinois	19	74	60	13
Mississippi	46	87	53	13
Louisiana	41	87	56	12
New York	18	42	58	19
New Jersey	16	61	62	11
California	7	23	37	21
Pennsylvania	13	55	80	29
North Carolina	26	66	63	24
Michigan	18	55	73	39
Ohio	14	56	80	40
Texas	12	30	44	16
Virginia	24	69	67	27
Georgia	36	81	58	17
Alabama	32	78	65	22

Source: www.childwelfare.com (State Welfare Report Cards, slide 11).

In both Mississippi and Louisiana Black children represent 87 percent of the welfare (TANF) population even though they are less than half of the state's child population. In these and most other states Black children are substantially overrepresented in the welfare population. The major reductions in income support for children, which welfare reform has brought about, have primarily impacted Black children.

Welfare reform resulted in many children who remained poor losing their welfare benefit—and the brunt of that loss was borne by poor Black children. Although some have suggested welfare reform has helped Black children, a careful and close review suggests quite the opposite. Black children have suffered the greatest loss of benefits—regardless of their poverty—as a result of welfare reform.

The data in table 10.9 demonstrate that the welfare program in the United States has its greatest impact on Black children (Hines, Lemon, Wyatt, and Merdinger, forthcoming). Although welfare impacts all race and ethnic groups it is concentrated among Black and Hispanic children.

Out-of-Wedlock Births

Before closing this discussion on the impact of welfare reform one important issue remains—its impact on out-of-wedlock births. One of the major concerns expressed during the welfare reform debate was the connection between increasing welfare dependency and out-of-wedlock births. The welfare reform legislation specifically addressed this problem and included incentives to states to lower the rates of out-of-wedlock births. Rector and Fagan (2001) have suggested that welfare reform contributed to reducing the number of out-of-wedlock births.

The data in Figure 10.16 show the change in out-of-wedlock births for the states with the largest declines in their welfare caseloads (Census Bureau, 2002). The data suggest that rather than declining, the number of births to unmarried women nationwide has increased despite the decline in welfare caseloads. In fact, for *all* of the states the percentage of out-of-wedlock births *increased*. In 1996, the national average was 32.4, which increased slightly to 33.0 by 1999.

It is difficult to detect long-term and consistent changes in out-of-wedlock births as a result of substantial reductions in the welfare caseloads. The data here are not conclusive but simply suggest that welfare reform may not have reduced out-of-wedlock births.

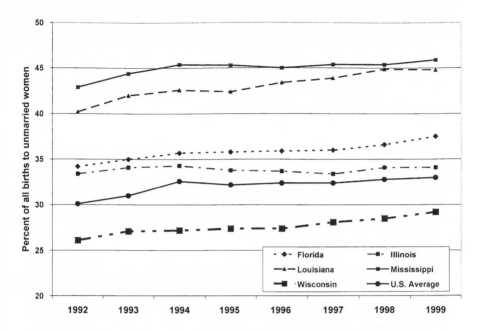

Figure 10.16 Changes in the Percentage of Births to Unmarried Women, 1992–1999

Source: Division of Vital Statistics, National Center for Health Statistics, Center for Disease Control (2002).

Discussion

> Just as the origins of the public aid and child welfare were linked at the beginning of the twentieth century, so their fates were linked at the century's end. If welfare was created to avoid the removal of needy children from their mothers, then eliminating welfare must have implications for child welfare policy.
>
> Dorothy Roberts, *Shattered Bonds*

Critics of welfare reform expressed concern that removing the entitlement status for welfare would give states carte blanche to reduce their welfare caseload. The data examined in this chapter suggest that many states simply reduced their welfare caseloads by no longer providing many poor children with welfare regardless of these children's economic circumstances. This would certainly seem to be the case in Wyoming and Idaho (see Lindsey and Martin, 2003). But it also seems to be true for many of the states with dramatic welfare caseload reductions that are not matched with similar declines in child poverty, as revealed by the number of child food stamp recipients or NSLP free lunch recipients (see table 10.10).

Table 10.10 Child Poverty and Participation in Means-tested Programs

	Child Population	2000 Children Below Poverty*	2002 Children Receiving Welfare	2002 Children Receiving Food Stamps	2002 NSLP Free Lunch Recipients
Florida	3,646,340	791,489	101,431	457,100	748,164
Illinois	3,245,451	498,804	142,943	443,172	571,668
Louisiana	1,219,799	312,008	51,914	314,237	349,192
Mississippi	775,187	184,010	27,736	171,197	251,886
Wisconsin	1,368,756	188,461	33,817	142,714	145,616
U.S. Total	72,294,000		3,916,000	9,728,879	12,580,270

*U.S. Census Bureau estimate.

The data in table 10.10 raise concern about the removal of children from the welfare caseload. For example, approximately 790,000 children live in poverty in Florida, yet only about 101,000 or 12.7 percent of these poor children receive welfare benefits.

Even though these children fail to receive welfare, about 457,000 receive food stamps and almost 750,000 receive a subsidized free lunch (keep in mind that only school-age children can receive the subsidized free lunch). Since all of these programs base eligibility on a similar means test, the discrepancy indicates, in a sense, denial of welfare benefits to likely eligible children. These findings are repeated for the other states.

Extreme Poverty Increasing for Black Children

Although Rector and Fagan (2002), Pardue (2003) and others have suggested that welfare reform has produced a decline in child poverty, especially among Black children, this view conflicts with the data on extreme child poverty for Black children. The Children's Defense Fund analyzed data from the Census Bureau's Current Population Survey and found that Black children living in extreme poverty (defined as less than half the poverty line income) has increased substantially since the passage of welfare reform (see table 10.11). The percentage has increased from 6.4 to 8.4 percent. Further, during this period the Children's Defense Fund calculations estimate that the number of extremely poor children not receiving welfare has risen sharply from 1,062,000 in 1996 to 1,649,000 in 2002. Thus, despite a period of substantial economic prosperity, the situation for the poorest children in the United States has apparently not improved.

Table 10.11 The Increase in Extreme Poverty for Children Since the Passage of Welfare Reform

	Black Children Living in Poverty	Percentage of Black Children Living Poverty	Percentage of all Children Living in Extreme Poverty	Extremely poor children not receiving welfare
1996	680,000	6.4%	3.6%	1,062,000
2001	932,000	8.4%	4.0%	1,649,000

Source: Children's Defense Fund (2003).

In fact, this data suggest that there has been a substantial increase in the number of Black children living in extreme poverty; only now the situation is compounded by the absence of welfare.

Conclusion

With the enactment of welfare reform the historic program that provided income protection to disadvantaged children was ended. With the dismantling of the old welfare system a new and more restrictive system has emerged. There has been increased participation of a number of single mothers in the labor market, and although census data are not conclusive, at the national level there has been a downward trend in the rate of poverty for the first several years since passage of welfare reform. However, child poverty rate declines do not appear to be related to the declines in welfare caseloads when examined at the state level.

It appears that millions of poor children no longer receive welfare, children who in the past would have received it. Data from the food stamp program indicates that the number of poor children who have lost welfare benefits, even though their economic situation has not improved, is about 2.7 million. Data from the National School Lunch Program indicates the number of poor children who have lost their welfare benefits, even though their economic situation has not improved, may be as high as 4.8 million. What has happened to these children who no longer receive welfare but who apparently are still very poor? That is a question that has yet to be answered.

The data examined here suggest that the consequence of welfare reform is not the achievement for poor children some have celebrated. The story of that achievement, at least for poor children, does not conform to the state level data. For some children in families where the mother has left welfare and gone to work, the promise of welfare reform may have been realized. But these children are the exceptions. Millions of impoverished children who used to receive income protection (welfare) now find themselves without it. From the perspective of these children, welfare reform appears to be, at the least, a substantial net financial loss. The most recent data, in fact, suggest that poverty, and in particular extreme poverty, has increased for Black children in recent years.

The social contract which America had forged with poor children over the years has been replaced. The terms and expectations of the new social contract, especially in regards to children, are unclear. It is being worked out at the state level and taking different form in each of the states. What is clear is that life is harder for poor children, especially poor children of color. What all this will mean in the long term is yet to be determined.

Welfare as we knew it has ended. We are entering a new era. The solution is not to reinstate welfare. Even if that were possible, it would not be desirable, for a number of reasons which we will get to in the next chapter. There are other policies and programs that can be easily instituted that would more effectively lift millions of children out of poverty. In the next chapter we explore what these are.

11

Two Simple Programs for Ending Child Poverty

What is needed is a consistent and coherent social policy for all children, a component of which would be a scheme of income guarantees that does not differentiate between poor and nonpoor children and provides the means for poor families to escape poverty. By implication this means a "universal" approach, one in which benefits are provided to all children without regard to their financial status.　　　　　George Hoshino, *AFDC as Child Welfare*

Three percent of Americans were behind on their car payments while 53 percent were behind on their child support payments.
　　　　　　　　　　　　　　　　　　　　　　Senator David Pryor

Although Social Security was signed into law in the United States in 1936, full implementation of the program was complicated by World War II, and it took several decades before large numbers of seniors were covered and began benefiting from the program. Thus, as late as the 1950s the economic condition for many senior citizens in the United States remained bleak, and many were without a reliable source of retirement income. The poverty rate for seniors 65 or older stood above 35 percent, higher than for any other group. The major income support program was a means-tested welfare program called Old Age Assistance which was administered by the same welfare agency that administered public assistance.[1]

Over the next several decades, however, Social Security began to dramatically reduce the number of seniors living in poverty. By 2000, more than 35 million seniors were receiving benefits totaling more than 350 billion dollars annually. In addition, Medicare, which serves the health insurance needs of seniors, had an annual budget exceeding $128 billion.

---

[1] The Supplemental Security Income (SSI) program replaced Old Age Assistance (OAA) in 1973. In 2000, more than 2 million seniors received benefits from SSI (Social Security Administration, 2001).

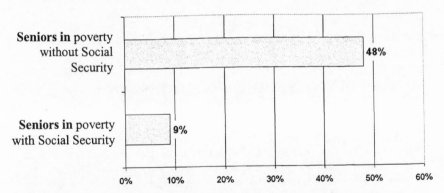

Figure 11.1 Impact of Social Security on Poverty Among Seniors
Source: Social Security Administration (2001).

The success of Social Security in reducing poverty among seniors and assuring a minimum level of income in retirement years has been nothing less than spectacular, fundamentally altering the economic situation of the elderly in the United States. Without Social Security, almost half of all elderly in the United States would today be living in poverty. Instead, the poverty rate for seniors is now less than 10 percent (see figure 11.1).

For almost a third of seniors, Social Security benefits represent more than 90 percent of their annual income. For another third it represents between 50 to 90 percent of their income, while for the remaining third Social Security is less than half of their retirement income (see figure 11.2).

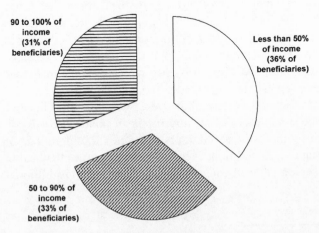

Figure 11.2 Importance of Social Security Income for the Aged, 2000
Source: Social Security Administration (2001).

The main advantage of Social Security is that it provides *universal coverage* and is *not means-tested*. Upon retirement seniors receive a basic income support benefit to which no stigma is attached, because the benefit derives in part from premiums the recipients have paid to the program throughout their working years (Steuerle and Bakija, 1994).[2] Social Security does not assure a life of abundance, but it has kept millions of seniors out of poverty, despair, and ill health during their retirement years. Not surprisingly, it is a model that is respected and emulated throughout the world (see table 11.1).

Table 11.1 Social Security Programs in Other Countries

	Year Began	Type	Source of Funds		
			Individual	Employer	Government
Australia	1908	Dual†			
Belgium	1900	Social Insurance	7.5%	8.9%	Annual subsidy
Canada	1927	Dual‡			Whole cost
Denmark	1891	Dual‡			
Finland	1937	Dual†	4.7%	2 to 4.9%	36% of pension
France	1910	Social Insurance	6.6%	8.2%	Variable
Germany	1889	Social Insurance	9.8%	9.8%	Subsidy
Greece	1934	Social Insurance	6.7%	8.9%	10%
Italy	1919	Social Insurance	8.9%	23.8%	Subsidy
Japan	1941	Social Insurance			
Netherlands	1919	Social Insurance	17.9%	7.0%	Subsidy
Norway	1936	Dual‡	7.8%	14.1%	Subsidy
Spain	1919	Social Insurance	4.7%	23.6%	Subsidy
Sweden	1913	Dual†	6.0%	5.9%	25%
United Kingdom	1908	Dual§	10.0%	12.2%	Subsidy
United States	1936	Social Insurance	7.65%	7.65%	

†Social insurance and mandatory earnings pension
‡Social insurance and universal pension
§Social insurance and social assistance
Online at www.ssa.gov/policy/docs/progdesc/ssptw/2002/europe/index.html.

---

[2] It has been estimated that the average Social Security recipient receives a benefit worth more than twice what would otherwise be expected based on contributions the retiree paid. Schorr (1987: 58) observes, "the average low-paid man retiring in 1982 received a benefit of $371 a month, of which his contributions paid for $105; thus he received a subsidy of $266." To correct the popular misconception that Social Security payments represent a fully paid-for premium, U.S. Representative Cooper has suggested that Social Security checks be printed in red ink after the recipient has collected all the money he or she paid into the system and the interest it accrued (Broder, 1991). Ackerman and Alstott (2002: 143–144) observed, "Americans who retired during the first fifty years of the program have received much more than they 'bought,' and future generations will receive less."

Children Not Included

While the United States has developed a broad and comprehensive set of universal social programs to protect the economic situation of seniors, there is no similar benefit package for children. Examining federal programs for seniors and children ages zero to six, what stands out is that the federal government does very little for young children (see table 11.2). To put if bluntly, the main reason that the United States, the richest country in the industrialized world, has the highest child poverty rates is that, in contrast to the elderly, social programs for children under the age of six are a patchwork of "means-tested" programs geared more toward making sure mothers work than to protecting the economic condition of children. In this regard, the United States stands apart from nearly every other modern industrialized nation.

The Failure of Means-Tested Welfare

In the United States poor single mothers have not been successful in collecting child support payments, and few receive the child support they are entitled to. As well, the major "children's allowance" is provided by way of an income tax deduction, in which the more a parent earns the greater the value of the benefit. If the parent has minimal or no income, the tax deduction benefit has no value.

Table 11.2 Income Support Programs for Young Children and Seniors

Seniors (N = 41 million)	Amount in Billions
Universal	
Social Security	$352.7
Medicare	128.5
Prescription Drug Benefit	?
Means-tested	
SSI	11.0
Children 0–6 (N = 25 million)	
Universal	
None	
Means-tested	
TANF	22.8
Head Start	3.5
Child Welfare	.2
Adoption Subsidies	.9

Source: Social Security Administration (2001).

Over the years welfare emerged as, in effect, a "bundled" benefit that compensated for both child support and the children's allowance with one single payment. But as we have seen, it has failed to move poor children out of poverty, both before and after its reform. The failure of welfare derives from the limitations of the residual model, which limits aid to those mothers who can prove they are poor and cannot take care of themselves. This creates an unintended incentive to fail. As Rector (2001) writes, "to 'earn' this welfare paycheck, the mother had to fulfill two conditions: She could not work and she could not marry an employed man."

The early debate between liberals and conservatives often centered on how much cash assistance to provide the poor. Only with Charles Murray's ideological treatise, *Losing Ground*, was the fundamental premise of providing income assistance to the poor questioned. Thus began a conservative campaign that brought about the end of welfare as we know it. We are now in a period when states are selectively but progressively dismantling income support for poor children and their mothers. It is highly unlikely that the original welfare program will be restored, despite evidence that poverty among children continues at high levels.

Critics were correct in their argument that welfare serves as an *impediment* to work. However, they were mistaken in understanding why it discourages work. The real problem with welfare is that it is taken back as the recipients improve their situation. A poor mother who receives welfare loses part (or all) of the welfare payment as she works. As the mother earns income, the government "claws back" the welfare payment it provides. This "claw back" has the effect of taxing the wage income the mother receives.

This action is illustrated by data from the Brookings Institute welfare study. Researchers from the Brookings Institute compiled income data of female heads of households with children. For mothers in the bottom fifth of this group they observed that their "earnings" increased from $1,774 in 1995 to $3,148 in 2000, a more than 75 percent increase in earnings. However, during this same period these mothers saw their welfare payments decrease from $4,758 in 1995 to $3,298 in 2000—a loss of $1,460, which is more than was gained by their increased earnings. Thus, even though these mothers increased their earnings by 75 percent, they experienced a net loss after taking into account their loss of "means-tested" benefits.

This same phenomenon occurred for female heads of households in the second fifth. Between 1995 and 2000 these mothers increased their earnings from $6,898 to $11,710, an increase of 70 percent. However, their means-tested benefits declined from $5,678 to $2,636, a loss of more than $3,000. As a result, the net benefit from increased earnings was more than cut in half by the "claw back" of welfare benefits.

Researchers at the Urban Institute (Giannarelli and Steuerle, 1994) modeled the impact of this process of taking back benefits on a sample of welfare recipients and calculated that it produced an average net tax rate in excess of 70 percent.

As the Brookings and Urban Institute data illustrate, providing income assistance to poor mothers using a "means-tested" welfare structure has the net effect, even if unintended, of imposing a very high tax on earnings. The consequence of such "clawing back" is to diminish the financial rewards which work would otherwise provide and thereby diminish individual work incentive.

Proven Programs for Ending Child Poverty

So why not take the opportunity that the demise of AFDC now thrusts upon us? Why not start talking about broad new ways—a widening of the idea of social security—to help the majority of American working parents, with extra help for the poorest offered in the context of such an overall effort?

Theda Skocpol, *The Next Liberalism*

Restoration of welfare would be neither feasible nor desirable, for with the effective dismantling of income support to poor mothers and their children through the 1996 welfare reform legislation, we are presented with a rare opportunity to restructure our approach to helping poor children. What is required is the development of income support programs that meet the needs that welfare provided, but without the limitations and harmful side effects that welfare induced. This will mean programs which ensure that poor mothers receive *both* child support and a children's allowance, and which are not "taken back" as the wage income of the welfare mother increases. Thus, if the welfare mother works and earns additional income, she should not lose the payments she receives for child support or a children's allowance, as is now the case with what is, in effect, a "bundled" welfare payment. Further, single mothers must begin having access to publicly subsidized child care, as is available for children ages six to eighteen in the United States and for pre-kindergarten children in Western Europe (see table 4.9).

In this effort most modern industrialized democracies provide good examples of income support programs that create a safety net for poor and disadvantaged children. In Western Europe these programs take the form of income support packages that include 1) assured child support, 2) a children's allowance, and 3) publicly subsidized child care.[3]

Following the lead of other industrialized democracies, our first step should be to make our children's allowance program, currently provided by way of a tax deduction, fair, equitable, and available to *all* children. Second, we should provide a child support program along the lines of what is provided in other modern industrial democracies. If these two programs are then combined with universal child care, the problem of child poverty which has been with us for so long will start coming to an end, and we will have obviated the need for any means-tested welfare program.

A Universal Children's Allowance

For families in Europe and other industrialized countries, the children's allowance is an important part of their income and is responsible for protecting the economic viability of many poor families. Children's allowance programs, which recognize the financial burden that parents have in raising children,[4] take the form of direct payments to every family for their children and are applied universally, from the poorest families to the wealthiest (Brazer, 1967; Garfinkel and Uhr, 1987). Since the program is not means-tested, it is not taken away when parent(s) work.

Underlying this children's allowance approach is the assumption that children represent a society's future. To ensure their care and well-being is to ensure the future of the society (Rejda, 1970). Just as Social Security plays a critical role for elderly families, especially those with limited income, the children's allowance program can play a critical role in lifting families with children out of poverty.

Children's allowance programs can be found in more than seventy nations, including all of Western Europe and North America (Canada, England, France, Mexico, Belgium, etc.) (see Burns, 1967; Kamerman and Kahn, 1983; McLanahan and Garfinkel, 1993: 28)[5] (see table 11.3). As mentioned, the children's allowance program is provided universally to all parents, and is *not* contingent on poverty.

---

[3] The exceptions include countries like Norway that provide a "negative income tax" which substitutes for these packages of income support programs.

[4] Longman and Graham (1998) estimate the cost of raising one child for a middle-class family is approximately $300,000 and about $225,000 for each additional child. Ackerman and Alstott (2002: 239) indicate this figure "omits foregone wages, college costs, and other added expenses, which together raise the cost of one child to a whopping $1.5 million."

[5] Germany provides a children's allowance of $450 a month during the first six months of a child's life and $166 a month thereafter (Haanes-Olson, 1972; Wilson, 1990). In addition, the standard tax deduction is $4,500 per child.

Table 11.3 Children's Allowance Programs

| | | Annual Benefit | | |
	Program Started	First child	Second child	Means-tested
Belgium		$ 933	$ 793	No
Canada	1944	$ 658	$ 658	Sliding scale
Denmark*	1952	$1,747	$ 1,252	No
Finland§	1948	$1,242	$ 1,524	No
France	1932	$1,251	$ 1,251	No
Germany	1954	$ 128	$ 128	No
Greece	1958	$ 86	$ 172	No
Netherlands	1939	$ 671		No
Norway**	1946	$2,536	$ 2,536	No
Spain	1938	$ 249	$ 249	Part is means-tested
Sweden	1947	$1,084	$ 1,084	No
United Kingdom	1945	$1,248	$ 832	Part is means-tested
United States	None			Tax deduction

*Denmark provides a variable family allowance for children based on age. Data displayed are for children 0–2 years old. Benefit for school-age children (7–17) is $1,252 per year.
§Finland provides a variable single parent supplement based on the number of children. The amount displayed here is for two children. Child care allowance for child under 3.
**Norway family allowance includes $1,053 supplement for children aged 1 to 3.

Source: Social Security Administration (2002).

All parents with children receive this income support whether they are wealthy or not. Child support assurance is, of course, limited to those children living primarily with one parent. But, even then, it is provided to all custodial parents irrespective of income.

In France, the children's allowance program provides all families, regardless of income and without any requirements, an annual benefit of $1,200 for each child. The objective is to assure that all families have a minimal amount of money to provide for the needs of their children, irrespective of income or employment. Several countries in Europe accomplish this same protection with a "negative income tax" program, which assures all families a minimal base of income.[6]

---

[6] The Netherlands provides a negative income tax. In Germany the government, in addition to providing the usual child allowance, provides $1,000 a year per child (under 8) to a parent who stays at home to take care of a child.

Table 11.4 Value of the Children's Allowance
Benefit Provided Through the Tax Deduction, 2002

Family Income	One Child	Two Children
15,000	0	0
20,000	10	20
50,000[§]	865	1,330
75,000	1,237	2,474

[§] Note The tax cuts legislation enacted in 2003 provided an additional $800 benefit for a married couple with two children earning $50,000 (Geary, 2003).
Note: For a married couple, filing jointly.

The U.S. Tax Exemption Approach

In the United States the current children's allowance takes the form of a tax exemption, which excludes more than $2,300 from federal, state, and local income for each child living as a dependent in a household. For children in families with an average or higher income, this exemption represents a substantial benefit but provides little for children in low-income and poor households. For example, the single mother working full-time all year at $7.50 an hour would earn $15,000 a year.[7] This mother and her children receive no benefit through the tax exemption. In contrast, a family with an income of $75,000 would receive a benefit of $1,237 from federal taxes for one child (table 11.4) and $2,474 for two children. Western European countries use a progressive approach that provides children from low-income and poor families with the larger children's allowance benefit.[8]

Administering the children's allowance in this tax deduction fashion has regressive consequences. It conditions receipt of the children's allowance to income earning activities that are beyond the control of the child, resulting in a situation where the children most in need receive the least, while the children least in need receive the most.

---

[7] The 1997 Taxpayer Relief Act provided a $500 tax credit for most children. However, the tax credit is only payable to families who owe federal taxes and, thus, provides *no* benefit to the poorest children (Plotnick, 2000). The 2003 tax legislation increases the tax credit to $600 and increases to $1,000 by 2006. The credit is not available to low-income and poor children.

[8] The Institute on Taxation and Economic Policy (2003) estimates that as a result of the tax legislation in 2003 the average tax cut will be $350 for those families in the bottom 60 percent and $17,302 for those in the top 10 percent over the 2003–2006 period.

Guaranteeing the Child's Exemption

The inequity of the child's exemption can be remedied by simply *guaranteeing* the exemption for all children as a tax credit not conditioned on parental work behavior. This would ensure that poor children, as well as wealthy children, receive an equal benefit. Implementing a program to do this would be a simple matter. When parents secured employment, they would declare the number of dependent children in their household. Based on this declaration, the parent, whether working full or part time, would receive the value of the exemption through reduced payroll deductions (which is what happens now). However, those parents who were unemployed or not in the labor market would receive regular (monthly) cash payments up to the value of the exemption in the form of a children's allowance. All children would thus be guaranteed a child's exemption of, say, $75 a month. An unemployed parent with two children would therefore receive a monthly children's allowance of perhaps $150.[9] This payment would be separate and independent of welfare (TANF) or other income transfer programs designed to help the single parent. Further, if a child were placed in foster care or an other substitute care arrangement, the guaranteed benefit would follow the child and be paid directly to the child's caretaker.

Unlike income transfers through welfare, the guaranteed child's exemption, because it would be applied *universally*, would not carry the stigma of "welfare" or public assistance. As well, it would not discourage work. If the child-caring parent worked, he or she would continue to receive the benefit. Further, the program would be efficient and inexpensive to administer, since it would not involve a large and complicated bureaucracy overseeing complex eligibility requirements or means testing. Finally, it would prove an efficient distribution mechanism in terms of promoting equity and fairness for all children by ensuring that poor children receive the same benefits as children from wealthier families.

Double the Exemption

One of the main tax advantages denied poor families with children in the United States is the benefit derived from the mortgage deduction.

---

[9] Over the years the value of the child's exemption has decreased substantially. The 1990, exemption of $2,150 was one-third the value of the child's exemption in 1948 (Taylor, 1991; National Commission on Children, 1991). Consequently, many have suggested doubling the exemption for children. The Progressive Policy Institute has recommended that the child exemption be increased from $2,300 to $6,000 or $7,000 per child in order to restore the exemption to the value it had in 1948 (Browning and Evison, 1993, 716).

Table 11.5 The Value of the Mortgage Deduction at
25 Percent Tax Bracket

Mortgage Amount	Value of Exemption
$50,000	$812
$75,000	1,219
$100,000	$1,625
$200,000	$3,250

Note: Assuming a 6.5 percent mortgage interest rate.

This can be substantial. For example, for a family with a $75,000 mortgage in the 25 percent tax bracket (average income tax), the mortgage deduction amounts to about $1,219 a year (see table 11.5). For a family with a home mortgage of $100,000, the deduction is more than $1,600 a year. A family with a home mortgage of $200,000 receives an annual federal benefit of $3,250. Clearly, for families with high-cost housing and mortgage payments, the benefit of the mortgage deduction is considerably more than the average annual welfare (TANF) benefit received by a mother with two children.

Further, since the deduction is often permitted against state and local income tax, it can be worth even more. As Jonathan Kozol (1991: 55) observes, "property-tax deductions granted [to homeowners] by the federal government were $9 billion. An additional $23 billion in mortgage-interest deductions were provided to homeowners: a total of some $32 billion. Federal grants to local schools, in contrast, totaled only $7 billion, and only part of this was earmarked for low income districts. Federal policy, in this respect, increases the existing gulf between the richest and poorest schools."

Since poor families are rarely able to benefit from a mortgage deduction, the deduction has had an unintended *dis*-equalizing effect among the population. To a poor family struggling to provide for its children and unable to buy a house, the tax advantage is effectively denied. Even if the poor family were able to purchase a house and acquire a mortgage, the benefit would be limited compared to the high-income family. The guaranteed child's exemption could be used to balance this disadvantage. In this regard, if the custodial parent did not claim a mortgage deduction, the family should be entitled to a *double* guaranteed child's exemption.[10] Permit-

---

[10] What little borrowing low-income families can do is usually limited to credit cards and other nonsecured loans that are not tax deductible. Consequently, the poor pay high interest rates and receive no tax benefits.

ting a double exemption would serve to more effectively equalize the distribution of tax benefits to all families.[11]

Overall, while the deduction mechanism in the tax law has been used successfully to achieve a variety of socially desirable purposes, its main limitation as applied to children is that it denies benefits to poor children for actions over which they have no control. For example, in addition to the mortgage deduction, the federal government provides a Dependent Care Tax Credit (DCTC) that in 2003 allows parents to deduct up to 35 percent of their child care expenses up to $3,000 per year for one child and up to $6,000 per year for two or more children.[12] Since it is a tax credit most poor families gain nothing. The estimated cost of this program is approximately $4 billion.

Limitations

It can be argued that the guaranteed child exemption might, as does welfare, serve as a disincentive for labor force participation by the parent, since the exemption eliminates "conditioning" the children's allowance on the parent's work effort. The guaranteed child exemption assumes children should not be denied income security because of their parent's actions.

Better ways exist to encourage labor force participation than conditioning a child allowance to it, which has the net effect of trying to motivate the parent by threatening to punish the child. Empirical studies of the labor market suggest that the best ways to encourage labor force participation are (1) to provide child care services, (2) to establish benefits that reward labor force participation (such as the Earned Income Tax Credit program), and (3) to pursue policies that increase the demand in the labor market for employment of single parents (Ellwood, 1989; Levitan, 1990).

---

[11] The mortgage deduction was placed in the tax code to stimulate and encourage home ownership, which has been very successful, since today the wealth of most U.S. families is represented by home ownership. Avery, Elliehausen, and Canner (1984a, b) observed that the average family net worth of homeowners was $50,125, compared to $15 for the average renter. Housing is where most families have built their savings. In 1988, 43 percent of total net worth in the United States derived from home ownership (*Wall Street Journal*, 1991). Phillips (1993: 180) observes, "Right up to the 95th percentile, the solid middle class was home-dependent because only the top 1 percent or 2 percent of U.S. households had most of their net worth in financial assets like stocks and bonds."

[12] The children must be under age 13. For parents with adjusted gross incomes above $43,000, the maximum credit is $600 for one dependent and $1,200 for two or more dependents. For a family with income of $50,000 the Dependent Care Tax Credit is of greater value than the tax deduction for the child. In a sense these families receive more than a double exemption (see table 11.4).

It is important to note that the "guaranteed child's exemption" is simply intended to ensure that poor children receive the same children's allowance benefits already provided to wealthier children.[13] The net effect of the guaranteed child's exemption would be to no longer *deny* benefits directed to and meant for children because of the actions of others, namely their parents, over whom they have no control. As a universal approach it would guarantee that all children would be treated equally and fairly without the stigmatization of a means-tested benefit.

Child Support—Collecting What's Due

Currently, only a modest fraction of poor children in single-parent families receive child support income from their non-custodial parent. The proportion of never-married mothers who receive child support payments is especially low. Research indicates that more than $34 billion in potential child support income goes unpaid each year and that almost two-thirds of single mothers receive no assistance.

Center on Budget and Policy Priorities, 1998

When a two-parent family breaks apart, the income-earning parent usually goes off and starts afresh, becoming, as it were, a free person—free of any labor-intensive child care responsibilities. The remaining parent is left with increased child care demands, limited employment opportunity, and reduced earning capacity. In most instances, the child-caring parent rarely receives adequate or equitable financial support for the children from the noncustodial parent through the current court-administered mechanisms of child support collection. Blank (1997) reports that less than half of the children who do not live with their fathers ever received a child support award from the courts. For children born out of wedlock, less than a quarter ever received a child support award. At a time when divorces were infrequent and children born out of wedlock rare, the problem could be managed by substituting a "bundled" welfare benefit for lost or uncollected child support. Over the years, with the increase in the number of children living in divorced or never married families, the problem of uncollected child support has become more severe.

---

[13] The provision of income support to low-income mothers is a separate issue and needs to be separated from the provision of the child's exemption.

Determining the Monthly Child Support Payment

The child support collection mechanism used in the United States emerged from the primary role that state courts play in domestic relations. When a husband and wife seek to divorce they usually turn to the courts. If there are assets involved, the court will assist in the division of those assets. The court is also instrumental in deciding child custody questions if they are in dispute. It is only logical that the courts continue their involvement in issues of child support.

The mechanisms the courts use for this determination, be it a standardized formulas, a set of guidelines to be interpreted by a judge, or a combination of these, is legislated by the various states. Many states now provide a Web-based calculator to determine the amount owed based on a variety of inputs such as number of children, age of children, noncustodial parents income, et cetera. [14]

Dismal Record of Collecting Support

While a court may stipulate a level of support, collecting that support has been another matter. Child support arrangements may be agreed to in court, but they are not always fully complied with. This is especially true for unmarried mothers with children for whom the problem becomes particularly acute. Despite the rhetoric about tracking down "dead beat dads" and making sure they contribute to the support of their children, the United States has one of the industrial world's lowest levels of child support collection.

In 2000, the Census Bureau estimated that child support collections in the United States should amount to $60 billion a year, of which $17.1 billion a year would actually be collected.

Despite this history, the federal government's Office of Child Support Enforcement (OCSE) has reported progress in collecting child support during the last decade. As seen in figure 11.4 there has been a consistent increase in the amount of child support collected but primarily for nonwelfare families. Unfortunately, those families in greatest financial need—welfare families—have seen little progress.

---

[14] A sense of the variation in approaches to calculating child support can be gained by reviewing the numerous Web-based calculators used to estimate child support payments in each state (see www.childwelfare.com/book).

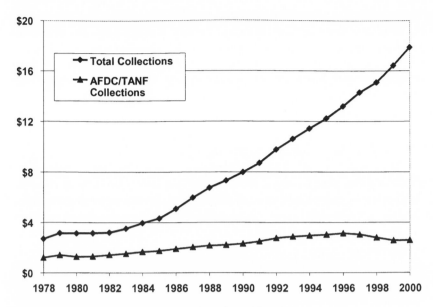

Figure 11.4 Child Support Collections (in Billions)
Source: Office of Child Support Enforcement (2002).

Currently the amount of child support collected is about one-quarter of what should fairly be collected. Delinquent child support payments now exceed $84 billion. There have been several high-profile collection efforts, but progress on reducing the amount of delinquent child support has been slow (Pear, 2002). Nevertheless, less than $4 billion of the $84 billion in arrears (or one-twentieth of the amount owed) is collected annually. As with welfare under TANF, child support is primarily a state responsibility. There is considerable variation among the 51 state systems (Garfinkel, Miller, McLanahan, and Hanson, 1998).

Much speculation has focused upon why some parents do not pay child support (Chambers, 1979; Johnson, Levine, and Doolittle, 1999). The most obvious answer is: Why should they? Aside from any moral obligation, which thus far has not proved sufficient, most fathers sense they have little to fear if they stubbornly refuse to pay.[15] The mother, after all, lacks

---

[15] Numerous books and Web sites provide advice and suggestions on strategies for avoiding child support enforcement efforts. Typical of these is attorney Ronald Isaac's "how to" guide for fathers wishing to avoid child support, entitled *How to Minimize Child Support*. Self-described as "a book giving proven tactics on how to avoid unreasonable child support payments" it includes sample pleadings and related documents. Topics include advice on 1) fighting out-of-state orders; 2) safeguarding your assets; 3) shifting income to spouses; 4) paying your new spouse rent and so on.

the traditional reciprocity arrangements available to other creditors in civil court. Unlike a bank out to collect on an automobile loan, she cannot obtain a court order to repossess anything. In fact, many fathers angrily believe the mother already possesses everything of value. The mother cannot even register delinquent payments with credit bureaus, something that might constitute an effective means of forcing payment.

Ability to Pay: The Cassetty Research

One of the more popular and detrimental myths about child support is that most noncustodial parents (fathers) do not pay child support because they simply do not have the money. After leaving their former spouse and children, it is argued, they incur new expenses and demands that prevent them from making adequate child support payments.[16] This issue was carefully examined by Cassetty (1978) using data from a longitudinal analysis of family income for 5,000 families using the Michigan panel income study.

Cassetty developed an "ability to pay" measure that involved two principles. First, payment of child support should never reduce the noncustodial parent's income below the poverty line (as defined for his or her current family). Second, the noncustodial parent should not be forced to pay support if the custodial parent's position, relative to the poverty line, was better than the noncustodial parent's. Following these two principles, Cassetty calculated the noncustodial parent's ability to pay by subtracting an amount equal to the parent's poverty level from his or her total income. Using the subsample of family divorces and separations in the longitudinal *Panel Study of Income Dynamics,* Cassetty examined the relative position of the noncustodial parent and the lone child-caring parent relative to the poverty line. She found that 80 percent of the noncustodial parents' households were better off financially after leaving their former families and far better off than the families they left behind. Could some of the noncustodial parent surplus, which derived in part from the lifting of child care expenses, be used to offset the declining financial condition of the single parent's family?

---

[16] In fact, there are wide variations in the earnings of noncustodial fathers. Garfinkel (1992: 130–131) indicates that the incomes of fathers of children born out of wedlock are low (about $6,000 to $10,000 a year) compared to divorced fathers (about $11,000 to $20,000 a year). This explains, in part, why a marriage does not take place for many women in this context; the father would be unable to adequately provide for the family. In fact, welfare, even with all its failings, may be viewed as a more reliable provider. This problem highlights how important ensuring employment opportunity is to efforts at welfare reform.

To examine this question, Cassetty applied the AAP index (estimate of Amount Able to Pay for child support) to the sample of family splits in the 5,000 families from the Michigan panel data. Her findings revealed the great disparity between what a noncustodial parent might be able to contribute, in a context of equity, and what the average noncustodial parent did in fact contribute. The disparity was greatest among the poor, where payments by noncustodial parents amounted to only 7 percent of what they might equitably have been expected to pay (a $24 monthly payment compared to an AAP calculation of $338). The more affluent parents, however, did not contribute much more. The affluent paid only 23 percent of what they might equitably have been expected to pay ($72 vs. $308).

The Cassetty data suggest that, overall, only 15 percent of expected child support payments are actually paid. That is, absent fathers kept for themselves 85 percent of what they might otherwise be expected to pay (using Cassetty's conservative estimate of what the noncustodial parent could pay). Thus, we can reasonably conclude that children are being denied child support, not because the funds are unavailable, but because the court-administered collection mechanism has proven ineffective.

Clearly there are some fathers who have a difficult time providing adequate child support (Rich, 2001). Blank (1997) reported that many unmarried fathers are homeless or otherwise in difficult financial situations. In the mid-1990s about 11 percent of unmarried fathers were under court supervision. For Black fathers 37 percent were under the supervision of the judicial system (that is, in jail or on parole or probation).

Child Support Collection as the Mother's Responsibility

The fundamental problem of the child support system is that collection of child support has historically been viewed as a civil matter in which the child-caring parent, usually the mother, is required to collect child support from the noncustodial parent, usually the father. Following are the steps a mother is usually required to follow in attempting to get any child support from a father unwilling to pay it.

1. She must acquire the services of an attorney. Since competent attorneys are expensive, this may require considerable outlay of her already limited financial resources, something she will have to weigh against the possible amount of child support it may produce.
2. She will have to meet with the attorney. While this may seem trivial, it can amount to a considerable burden to a woman already

    overburdened with a job, child care responsibilities, and maintaining a household.

3.   She will have to provide all necessary documentation proving nonpayment, taking care to observe any technical requirements of the court designed to safeguard the rights of the father.
4.   She may have to assist in locating the father, who may have gone off to another state, and she may require the services of a private investigator.
5.   The mother will find herself having to assume an adversarial stance toward the father, which could well aggravate an already tense and difficult relationship, thereby significantly undermining any hope of reconciliation and accord.

Even should the mother finally get the father into court, and the court order him to pay child support, there is no assurance he will ever do so. Should this happen, she can, if she wishes, turn to local civil authorities for help in forcing the noncustodial parent to pay court-ordered child support. The amount of manpower and resources devoted to this endeavor is significant. In 1990, Sisman reported that on any given day in many large metropolitan areas, such as Los Angeles County, half or more of the district attorneys are working to collect money from absent parents in child support cases.[17] But even with this enormous legal effort, the results are discouraging, because such enforcement frequently costs more than paying child support directly to single mothers and their children. To be cost-effective, child support enforcement programs must select only cases where a reasonable probability of obtaining child support payments exists. Such a policy is, of course, unfair and counter to the legal doctrine that requires the law be applied equally to everyone. Further, it is children from poor families that most need assistance in child support collections but who are the least likely to represent cases that would prove cost-effective for collection efforts.

Faced with such an exhausting and costly legal gauntlet which, after all is said and done, may not lead anywhere, many single mothers conclude that it is easier to make ends meet without child support than to fight to collect it, thereby avoiding (at least) an even greater measure of anger and bitterness.

The only mothers who are assured that their collection efforts will not directly cost them are mothers receiving welfare, whose legal fees are paid

---

[17] In 2000, California replaced the county run system based on district attorney collections with a state run system. However, in 2003 state budget cuts resulted in substantial staff reductions which imperiled the effectiveness of the new system. In Los Angeles County less than one third of child support payments were collected (Martin and Fox, 2003).

by the state.[18] However, when support payments are secured by the courts, most of the money collected goes not to the mother, but is kept by the welfare system and applied against the legal and welfare costs. Further, the payments are frequently unreliable and tend to diminish over time (Cassetty, 1978: 39).

An Easy, Reliable Collection System

The collection of child support payments is—like bank deposit insurance, defense, road building, social insurance for seniors, and public education—too important to society to leave to voluntary compliance. What is needed is an easy and reliable means of collecting child support payments from noncustodial parents that does not intrude on the relationship between the noncustodial parent and the child. Also, it should no longer avail free, noncustodial parents a means of cleverly escaping responsibility. Often the hurt and anger and other emotions which have surrounded the separation of the parents prevent rational discussion of child support. What is required is an approach which removes the child support responsibility from this volatile emotional context and assures regular payments to support the needs of the children.

Also, we must accept that the mother is *not* responsible for collecting child support, since, as we have seen, she has little or no means of doing so. The father is responsible for paying child support. If he does not pay, it should be the government's responsibility to collect, since they have mechanisms for effective and efficient collection.

How Other Countries Do It

In almost all other developed countries the government assures that a minimal child support payment is collected through something called "advance maintenance payments." Under this approach, the mother receives a minimal child support payment which the state then has responsibility for collecting from the father. Given the authority and various collection strategies available to the government, high rates of collection with minimal administrative costs have been achieved.

---

[18] The federal Office of Child Support Enforcement reports that the cost-effectiveness ratio for "Non TANF" cases is 3.38, while it is .57 for "TANF/FC" cases. In short, enforcement efforts are only cost effective in "Non TANF" cases.

Germany: Advance Maintenance Payments

Typical of most countries in Europe, Germany uses an advance maintenance payments program. If a single parent does not receive child support equal to at least the established amount due from the nonresident parent, then the children receive an advance maintenance payment. The children living with one parent are eligible for an advance maintenance payment of up to $185 a month for a period of up to six years. After advancing the mother with the maintenance payment, the government then takes responsibility for collecting the funds it has advanced for the children from the nonresident parent. This policy ensures that all children in single parent families in Germany receive at least a minimal level of child support.

New Zealand

In New Zealand a single mother must follow only three simple steps to obtain child support:

- First, the mother files an application for child support at the tax office (Inland Revenue).
- Second, the tax office uses a standard formula[19] to determine the amount of child support due. A letter is then sent to both mother and father telling them how much is due.
- Third, the tax office collects the child support payment from the father and passes it to the mother.

Most European countries use an advance maintenance payment scheme like that described for Germany and New Zealand which assures that child support is paid (see table 11.6). Within this scheme the single mother is provided with a minimal child support payment which the government then attempts to collect from the absent father. Most of the countries use their national tax or revenue office to collect the payment.

The Netherlands provides single mothers with a social assistance payment equal to 90 percent of the minimum wage.[20] The single mother is not required to seek employment until her youngest child is over five years old. Thus, the substantial social assistance payment obviates the need to provide an advanced maintenance payment in the Netherlands.

---

[19] To calculate the amount of child support due the tax office (Inland Revenue) determines the father's taxable income. From this they deduct a living allowance and multiply the result by a percentage rate.

[20] The national government guarantees 70 percent of the minimum wage, and the local governments are asked to fund the remaining 20 percent (Barnes, Day and Cronin, 1998).

Table 11.6 Countries that Take Public
Responsibility for Collecting Child Support

	Provide an Advance Maintenance Payment
Austria	Yes
Belgium	Yes
Denmark	Yes
Finland	Yes
France	Yes
Germany	Yes
Netherlands	No
Norway	Yes
Sweden	Yes
United Kingdom	Yes
United States	No

Source: Corden (1999: Table 2.3).

How the United Kingdom Changed

The United Kingdom had a child support collection system similar to that in the United States, and, like the United States, had a dismal record of collecting child support. In 1998, a parliamentary study group published a green paper examining the child support system (Child Support Agency, 1998). The report detailed the low compliance of absent fathers with the current child support system and the ineffectiveness of the various enforcement strategies that Britain had employed. After reviewing several approaches, the report recommended removing the responsibility for collecting child support from the mother and placing it with the government. A child support collection system operated by the government was proposed that would provide an automatic payment to the single mother. It would then use the national tax system to collect the payment from the absent father.

The advantage of this approach is that it takes the volatile task of assessing and collecting child support away from the single mother, who is often a partisan in the breakup of the family, and places it in the hands of the government. Children, it was argued, are entitled to child support and it should not be the responsibility of the mother to collect it. Further, having the mother collect it often leads to unnecessary antagonism and discord.

Proponents of the new system feared that the public might resist the proposal. However, the proposal was met with widespread support and only limited resistance, and subsequently it was enacted. Two years later a government white paper was published outlining a plan for switching over to the new system by 2002 (see www.csa.gov.uk).

Implementing Advance Maintenance Payment in the United States

In the United States the time is right to consider a child support system operated through the federal tax system. The mechanism by which child support could be efficiently and effectively collected and redistributed through taxation is not complicated. Basically, fathers would be shifted to a "child support" tax table at the time of separation or divorce, thereby subjecting them to a slightly higher tax rate based on their gross earnings and the number of children concerned. Their employer would withhold the additional money for child support along with other withholding taxes.

Benefits to custodial parents or guardians would be set according to a fixed national schedule. Noncustodial parents would pay, say, an additional 12 percent in federal income tax.[21] The single parent might receive, for example, $150 for the first child, and $100 for the second and for each additional child a month.[22] The payment would be provided to every custodial parent regardless of income. The mandatory payroll deduction could only be disregarded if the noncustodial parent obtained a waiver from the court because other appropriate payment arrangements had been made. In the case of wealthy and upper-income fathers, the deduction would not prevent the mother from obtaining additional support through civil litigation. While the support assured in this manner would perhaps not amount to a great deal for wealthy parents, it would ensure that every single parent received the minimal child support required to meet the financial needs of the children in their custody.[23]

---

[21] Jones, Gordon, and Sawhill (1976) found that the income of most single noncustodial fathers rises an average of 12 percent while the income of their related custodial spouses declines. Perhaps a sliding scale could be used beginning at 5 percent up to $20,000, then 7.5 percent for income to $30,000, 10 percent up to $40,000, and 12 percent thereafter until the child support costs are paid.

[22] Irwin Garfinkel (1992: 47) proposes a child support assurance system that would guarantee each child between $2,000 to $2,500 per year for the first child and $1,000 for each additional child. The program is similar to the advance maintenance payment approach except that it determines the amount due using a formula and then collects that amount.

[23] If the noncustodial parent moves out of state, the custodial parent would not be required to use the collection mechanisms of the state where the noncustodial parent moved to because the federal tax system would automatically collect the necessary funds regardless of locality.

The advance maintenance payment program would be based upon several principles:

- First, the noncustodial parent should not be allowed to abandon responsibility for the economic well-being of their children.
- Second, the enforcement of child support payments should not prove a severe financial burden on the noncustodial parent or discourage their participation in the labor force.
- Third, the burden of ensuring collection of child support should not be carried solely by the child-caring parent, or, failing such collection, shift to become, indirectly through the TANF program, a burden carried by the general public.
- Fourth, payment of child support should not be linked to other issues such as visitation rights.

The advance maintenance payment program suggested here assumes that responsibility for collecting child support is a public trust that rests with society at large, whose future depends ultimately upon the health and well-being of its children. The mechanisms used to accomplish this transfer of child support income must be elevated in significance so that noncompliance is removed as the central issue. The role of the government must become one of facilitating and enforcing an important and necessary obligation in as efficient a manner as possible.[24] Such a collection approach would not involve new public tax dollars to provide income support. It merely represents a reform mechanism for more effective collection and distribution of income.

Initially, the advance maintenance payment program might cause some disruption in current child support arrangements. Many noncustodial spouses presently paying child support might ask for a reduction in their payment level to reflect the tax that would be levied against them. This could be achieved by a consent order signed and agreed to by the child-caring parent. The program would not abolish the right of child-caring parents to take legal action to obtain standards of child support compatible with the noncustodial spouse's earning capacity. Rather, the program would provide a floor of support which could, through the courts, be augmented. Should two parents work out a mutually acceptable agreement for child support payments, such evidence could be used to release the noncustodial parent from the incremental tax rate.

Finally, a universal coverage program would also help eliminate an aggravating problem that exists at every socioeconomic level of society: love

---

[24] Other countries, such as New Zealand, administer the obligation in this manner (Kamerman and Kahn, 1983; Stuart, 1986).

that has somehow twisted into hate; two people trapped in unrelenting bitterness and acrimony, husbands unwilling to pay "the least dime to that [expletive deleted]," wives angry about the "dead beat [expletive deleted] who ran out on his family." In the middle are the children, growing more disillusioned and despairing at what the future holds for them. In their eyes can be seen the pain of a heartless and brutal policy that has failed to protect those least able to protect themselves.

Developing equitable and effective child support collection can be achieved at little or no public expense. Establishing a universal child support collection program by way of an advance maintenance payment approach would reduce the expense of child support collections by replacing the current inefficient court system with a simple modification of the federal income tax laws. Just as the federal government collects its taxes when income is earned, so must children be entitled to collect their child support from income as it is earned. Implementing such a program would shift a substantial burden of income support for children from the general public to nonpaying noncustodial parents and produce considerable tax savings.

Alternative Approach: Child Support Assurance

Garfinkel (1992) proposed a Child Support Assurance System (CSAS) that would accomplish much the same goal as the advance maintenance payment program outlined above. Based on the same principal of federally insured child support collection proposed by Schorr (1965) several decades earlier, the program would require that all noncustodial parents (Garfinkel uses the term "nonresident parents") provide a proportion of their gross income for the care and support of their children at a rate that would be determined by legislation, and that would be withheld from income. The child would receive the full amount directly from the government. A variant of this approach has been implemented in Wisconsin and has proven successful.

Conclusion

The United States is currently the only country in the industrialized world which provides no children's allowance to those children who most need it, and virtually no assurance of child support collection to single mothers. The current tax exemption approach to a children's allowance effectively means no benefit for poor children. As it is tied to substantial reportable income, it benefits only families with modest or high earnings.

Likewise, the current performance of the court-based child support collection system for poor children leads to virtually no assistance for the mothers who need it. While there may be situations where a court-administered payment collection system is appropriate, collection of child support is not one of them. It has proven too cumbersome and slow, and by placing the burden of collection on the mother, the approach only serves to exhaust resources and further antagonize relationships between separated parents. In fact, every effort should be made to reduce the need for court involvement.

It is the absence of support in these two areas—children's allowance and assurance of child support collection—which largely explains why there has been such a heavy reliance on means-tested welfare. Indirectly, welfare has been used as a substitute for these two essential income support programs (in effect, a bundled benefit). The principal limitation of a means-tested benefit like welfare is that it sets up a kind of tax scheme that reduces incentives for both working and getting remarried. When the individual collecting welfare begins working, their welfare benefit is quickly clawed back. Further, the means-tested benefit is often viewed as charity and, thus, can be demeaning to the beneficiary.

In most European countries children receive both a *children's (or family) allowance* and an *advance maintenance payment* of child support. For the most part these are provided as universal programs. This universality means that they are given to both poor and wealthy alike, and not as charity, so no stigma is attached. The universality also means that the programs are not means-tested and taken away when a child's single mother goes to work or gets remarried. The mother continues to receive the full benefits even after she obtains additional income.

The almost complete failure to provide these two programs explains why the United States—the richest country in the world—has the highest rates of child poverty. Our view is that we should provide just such programs—a children's allowance plus an advance maintenance payment for child support. As seen in table 11.7, in combination the two programs, along with universal child care, would provide benefits that are *higher* than is currently provided in most states through welfare (TANF).

Table 11.7 Proposed Universal Programs to End Child Poverty

| | Monthly Benefit | |
	One Child	Two Children
Advanced Maintenance Payment	$150	$250
Guaranteed Child Exemption	100	200
Universal Child Care (ages 3 to 5)	200	400
	------	-----
Total	450	850

Average TANF payment for mother with two children	
Mississippi	$140
Wyoming	142
Texas	162
Illinois	233
Florida	250
Wisconsin	447
New York	457
California	491
Massachusetts	518

Further, funding the programs would cost substantially less than is currently spent to administer welfare (TANF). The programs would not necessitate obtrusive government interference in the lives of families, but, being universal entitlements, would be easy to administer, producing substantial savings by all but eliminating the administrative bureaucracy required for welfare and the cumbersome child support enforcement agencies.

For poor children and their mothers the combination of these benefits would make the kind of difference that Social Security has made for the elderly. Together they would dramatically reduce the poverty and hardship of low-income and poor mothers and their children, ending the disparity in child poverty rates that exists between the United States and other industrialized countries.

These two programs—an advance maintenance payment and a guaranteed child's exemption—would restore the social contract that provides to all children, regardless of their parents status and income, equivalent benefits to public programs.

12

Child Future Savings Account:
Social Security for Children

In contrast to most public programs this one does not restrict the rights of private property on behalf of some collective good. It is based on the opposite premise: property is so important to the free development of individual personality that everybody ought to have some. Without stakeholding, formal freedom easily degenerates into a farce—as Anatole France once jested, the equal right to sleep under the bridges of Paris.

. . . a propertyless person lacks crucial resources needed for self-definition. He can never taste the joys and sorrows of real freedom—and the possibilities of learning from his own successes and mistakes. He is condemned to a life on the margin, where the smallest shocks can send him into a tailspin. He can never enjoy the luxury of asking himself what he really wants out of life, but is constantly responding to the exigent demands of the marketplace.

Bruce Ackerman and Anne Alstott, *The Stakeholder Society*

In 1966, James Coleman published his historic study of the factors which influence the success of children in school. The report, *On Equality of Educational Opportunity*, is viewed by many as the most important educational research of the twentieth century. The report found that the best predictors of success in school were not the amount of money spent on school facilities or teacher salaries, but rather the child's family background and the socioeconomic status of the school.

Elsewhere it has been observed that at the very earliest years of childhood children know whether or not they have hope and opportunity (Kelly, 2003). This knowledge and understanding shapes their development and outlook (Seigal, 1985). When children begin school they usually start, as Jonathan Kozol (1991: 57) observes, "with a degree of faith and optimism, and they often seem to thrive during the first few years. It is sometimes not until the third grade that their teachers start to see the warning signs of failure. By the fourth grade many children see it too . . . By fifth grade, many children demonstrate their loss of faith by staying out of school."

339

It cannot be overemphasized that the primary victims of poverty in America are not working-age men or single mothers, but children who grow up in circumstances devoid of hope or opportunity. The result has been a social misfortune whose proportions are deepening and which we are only beginning to appreciate. Although its physical form can be seen in the blighted neighborhoods of most major cities, its impact on the hopes and dreams of the poor, especially poor children, is not so visible. Investing the minimal amount in the development of poor children is unwise in the extreme, since children represent one of society's most valuable human resources (Denison, 1985).

Children from low income and poor families arrive at elementary school disadvantaged and unprepared (Hart and Risley, 1995). From the start they lag behind children from less stressful and impoverished home situations. As the Coleman study points out, the schools are hard pressed to overcome these disadvantages. To illustrate the disadvantage of children from poor neighborhoods one has only to examine the reading and math scores of children entering the Los Angeles Unified School District (LAUSD).[1]

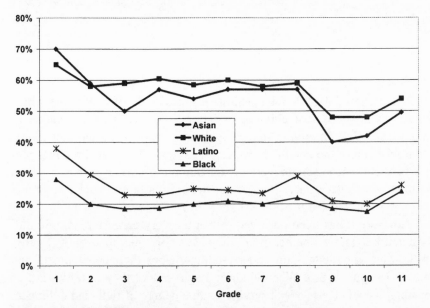

Figure 12.1 Reading Scores on the Stanford 9 (LAUSD)
Source: Meersman (1999).

---

[1] In 2000, the Los Angeles Unified School District served over 700,000 children.

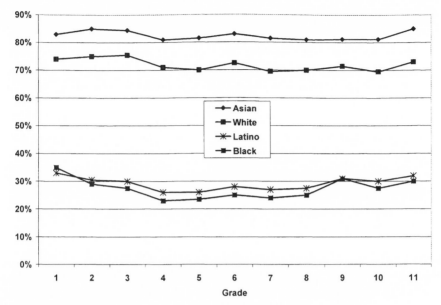

Figure 12.2 Math Scores on the Stanford 9, 1998–1999 (LAUSD).
Source: Meersman (1999).

As seen in Figures 12.1 and 12.2, Latino and Black children enter first grade well behind white and Asian children. In California, the median income of white and Asian families is substantially higher than the median income of Latino and Black children.[2] The constraints on family income are reflected in the performance of these children when they enter school.[3] Little change in the overall disparity between these groups occurs over the next dozen years of schooling. The difference in performance on reading and math tests recorded upon entry into first grade remain as the children prepare to leave high school. This is a discouraging finding. It emphasizes the need to provide children with a quality preschool experience, hope and a sense of opportunity (Hart and Risley, 1999). The public school system,

---

[2] In 2000, the median family income in California for whites was $65,342 [54,698]; for Asians, $61,385 [59,324]; for Latino, $35,980 [34,397]; and for Black, $39,726 [33,255]. U.S. values are reported in square brackets (Lopez, 2003).

[3] Hart and Risley (2003: 4) observe, "During the 1960s War on Poverty, we were among the many researchers, psychologists, and educators who brought our knowledge of child development to the front line in an optimistic effort to intervene early to forestall the terrible effects that poverty was having on some children's academic growth. We were also among the many who saw that our results, however promising at the start, washed out fairly early and fairly completely as children aged."

which used to be viewed as the great equalizer, no longer seems effective in providing disadvantaged children with an opportunity to alter the circumstances which they were born into.

To allow for children from disadvantaged backgrounds to succeed will require more than additional spending on education. Without question, adequate school funding is vital. But to alter the life trajectories of young people will require a fundamentally different approach.

Our first step is to acknowledge that a *structural problem* is the root cause of the continuing child poverty in our county. Our residual approach to children and their needs says, in effect, that poverty is somehow the fault of the child, who must demonstrate eligibility for public aid before support is forthcoming.

Fundamental Reform Is Required

Although the child support and children's allowance reforms proposed in the previous chapter are important programs that will help reduce child poverty, they will not eliminate the root cause of child poverty. We need a bold new approach that implements fundamental reform—a Marshall Plan of sorts directed at child poverty that has the potential of substantially changing the socioeconomic status of poor children.

To be effective any program must begin in childhood and continue through late adolescence. Programs that provide opportunity during the child's transition to adult life, their emancipation from the family and embarkation into adult responsibilities, are essential ingredients for any comprehensive child welfare reform. Unless imaginative programmatic efforts to break the cycle of poverty are undertaken, that will provide children the *escape velocity* to break out of patterns established over years, even generations, we have little chance of ending poverty among children.

As we have seen, society does not want to encourage the formation of non-self-supporting households, since once these have been created little can be done to change them. Current social programs provide few positive incentives that discourage early child bearing. Instead, public assistance programs approach the problem using disincentives, that is, offering only the most meager of income supports to single mothers and their children. In recent years, since its reform, welfare has become even more meager. Ackerman and Alstott (1999: 196) observe, "America is so ungenerous in its welfare policies at present that it is hard to imagine it getting much stingier." The logic is that the less attractive life on welfare appears, the greater the likelihood that young women will avoid it.

Efforts to provide income protection for children through welfare payments confront the essential dilemma of how to target money that will effectively shield children from poverty and abuse without encouraging their single mothers, who receive the money, to have more children. Murray (1984: 203–204) addressed this issue:

> In deciding upon my stance in support or opposition of a policy that automatically provides an adequate living allowance for all single women with children, I am informed that one consequence of this policy is that large numbers of the children get better nutrition and medical care than they would otherwise obtain. Using this known fact and no others, I support the program. Now let us assume two more known facts, that the program induces births by women who otherwise would have had fewer children (or had them under different circumstances), and that child abuse and neglect among these children runs at twice the national average. Does this alter my judgment about whether the allowance is a net good? What if the incidence of abuse and neglect is three times as high? Five times? Ten times? A hundred times? The crossover point will be different for different people. But a crossover point will occur. At some point, I will say that the benefits of better nutrition and medical care are outweighed by the suffering of abused and neglected children. The first conclusion is that transfers are inherently treacherous. They can be useful; they can be needed; they can be justified. But we should approach them as a good physician uses a dangerous drug—not at all if possible, and no more than absolutely necessary otherwise.

The current meager public assistance benefits provided after welfare reform attempt to balance the need to provide minimal income protection for children with the need to discourage further childbearing by single mothers. Usually the balance neither provides adequate income protection for the children nor discourages disillusioned and alienated young women from having children they cannot adequately provide for.

A way out does exist. To understand what it is, we must appreciate what social resources and choices young people require in making the critical and difficult transition from childhood to adulthood.

Transitioning Young People to Self-Supporting Adult Life

Before they are even born, children require proper health care. This need is recognized in the provision of prenatal care[4] and counseling offered pregnant women. After children are born, adequate nutrition, health care (in-

---

[4] Women, Infants and Children (WIC).

cluding immunizations), and nurturing by the mother are essential. In the second year of life the list of the child's needs expands to include such services as day care and Head Start, which not only enable the parent to return to the work force, but provide essential mental and physical stimulation for the child's proper growth and development (Tobin, Wu, and Davidson, 1989).

When they reach school age, children require quality educational opportunities, not only for their own sake, but for society's as well. Free public education is provided in most parts of the world and often begins at three years of age.[5] In the United States free public education is provided for every child from age six to eighteen (Lindsey, 1991b; Children's Defense Fund, 2002).[6] Public education is regarded as an essential investment that prepares the child for responsible, self-reliant, and productive participation in our free market based society.[7]

High school begins the young person's transition to adult life. At this stage adolescents undergo major psychological and physiological growth and change. They develop a sense of personal identity (Erikson, 1959) and begin to consider the career options and opportunities open to them when they leave home: college, vocational training, job apprenticeships. For a few, adolescence is a time of experimentation with deviant behavior (Matza, 1964), as witnessed by the high rates of delinquency during this age.

When young people graduate from high school they begin the most important and difficult transition in their lives. They embark on their adult career, which, ideally, should be characterized by independence and self-sufficiency. If they have prepared for this transition, they will likely become productive and contributing adults. If not, they will be vulnerable to dependency and failure in a society that demands independence and self-reliance. In a free market economy, the passage from adolescence to adulthood requires more than years of physical, intellectual, and emotional development. It requires that young people have the financial resources that

---

[5] While most European countries provide publicly funded child care for 3- to 5-year-olds, the United States provides the least (chapter 4, table 4.9 of this book; Kamerman and Kahn, 1988).

[6] The average public expenditure for children is $7,000 a year. Kozol (1991) points out that the inequalities in education begin with funding. Some wealthy school districts spend more than $15,000 per student, while other poor districts spend less than $4,000 per student.

[7] Although a single parent on welfare with two children will likely receive less than $5,000 a year in welfare assistance to provide for shelter, clothing, electricity, phone, heating, transportation, and other living expenses, the public school system will likely spend more than $14,000 a year for educating her two children.

will permit emancipation from nearly two decades of dependence on their family, and that will enable them to sever ties with home and family and to embark successfully on an independent life.

Currently, only children from upper-middle-class and wealthy families can safely rely on such resources. For children from poor and low-income families, the resources, and hence opportunities, are too often absent. In many ways, the social and economic situation that poor youth face at this stage in their lives can be compared to a Monopoly board game. In Monopoly all players begin the game having $1,500, which, according to the game's logic, ensures that everyone has an equal opportunity of winning. One can imagine the effect if the rules allowed only selected players to start with $1,500, while others started with nothing. Those players who must roll the dice and move their token, knowing that they had no money to buy property or even pay rent, would soon regard the game as not much fun and begin "dropping out."

So it is with the "real life" economic game in which young people in a market economy find themselves. Too many children, realizing as they grow up that they will not have the resources and opportunities to move into productive adulthood, turn to early childbearing and public assistance, or worse, to drugs and crime. The Children's Defense Fund (1986) examined this issue with data from the *National Longitudinal Survey of Young Americans.* They compared teenage girls from poor families who lacked basic academic skills with those from affluent families and more skilled peers. They found that the poor teenage girls were nearly six times more likely to become pregnant. With little confidence in their future, teenagers living in poverty lacked the incentives to delay parenthood.

State Provisions for Youth Transitioning to Adulthood

Higher education provides one of the most promising avenues to success for young people. In today's world a college education has become an important building block for a successful career and has substantial impact on lifetime earnings (see Figure 12.3). Most states have developed public universities that are largely subsidized through public expenditures.

Although there is great variation in median income for different racial and ethnic groups (see footnote 2, this chapter), much of the difference can be explained by educational attainment. As seen in figure 12.4, the variation is largely the result of educational and, to a lesser degree, by race and ethnicity.

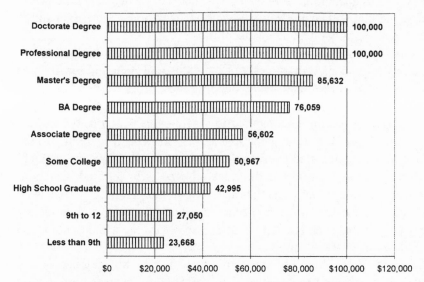

Figure 12.3 Education and Median Income of Families, 1999

Source: U.S. Census Bureau (2000, P60-209).
Online at www.census.gov/prod/2000pubs/p60-209.pdf.

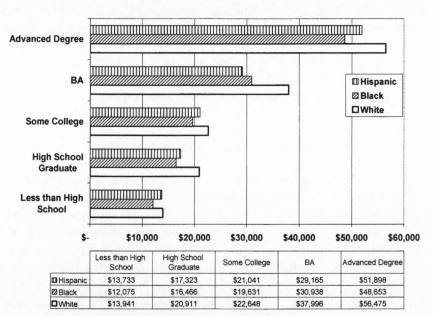

	Less than High School	High School Graduate	Some College	BA	Advanced Degree
Hispanic	$13,733	$17,323	$21,041	$29,165	$51,898
Black	$12,075	$16,466	$19,631	$30,938	$48,653
White	$13,941	$20,911	$22,648	$37,996	$56,475

Figure 12.4 Income, Race/Ethnicity and Education

Source: U.S. Census Bureau (2001).
Online at www.census.gov/population/socdemo/education/table19.dat.

I teach at the University of California in Los Angeles. I have been struck by the variations in access to higher education and foster care in California. In one sense, the University of California is a child welfare institution. It provides all the young people in the state with an opportunity to attend a top national university at very low cost. In fact, in California the provision of Cal Grants and other financial aid means that access to the university is restricted only by the admission decision. Once a young person is admitted, adequate financial aid is available to assure that all who are admitted will be able to attend regardless of their families financial circumstances.[8] In this sense, the university serves as a beacon of opportunity for all the children of the state.

The major service provided by the child welfare system is foster care. In California the public expenditure for children in foster care is similar to the public expenditure for the University of California. The average annual public expenditure per child for foster care exceeds $22,000 (Steering Committee, Study of Out-Of-Home Care Placement Costs, 1990; Barth, 1995). The average annual expenditure for each student in the University of California is less than $15,000.[9] Both foster care and a university education are provided to young people based on their admission into the particular system. Both systems are operated at public expense. Both systems are designed to improve the well-being of those served.

However, the University of California and the public child welfare system serve different populations. As seen in Figure 12.5, Black children are substantially underrepresented at the University of California, while they are substantially overrepresented in the foster care system. A willingness to spend on the poor is not the issue. The state spends substantially more, on a per child basis, on the foster care system which primarily serves the poor. Yet few view this distribution as advantageous to Black children.[10] While there has been a long standing concern with assuring access to the University of California for all children regardless of race or ethnicity, there has been little concern about access to the public child welfare system or with the imbalance between these two systems.

---

[8] This is true for most public universities. I should note that I am a beneficiary of the opportunity California provided (B.A., University of California, Santa Cruz, 1969).

[9] In 2001, the University of California enrolled approximately 114,000 full time undergraduate students, while the child welfare system in the state provided for approximately 93,000 children in foster care.

[10] Similar comparisons can be drawn between the state corrections system and the university. Macallair, Taqi-Eddin and Schiraldi (1999: 1) report that "the ratio of imprisoned African-American males to those in state universities [both California State University and the University of California] is currently 5 to 1."

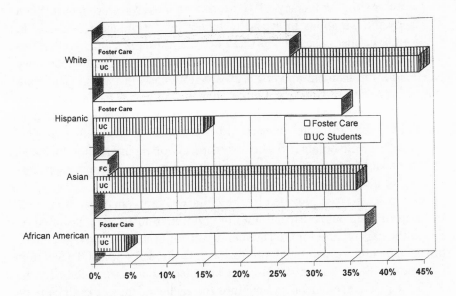

Figure 12.5 Percent of Population in Foster Care and Undergraduates at the University of California by Race/Ethnicity (2000)

Source: University of California, Office of the President. (2003); Needell et.al. (2003).

Buried in the troubling feeling Figure 12.5 produces is the seed for fundamental reform of the child welfare system.[11] Is it possible to have the public infrastructure of support for disadvantaged children look and perform more like the public infrastructure for advantaged children? The answer is yes, if we can move away from the residual model.

The public child welfare system will have a different impact on the life trajectory of the children it serves only if it develops avenues of opportunity that ensure that Black and Latino children and, more generally, economically disadvantaged children have access to higher education. As we have seen in the beginning of this chapter, Black and Latino children are already at a substantial disadvantage when they arrive at elementary school, a situation that is unlikely to change substantially over the years, as the data in Figures 12.1 and 12.2 demonstrate.

---

[11] In 2000, the freshman class at UCLA included 4 percent Black students and 15 percent Hispanic, while Los Angeles County included 10 percent Black and 57 percent Hispanic 18-year-olds. The population of the county in 2000 was about 9.5 million. Although UCLA serves a statewide, as well as national and international student body, more than half of freshmen class came from within the county.

The alienation of youth, especially low-income minority youth, is one of the most destructive consequences of the existing inequality, and the society that is unwilling to provide for initial "equal" opportunity, or at least a fair start, soon finds itself having to pay substantially more for child protective services, foster care, public assistance, drug rehabilitation programs, and overcrowded prisons.

So what can be done?

Solutions—Seedbed for Change

In their book, *The Stakeholder Society*, Ackerman and Alstott (1999), two professors at Yale's law school, propose a program that would provide all children a major stake in American society, "a one-time grant of eighty thousand dollars as the child reaches early adulthood." The only requirement to gain access to their stake is that the children graduate from high school. Ackerman and Alstott suggest that without such a program it is unlikely that disadvantaged young people will ever have a chance to achieve the American dream.

They propose that the grant be viewed not as a gift but rather as the initial stake needed for a chance at success in the free enterprise market economy in the United States. They provide for a number of conditions for accessing the grant. The young person would be able to access no more than $20,000 a year. They would be obliged to pay the money received back later in life as their earning power and ability to pay increased.

Although the "stakeholder" proposal may seem impractical and expensive it is not without precedent. The economic historian Denison (1985) has suggested that much of the great economic achievement of the United States during the half century between 1930 and 1980 can be credited to the idea of universal free education pioneered in the United States.[12] When first adopted, many viewed such a program as too costly and idealistic. Today, however, public school education is taken as a right of citizenship. It is viewed as key to providing equal opportunity to all children.

---

[12] During the twentieth century educational attainment in the United States has substantially increased. Before the twentieth century most people did not receive more than an eighth grade education. Less than a quarter of citizens graduated from high school, and about 10 percent went on to college. People born between World War I and World War II were much more likely to graduate from high school (61 percent) and about a fifth went on to college. The majority of people born after World War II and before 1963—the so-called baby boomers—not only graduated from high school (87 percent) but attended college (27 percent) as well. As a result, America leads the world in educational attainment and national income per capita (Denison, 1974, 1985).

529 College Savings Plan

If you start with $100 and contribute the same amount monthly to your child's account, you'll have accumulated over $60,000 at 10% interest over 18 years.

Laura Pickford Ramirez, *529 Plans*

In 1995, the General Accounting Office (GAO) conducted a study of the college savings plans various states offered to parents. Several years later Congress relied on the experience of the states and the GAO Report in drafting the 529 section of the tax code. Similar to Canada's Registered Educational Savings Plan, this provision provides for a tax-free 529 College Savings Plan.[13] The 529 plan allows a parent (or any relative) to invest money tax free in a college saving account so that when the child is ready to go to college the money necessary to attend will be available. In essence, the 529 College Savings Plan is a federally subsidized child savings account. It has the following features:

- 529 plans allow money in the account to grow tax free.[14]
- Withdrawals used to cover college costs are not taxable.
- Parent (or account owner) maintains control of the account until the child reaches age 18, 21, or 25.
- The account can accumulate as much as $300,000 per child.[15]
- If the child opts not to go to college, the parent can transfer the funds to another beneficiary.
- Funds in the account are professionally managed.
- Assets in the account are considered to be the property of the account owner (parent), which means that only 6 percent of the account balance will be considered in the financial aid eligibility calculation.
- Most states provide identical tax breaks on state income taxes for 529 withdrawals, but 23 states go further and provide upfront tax deductions.

---

[13] Provisions for the 529 account were included in the 2001 Tax Relief Act (Max, 2001). The program was imaginatively named after the section of the Internal Revenue Service (IRS) tax code that created it.

[14] An easy way to augment the 529 College Savings Plan is to sign up with Upromise (www.upromise.com) and let selected companies contribute to your child's account. Companies such as AT&T, America Online, Mobil, Exxon, JCPenney.com, and many more will contribute to your child's 529 account based upon a percentage of your purchases. Grocery stores and pharmacies also will contribute a percentage of your bill. Also, various manufacturers will contribute when you buy their products. These include Huggies diapers, Minute Maid, Kellogg's, Tylenol, and many more.

[15] Limits are set by individual states. In 2002, the amount ranged from $100,000 to $305,000.

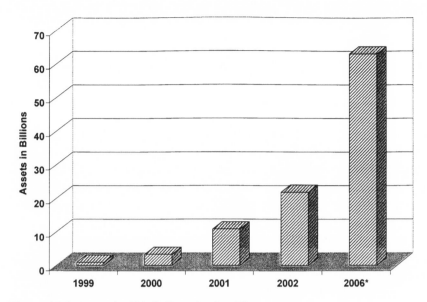

Figure 12.6 Assets in 529 College Saving Plans
Source: Kristof (2002). *The estimate for 2006 is from Cerulli Associates.

As of June 30, 2002, a total of $21.8 billion was invested in 529 plans, compared to $11 billion a year earlier in June 2001 (Cooper, 2002). Cerulli Associates (2002) estimates that by 2006 more than $63 billion will be invested in 529 plans (see figure 12.6). As with Canada's Registered Educational Savings Plan, most of the children for whom accounts have been opened and made available are from upper-income and wealthy families. Children from low-income and disadvantaged families are essentially denied the benefits of this major federally subsidized college savings plan.

Programs like the 529 College Saving Plan are a great idea, but unless there is a mechanism that allows working-class, low-income, and poor children to participate, these plans will simply accelerate and extend the inequality that already exists. What was meant to have a positive impact on society could end up having a negative impact if some way for all children to fully participate is not found. The gulf between children who have and children who don't will widen even more.

Social Security: A Proven Model

We need not look far to find a plan that will ensure that all children have a chance at success in life. Social Security, the "social savings" program that has proven successful in providing for the economic needs of the elderly in the United States, provides an ideal model for a similar children's program.

Before Social Security, the elderly were responsible for setting aside sufficient resources for their retirement. However, because too many individuals failed to do this, substantial poverty existed among the elderly. As we have mentioned before, Social Security eliminated such poverty by requiring that everyone save for their retirement by contributing to a "social savings" program during their working years which then provides benefits for them when they retire.

Social Security is a "social" insurance program, as opposed to an insurance program, which means that it serves a collective social purpose. Contributions to Social Security do not go into a special trust fund earmarked for the individual who has made the contribution. Instead, they go into a general fund from which they are distributed to current beneficiaries. The program operates on a pay-as-you-go basis, with retired beneficiaries being paid from contributions collected from the current working generation. Thus, benefits are only marginally related to contributions, and many current beneficiaries receive payments well in excess of what similar contributions to a private system would have entitled them to. Economist Joseph Pechman (1989: 171) points out that Social Security beneficiaries in the United States "as a group receive far larger benefits than those to which the taxes they paid, or that were paid on their behalf, would entitle them." He argues that instead of viewing Social Security as an "insurance" program for old age, it is better to understand it as an "institutionalized compact between the working and non-working generations" (p. 175).

Although some theorists have viewed Social Security as an unwanted intrusion by government into the affairs of the individual and have urged that it be voluntary (Feldstein, 1974), the success of the program in insuring income protection to the elderly has led to its continued widespread support. Indeed, there are no efforts to discourage participation. Quite the contrary, Social Security stipulates universal coverage, providing benefits for all irrespective of their income.

As a social savings program, Social Security provides a guaranteed minimum income for all beneficiaries, while also providing differential benefits related to the contributions the individual has made. Most importantly, Social Security does not have the stigma of a "public assistance" program, but retains the dignity of an "earned pension." Advocates and partisans who fight on behalf of the elderly for improved Social Security benefits are not viewed as asking for charity, only demanding what their constituency has earned. Over the years no other social program has achieved more widespread public support (Marmor, Mashaw, and Harvey, 1990). Social Security enjoys wide support because it is viewed not as a means tested income transfer program but as a social insurance program paid for by the beneficiaries (Aaron, 1982).[16]

The situation is in contrast to that of single mothers and their children receiving public assistance, who are viewed as people asking for a hand-out. Of course, the desire to lend a helping hand, especially to children, is what gives impetus to public assistance programs. As Murray (1984: 235–236) observed, "Most of us want to help. It makes us feel bad to think of neglected children and rat-infested slums, and we are happy to pay for the thought that people who are good at taking care of such things are out there. If the numbers of neglected children and number of rats seem to be going up instead of down, it is understandable that we choose to focus on how much we put into the effort instead of what comes out. The tax checks we write buy us, for relatively little money and no effort at all, a quieted conscience. The more we pay, the more certain we can be that we have done our part, and it is essential that we feel that way regardless of what we accomplish."

Because welfare is a means tested income transfer program, it is vastly different from Social Security. The single mothers and children who bene-fit from welfare (TANF) have made no contributions that might warrant a payment to them; they are simply poor. Thus, they are viewed by many as a "burden" on the back of the already overburdened tax payer. As we have seen, the answer in the United States has been to make public assistance so unattractive that those receiving it will want to stop (Jencks, 1993). The paradoxical result, however, has been a poverty trap with a grip so tight that once people get in, they are rarely able to muster the resources, en-ergy, or will to get out.

A Bold Approach:
Developing a Child Future Savings Account

In recent years Michael Sherraden (1991, 2002) and others have been pro-posing a shift in social welfare policy from the means tested income trans-fer approach (welfare) to an asset based approach (investment and saving). The focus of an asset-based approach is to provide individuals with the assets and savings needed to succeed in a free enterprise market economy.

---

[16] See Ozawa (1977) for further discussion of the regressive tax component elements of the Social Security program.

Rather than focusing on providing the minimal resources to ensure the daily needs of the poor, an asset based approach focuses on encouraging individuals to build up an asset base that will ensure their long term well-being. This is the underlying assumption of Social Security.

Whereas the original Social Security Act provided a "social insurance" approach to provide income assistance to the elderly, the same Social Security Act provided a means tested income transfer program to provide income support to poor mothers and their children. Over the years the "social insurance" approach has proven effective for seniors. The program is widely credited with ending poverty among seniors. In contrast, the means tested income transfer program for poor mothers and their children (AFDC) has been viewed as a failure and even credited by some with making the situation of those it served worse. In 1996, with the passage of welfare reform, AFDC was eliminated and replaced with a more restrictive state operated welfare program (TANF). The entitlement status of welfare ended, and the number of children on welfare plummeted. The original welfare program that had been included in the Social Security Act (1936) was gone.

The old welfare system had some advantages but it was also an impediment to fundamental reform. Now, with it gone, the stage is set for a bold new approach to ending child poverty. What might this new approach look like?

Something Like Social Security for Children

Just as Social Security requires citizens to prepare for their retirement years by setting up a social savings account, a similar Child Future Savings (CFS) account might be created that would provide a savings account for young persons to ensure they have the funds necessary at the age of 18 to embark successfully on adult life, regardless of the economic situation they are born into. It would provide poor children an opportunity to break free of the cycle of poverty by ensuring that they would have money for a college education or some other training opportunity.

At birth, every child, regardless of the current economic status of their family, would have a custodial account—a Child Future Savings account—opened in their name with an initial deposit of $1,000 assured by the government. The funds would be deposited in a registered brokerage firm account selected by the parent. Each year the account would receive an additional $500 deposit assured by the government from funds collected in the same fashion used by Social Security. In a sense, the child future savings account (CFS) would be a 529 plan guaranteed for all children.

The child's parents could, if they wished, contribute privately to the account, as could the child through his or her earnings, although such contributions would not diminish the government contribution. At age eighteen, the accumulated funds would be made available to the young person for approved career program expenditures, such as college tuition, vocational training, job-readiness programs, and so on.[17] By the time the child reached eighteen, a typical CFS deposit might have an accumulated balance of nearly $40,000 (see figure 12.7).

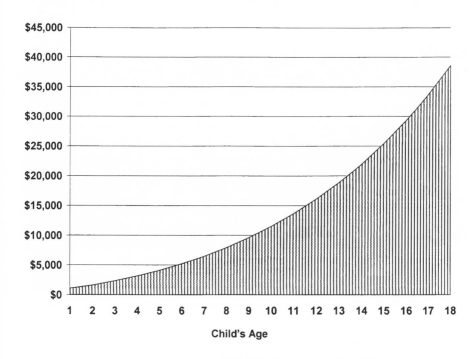

Figure 12.7 Projected Growth of a Child Future Savings Account

---

[17] The purpose of the Child Future Savings account is to provide young people with the resources needed for effective transition to adulthood. The funds are not for consumer needs and would not be made available for consumer items, but only for purposes that represent an investment in the young person's future.

Cost of the Program

Given roughly 4 million births a year in the United States, new CFS accounts would cost an estimated $4 billion annually. Maintaining the annual contribution to the accounts for the other roughly 65 million children under the age of eighteen would add another $33 billion, for a total annual cost of roughly $37 billion.

Following a start-up expense, the program would be funded entirely by children *repaying* their benefits during adulthood, using a collection mechanism similar to that used by the Social Security Administration, in which a payroll contribution of less than one half of 1 percent would be made by employee and employer.

Parents' Contribution

The cost could be reduced considerably by requiring parents to contribute to the cost of their child's CFS through a graduated tax schedule. For instance, parents with incomes above $30,000 might be asked to contribute at the rate of 1 percent of all taxable income above $30,000 (with appropriate adjustments for family composition). The rate of contribution could be increased by one half percent for each additional $10,000 of income (see table 12.1).

Table 12.1 Projected Tax Schedule

Family Income	Tax Contribution
$30,000	0
35,000	50
40,000	100
45,000	175
50,000	250
55,000	350
60,000	450
65,000	575
70,000	700
75,000	850
80,000	1,000

Such an approach which shared the cost of the child future savings account with parents would fund more than half the total cost of the program. Thus, the remaining cost of the program that would need to be funded through a payroll tax would be less than $15 billion (or less than one half of one percent from both employer and employee).

Canada's Approach: Registered Educational Savings Plan (RESP)

In Canada, a scheme resembling the proposed child future savings plan already exists. Parents can save money in a tax exempt Registered Educational Savings Plan (RESP), which allows them to contribute up to 4,000 Canadian dollars a year (2,528 U.S. dollars) fully tax deductible into a custodial account opened in the child's name with a registered security dealer. Funds in the account can be invested in stocks, bonds, mutual funds, and money market instruments.

Canada's Royal Bank advises parents that if they contribute the allowable $4,000 a year (2,528 U.S. dollars) for 21 years the funds in the account will likely grow to more than $250,000 (158,000 U.S. dollars)— "more than enough to ensure that your child or grandchild will be able to continue their education." Only a small fraction of Canadian families have been taking advantage of this government subsidized savings plan.[18]

Advantage of the CFS Plan

The primary advantage of the child future savings plan is that it provides the opportunity to save for college to *all* children regardless of their socioeconomic status. Because recipients of CFS would repay their benefits through payments made during their working adulthood, the Child Future Savings program represents an approach that, like Social Security, reinforces the broad social reciprocal contract between the generations. Further, the children would likely go on to pay substantially more taxes as productive citizens, and be less likely to incur social costs (i.e., welfare assistance or correctional system costs).[19]

---

[18] In 1998 Canada added a Canada Education Savings Grant (CESG) of 20 percent on annual contributions of up to $2,000 to the RESP.

[19] The best assurance of a sound Social Security system is a productive work force. Since Social Security is a contract between generations, the approach proposed here would strengthen the overall Social Security program by assuring that the generation coming of age would be able to meet its obligation to the generation retiring. Commenting on the high

Wealth Builder Approach

Financial well-being has two dimensions—income and wealth—one short term and the other long term. Income assistance payments that address the short-term income dimension by providing families with money for immediate basic needs such as shelter, food, and clothing do little to foster long-term accumulation of assets or wealth (Sherraden, 1990). The CFS account is essentially a long term wealth builder approach, something frequently overlooked by programs that attempt to ameliorate poverty. The account would be managed separately from current income security programs like Social Security or TANF, with rules developed and administered by a governing board to oversee the program's operation.[20]

Ideally, CFS funds would be held in custodial accounts at private brokerage firms where they could be invested in stocks, bonds, or mutual funds, in much the same way that college savings are invested in 529 College Savings Plans in the United States or Registered Education Savings Plans (RESPs) in Canada. Parents might select among approved mutual funds in which to invest their child's account balances. The child would be encouraged to participate in the investment decision-making process, perhaps receiving semiannual statements of their account balance that would reinforce the lessons of saving and investing.[21] By working with their own funds, children would be learning lessons and habits which could serve them in our society throughout their lives. In a sense, the CFS account is conceived more as a "capital building" account than a "savings account."

Responsibility for overseeing the program might be assigned to the child welfare system, where child welfare social workers would provide advice to the parent and child in making investment choices and developing a plan for productive and approved uses of funds in the child's account. In this manner, the child would establish a meaningful base for accumulating asset wealth and ownership in our economy.

---

rate of poverty among Canadian children, Eichler (1988: 49) observes, "The future consequences of neglecting to provide for our young could possibly disrupt the entire society. After all, it is the younger ones who have to produce the goods from which pensions are paid."

[20] The needs of children and the elderly are substantially different. Consequently, these programs should be kept separate. The approach proposed here is simply to model current child welfare income security programs along the lines of the successful Social Security program.

[21] The low savings rate in North America has been of particular concern because these savings fund growth and investment. As Thurow (1992: 160) points out, "Of twenty-one industrial countries, no country had a savings rate lower than that of the United States in the late 1980s."

The United States is a free enterprise market economy in which virtually all business and industry are privately owned, with small public sector involvement. To participate meaningfully in the nation's wealth, individuals must come to know and understand early in their lives the procedures and instruments used to allocate and manipulate ownership and wealth. Today, most young people know very little about stock ownership, what it is, how it works, and the good of it.[22] This is comparable to an island child growing up in Micronesia not knowing how to fish, or a child raised on a ranch in Argentina knowing nothing of cattle. Although many young people in our society may have a passing acquaintance with the language of business and investment, and may even participate in a stock purchase simulation in school, most never learn the importance of stock ownership in obtaining a share of the productive assets of the nation.

The CFS account would give young people a reason to learn about stocks, bonds, and investing because they would have funds to invest. If young people developed better skills and knowledge about investing and saving, the long-term collective benefit of their knowledge would be a nation better able to save, invest, and compete in the global marketplace.[23] Because children would "have a stake" in their society, they would learn the importance of saving and investing, and how the free enterprise system in which they live works.[24] It is extremely important that children living in a free market economy not grow up alienated by ignorance of the very instruments of power and wealth that represent ownership in their society (Kelley, 2003; Kiyosaki, 2000).

Finally, the money saved in the CFS accounts would be directly invested in the nation's economy and thus would promote increased economic growth and development. The savings and investment this approach would produce would also increase the nation's savings rate. In this sense, the Child Future Savings account is a "catalytic reform." It would lead to broad economic growth for the national economy.

---

[22] Home ownership has been the other major avenue to obtaining a share of the enormous amount of privately held wealth.

[23] In his book, *Rich Dad, Poor Dad*, Richard Kiyosaki suggests that the first step in financial education for young people is to simply introduce financial terms into your conversations with them. Young people should understand such simple concepts as assets and liabilities, savings and investment, and debt and credit.

[24] In this regard, see the recent work on developing a "stake" through an asset-based welfare approach by Sherraden (1991, 2002).

Variant Proposals

The aim of the CFS account is not new. Economists and others have long recognized the value of such an approach (Haveman, 1988; Sherraden, 1990; Thurow, 1992).[25] In 1970, Nobel Prize–winning economist James Tobin proposed:

> After high school, every youth in the nation—whatever the economic means of his parents or his earlier education—should have the opportunity to develop his capacity to earn income and to contribute to the society. To this end the federal government could make available to every young man and woman, on graduation from high school and in any case at the age of 19, an endowment of, for example, [roughly $30,000 in 2002 dollars].
>
> This proposal has a number of important advantages. Individuals are assisted directly and equally, rather than indirectly and haphazardly, through government financing of particular programs. The advantages of background and talent that fit certain young people for university education are not compounded by financial favoritism. Within broad limits of approved programs, individuals are free to choose how to use the money the government is willing to invest in their development. No individual misses out because there happens to be no training courses where he lives, or because his parents' income barely exceeds some permissible maximum. (p. 92)

Lester Thurow (1992: 279) proposed an approach nearly identical to CFS:

> The Social Security system could be expanded beyond health care and pensions for the elderly to include training for the young. Upon birth, every young person would have a training account set up in his [or her] name for use after graduation from high school in which a sum of money equal to the amount of public money that is now spent on the average college graduate (about $17,500) would be deposited. Over their lifetime, individuals could draw upon this fund to pay for university training or to pay their employer for on-the-job skill training. Repayment would occur in the form of payroll tax deductions.

The idea of CFS derives from one of America's oldest pioneer traditions. Like the grubstake provided the prospector a century ago, CFS funds

---

[25] Thomas Paine argued for a similar approach two centuries ago in his treatise *Agrarian Justice*. Specifically, he argued that every person on their twenty-first birthday "should be entitled to receive fifteen pounds sterling each" (see Agassi, 1991: 453). The funds for this provision were to derive from a 10 percent inheritance tax on estates.

would constitute the resources each young person would need upon graduation from high school to embark upon their future. Like the prospector, the youthful beneficiary would, during the course of his or her adult working life, repay the cost of the grubstake, so that others who followed would continue to benefit.

Building Hope

Especially for children born at the bottom, the stake will stand as a symbol of hope. However grim their present situation, they will know that America has not given up on them. If they stay in school and work hard, they will receive the wherewithal to pursue the American Dream. It would be a serious mistake to underestimate the motivating power of this message.
Bruce Ackerman and Anne Alstott, *The Stakeholder Society*

The most important aspect of this approach may not be its financial benefits, which will be substantial, but its impact on personal and social development. The psychological and personality development benefits may far outweigh the financial rewards (Coleman et al., 1966; Moore et al,. 2001). The most significant aspect of the Child Future Savings account program may be through instilling hope and opportunity in millions of young people who would otherwise have little (Schreiner, Clancy, and Sherraden, 2003; Siegal, 1985). Even the poorest children would know that, upon graduation from high school, opportunity would be waiting for them.

A program that demonstrates the viability of the CFS approach was initiated and funded by Eugene Lang, a self-made millionaire and philanthropist (Ellwood, 1988: 215–216). Lang promised the students of the inner-city Harlem school that he had attended that he would pay the cost of a college education for any student who graduated and was subsequently admitted to a college or university. Prior to this time, the school's dropout rate had been close to 50 percent, with few students going on to college—a statistic mirrored in national data. Following Lang's offer, the dropout rate plummeted to barely 5 percent. Nearly all students began graduating, with most accepting Lang's offer and continuing on to college. The success of Lang's venture has led to the formation of the "I Have a Dream" Foundation. The program has been replicated in twenty-four cities serving 5,000 young people and financed from private giving (Bowen, 1987; Solomon, 1989).

Staying in School. At 29 percent, the United States has one of the highest high school dropout rates in the world. This compares to 6 percent in Japan, 9 percent in Germany, and 20 percent in Canada (Thurow, 1992: 159).[26] The CFS program would go a long way toward reducing this dropout rate, providing young people an incentive to stay in school and discouraging early pregnancy and family formation. Young men and women, despite an impoverished family situation, would know that when they graduated from high school, they would have the resources to attend training school, apprentice training, community college, or a university.[27] If a young woman chose to have a child out of wedlock, she might be required to share the costs of rearing that child, using funds from her accumulated CFS account, supplemented with funds from the father's CFS account. Thus, the mother and putative father would understand beforehand that having children before finishing high school or before marriage would severely limit their future opportunities. The costs of their behavior would be directly borne by them. The empirical research suggests that as they became aware of opportunities other than that offered by early parenthood on public assistance, fewer would allow themselves to get trapped.

Promote Entrepreneurship. Young people today have no assurance, even with a college education, that a job will be available for them when they are ready to enter the labor market. With the advance of high technology and the information age combined with the broad reach of global markets, labor market conditions have been changing. Large corporations have been reducing the size of their work force. Increasing numbers of young people may have to rely on their own initiative and imagination to create opportunities for themselves. They may need to develop new opportunities such as starting their own business or pooling their resources with friends and associates to buy a franchise business. However, starting a business or buying a franchise requires start-up capital. One of the important uses of the CFS account funds would be to provide young people who chose to try

---

[26] Thurow (1992: 40) observes, "in the twenty-first century, the education and skills of the work force will end up being the dominant competitive weapon."

[27] Thurow (1992, 52) points out that in the new global economy "the education of the bottom 50 percent of the population moves to center stage." It is not just the education of management that is required in the new world order, but the education of the whole population (Friedberg, 1988; Solomon, 1989). "In the end the skills of the bottom half of the population affect the wages of the top half. If the bottom half can't effectively staff the processes that have to be operated, the management and professional jobs that go with the processes disappear" (Thurow, 1992: 55). Later Thurow (p. 247) observes, "Japanese high school students come near the top in any international assessment of achievement, and the nation's ability to educate the bottom half of the high school class is simply unmatched anywhere in the world."

their hands at entrepreneurship with start-up capital. Whatever the young person's choice, the role of the social worker would be to both encourage the young person to stay in school as well as to ensure careful and proper use of the available funds for transition into self-supporting adult roles.

Grubstake. Children living in impoverished homes and blighted neighborhoods have little hope and even less to lose. As they watch television they realize all too well that in a society possessing abundant wealth, they have been dealt a losing hand. It is not surprising that so many are tempted by gang involvement, drug use or drug dealing, and criminal behavior, none of which are effectively countered by any fear of loss. Why, the young person asks, should I worry when I have nothing to lose? The CFS account attempts to change this equation by making even the most impoverished child a stakeholder in society. When they see they have real hope and opportunity, they will realize they have a lot to lose, and yet still more to gain, and will be far more likely to contribute positively toward their community.

Thurow (1992) has pointed out that to make new citizens into productive workers requires substantial investment in the social and economic infrastructure: new schools, additional housing, plant and equipment to support employment, and so on. He estimates that each new citizen born in America will require $20,000 for housing, $20,000 for food, $20,000 for public infrastructure, $100,000 for education, and $80,000 for plant and equipment to permit productive participation in advanced postmodern society. He concludes that "basically each new American will require an investment of $240,000 before he or she is capable of fitting into the American economy as a self-sufficient, average citizen-worker" (p. 206).

The CFS account is essentially an investment in infrastructure development—the infrastructure being the human resources represented by our children. It provides the additional marginal investment that would greatly leverage the nearly $250,000 that will be required for each new citizen.

In some ways, we already do much of what the CFS account proposes through a patchwork of job training programs, higher education training grants, loan programs, and loan guarantees. The CFS account would simply consolidate and unify many separate programs into a single approach that would reduce the vast and confusing patchwork of programs with confusing and different rules, eligibility requirements, and standards. The CFS account puts the young person at the center of control and demands responsible individual action. It is a program designed to provide young people with hope and vision and to assure the resources required to achieve them.

The CFS account would allow young people to start their careers without incurring substantial debt. The transition from adolescence to adulthood in a free enterprise economy requires substantial investment. Today, most young persons wanting to attend college or obtain vocational training must have financial assistance. Young people from low-income and middle-income families face a difficult time. While they may be eligible for financial aid programs, such means-tested programs often promote dependency and a reliance on government aid. Further, young people who take on substantial debt to fund their college education too often mortgage their future and much of their hope.[28] The CFS program would free young people from incurring such heavy burdens early in their careers.

Limitations

Limitations to the CFS program do exist. For one, it does not address the current and pressing problems that children may be suffering now: substandard housing, poor health, inadequate nutrition, violent surroundings, and ineffective schooling. It may seem insensitive in the face of such urgent needs to focus on building a savings account for future needs. Although the immediate needs of children are vitally important and should receive priority (as discussed in chapter 11), we must not neglect long-term, preventative solutions that will eventually get to the root causes of poverty. We have seen this with respect to Social Security for the elderly. Like a physician attending a diseased patient, child welfare would be delinquent in its service should it provide only immediate comfort and care while neglecting to search for the cause of illness and a permanent cure. The problem of child poverty will never end unless we adapt long-term solutions addressed to root causes.

The objection can also be made that if children gain money too easily, they will have little appreciation for the labor and toil it represents.[29] This is a crucial issue because if children are able to build substantial savings

---

[28] Approaches to provide funds for college or vocational training that open a "line of credit" encourage the habit of borrowing. Young people learn to borrow and spend only to accumulate debt. Further, this "debtor" approach may result in children believing that they have mortgaged their future once the "credit line" has been fully used. The advantage of the social savings approach is that it encourages the habit of saving and teaches young people about investing. These are lessons and habits that will serve them in the future (Kiyosaki, 2000).

[29] Ackerman and Alstott (1999) address this and other concerns raised about their "stakeholder" proposal. See their book for additional discussion of this issue.

with little or no effort, they may mistakenly believe that money and savings will always be easy to come by—a lottery in which everyone wins. Money easily gained can become money easily lost. There is no simple reply to this objection. It will be important for schools, parents, and society as a whole to emphasize this value of savings to children, assuring them that the funds in their account will have to be repaid through contributions made during their working years. Children would have to know that the CFS funds represent a "compact between the generations," a statement of faith in their future and potential, an investment made by one generation in the future of the next.

Implementation

As a long-term solution, the child future savings account would not immediately end poverty among children. As with Social Security, several years would pass before effects would be felt. One immediate concern would be those children currently too old to effectively participate. One solution might be to phase the program in for all children under six years of age and to make it voluntary for all children over six. All children would have an account opened for them unless they expressly asked not to participate. An educational loan fund could be made available to all children who have not been able to accumulate savings for their adult education and training. Over time, younger children would have accumulated funds in their accounts and thus would need to borrow less. After full implementation, the need for an educational loan fund would likely disappear altogether.

Child Trust Fund in Britain

The Child Trust Fund is a groundbreaking new initiative which will strengthen financial education, promote positive attitudes to saving and ensure that all children, regardless of family background, will benefit from access to a stock of financial assets when they start their adult lives. It is based around the Government's belief in progressive universalism—benefiting every child while offering more help to those in most need.
    Ruth Kelly, *Strengthening the Saving Habit of Future Generations*

In 2003, Prime Minister Tony Blair, in a historic and bold social policy move, launched a progressive universal children's savings account for the United Kingdom (Gaven, 2003; Nissan and Le Grand, 2000). Working with Michael Sherraden and others, the prime minister started a program to create a child trust fund for every child in the United Kingdom (Kelly and Lissauer, 2000; Sherraden, 2002b). The program provides all children in the nation a savings and investing account for their future. Some components of the program are still being developed.

How the Child Trust Fund Works

Initial Endowment. Every child born in the United Kingdom beginning in September 2002 will have a Child Trust Fund account opened at birth. The initial endowment will be £250 (414 U.S. dollars). Children from low-income families will qualify for £500 ($828), although estimates are that about two-thirds of families will be eligible for the £500 amount. Parents, family members and friends will be able to contribute up to an additional £1000 ($1,656).

Account Type. Accounts will be made available through open competition. The government is considering submissions from various financial institutions with provision to go to authorized providers.

Access. Children will not be able to access the funds until they are age eighteen. Funds can be used for any purpose or may be rolled over into other savings accounts.

It is estimated that if parents (or grandparents, other family or friends) "paid their weekly child benefit into the fund [£10 or $16.50], the fund would have grown to a substantial £27,000 [$44,625] by age 18, presuming 7 % annual growth" (BBC New, 2003).

In many respects, the Child Trust Fund is similar to the Child Savings Account proposed in this chapter. The funding for the Child Trust Fund is less than proposed for the Child Future Savings Account but, as Fred Goldberg (2002) observes, it is important "to put the plumbing in place" that will provide all children with an account (cited in Sherraden, 2002). Sherraden (2002: 4) continues that once "the accounts are in place, there will be creative policy making and private initiative, impossible to define or predict ahead of time, to fund accounts."

It is reasonable to expect that with the development of this program in the United Kingdom other nations in Europe will follow.

With the demise of the public welfare program the stage is set for a new era of social policies and programs for children in the United States. It is important in this new era to be cognizant of the limitations of casework and therapeutic approaches to providing social services to the poor. It is not clear that these approaches have developed an effective technology for change or intervention. Until there is evidence of their effectiveness they will likely be limited to a small residual group.

The promise of the asset based social policy approach discussed above is that it builds the foundation for fundamental change of the economic circumstances of poor and disadvantaged children. This approach beckons a new child welfare system that holds the potential of transforming life for children now mired in poverty. With the opening of a child trust fund for every child, the United Kingdom is at the inflection point for change for disadvantaged children. It may take a number of years for the program to take effect, but, as with Social Security in the United States (see figure 8.9, page 228 where the inflection point was also at the outset of the program), once the program takes hold it will produce fundamental change for all children and lead to a long term decline in child poverty.

Conclusion

The future of society is determined by the achievements of its young people. Children who grow up in poverty—about one-fifth of all young people in America—are, through current social programs, being effectively denied both hope and opportunity. The result is despair and resentment against the society in which they have so little stake.

The child future savings account proposed in this chapter represents a "social investment" approach to safeguarding the futures of children. The program conforms to and takes advantage of the inherent nature of the free enterprise market economy. It does not rely on a residual approach but attempts to prevent the need for residual services by building a structure that reduces the number of children unable to achieve economic self-reliance. The intent is to lead children to economic self-sufficiency where they can make positive contributions to the collective good.

The CFS account would guarantee all children the resources required at a critical stage in their lives to make the difficult transition to effective, self-reliant, and productive citizenship. It would permit them to realize opportunities in the free enterprise market economy without reference to the economic status of their parents, thereby ensuring all an equal opportunity and a fair start. It would be the fulcrum of opportunity that frees all children to fully engage their potential.

As with Social Security for the elderly, the CFS account would be paid for by the beneficiaries themselves during their working lives, the assumption being that young people who had the resources to properly prepare themselves for a career or occupation would earn more income and, thus, pay into the program throughout their working life. The program would, within a generation, significantly reduce, even eliminate, poverty among children, at least to the extent we have seen it reduced among the elderly. Many of the social problems currently attendant upon that poverty would vanish.

The lesson from the Child Trust Fund in the United Kingdom is that fundamental change is not only possible, but is underway. We have an opportunity in the United States to embark on a new era of public policies for children that take advantage of the inherent features of the free enterprise market economy. With welfare reform we have begun to dismantle the failed means tested income transfer approach of the previous century. But we have yet to replace it with a more effective approach which will provide for our collective responsibility to all children, but particularly children from disadvantaged and impoverished families.

The United States and the United Kingdom are investing billions of federal dollars in new programs for children. While the United States is implementing the 529 College Savings Plan, the United Kingdom is putting in place a Child Trust Fund. One program is essentially limited to children from families that are well off, while the other serves all children. One program will increase the advantage of children from privileged backgrounds; the other will extend opportunities for all children.

As Social Security serves to secure the retirement years of all seniors, a program like the child future savings account could secure the hope of all children to embrace the opportunity of life in America—it would restore the American Dream for all.

Closing

> No one expected the civil rights movement of the 1960s, and no one pre-
> dicted the Berlin wall would come down . . . Knowledge is responsibility. If
> social workers are persuaded that the situation of children is grave, we may
> and perhaps we must conduct a virtual insurrection against public mistreat-
> ment of children.
>
> Alvin Schorr, *Prospects for Public Child Welfare*

*The year is 2021. No child has been born for a quarter of a century. The
human race—quite literally—faces extinction.*

So begins the novel, *The Children of Men*, by P. D. James, in which we
see our world coming to an end. There are no children; their innocence and
playful laughter have disappeared. The joy and purpose of human life are
fading.

The story is a compelling vision which reminds us that, indeed, children are the ingredients of our future. Without them, we have no future. It
is also a reminder that while our children will see a future world we will
not, we participate in creating their coming world. Our collective actions
determine, in large part, the joys or hardships they will experience.

What kind of world are we creating? America is an incredibly wealthy
country, the wealthiest in the history of the world. Its productive energies
have been harnessed and guided by a free enterprise market economy and
a deep and unrelenting commitment to democracy, which have allowed it
to become, in large measure, the economic engine of the world. The families of the top economic 1 percent have a median net worth of over $10
million, and there are almost a million families in the top 1 percent. An
economy that can produce such wealth cannot but help be the world's envy
and steward.

The concern of this book is the large number of children who have
been left out of this great economic achievement. By and large, the poor in
America are single mothers with children, whose difficulty is for the most
part structural. They exist in an economic system that scarcely allows their
participation and is too often unforgiving of failure.

For families that have broken apart, or perhaps have never fully assembled, it is usually the mother, driven by maternal instincts, who takes
responsibility for caring for a child. Yet this maternal instinct is a heavy
burden—an albatross around her heart. Raising children is difficult and

expensive, a labor-intensive activity. Children compel our attention and exhaust our energy. Young children cannot be left alone, but require supervision and care around the clock. Thus, finding work outside the home and maintaining that work involves substantial child care expense for the mother. In addition, she has a home to maintain and the healthy development of children to ensure. Without a partner to carry part of the burden, she has few resources with which to succeed. And it is her children who will feel her pain and failure.

In an ideal world we would like all children to be raised in two-parent families. Two parents are able to share the responsibilities and burdens (and joys) of raising children. They can share child-caring duties. They can share the myriad of household chores. They can take turns working outside the home. Today the average family has both parents working outside the home and sharing child care and household chores.

When one parent is left to raise the child by herself it is rarely by choice. The Murphy Browns are the exception. Most single mothers are thrust into the situation almost by accident, by circumstances that spin out of their control. They assume the burden of raising their children because it is the right thing to do. They accept this responsibility at considerable expense to their personal economic prospects. Unfortunately, public policy can do little about the single parent families that result from divorce or from young women who elect to keep children from unplanned pregnancies.

What happens to poor children who reside primarily in single parent families represents the major blight on the landscape of American economic achievement. Our public policies with respect to these families have been a failure, which is seen most vividly in the blighted futures of the children in these families. For decades these families were served by a limited and ill-conceived welfare program which, as its critics complained, encouraged dependency and failed to promote economic self-sufficiency.

With the end of welfare, the children of poor families have entered a new era—of deeper poverty and an even deeper chasm between their futures and those of children from wealthy and upper-income families. Our public policies provide substantial social programs and policies to ensure the futures of the latter children. We have 529 college savings plans, which allow parents to set aside, on a tax-free basis, funds for their children's future college expenses. Plus, economically advantaged parents benefit from substantial child dependent deductions and deductions for child care expenses. The children living in poor single parent families are effectively denied these benefits.

I must confess to you today that not long after talking about the dream, I started seeing it turn into a nightmare as I moved through the ghettos of the nation and saw my black brothers and sisters perishing on a lonely island of poverty in the midst of a vast ocean of material prosperity.

Martin Luther King, Jr., *Why We Can't Wait*

Without question race and ethnicity is an issue for these children. Black and Hispanic children are several times more likely to live in poverty compared to white children. Black and Hispanic children are far more likely to grow up in high-poverty neighborhoods characterized by failing schools, high rates of crime, drug and alcohol abuse, unemployment, and despair. The residual social programs designed to cope with these problems—foster care and welfare—are substantially overpopulated by Black and Hispanic children. As we have seen, when welfare reform removed children from income assistance programs, it was Black children who were most affected. Four decades ago the civil rights movement led a struggle against the discrimination and prejudice which crippled the hopes and dreams of these children. Yet, today many of the same attitudes, problems, and failing institutions remain.

In this land of enormous wealth there is also poverty and despair. Much of this poverty is concentrated among children, and particularly children of color. Poverty is particularly pernicious in its effects on children because it alters the trajectory of their lives. High rates of poverty, particularly among children, are the seedbed of inequality. As we have seen, during recent decades inequality in the United States has increased. The cause of this inequality can be partly traced to changing tax policies that favor asset holders. But America is a land where we wish to encourage the building of wealth. It is not the success of those at the top that produces the vast inequality—or at least the pernicious inequality. Rather, it is the failure to participate in the wealth of the nation by so many at the bottom which is the heart of the problem. The answer is to be found in social policies and programs that facilitate and expand participation in saving and investing, particularly for poor children, and that allows them to obtain a stake in the vast wealth created by our free enterprise market economy.

******

In this book I have examined the platform of opportunities provided by the public child welfare system in the United States. The early history is the story of a residual child welfare system that went to great pains to ensure that children who were left out—who were abandoned or orphaned—were properly cared for. Over the years this effort led to the development of child welfare agencies and a cadre of child welfare caseworkers. After World War II these workers began organizing into a profession that conducted research on the effectiveness of various public efforts to care for children. The results of this research highlighted the limits of public intervention in the personal lives of families using the casework method. During the sixties and seventies there was considerable large-scale research examining the different ways the public child welfare agencies could be improved. These later studies set the stage for change: substantial progress could have been made at that time.

But a dramatic discovery emerged out of the medical centers in 1962—the "Battered Child Syndrome" and child abuse—which galvanized the public into protecting young children instead of helping them. With a ferocity similar to the outrage against the terrorists who struck on September 11, 2001 the public demanded action to protect children. Every effort was made to do whatever possible to protect young children in their home.

It was a noble effort, one which required that we take collective responsibility to protect children, particularly the very young and defenseless. The result, however, was the end of modern child welfare system and the transformation of the public child welfare agency, which had previously focused on aiding and assisting disadvantaged and poor children, into a quasipolice, child protective service agency that responded solely to reports of child abuse. There is no longer a child welfare agency that provides services to needy and disadvantaged families, which will help them cope in times of severe economic downturn in their personal fortunes. The notion of the proverbial social worker rolling up his or her sleeves to assist families in getting back onto their feet and reentering the economic mainstream no longer applies.

******

In the later chapters of this book I examined the social programs and policies that hold out a real prospect of producing fundamental change for poor families. It is perplexing to read the statistics published by the United Nations that assert that, of all the developed countries, the United States, the richest country in the world, has the highest poverty rates for children—and the lowest poverty rates for seniors. How can this be?

The difference is the approach we have taken toward poverty among seniors and poverty among children. We have relied on universal social policies to end poverty among seniors. In the early part of the century the elderly in the United States had the highest poverty rates. It would have been understandable, and simple, to simply raise our hands in futility and complain that nothing could be done. But the Social Security Act of 1936 created the foundation for ending poverty among the elderly, and by the early sixties it was beginning to substantially reduce poverty among seniors. Today, Social Security is widely credited with virtually ending poverty among seniors.

In contrast, we have relied on a patchwork of "means-tested" residual programs for children and single parents—foster care and welfare—which, by and large, have been a failure. We ended poverty among seniors. There is no reason why we can't do it for children. That is the message of this book.

Ending child poverty is possible. It will require simple and feasible changes to our current child support program. Instead of relying on an expensive, cumbersome, ineffective, and unfair court-based child support collection system, we need to follow the examples set by other developed countries which have achieved success in collecting child support. In chapter 11, I argued that we should adopt an "advance maintenance payment" approach as is used in most European countries (including just recently England) as well as New Zealand and Australia. This approach would shift responsibility for collecting child support from the custodial parent, usually the mother, to the state. The experience of these other countries has been that the state has the mechanisms and persistence to ensure collection at minimal administrative cost.

In chapter 11, I argued for changing our approach to providing a children's allowance. Currently we use a tax deduction approach. The difficulty with this approach is that its net effect is to provide the highest benefits to the children in the wealthiest families and virtually no benefit to children in the poorest families (Robin Hood in reverse). To fix this problem we should simply *guarantee the children's allowance* to all children regardless of their parents' economic circumstances. This is the right and fair thing to do.

I also identify the limits of tax policies that lead to unequal benefits for poor children. I propose a simple double exemption approach to adjust these policies which would go a long way toward producing fair and equal treatment for all children.

Fixing these two simple programs—child support and children's allowance—could substantially improve the economic circumstances of poor children. The economic support provided by these two universal programs would, in most cases, be more than is currently provided by welfare (TANF). The main advantage with these programs is that they are not means-tested and thus would not be "clawed back" as the parent works. The major disadvantage of welfare is that it is means-tested, which means that as the mother works and her "means" increase, her welfare benefit is reduced. Taking back the means-tested welfare benefit is experienced as a

"tax" on her earnings. As numerous studies have pointed out, the consequence has been a net tax rate for welfare mothers that often exceeds 50
percent and frequently more than 70 percent. This is the highest net tax
rate in the country. When tax rates are this high they discourage work.

Thus, with two simple program reforms—child support and children's
allowance—poor families would receive universal entitlements that would
not be clawed back. Combined with universal child care, these reforms
would provide an economic foundation that would allow poor families,
especially single mothers, to seek work and to benefit from that work
without penalty.

******

The lesson from the history of ending poverty among seniors is that a "social savings" approach works best in bringing about fundamental change.
In chapter 12, I argued for a "social savings" approach for children. One of
the most important times in a child's life is when they leave home and embark on their own independent adult careers. Many young people will attend college. Others will enroll in vocational training or apprenticeship
programs. Others will enter the workforce or perhaps volunteer for military service.

For most young people, resources will be required that ensure them a
chance of success. I proposed a "Child Future Savings" plan, which is
similar in concept to the current 529 college savings plan. The 529 plan
was recently reformed to allow parents to set aside, on a tax-free basis, up
to $300,000 in each child's account for later college expenses. For the one-
year period from June 2001 to June 2002 more than $12 billion was depos-
ited into these federally subsidized tax-free accounts. The 529 plan is a
wonderful program, and clearly, many knowledgeable parents view this
approach as vital and worth investing in. It taps into the achievements of
the free enterprise market economy. It allows selected parents to ensure
that their children will have the resources needed to take advantage of the
opportunities this rich and bountiful country provides.

From a wider social perspective, however, the approach is flawed because the benefits are concentrated and essentially limited to children from
upper-income and wealthy families. Children from poor and disadvantaged
families are left out. This is paradoxical in the sense that the children with
the greatest need for this type of program are again least able to participate, while those least likely to require the benefits of this program are
most likely to receive them.

In contrast, the "child future savings" plan proposed in chapter 12
would be universally implemented for all children, and would assure equal

economic opportunities for everyone. The plan aims to achieve the same goal as the 529 plan, but for all children regardless of their parents' wealth and income. This is the way it should be. In a land of opportunity it is essential to assure opportunity for all children.

The United Kingdom has implemented a child trust fund for every child born since September 2002. This bold and courageous policy initiative by Prime Minister Tony Blair demonstrates that fundamental change is not only possible but is underway. It would be easy to underestimate the significance of this change. When Bismark introduced social security in Germany in 1889, the modern social welfare state was born. Social security has emerged as a requirement of modern industrial economies. Like social security, the child trust fund represents a fundamental break with approaches of the past and is likely to unleash a revolution in social policies and programs that serve children.

******

Today, in the United States the major remaining social failure has been our inability to make progress in the war against poverty, especially child poverty. During the 1960s Lyndon Johnson conducted a "war" on poverty. The war took the form of large publicly managed social programs. Some progress was achieved, but, as Ronald Reagan would comment decades later, "We conducted a war on poverty and poverty won." Poverty did win. And the victims were mainly children—in particular, disadvantaged children living in single parent families, with an overrepresentation of children of color.

Many of the approaches toward letting people change their circumstances, which social work has promoted, have failed. These programs simply have not produced or facilitated change. But there have been successes. Reform efforts must look to those programs that have succeeded, while casting aside those programs that have not. Beyond that, we must turn to and follow the lead of empirical research.

It *is* possible to end child poverty. It has been done with other groups. And if child poverty were ended, the United States would enter a new era of prosperity, a new world impossible even to envision today. America would advance in ways it is difficult to imagine. We would be creating a future for our children that would truly be something to be proud of. We only need the will and determination to do it.

Fundamental child welfare reform along the lines discussed here could sew the seeds for enlightened social advancement. It has happened before. Historian Michael Katz (1986: 113) observed, "Throughout the country, by the 1890s, children had captured the energy and attention of social reformers with an intensity never matched in other periods of American history. Almost overnight, it seemed, children became the symbol of a resurgent reform spirit, the magnet that pulled together a diverse but very effective coalition." It was this early wave of compassion that led to the development of the modern public education system and, later, the public child welfare system in the United States.

Children stand again, as they did a century ago, "as the fulcrum that can move society from an era of material self-absorption to an era of civic-minded government" and collective responsibility for building the infrastructure required to ensure that all children have a fair start and equal opportunity. Momentum for change has been building. An opportunity to renew our faith in free enterprise and democracy is once again before us. We define our horizons by the decisions we make, and in that the possibilities for humankind are boundless. Acting collectively, we *can* build a fundamentally different and better future for all our children.

References

Abbott, E. (1942). *Social welfare and professional education.* Chicago: University of Chicago Press.

Abbott, G. (1938). *The child and the state.* Chicago: University of Chicago Press.

Abbott, G. (1941). *From relief to Social Security: The development of the new public welfare services and their administration.* Chicago: University of Chicago Press.

Ackerman, B., and Alstott, A. (1999). *The stakeholder society.* New Haven, CT: Yale University Press.

Acs, G., and Loprest, P. (2002). *Initial synthesis report of the findings from ASPE's "leavers" grants.* Washington, DC: Urban Institute.

Adams, G., and Schulman, K. (1998). *Child care challenges.* Washington, DC: Children's Defense Fund.

Adams. P. (1992). *Marketing social change: The case of family preservation.* Paper presented at the Annual Program Meeting of the Council on Social Work Education, Kansas City, March 1.

Addams, J. (1902). *Democracy and social ethics.* New York: Macmillan.

Addams, J. (1910). *Twenty years at Hull House.* New York: Macmillan.

Adelson, L. (1961). Slaughter of the innocents: A study of forty-six homicides in which the victims were children. *New England Journal of Medicine 246:*1345–1349.

Administration for Children and Families. (2002). *National Foster Care and Adoption Information.* Washington, DC: U.S. Department of Health and Human Services. Foster care data available online at www.acf.dhhs.gov/programs/cb/dis/tables/sec11gb/national.htm.

Administration for Children and Families. (2002). *Total number of families and recipients for 1st quarter FY 2002.* Washington, DC: U.S. Department of Health and Human Services. TANF data available online at aspe.hhs.gov/hsp/indicators02/appa-TANF.pdf.

Administration for Children, Youth, and Families. (1984). *Report to Congress on PL 96-272, the Adoption Assistance and Child Welfare Act of 1980.* Washington, DC: Department of Health and Human Services.

Adoption Assistance and Child Welfare Act of 1980, Public Law 96-272, H.R. 3434, 94 Stat. 500 (June 17).

Agassi, J. B. (1991). The rise of the ideas of the welfare state. *Philosophy of the Social Sciences 21:*444–457.

Akerlof, G. A., and Yellen, J. L. (1996). *An analysis of out-of-wedlock births in the United States.* Policy Brief #5, August. Washington, DC: Brookings Institution.

Alfaro, J. D. (1988). What can we learn from child abuse fatalities? A synthesis of nine studies. In D. J. Besharov, ed., *Protecting children from abuse and neglect: Policy and practice,* 219–264. Springfield, IL: Charles C. Thomas.

Allan, L. J. (1978). Child abuse: A critical review of the research and theory. In J. P. Martin, ed., *Violence in the family.* New York: Wiley.

Amacher, K. A., and Maas, H. S. (1985). Children, youth, and social work practice. In S. A. Yelaja, ed., *An introduction to social work practice in Canada,* 217–233. Scarborough, Ontario: Prentice-Hall.

Amato, P. R. (1998). More than money? Men's contributions to their children's lives. In A. Booth and A. C. Crouter, eds., *Men in families: When do they get involved? What difference does it make?* 248–258. Mahwah, NJ: Lawrence Erlbaum.

American Humane Association. (1977). *Statistics for 1977.* Denver, CO: Author.

American Humane Association. (1978). *National analysis of official child neglect and abuse reporting.* Denver, CO: Author.

American Humane Association. (1988). *National analysis of official child neglect and abuse reporting, annual report, 1986.* Denver, CO: Author.

Anderson, E. (1990). *Streetwise: Race, class, and change in an urban community.* Chicago: University of Chicago Press.

Anderson, E. (1994). Looking out for our nation's welfare. *Register Guard,* January, 9:F1 and F4.

Anderson, R., Ambrosino, R., Valentine, D., and Lauderdale, M. (1983). Child deaths attributed to abuse and neglect: An empirical study. *Children and Youth Services Review 5:*75–89.

Annie E. Casey Foundation. (2002). *Children at risk: State trends 1990–2000.* Baltimore, MD: Author. Online at www.kidscount.org.

Antler, J., and Antler, S. (1979). From child rescue to family protection: The evolution of the child protection movement in the United States. *Children and Youth Services Review 1:*177–204.

Apsler, R., Cummins, M. R., Carl, S. (2002). Fear and expectations: Differences among female victims of domestic violence who come to the attention of the police. *Violence and Victims 17:* 445–53.

Archard, D. (1993). *Children: Rights and childhood.* London: Routledge.

Asen, R. (2002). *Visions of poverty: Welfare policy and political imagination.* East Lansing: Michigan State University Press.

Avery, R. B., Elliehausen, G. E., and Canner, G. B. (1984a). Survey of consumer finances, 1983. *Federal Reserve Bulletin,* September, 679–682.

Avery, R. B., Elliehausen, G. E., and Canner, G. B. (1984b). Survey of consumer finances, 1983: A secondary report. *Federal Reserve Bulletin,* December, 857–869.

Bachrach, C. (1986). Adoption plans, adopted children and adoptive mothers. *Journal of Marriage and the Family 48:*243–253.

Bachrach, C. A. (1998). The changing circumstances of marriage and fertility in the United States. In R. A. Moffitt, ed., *Welfare, the family, and reproductive behavior.* Washington, DC: National Research Council, 1998.

Bachu, A. (1999). *Trends in premarital childbearing: 1930 to 1994.* P23-197. Washington, DC: U.S. Census Bureau.

Bagley, C., and King, K. (1990). *Child sexual abuse: The search for healing.* London: Tavistock/Routledge.

Baker, M. (1985). *What will tomorrow bring? A study of the aspirations of adolescent women.* Ottawa: Canadian Advisory Council on the Status of Women.

Bakwin, H. (1952). Roentgenographic changes in homes following trauma. *Journal of Pediatrics 42:7–15.*

Bakwin, H. (1956). Multiple skeletal lesions in young children due to trauma. *Journal of Pediatrics 39:7–15.*

Baldwin, J. A., and Oliver, J. E. (1975). Epidemiology and family characteristics of severely abused children. *British Journal of Preventive and Social Medicine 29:205–221.*

Bane, M. J., and Jargowsky, P. A. (1988). The links between government policy and family structure: What matters and what doesn't. In A. J. Cherlin, ed., *The changing American family and public policy,* 219–261. Washington, DC: Urban Institute Press.

Banting, K. G. (1987). *The welfare state and Canadian federalism. 2d ed.* Kingston and Montreal: McGill-Queen's University Press.

Barmeyer, G. H., Alderson, L. R., and Cox, W. B. (1951). Traumatic periostitis in young children. *Journal of Pediatrics 38:184–190.*

Barnes, H., Day, P., and Cronin, N. (1998). *Trial and error: A review of UK child support policy.* Occasional Paper 24. London: Family Policy Studies Centre.

Barth, R. P. (1995). *Foster care dynamics and family preservation.* Presentation to the California Family Impact Seminar, Sacramento, California, November 21.

Barth, R. P. (1997). Permanent placements for young children placed in foster care: A proposal for a child welfare services performance standard, *Children and Youth Services Review 19:615–631.*

Barth, R. P. (2002). *Institutions vs. foster care: The empirical base for a century of action.* Chapel Hill, N.C.: Jordan Institute for Families, School of Social Work, University of North Carolina, June 17.

Barth, R. P., and Berry, M. (1987). Outcomes of child welfare services under permanency planning. *Social Service Review 61:71–90.*

Barth, R., Berrick, J. D., and Courtney, M. (1990). *A snapshot of California's families and children: Pursuant to the child welfare reforms of the 1980s.* A presentation to the California Child Welfare Strategic Planning Commission, February 22.

Bawden, D. L., and Sonenstein, F. L. (1992). Quasi-experimental designs. *Children and Youth Services Review 14:137–144.*

Bean, P., and Melville, J. (1989). *Lost children of the empire.* London: Unwin Hyman Ltd.

Becker, E., Rankin, E., and Rickel, A. U. (1998). *High risk sexual behavior: Interventions with vulnerable populations.* New York: Plenum Press.

Becker, G. (1981). *A treatise on the family.* Cambridge, MA: Harvard University Press.

Bell, W. (1965). *Aid to dependent children.* New York: Columbia University Press.

Bellamy, D. (1983). Social policy in Ontario. In Ontario Social Development Council, *The province of Ontario, Its social services, A handbook on the human services,* 31–51. Toronto: Ontario Social Development Council.

Bellamy, D., and Irving, A. (1986). Pioneers. In J. C. Turner and F. J. Turner (eds.), *Canadian social welfare,* 29–49. Dons Mills, Ontario: Collier Macmillan Canada.

Bergquist, C., Szwejda, D., and Pope, G. (1993). *Evaluation of Michigan's Families First program: Summary report.* Lansing, MI: Michigan Department of Social Services.

Berk, R. A., Campbell, A., Klap, R., and Western, B. (1992). The deterrent effect of arrest in incidents of domestic violence-a Bayesian-analysis of 4 field experiments. *American Sociological Review 57:*698–708.

Berlin, G. (1992). Choosing and measuring interventions. *Children and Youth Services Review 14:*99–118.

Berrick, J. D. (1997). *Faces of poverty: Portraits of women and children on welfare.* New York: Oxford University Press.

Berry, M. (1990). Keeping families together: An examination of an intensive family preservation program. Unpublished doctoral dissertation. University of California, Berkeley.

Berry, M. (1991). The assessment of imminence of risk of placement: Lessons from a family preservation program. *Children and Youth Services Review 13:*239–256.

Berry, M. (1992). An evaluation of family preservation services: Fitting agency services to family needs. *Social Work 37:*314–321.

Berry, M. (1993). The relative effectiveness of family preservation services with neglectful families. In E. S. Morton and R. K. Grigsby, eds., *Advancing family preservation practice,* 70–98. Newbury Park: Sage.

Besharov, D. J. (1983). *Criminal and civil liability in child welfare work: The growing trend.* Washington, DC: American Bar Association.

Besharov, D. J. (1987). *Defending child abuse and neglect cases: Representing parents in civil proceedings.* DC Superior Court. Washington, DC: Counsel for Child Abuse and Neglect.

Besharov, D. J. (1988a). Introduction. In D. J. Besharov, ed., *Protecting children from abuse and neglect: Policy and practice,* 3–8. Springfield, IL: Charles C. Thomas.

Besharov, D. J. (1988b). The misuse of foster care: When the desire to help children outruns the ability to improve parental functioning. In D. J. Besharov, ed., *Protecting children from abuse and neglect: Policy and practice,* 185–206. Springfield, IL: Charles C. Thomas.

Besharov, D. J. (1990a). Gaining control of child abuse reports. *Public Welfare 48:*34–40.

Besharov, D. J. (1990b). *Recognizing child abuse.* New York: Free Press.

Besharov, D. J. (1991). D. J. Besharov's response to the symposium review by D. Daro and R. Becerra, *Children and Youth Services Review 13:*306–309.

Besharov, D. J. (1993). Escaping the dole: For young unmarried mothers, welfare reform alone can't make work pay. *Washington Post*, December 12, C3.

Best, J. (1990). *Threatened children: Rhetoric and concern about child-victims.* Chicago: University of Chicago Press.

Bianchi, S. M., Milkie, M. A., Sayer, L. C., and Robinson, J. P. (2000). Is anyone doing the housework? Trends in the gender division of household labor. *Social Forces 79*:191–228.

Blank, R. (1997). *It takes a nation: A new agenda for fighting poverty.* Princeton, NJ: Princeton University Press.

Blankenhorn, D. (1995). *Fatherless America: Confronting our most urgent social problem.* New York: Harper-Collins.

Blenkner, M., Bloom, M., and Nielsen, M. (1971). A research and demonstration project of protective services. *Social Casework 52:*483–499.

Boehm, B. (1970). The child in foster care. In H. D. Stone, ed., *Foster care in question: A national reassessment by twenty-one experts,* 220–227. New York: Child Welfare League of America.

Bolton, F. G., Laner, R., and Gai, D. (1981). For better or worse? Foster parents and foster children in an officially reported child maltreatment population. *Children and Youth Services Review 3:*37–53.

Bowen, E. (1987). Needy kids, perpetual aid. *Time,* November 30, 70.

Bowlby, J. (1958). The nature of the child's tie to his mother. *International Journal of Psychoanalysis 39:*350–373.

Bowlby, J. (1969). *Attachment and loss. Vol. 1. Attachment.* New York: Basic Books.

Boyle, M. H., Offord, D. R., Hofman, H. G., Catlin, G. P., Byles, J. A., Cadman, D. T., Crawford, J. W., Links, P. S., Rae-Grant, N. I., and Szatmari, P. (1987). Ontario child health study. I. Methodology. *Archives of General Psychiatry 44:*826–832.

Brace, C. L. (1859). *The best method of disposing of pauper and vagrant children.* New York: Wyncoop and Hallenbeck.

Brace, E., ed. (1894). *The life of Charles Loring Brace: Chiefly told in his own letters.* London: S. Low, Marston and Company.

Bradbury, B., Jenkins, S., and Micklewright, J. (2001). *The dynamics of child poverty in industrialized countries.* New York: Cambridge University Press.

Bradbury, D. E. (1962). *Five decades of action for children.* Washington, DC: U.S. Department of Health, Education, and Welfare, Children's Bureau.

Bradbury, D., and Eliot, M. (1956). *A formal history of the Children's Bureau.* Online at www.ssa.gov/history/pdf/child1.pdf.

Braun, D. (1997). *The rich get richer: The rise of income inequality in the United States and the World.* Chicago: Nelson-Hall.

Brazer, H. E. (1967). Tax policy and children's allowance. In E. M. B. Burns, ed., *Children's allowances and the economic welfare of children,* 140–149. New York: Citizen's Committee for Children of New York.

Bremner, R. H., ed. (1971). *Children and youth in America: A documentary history. Vol. II: 1866–1932, Parts one through six.* Cambridge, MA: Harvard University Press.

Briar, S. (1963). Clinical judgment in foster care placement. *Child Welfare 42:*161–169.

Brieland, D. (1965). An assessment of resources in child welfare research. In M. Norris and B. Wallace, eds., *The known and the unknown in child welfare research: An appraisal,* 188–196. New York: Child Welfare League of America.

Broder, D. (1991). Unless we act now, nation's future looks bleak. *Washington Post,* June 15.

Brookings Institution. (2002). *Brookings welfare reform and beyond initiative.* Washington, DC: Brookings Institution.

Brooks, D., and James, S. (2003). Willingness to adopt black foster children: Implications for child welfare policy and recruitment of adoptive families. *Children and Youth Services Review 25:*463–487.

Brown, G. E. (1968). *The multi-problem dilemma.* Metuchen, NJ: The Scarecrow Press.

Browning, D., and Evison, I. (1993). The family debate: A middle way. *Christian Century 110:*712–716.

Brownstein, R. (2002). The prescription drug plan that is eating Washington. *Los Angeles Times,* July 22.

Bruchey, S. (1988). *The wealth of the nation: An economic history of the United States.* New York: HarperCollins.

Bruno, F. J. (1957). *Trends in social work, 1874–1956: A history based on the proceedings of the National Conference of Social Work.* New York: Columbia University Press.

Buchan, W. (1783). *Domestic medicine: Or a treatise on the prevention and cure of diseases.* London: Milner.

Buchanan, J. M., and Lee, D. R. (1982). Politics, time and the Laffer Curve. *Journal of Political Economy 90:*816–819.

Buehler, C., Orme, J. G., Post, J., and Patterson, D. A. (2000). The long-term correlates of family foster care. *Children and Youth Services Review 22:*595–625.

Burt, M. R., and Bayleat, R. R. (1978). *A comprehensive emergency services system for neglected and abused children.* New York: Vantage Press.

Burt, M. R., and Blair, L. H. (1971). *Options for improving care of neglected and dependent children.* Washington, DC: Urban Institute.

Burt, R. A. (1971). Forcing protection on children and their parents: The impact of Wyman v. James. *Michigan Law Review 69:*1259–1310.

Burtless, G. (2002). *Growing American inequality: Sources and remedies.* Washington, DC: The Brookings Institution.

Burtless, G. (2002). *Has widening inequality promoted or retarded U.S. growth?* Washington, DC: The Brookings Institution.

Bush, M. (1987). *Families in distress.* Los Angeles and Berkeley: University of California Press.

Butler, A. (1992). The changing economic consequences of teenage childbearing. *Social Service Review 66:*1–31.

Caffey, J. (1946). Multiple fractures in the long bones of infants suffering from chronic subdural hematoma. *American Journal of Roentgenology 56:*163–173.

Caffey, J., and Silverman, W. A. (1945). Infantile cortical hyperostos: Preliminary report on a new syndrome. *American Journal of Roentgenology 55:*1–16.

Calasanti, T. M., and Bailey, C. A. (1991). Gender inequality and the division of household labor in the United States and Sweden: A socialist-feminist approach. *Social Problems 38:*34–53.

Callahan, M. (1985). Public apathy and government parsimony: A review of child welfare in Canada. In K. L. Levitt and B. Wharf, eds., *The challenge of child welfare,* 1–27. Vancouver: University of British Columbia.

Cameron, J. M. (1978). Radiological and pathological aspects of the battered child syndrome. In S. M. Smith, ed., *The maltreatment of children,* 69–81. Baltimore: University Park Press.

Campbell, D. T., and Stanley, J. C. (1963). *Experimental and quasi-experimental designs for research.* Chicago: Rand McNally.

Cancian, M., Haveman, R., Meyer, D., and Wolfe, B. (2002). Before and after TANF: The economic well-being of women leaving welfare. Discussion paper no. 1244–02. Madison, WI: Institute for Research on Poverty.

Capizzano, J., and Adams, G. (2000a). *The hours that children under five spend in child care: Variations across states* (No. B–8). Washington, DC: Urban Institute.

Capizzano, J., and Adams, G. (2000b). *The number of child care arrangements used by children under five: Variations across States* (No. B–12). Washington, DC: Urban Institute.

Capizzano, J., Adams, G., and Sonenstein, F. (2000a). *Child care arrangements for children under five: Variations across States* (No. B–7). Washington, DC: Urban Institute.

Casper, L. M., Hawkins, M., and O'Connell, M. (1991). *Who's minding the kids?: Child care arrangements.* Washington, DC: Bureau of the Census.

Cassetty, J. (1978). *Child support and social policy.* Lexington, MA: D.C. Heath.

Center on Budget and Planning Priorities. (1998). *Developing innovative child support demonstrations for non-custodial parents.* Washington, DC: Author.

Chambers, D. L. (1979). *Making fathers pay: The enforcement of child support.* Chicago: University of Chicago Press.

Charnley, J. (1955). *The art of child placement.* Ann Arbor: University of Michigan Press.

Chase-Lansdale, P. L., Coley, R. L., Lohman, B. J., and Pittman, L. D. (2003). *Welfare reform: What about the children.* Policy brief 02-1. Baltimore, MD: Welfare, Children and Families.

Chawla, R. K. (1990). The distribution of wealth in Canada and the United States. *Perspectives 2:*29–41.

Cherlin, A. J. (1992). *Marriage, divorce, remarriage.* Cambridge, MA: Harvard University Press.

Cherlin, A. J. (2002). *Public and private families: An introduction.* New York: McGraw-Hill.

Chess, W. A., Hale, K., Carroll, K., Baker, D. R., Wilson, M., Spyres, E., and Jayaratne, S. (1993). *The family focus services program: Final report.* Norman, OK: Oklahoma Department of Human Services.

Child Abuse Study Group. (1990). *Taking child abuse seriously.* London: Unwin Hyman.

Child Support Agency. (1998). *Children first: A new approach to child support.* Green paper. (www.csa.gov.uk)

Child Support Agency On-Line. (2002). *A new contract for welfare: children's rights and parents' responsibilities: A Summary.* White paper. (www.csa.gov.uk)

Child Trends. (2001). Teen birth rate. *CTS facts at a glance* (August).

Children's Bureau. (1980). *Child welfare training: Comprehensive syllabus for a child welfare training program.* DHHS Publication No. (OHDS) 80-30276, Washington, DC: U.S. Department of Health and Human Services.

Children's Defense Fund. (1986). *Preventing adolescent pregnancy: What schools can do.* Washington, DC: Author.

Children's Defense Fund. (1994). *The state of America's children 1994.* Washington, DC: Author.

Children's Defense Fund. (2003). *Number of Black children in extreme poverty hits record high.* Washington, DC: Author.

Children's Defense Fund. (2002). *Richest taxpayers to get a shocking 52 percent of the Bush Tax Cut by 2010.* (June 12). Washington, DC: Author.

Clark, K. B. (1965). *Dark ghetto: Dilemmas of social power.* New York: Harper and Row.

Clarke, A. M., and Clark, C. B. eds., (1976). *Early experience: Myth and evidence.* London: Open Books.

Clarke-Stewart, A. (1993). *Daycare.* Cambridge, MA: Harvard University Press.

Clement, P. F. (1978). Families in foster care: Philadelphia in the late nineteenth century. *Social Service Review 53:*406–420.

Clinton Administration. (1994). *Possible elements in the welfare reform proposal: A new vision.* (March 22). Washington, DC: Author.

Cohen, J. S., and Westhues, A. (1990). *Well-functioning families for adoptive and foster children: A handbook for child welfare workers.* Toronto: University of Toronto Press.

Cohen, P. (2002). The marriage problem: "I Do" to "I Don't". *New York Times,* March 24.

Cohn, A. H., and Daro, D. (1987). Is treatment too late?: What ten years of evaluative research tell us. *Child Abuse and Neglect 11:*433–522.

Coleman, J. S., Campbell, E. Q., Hobson, C. J., McPartland, J., Mood, A. M., Weinfeld, F. D., and York, R. L. (1966). *Equality of educational opportunity.* Washington, DC: U.S. Government Printing Office.

Collier, W. V., and Hill, R. H. (1993). *Family ties. Intensive family preservation services program. An evaluation report.* NY: New York Department of Juvenile Justice.

Colon, F. (1981). Family ties and child placement. In P. A. Sinanoglu and A. N. Maluccio, eds., *Parents of children in placement: Perspectives and programs*, 241–267. New York: Child Welfare League of America.

Coltrane, S. (1997). *Family man: Fatherhood, housework, and gender equity.* New York: Oxford University Press.

Committee for Economic Development. (1987). *Children in need: Investment strategies for the educationally disadvantaged.* Washington, DC: Author.

Congressional Budget Office. (1997). *The changing distribution of federal taxes: 1975–90*, October, table 8, 48. Washington, DC: Author.

Congressional Budget Office. (1992). *Green book.* Washington, DC: Author.

Conley, D. (1999). *Being black, living in the red: Race, wealth and social policy in America. Berkeley:* University of California Press.

Conway, J. F. (1990). *The Canadian family in crisis.* Toronto: James Lorimer and Company.

Cook, R. (1992). *A national evaluation of Title IV-E foster care independent living programs for youth: Phase 2 final report.* Rockville, MD: Westat.

Cooper, D. M. (1993). *Child abuse revisited: Children, society and social work.* Buckingham, England: Open University Press.

Cooper, P. P. (2002). Billions flow into 529 accounts, as returns flunk math for college. *The Philadelphia Inquirer*, November 3, 2002.

Corbit, G. (1985). The hidden unemployables. Paper delivered at the University of Calgary, January 21.

Corcoran, M., and Chaudray, A. (1997). They dynamics of child poverty. *Future of Children 7*:40–54. Online at www.futureofchildren.org.

Corden, A. (1999). *Making child maintenance regimes work.* London: Family Policy Studies Centre.

Costin, L. (1992). Cruelty to children: A dormant issue and its rediscovery, 1920–1960. *Social Service Review 66:*177–198.

Costin, L., and Rapp, C. (1984). *Child welfare policies and practices.* New York: McGraw-Hill.

Council of Europe. (1999). *Recent demographic developments in Europe, 1999.* Council of Europe Press.

Cournand, A., and Meyer, M. (1976). The scientist's code. *Minerva 14:*79–96.

Courtney, M. E., and Dworsky, A. (2001). *Children in out-of-home care in Wisconsin, 1990–1999.* Madison, WI: Department of Health and Family Services.

Courtney, M. E., Piliavin, I., Grogan-Kaylor, A., and Nesmith, A. (1998). *Foster youth transitions to adulthood: Outcomes 12 to 18 months after leaving out-of-home care.* Madison, WI: Institute for Research on Poverty.

Courtney, M. E., and Skyles, A. (2003). Racial Disproportionality in the Child Welfare System. *Children and Youth Services Review 25:*355–358.

Crump, A. D., Hynie, D. L., Aarons, S. J., Adair, E., Woodward, K., and Simons-Morton, B. G. (1999). Pregnancy among urban African-American teens: Ambivalence about prevention. *American Journal of Health and Behavior 23:*32–42.

Cunningham, M. L., and Smith, R. J. (1990). *Family preservation in Tennessee: The home ties intervention.* Knoxville: University of Tennessee Social Work Office of Research and Public Services.

Danziger, S., and Gottschalk, P. (1986). *How have families with children been faring?* Institute for Research on Poverty Discussion Paper 801–806. Madison, WI: University of Wisconsin.

Danziger, S., and Stern, J. (1990). *The causes and consequences of child poverty in the United States.* Innocenti Occasional Papers, No. 10. Florence, Italy: Spedale degli Innocenti.

Danziger, S., and Weinberg, D. H., eds. (1986). *Fighting poverty.* Cambridge, MA: Harvard University Press.

Danziger, S., Jakubson, G., Schwartz, S., and Smolensky, E. (1982). Work and welfare as determinant of female poverty and household headship. *The Quarterly Journal of Economics 98:*519–534.

Darity, W., Jr., and Myers, S., Jr. (1983). Changes in Black family structure: Implications for welfare dependency. *American Economic Review Proceedings 73:*59–64.

Darity, W. A., Myers, S. L., and Elgar, E. (1998). *Persistent disparity: Race and economic inequality in the United States Since 1945.* Northampton, MA: Edward Elgar.

Daro, D. (1988). *Confronting child abuse: Research for effective program design.* New York: Free Press.

Daro, D. (1991). Review of *Recognizing child abuse,* by D. J. Besharov, *Children and Youth Services Review 13:*301–304.

Daro, D., and McCurdy, M. A. (1991). *Current trends in child abuse reporting and fatalities: The results of the 1990 annual fifty state survey.* Working paper No. 808. Chicago: National Committee for the Prevention of Child Abuse.

Daro, D., and Mitchel, L. (1990). *Current trends in child abuse reporting and fatalities: The results of the 1989 annual fifty state summary.* Chicago: National Committee for the Prevention of Child Abuse and Neglect.

Dattalo, P. (1991). The gentrification of public welfare. Unpublished paper. Richmond, VA: Virginia Commonwealth University.

Davis, D. (Producer) (1988). The unquiet death of Eli Creekmore. KCTS-TV, Seattle, Washington.

DeFrancis, V. (1956). *Child protective services in the United States.* Denver, CO: Children's Division, American Humane Association.

DeFrancis, V. (1966). *Child abuse legislation: Analysis of mandatory reporting laws in the United States.* Denver, CO: Children's Division, American Humane Association.

DeFrancis, V. (1967). *Child protective services in the United States: A nationwide survey.* Denver, CO: Children's Division, American Humane Association.

Denison, E. F. (1974). *Accounting for United States Economic Growth, 1929–1969.* Washington DC: Brookings Institution.

Denison, E. F. (1985). *Trends in American economic growth, 1929–1982.* Washington, DC: Brookings Institution.

DeParle, J. (1992). Why marginal changes don't rescue the welfare system. *The New York Times,* March 1, E3.

Desowitz, R. S. (1987). *The thorn in the starfish.* New York: W.W. Norton.

Dingwall, R. (1989). Some problems about predicting child abuse and neglect. In O. Stevenson, ed., *Child Abuse: Professional practice and public policy,* 28–53. London: Havester Weatsheaf.

Dingwall, R., Eekelaar, J., and Murray, T. (1983). *The protection of children: State intervention and family life.* Oxford: Basil Blackwell.

Donnelly, A. H. C. (1991). What we have learned about prevention: What we should do about it. *Child Abuse and Neglect 15:*99–106.

Donnelly, B. P. (1980). *A policy review of California's foster care placement and payment systems.* Report No. S80-6 (May 1980). State of California, Department of Finance, Program Evaluation Unit.

Donzelot, J. (1979). *The policing of families.* New York: Pantheon.

Downs, S., and Taylor, C. (1978). *Resources for training: Permanent planning in foster care.* Portland, OR: Regional Research Institute for Human Services, Portland State University.

DuBois, W. E. B. (1896). *The Philadelphia Negro.* New York: Lippincot.

Duncan, G. J., and Brook-Gunn, J. (1997). *Consequences of growing up poor.* New York: Russell Sage Foundation.

Duncan, G. J., and Hoffman, S. D. (1985). Economic consequences of marital stability. In M. David and T. Smeeding, eds., *Horizontal equity, uncertainty and well-being, 427–470.* Chicago: University of Chicago Press.

Duncan, G. J., and Hoffman, S. D. (1989). *Welfare benefits, economic opportunities, and the incidence of out-of-wedlock births among Black teenage girls, mimeo.* Institute for Social Research, University of Michigan.

Duncan, G. J., and Rodgers, W. (1991). Has children's poverty become more persistent? *American Sociological Review 56:*538–550.

Duquette, D. N. (1980). Liberty and lawyers in child protection. In C. H. Kempe and R. E. Helfer, eds., *The battered child,* 3d ed. rev. and expanded, 316–329. Chicago: University of Chicago Press.

Dworsky, A., and Courtney, M. E. (2000). *Self-sufficiency of foster youth in Wisconsin, Analysis of employment insurance wage data and public assistance data.* Online at aspe.hhs.gov/hsp/fosteryouthWI00.

Dybwad, G. (1949). The challenge to research. *Child Welfare 28:*9–15.

Eckenrode, J., Powers, J., Doris, J., Munsch, J., and Bolger, N. (1988). Substantiation of child abuse and neglect reports. *Journal of Consulting and Clinical Psychology 56:*9–16.

Edelman, M. W. (1987). *Families in peril: An agenda for social change.* Cambridge, MA: Harvard University Press.

Edelman, M. W. (2002). *The shame of child poverty in the richest land on earth.* Washington, DC: Children's Defense Fund.

Edelman, M. W. (1995). Say no to this welfare reform: An open letter to the President. *Washington Post,* November 3.

Edin, K. (1995). Single mothers and child support: The possibilities and limits of child support policy. *Children and Youth Services Review 17:*203–230.

Ehrenreich, B. (2001). *Nickel and dimed: On (not) getting by in America.* New York: Metropolitan Books.

Eichler, M. (1988). *Families in Canada today: Recent changes and their policy consequences,* 2d ed. Toronto: Gage.

Ellwood, D. T. (1986). *Targeting the would-be long term recipient: Who should be served?* Report to the U.S. Department of Health and Human Services. Princeton, NJ: Mathematica Policy Research.

Ellwood, D. T. (1988). *Poor support.* New York: Basic Books.

Ellwood, D. T. (1989). Poverty through the eyes of children. Unpublished manuscript, John F. Kennedy School of Government, Harvard University, Cambridge, MA.

Ellwood, D. T., and Crane, J. (1990). Family change among Black Americans: What do we know? *Journal of Economic Perspectives 4:*6–84.

Elmer, E. (1967). *Children in jeopardy-A study of abused minors and their families.* Pittsburgh, PA: University of Pittsburgh Press.

Emlen, A. (1974). Day care for whom? In A. L. Schorr, ed., *Children and decent people,* 88–112. New York: Basic Books.

Emlen, A. (1976). *Barriers to planning for children in foster care. Vol. 1.* Portland, OR: Regional Research Institute for Human Services, Portland State University.

Emlen, A., Lahti, J., Downs, G., McKay, A., and Downs, S. (1977). *Overcoming barriers to planning for children in foster care.* Portland, OR: Regional Research Institute for Human Services, Portland State University.

England, H. (1986). *Social work as art: Making sense for good practice.* London: Allen and Unwin.

Epstein, W. M. (1983). Research biases. *Social Work 28:*77–78.

Epstein, W. M. (1999). *Children who could have been: The legacy of child welfare in wealthy America.* Madison, WI: University of Wisconsin Press.

Epstein, W. M. (2002). *American policy making: Welfare as ritual.* Lanham, MD: Rowman and Littlefield.

Epstein, W. M. (2003a). The futility of pragmatic reform: The Casey Foundation in New York City. *Children and Youth Services Review 25:*683–701.

Epstein, W. M. (2003b). Personal communication, June 2.

Erikson, E. (1959). *Identity and the life cycle.* New York: International University Press.

Espenshade, T. J. (1979). The economic consequences of divorce. *Journal of Marriage and the Family 41:*615–625.

Ezell, M., and McNeese, C. A. (1986). Practice effectiveness: Research or rhetoric? *Social Work 31:*401–402.

Fagan, P. F. (1999). *How broken families rob children of their chances for future prosperity. Backgrounder* No. 1283. Washington, DC: Heritage Foundation.

Fagan, P. F., and Rector, R. (2000). *The effects of divorce on America. Backgrounder* No. 1373. Washington, DC: Heritage Foundation.

Falconer, N. E., and Swift, K. (1983). *Preparing for practice, The fundamentals of child protection.* Toronto: Children's Aid Society of Metro Toronto.

Faller, K. C. (1985). Unanticipated problems in the United States child protection system. *Child Abuse and Neglect 9:*63–69.

Faludi, S. (1991). *Backlash: The undeclared war against American women.* New York: Crown Publishers.

Fanshel, D. (1971). The exit of children from foster care: An interim research report. *Child Welfare 50:*65–81.

Fanshel, D. (1976). Discharge and other status outcomes. *Child Welfare 55:*143–171.

Fanshel, D. (1981). Decision-making under uncertainty: Foster care for abused or neglected children. *American Journal of Public Health 71:*685–686.

Fanshel, D., and Shinn, E. (1972). *Dollars and sense in the foster care of children: A look at cost factors.* New York: Child Welfare League of America.

Fanshel, D., and Shinn, E. (1978). *Children in foster care: A longitudinal investigation.* New York: Columbia University Press.

Federal Bureau of Investigation. (1962–2000). *Uniform crime reports for the United States.* Washington, DC: U.S. Department of Justice, Federal Bureau of Investigation.

Federal Bureau of Investigation. (2000). Supplementary Homicide Reports, 1976–2000. Washington, DC: U.S. Department of Justice, Bureau of Justice Statistics. On the web at www.ojp.usdoj.gov/bjs/homicide.

Fein, E., Maluccio, A. N., Hamilton, J. V., and Ward, D. E. (1983). After foster care: Outcomes of permanent planning for children. *Child Welfare 62:*485–462.

Fein, L. G. (1979). Can child fatalities, end product of child abuse, be prevented? *Children and Youth Services Review 1:*1–53.

Feldman, L. H. (1990). *Evaluating the impact of family preservation services in New Jersey.* Trenton, NJ: Bureau of Research, Evaluation, and Quality Assurance, Division of Youth and Family Services.

Feldman, L. H. (1991). *Assessing the effectiveness of family preservation services in New Jersey within an ecological context.* Trenton, NJ: New Jersey Department of Human Services, Division of Youth and Family Services.

Feldstein, M. (1974). Social Security, induced retirement, and private savings: New time-series evidence. *Journal of Political Economy 84:*905–926.

Ferguson, D. H. (1961). Children in need of parents: Implications of the Child Welfare League Study. *Child Welfare 40:*1–6.

Finkelhor, D. (1990). Is child abuse over reported? *Public Welfare 48:*22–29.

Finkelhor, D., Hotaling, G., and Sedlak, A. (1990). *Missing, abducted, runaway, and thrownaway children in America: First report, numbers and characteristics national incidence studies.* Washington, DC: U.S. Dept. of Justice, Office of Justice Programs, Office of Juvenile Justice and Delinquency Prevention.

Firestone-Seghi, L. (1979). Assessing results of the Alameda Project. *Children and Youth Services Review 1:*429–435.

Fischer, J. (1971). *Framework for the analysis of outcome research.* Honolulu: School of Social Work, University of Hawaii.

Fischer, J. (1973). Is casework effective? A review. *Social Work 18:*5–20.

Fischer, J. (1983). Evaluations of social work effectiveness: Is positive evidence always good evidence? *Social Work 28:*74–77.

Fisher, S. H. (1958). Skeletal manifestations of parent induced trauma in infants and children. *8th Medical Journal 51:*956–960.

Fontana, V. J. (1971). *The maltreated child.* Springfield, IL: Charles C. Thomas.

Food Research and Action Center (2002a). *State of the state: A profile of food and nutrition programs across the nation.* Washington, D.C.: FRAC Publications.

Food Research and Action Center. (2002b). *School breakfast scorecard: 2001.* 11th ed. Washington, DC: FRAC Publications.

Forrest, J. D., and Singh, S. (1990). The sexual and reproductive behavior of American women, 1982–1988. *Family Planning Perspectives 22:*206–214.

Forsythe, P. (1992). Homebuilders and family preservation. *Children and Youth Services Review 14:*37–47.

Frank, R. H. (1985). *Choosing the right pond: Human behavior and the quest for service.* New York: Oxford University Press.

Franklin, A. W., ed. (1975). *Concerning child abuse.* London: Churchill-Livingstone.

Fraser, M., Pecora, P., and Haapala, D. (1991). *Families in crisis.* New York: Aldine de Gruyter.

Fraser, S., ed. (1995). *The bell curve wars.* New York: Basic Books.

French, D. (1949). *The contribution of research to social work.* New York: American Association of Social Workers.

Friedberg, A. (1988). *The weary titan: Britain and experience of relative decline, 1895–1905.* Princeton, NJ: Princeton University Press.

Friedman, M., and Friedman, R. (1979). *Free to choose.* New York: Harcourt Brace Jovanovich.

Frost, N., and Stein, M. (1989). *The politics of child welfare: Inequality, power, and change.* New York: Harvester Wheatsheaf.

Furstenberg, F. F., Jr. (1991). As the pendulum swings: Teenage childbearing and social concern. *Family Relations 40:*127–138.

Furstenberg, F. F., Jr. (2002). What a good marriage can't do. *New York Times,* August 13.

Furstenberg, F. F., Jr., Brooks-Gunn, J., and Morgan, S. P. (1987). *Adolescent mothers in later life.* New York: Cambridge University Press.

Galbraith, J. K. (1967). *The new industrial state.* Boston: Houghton-Mifflin.

Galinsky, E., Bond, J. T., and Friedman, D. E. (1993). *The changing workforce: Highlights of the National Study.* New York: Families and Work Institute.

Galston, W. (1990). A liberal-democratic case for the two-parent family. *The Responsive Community* 14-26.

Gambrill E., and Shlonsky, A. (2000). Assessing risk in child maltreatment. *Children and Youth Services Review 22* (11–12).

Gambrill, E. (1990). *Critical thinking in clinical practice: Improving the accuracy of judgments and decision about clients.* San Francisco: Jossey-Bass.

Gambrill, E. (1997). *Social work practice: A critical thinker's guide.* New York: Oxford University Press.

Gambrill, E. D., and Stein, T. J. (1981). Decision making and case management: Achieving continuity of care for children in out-of-home placement. In A. N. Maluccio and P. A. Sinanoglu, eds., *The challenge of partnership: Working with parents of children in foster care,* 109–139. New York: Child Welfare League of America, Inc.

Garbarino, J., Carson, B., and Flood, M. F. (1983). A protective service system. *Children and Youth Services Review 5:*49–63.

Garbarino, J., and Sherman, D. (1980). Identifying high-risk neighborhoods. In J. Garbarino, S. H. Stocking, and Associates, eds., *Protecting children from abuse and neglect: Developing and maintaining effective support systems for families,* 94–108. San Francisco: Jossey-Bass.

Garbarino, J., and Stocking, S. H. (1981). The social context of child maltreatment. In J. Garbarino, S. H. Stocking, and Associates, eds., *Protecting children from abuse and neglect: Developing and maintaining effective support systems for families,* 1–14. San Francisco: Jossey-Bass.

Garfinkel, I. (1968). Negative income-tax and children's allowances programs-Comparisons. *Social Work 13:*33–39.

Garfinkel, I. (1992). *Assuring child support: An extension of child security.* New York: Russell Sage Press.

Garfinkel, I., and McLanahan, S. (1986). *Single mothers and their children: A new American dilemma.* Washington, DC: Urban Institute Press.

Garfinkel, I., and Uhr, L. (1987). A new approach to child support. *Public Interest 75:*111–122.

Garfinkel, I., McLanahan, S., Tienda, M., and Brooks-Gunn, J. (2001). Fragile families and welfare reform. *Children and Youth Services Review 23:* (4–5).

Garfinkel, I., Meyer, D. R., and Sandefur, G. D. (1992). The effects of alternative child support systems on Blacks, Hispanics, and Non-Hispanic Whites. *Social Service Review 66:*505–523.

Garfinkel, I., Miller, C., McLanahan, S., and Hanson, T. (1998). Deadbeat dads or inept states? *Evaluation Review 22* (6).

Gart, J. J. (1971). The comparison of proportions: A review of significance tests, confidence intervals, and adjustments for stratification. *Review of the International Statistical Institute 39:*148–169.

Gauthier, A. H. (1999). Historical trends in state support for families in Europe (post-1945). *Children and Youth Services Review 21:*937–965.

Geary, L. H. (2003). What it all means for families, married couples and investors. Plus: Tax savings calculator. May 30, *CNN/Money.*

Gelles, R. J. (1996). *The book of David: How preserving families can cost children's lives.* New York: Basic Books.

Gelles, R. J. (2000). Public policy for violence against women: 30 years of successes and remaining challenges. *American Journal of Preventive Medicine 19:*298–301.

Gelles, R. J., and Straus, M. A. (1987). Is violence toward children increasing? A comparison of 1975 and 1985 national survey rates. *Journal of Interpersonal Violence 2:*212–222.

Gelles, R. J., and Straus, M. A. (1988). *Intimate violence: The causes and consequences of abuse in the American family.* New York: Simon and Schuster.

General Accounting Office. (1976). *Administration of Children, Youth and Families-Need to better use its research results and clarify its role.* HRD-77-76. Washington, DC: Author.

Giannarelli, L., and Steuerle, C. E. (1995). *The twice-poverty trap: Tax rates faced by AFDC recipients.* Research Report. Washington, DC: Urban Institute.

Gibbons, J. (1997). Relating outcomes to objectives in child protection policy. In N. Parton, ed., *Child protection and family support: Tensions, contradictions and possibilities,* 78–91. London: Routledge.

Gil, D. (1970). *Violence against children.* Cambridge, MA: Harvard University Press.

Gilbert, N. (2002). *Transformation of the welfare state: The silent surrender of public responsibility.* New York: Oxford University Press.

Gilbert, N., and Gilbert, B. (1991). *The enabling state: Modern welfare capitalism in America.* New York: Oxford University Press.

Gilder, G. (1981). *Wealth and poverty.* New York: Basic Books.

Gilder, G. (1984). *The spirit of enterprise.* New York: Simon and Schuster.

Giovannoni, J. M. (1989). Substantiated and unsubstantiated reports of child maltreatment. *Children and Youth Services Review 11*:299–318.

Giovannoni, J. M., and Becerra, R. (1979). *Defining child abuse.* New York: Free Press.

Glazer, N. (1974). The schools of the minor professions. *Minerva 12*:346–364.

Glendon, M. (1987). *Abortion and divorce in Western law.* Cambridge, MA: Harvard University Press.

Glickman, E. (1957). *Child placement through clinically oriented casework.* New York: Columbia University Press.

Godfrey, R., and Schlesinger, B. (1965). *Child welfare services: Winding paths to maturity.* Toronto: Canadian Conference on Children.

Goerge, R. M. (1990). The reunification process in substitute care. *Social Service Review 64*:422–457.

Golden, O. (1992). *Poor children and welfare reform.* Westport, CT: Auburn House Publishing.

Golding, P., and Middleton, S. (1982). *Images of welfare: Press and public attitudes to poverty.* London: Martin Robertson.

Goldstein, H. (1992). If social work hasn't made progress as a science, might it be an art? *Families in Society 73*:48–55.

Goldstein, J., Freud, S., and Solnit, A. (1998). *The best interests of the child: The least detrimental alternative.* New York: Simon and Schuster.

Goldstein, J., Freud, A., and Solnit, A. (1973). *Beyond the best interests of the child.* New York: Free Press.

Goldstein, J., Freud, A., and Solnit, A. (1979). *Before the best interests of the child.* New York: Free Press.

Goldstein, J. R. (1999). The leveling of divorce in the United States. *Demography 36*:409–414.

Goldstein, N. C. (1991). Why poverty is bad for children. Unpublished Ph.D. dissertation. Cambridge, MA: Harvard University Press.

Goldstein, R. (1999). *Child abuse and neglect: Cases and materials.* St. Paul: West Publishing.

Goodwin, L. (1972). Welfare mothers and the work ethic. *Monthly Labor Review 95:*35–37.

Gordon, H. L. (1960). The challenge of new knowledge to the field of child care. *Journal of Social Work Process 11:*25–67.

Gordon, H. L. (1948). Editorial comment: Towards improved services to children. *Child Welfare 27:*7–10.

Gordon, H. L. (1956). Casework services for children. Boston: Houghton-Mifflin.

Gordon, L. (1988). *Heroes of their own lives: The politics and history of family violence, Boston 1880–1960.* New York: Penguin Books.

Gould, S. J. (1994). Curveball. *New Yorker,* November 28.

Gramlich, E., and Long, M. (1996). *Growing income inequality: Roots and remedies.* Washington, DC: Urban Institute. Online at www.urban.org/url.cfm?ID=306768

Gray, S. S., Hartman, A., and Saalberg, E. S. (1985). *Empowering the Black family: A roundtable discussion with Ann Hartman, James Leigh, Jacquelynn Moffett, Elaine Pinderhughes, Barbara Solomon, and Carol Stack.* Ann Arbor, MI: National Child Welfare Training Center.

Green Book. (1998, 2000). See United States House of Representatives. (1998). *Green Book.*

Greenhouse, S. (1993). If the French can do it, why can't we? *New York Times Magazine,* November 14, Sec. 6, 59–62.

Greenland, C. (1987). *Preventing CAN deaths: An international study of deaths due to child abuse and neglect.* London: Tavistock Publications.

Groenveld, L. P., and Giovannoni, J. M. (1977). Disposition of child abuse and neglect cases. *Social Work Research and Abstracts 13:*24–31.

Gruber, A. R. (1978). *Children in foster care: Destitute, neglected, betrayed.* New York: Human Sciences Press.

Gwinn, J. L., Lewin, K. W., and Peterson, H. G. (1961). Roentgenographic manifestations of unsuspected trauma in infancy: A problem of medical, social and legal importance. *Journal of the American Medical Association 176:*926–929.

Haanes-Olson, L. (1972). Children's allowance: Their size and structure in five countries. *Social Security Bulletin 5:*17–28.

Hacker, A. (1992). *Two nations: Black and white, separate, hostile, unequal.* New York: Ballantine Books.

Hagan, H. R. (1957). Distinctive aspects of child welfare. *Child Welfare 36:*1–6.

Halper, G., and Jones, M. A. (1981). *Serving families at risk of dissolution: Public preventive services in New York City.* New York: Human Resources Administration, Special Services for Children.

Hampton, R. L., and Newberger, E. H. (1985). Child abuse incidence and reporting by hospitals: Significance of severity, class, and race. *American Journal of Public Health 75:*56–60.

Handler, J. F., and Hasenfeld, Y. (1991). *The moral construction of poverty: Welfare reform in America.* New York: Sage.

Handler, J. F., and Hasenfeld, Y. (1997). *We the poor people: Work, poverty, and welfare.* New Haven, CT: Yale University Press.

Hardicker, P., Exton, K., and Barker, M. (1991). *Policies and practices in preventive child care.* London: Gower.

Harding, N. (1992). The Marxist-Leninist detour. In J. Dunn, ed., *Democracy: The unfinished journey, 508 BC to AD 1993,* 155–187. New York: Oxford University Press.

Harlow, H. (1958). The nature of love. *American Psychologist 13:*673–685.

Harlow, H. (1961). The development of affection patterns in infant monkeys. In B. M. Foss, ed., *Determinants of infant behavior,* Vol. 1. London: Methuen.

Harlow, H. F., and Zimmerman, R. R. (1959). Affectional responses in the infant monkey. *Science 130:*421–432.

Hart, B., and Risley, T. R. (1995). *Meaningful differences in the everyday experience of young American children.* Baltimore: Brookes Publishing.

Hart, B., and Risley, T. R. (1999). *The social world of children learning to talk.* Baltimore: Brookes Publishing.

Hart, B., and Risley, T. R. (2003). The early catastrophe: The 30 million word gap by age 3. *American Educator 27:*4–9.

Hartman, A. (1971). But what is social casework? *Social Casework 52:*411–419.

Haveman, R. (1988). *Starting even: An equal opportunity program to combat the nation's new poverty.* New York: Simon and Schuster.

Hazlitt, H. (1973). *The conquest of poverty.* New Rochelle, NY: Arlington House.

Hein, J. (2001). Taming the welfare state: New York City, once America's "welfare capital," has become the epicenter of reform. *American Outlook,* May/June.

Hein, J. (2001). United States Department of Health and Human Services: TANF Reauthorization Listening Session, Prepared Testimony of Jay Hein. Philadelphia, Pennsylvania, November 26, 2001.

Heineman, M. (1981). The obsolete scientific imperative in social work research. *Social Service Review 55:*371–397.

Helburn, S. W., and Bergmann, B. R. (2002). *America's childcare problem: The way out.* New York: St. Martin's Press.

Helfer, R. (1978). *Report on the research using the Michigan Screening Profile of Parenting (MSPP).* Washington, DC: National Center on Child Abuse and Neglect.

Heneghan, A. M., Horwitz, S. M., and Leventhal, J. M. (1996). Evaluating intensive family preservation programs: A methodological review. *Pediatrics 97:*535–542.

Henggler, S. W., Melton, G. B., and Smith, L. A. (1992). Family preservation using multisystematic therapy: An effective alternative to incarcerating serious juvenile offenders. *Journal of Consulting and Clinical Psychology 60:*953–961.

Hennepin County Community Services Department. (1980). *Family study project: Demonstration and research in intensive services to families.* Minneapolis: Author.

Henriksen, H., and Holter, H. (1978). Norway. In S. Kamerman and A. J. Kahn, eds., *Family policy: Government and families in fourteen countries,* 49–67. New York: Columbia University Press.

Henshaw, S. K., and Van Vort, J. (1989). Teenage abortion, birth and pregnancy statistics: An update. *Family Planning Perspective 21:*85–88.

Hepworth, H. P. (1985). Child neglect and abuse. In K. L. Levitt and B. Wharf, eds., *The challenge of child welfare,* 28–52. Vancouver: University of British Columbia.

Herrnstein, R. J., and Murray, C. (1994). *The bell curve: Intelligence and class structure in American life.* New York: Free Press.

Hewitt, C. (1983). Defending a termination of parental rights case. In M. Hardin, ed., *Foster children in the courts,* 229–263. Boston: Butterworth Legal Publishers.

Hewlett, S. A. (1991). *When the bough breaks: The cost of neglecting our children.* New York: Basic Books.

Hines, A. M., Lemon, K., Wyatt, P., and Merdinger, J. (forthcoming). Factors related to the disproportionate involvement of children of color in the child welfare system: A review and emerging themes. *Children and Youth Services Review.*

HM Treasury. (2001). Helping people to save. London: HM Treasury. Online at www.hm-treasury.gov.uk/pbr2000/savings.pdf.

Horwitz S. M., Balestracci, K. M., and Simms, M. D. (2001). Foster care placement improves children's functioning. *Archives of Pediatric Adolescent Medicine 155:*1255–60.

Hoshino, G. (1974). AFDC as child welfare. In A. Schorr, ed., *Children and decent people,* 113–141. New York: Basic Books.

Howells, J. G. (1975). *Remember Maria.* London: Butterworths.

Howitt, D. (1992). *Child abuse errors: When good intentions go wrong.* New York: Harvester Wheatsheaf.

Howling, P. T., Wodarski, J. S., Kurtz, P. D., and Gaudin, J. M. (1989). Methodological issues in child maltreatment research. *Social Work Research and Abstracts 25:*3–7.

Hotz, V. J., McElroy, S. W., and Sanders, S. G. (1997). The impacts of teenage childbearing on the mothers and consequences of those impacts for government. In R. E. Maynard, ed., *Kids having kids: Economic costs and social consequences of teen pregnancy.* Washington, DC: Urban Institute Press.

Hunter, W. M., Coulter, M. L., Runyan, D. K., and Everson, M. D. (1990). Determinants of placement for sexually abused children. *Child Abuse and Neglect 14:*407–417.

Hutchison, E. D. (1989). Child protective screening decisions: An analysis of predictive factors. *Social Work Research and Abstracts 25:*9–15.

Hutchison, E. D. (1990). Child maltreatment: Can it be defined? *Social Service Review 64:*61–78.

Hutchison, E. D. (1992). Child welfare as a woman's issue. *Families in Society 73:*67–78.

Hutchison, E. D. (1993). Mandatory reporting laws: Child protective case finding gone awry? *Social Work 38:*56–63.

Huxley, P. (1986). Statistical errors in the British Journal of Social Work, volumes 1–14. *British Journal of Social Work 16:*645–658.

Huxley, P. (1988). "Quantitative-descriptive" articles in the British Journal of Social Work, volumes 1–14. *The British Journal of Social Work 18:*189–199.

James, P. D. (1993). *The children of men.* New York: Penguin.

Janko, K. S. (1991). The social construction of child abuse: A qualitative investigation of child maltreatment. Unpublished Ph.D. dissertation, University of Oregon.

Jargowski, P. A. (1997). *Poverty and place: Ghettos, barrios, and the American city.* New York: Russell Sage Foundation.

Jencks, C. (1992). *Rethinking social policy: Race, poverty, and the underclass.* Cambridge, MA: Harvard University Press.

Jenkins, S. (1974). Foster care. In A. Schorr, ed., *Children and decent people,* 24–52. New York: Basic Books.

Jenkins, S., and Norman, E. (1972). *Filial deprivation.* New York: Columbia University Press.

Jenkins, S., and Norman, E. (1975). *Beyond placement: Mothers view foster care.* New York: Columbia University Press.

Jenkins, S., and Sauber, M. (1966). *Paths to child placement.* New York: Community Council of Greater New York.

Jeter, H. R. (1960). *Children who receive services from public child welfare agencies.* Washington, DC: Children's Bureau.

Jeter, H. R. (1963). *Children, problems and services in child welfare programs.* Washington, DC: Children's Bureau.

Johnson, C. M., Sum, A. M., and Weill, J. D. (1988). *Vanishing dreams: The growing economic plight of America's young families.* Washington, DC: Children's Defense Fund.

Johnson, D., and Fein, E. (1991). The concept of attachment: Applications to adoption. *Children and Youth Services Review 13:*397–412.

Johnson, E. S., Levine, A., and Doolittle, F. C. (1999). *Fathers' fair share: Helping poor fathers manage child support.* New York: Russell Sage Foundation.

Johnson, K. (1999). Can "child support" live up to its name? *USA Today,* October 20.

Jones, R., as told to L. Welch. (2003). The guardian: Working on behalf of children, I'm always on the case—even if everyone else is on mine. *The New York Times Magazine,* February 2, 86.

Jones, A., and Rutman, L. (1981). *In the children's aid: J.J. Kelso and child welfare in Ontario.* Toronto: University of Toronto Press.

Jones, C. A., Gordon, N. M., and Sawhill, I. V. (1976). *Child support payments in the United States.* Washington, DC: Urban Institute.

Jones, M. A., Neuman, R., and Shyne, A. (1976). *A second chance for families: Evaluation of a program to reduce foster care.* New York: Child Welfare League of America.

Kadushin, A. (1959). The knowledge base of social work. In A. J. Kahn, ed., *Issues in American social work,* 39–79. New York: Columbia University Press.

Kadushin, A. (1965). Introduction of new orientations in child welfare research. In M. Norris and B. Wallace, eds., *The known and the unknown in child welfare research: An appraisal,* 28–39. New York: Child Welfare League of America.

Kadushin, A. (1967). *Child welfare services.* New York: Macmillan.

Kadushin, A. (1976). *Emotional abuse.* Unpublished paper presented at a joint U.S. National Center on Child Abuse and Neglect and National Institute of Mental Health Workshop on Emotional Maltreatment, Houston, Texas, April.

Kadushin, A. (1978). Child welfare strategy in the coming years: An overview. In F. Farro, ed., *Child welfare strategy in the coming years,* 1–50. Children's Bureau (OHDS) 78-30158. Washington, DC: U.S. Department of Health, Education, and Welfare.

Kadushin, A., and Martin, J. A. (1981). *Child abuse: An interactional event.* New York: Columbia University Press.

Kadushin, A., and Martin, J. A. (1988). *Child welfare services.* 4th ed. New York: Macmillan.

Kadushin, A., ed. (1967). *Child welfare services: A sourcebook.* New York: Macmillan.

Kafka, F. (1995). *The trial.* New York: Knopf Publishing

Kahn, A. J. (1956). Facilitating social work research. *Social Service Review* *30:*331–343.

Kahn, A. J. (1976). Social service delivery at the neighborhood level: Experience, theory, and fads. *Social Service Review 50:*23–56.

Kahn, A. J., and Kamerman, S. B. (1975a). *Not for the poor alone.* Philadelphia: Temple University Press.

Kahn, A. J., and Kamerman, S. B. (1975b). *Social policies in the United States: Policies and programs.* Philadelphia: Temple University Press.

Kahn, A. J., ed. (1973). *Shaping the new social work.* New York: Columbia University Press.

Kamerman, S. B., and Kahn, A. J. (1983). *Income transfers for families with children: An eight country study.* Philadelphia: Temple University Press.

Kamerman, S. B., and Kahn, A. J. (1988b). *Mothers alone: Strategies for a time of change.* Dover, MA: Auburn House Publishing.

Kamerman, S. B., and Kahn, A. J. (1990). Social services for children, youth and families in the United States. Special Issue of *Children and Youth Services Review 12:*1–184.

Kamerman, S. B., and Kahn, A. J., eds. (1978). *Family policy: Government and families in fourteen countries.* New York: Columbia University Press.

Kamerman, S. B., and Kahn, A. J., eds. (1988a). *Child support: From debt collection to social policy.* Newbury Park, CA: Sage.

Kaplan, D., and Reich, R. (1976). The murdered child and his killers. *American Journal of Psychiatry 133:*809–813.

Karpf, M. J. (1931). *The scientific basis of social work.* New York: Columbia University Press.

Karski, R. W., Gilbert, N., and Frame, L. (1997). Evaluating the Emergency Response System's screening, assessment, and referral of child-abuse reports. *CPS Brief 9*: 1–11.

Katz, M. B. (1986). *In the shadow of the poorhouse*. New York: Basic Books.

Katz, M. B. (1986). *The undeserving poor: From the war on poverty to the war on welfare*. New York: Pantheon Books.

Katz, M. H., Hampton, R. L., Newberger, E. H., Bowles, R. T., and Snyder, J. C. (1986). Returning children home: Clinical decision making in cases of child abuse and neglect. *American Journal of Orthopsychiatry 56*:253–263.

Kaus, M. (1992). The end of equality. New York: Basic Books.

Keister, L. A. (2000). *Wealth in America: Trends in wealth inequality*. Cambridge: Cambridge University Press.

Kelly, G., and Lissauer, R. (2000). *Ownership for all*. London: Institute for Public Policy Research.

Kelly, R. (2003). *Strengthening the saving habit of future generations*. London: Inland Revenue. Online at www.inlandrevenue.gov.uk/budget2003/pn03.htm.

Kempe, C. H., and Silver, H. (1959). The problem of parental criminal neglect and severe abuse of children. *AMA Journal of Diseases of Children 98:*528.

Kempe, C. H., Silverman, F., Steele, B., Droegmueller, W., and Silver, H. (1962). The battered-child syndrome. *Journal of the American Medical Association 181:*17–24.

Kempe, R. S., and Kempe, C. H. (1978). *Child abuse*. New York: Open Books.

Kendrick, M. (1990). *Nobody's children: The foster care crisis in Canada*. Toronto: Macmillan of Canada.

Kennickell, A. B., and Woodburn, R. L. (1997). Consistent weight design for the 1989, 1992, and 1995 for the Survey of Consumer Finances. Preliminary draft of working paper, Board of Governors of the Federal Reserve System (August).

Kessler-Harris, A. (1982). *Out to work: A history of wage-earning women in the United States*. New York: Oxford University Press.

Keynes, J. M. (1964). *The general theory of employment, interest and money*. New York: Harcourt, Brace and World.

Kiernan, K. (2000). European perspectives of union formation. In L. Waite, C. Bachrach, M. Hindin, E. Thompson, and A. Thompson, eds., *Ties that bind: Perspectives on marriage and cohabitation*. New York: Aldine de Gruyter.

Kindleberger, C. (1996). *World economic primacy*. New York: Oxford University Press.

King, M. L., Jr. (1963). *Why we can't wait*. New York: Harper and Row.

Kinney, J. M., Haapala, D., and Booth, C. (1991). *Keeping families together: The Homebuilders Model*. Hawthorne, NY: Aldine de Gruyter.

Kinney, J. M., Madsen, B., Fleming, T., and Haapala, D. (1977). Homebuilders: Keeping families together. *Journal of Clinical and Counseling Psychology 43:*667–673.

Kirby, D., and Coyle, K. (1997). School-based programs to reduce sexual risk-taking behavior. *Children and Youth Services Review 19*:415–436.

Kirby, D., and Coyle, K. (1997). Youth development programs. *Children and Youth Services Review 19:*437–454.

Kiyosaki, R. T., and Lechter, S. L. (2000). *Rich dad, poor dad.* New York: Time Warner Books.

Kline, D., and Overstreet, H. (1972). *Foster care or children: Nurture and treatment.* New York: Columbia University Press.

Knitzer, J., Allen, M. A., and McGowan, B. (1978). *Children without homes.* Washington, DC: Children's Defense Fund.

Kolko, G. (1962). *Wealth and power in America: An analysis of social class and income distribution.* New York: Greenwood Publishing.

Kozol, J. (1991). *Savage inequalities: Children in America's schools.* New York: Crown Books.

Kristof, K. (2002). 529s ease burden of college costs. *Los Angeles Times*, December 15.

Kristol, I. (1971). The best of intentions, the worst of results. *The Atlantic Monthly*, August.

Krugman, P. R. (1992). *The age of diminished expectations: U.S. economic policy in the 1990s.* Cambridge, MA: MIT Press.

Kuhn, T. S. (1962). *The structure of scientific revolutions.* Chicago: University of Chicago Press.

Kunzel, R. G. (1993). *Fallen women, problem girls: Unmarried mothers and the professionalization of social work, 1890–1945.* New Haven, CT: Yale University Press.

Landsman, M. J. (1985). *Evaluation of fourteen child placement prevention projects in Wisconsin, 1983–1985.* Iowa City, IA: National Resource Center on Family Based Services.

Larner, M. B., Stevenson, C. S., and Behrman, R. E. (1998). Protecting children from abuse and neglect: Analysis and recommendations. *The Future of Children 8.* Online at www.futureofchildren.org.

LaRoe, R., and Pool, J. C. (1988). Gap grows between rich, poor. *Columbus Dispatch*, July 16.

Lealman, G. T., Haigh, D., Phillips, J. M., Stoan, J., and Ord-Smith, C. (1983). Prediction and prevention of child abuse: An empty hope. *Lancet 8339*:1423–1424.

Lee, F. (2003). Does class count in today's land of opportunity? *New York Times*, January 17, A17 and A19.

Lefaucheur, N., and Martin, C. (1993). Lone parent families in France: Situation and research. In J. Hudson and B. Galaway, eds., *Single parent families: Perspectives on research and policy*, 31–50. Toronto: Thompson Educational Publishing.

Leiby, J. (1978). *A history of social welfare and social work in the United States.* New York: Columbia University Press.

Lemov, P. (1989). Bringing children of the underclass into the mainstream. *Governing*, June, 34–39.

Lengyel, T. E., and Campbell, D., eds., (2002). *Welfare policy through the lens of personal experience.* Milwaukee, WI: Alliance for Children and Families.

Leonhardt, D. (2003). Defining the rich in the world's wealthiest nation. *New York Times*, January 12, Sec. 4, pp. 1 and 16.

Levine, R. S. (1973). Caveat parens: A demystification of the child protection system. *University of Pittsburgh Law Review 35:*1–52.

Levitan, S. A. (1990). *Programs in aid of the poor.* Baltimore, MD: The John Hopkins University Press.

Levy, F. (1987). *Dollars and dreams: The changing American income distribution.* New York: W.W. Norton.

Lewis, A., and Schneider, W. (1985). Hard times: The public on poverty. *Public Opinion 7:*2–7.

Liljestrom, R. (1978). Sweden. In S. Kamerman and A. J. Kahn, eds., *Family policy: Government and families in fourteen countries,* 19–48. New York: Columbia University Press.

Lindblom, C. E., and Cohen, D. K. (1979). *Usable knowledge: Social science and social problem solving.* New Haven: Yale University Press.

Lindsey, D. (1978). *The scientific publication system in social science: A study of the operation of leading professional journals in psychology, sociology, and social work.* San Francisco: Jossey-Bass.

Lindsey, D. (1982). Achievements for children in foster care. *Social Work 27:*491–496.

Lindsey, D. (1991a). Adequacy of income and the foster care placement decision: Using an odds ratio approach to examine client variables. *Social Work Research and Abstracts 28:29–36.*

Lindsey, D. (1991b). Building a great public university: The role of funding at British and American universities. *Research in Higher Education 32:*217–244.

Lindsey, D. (1991c). Does increased reporting reduce child abuse fatalities? An examination of national statistics. Unpublished manuscript. School of Social Welfare, University of California, Berkeley.

Lindsey, D. (1991d). Factors affecting the foster care placement decision: An analysis of national survey data. *American Journal of Orthopsychiatry 61:*272–281.

Lindsey, D. (1991e). Reliability of the foster care placement decision: A review. *Research in Social Work Practice 2:*65–80.

Lindsey, D., and Kirk, S. A. (1992). The role of social work journals in the development of a knowledge base for the profession. *Social Service Review 66:*295–310.

Lindsey, D., and Ozawa, M. N. (1979). Schizophrenia and SSI: Implications and problems. *Social Work 24:*120–126.

Lindsey, D., and Regehr, C. (1993). Protecting severely abused children: Clarifying the role of criminal justice and child welfare. *American Journal of Orthopsychiatry 63:*509–517.

Lindsey, D., and Trocmé, N. (1994). Have child protection efforts reduced child homicides? An examination of data from Britain and North America. *British Journal of Social Work 24:*715–732.

Lindsey, D., Martin, S. K., and Doh, J. (2002). The failure of intensive casework services to reduce foster care placements: an examination of family preservation studies, *Children and Youth Services Review 24:*743–775.

Lindsey, D., and Martin, S. K. (2003). Deeping child poverty: The not so good news about welfare reform. *Children and Youth Services Review 24:* 163–177.

Lis, E. F., and Frauenberger, G. S. (1950). Multiple fractures associated with subdural hematoma in infancy. *Paediatrics 6:890–892.*

Longfellow, C. (1979). Divorce in context: Its impact on children. In G. Levinger and O.C. Moles, eds., *Divorce and separation: Context, causes, and consequences,* 287–306. New York: Basic Books.

Longman, P. J., and Graham, A. (1998). The cost of children, *U.S. New and World Report*, March 30.

Lopez, A. (2003). *Race and income in California: Census 2000 profiles.* Center for Comparative Studies in Race and Ethnicity. Stanford, CA: Stanford University. Online at www.stanford.edu/dept/csre/reports/report_13.pdf.

Low, S. (1958). *Staff in public child welfare programs–1956, with Trend Data 1946–1956.* Children's Bureau Statistical Series, No. 41. Washington, DC: U.S. Children's Bureau.

Lowry, M. R. (1998). Commentaries: How we can better protect children from abuse and neglect. *Future of Children* 8. Online at www.futureofchildren.org.

Luker, K. (1996). *Dubious conceptions: The politics of teenage pregnancy.* Cambridge, MA: Harvard University Press.

Lyle, C.G., and Nelson, J. (1983). *Home based vs. traditional child protective services: A study of home based services demonstration project in the Ramsey County Community Human Services Department.* Unpublished paper. St. Paul, MN: Ramsey County Community Human Services Department.

Lynch, M. A. (1985). Child abuse before Kempe: An historical literature review. *Child Abuse and Neglect 9:*39–54.

Maas, H. S., and Engler, Jr., R. E. (1959). *Children in need of parents.* New York: Columbia University Press.

Macallair, D., Taqi-Eddin, K., and Schiraldi, V. (1999). Class dismissed: Higher education vs. corrections. San Francisco: The Justice Policy Institute. Online at http://www.cahro.org/html/decjan99-3.html.

MacMillan, H. L., MacMillan, J. H., Offord, D. R., Griffith, L., and MacMillan, A. (1994). Primary prevention of child physical abuse and neglect: a critical review. Part I. *Journal of Child Psychology and Psychiatry 35:*835–56.

Magura, S. (1981). Are services to prevent foster care effective? *Children and Youth Services Review 3:*193–212.

Mahoney, K., and Mahoney, M. J. (1974). Psychoanalytic guidelines for child placement. *Social Work 19:*688–696.

Mahoney, M. J. (1976). *The scientist as subject.* Cambridge, MA: Ballinger.

Malthus, T. R. (1941). *Essay on the principle of population.* [1798]. New York: E.P. Dutton.

Maluccio, A. N. (2002). Family preservation or adoption? An essay review, *Children and Youth Services Review 24:*287–292.

Maluccio, A. N., and Anderson, G .R. (2000). Future challenges and opportunities in child welfare. *Child Welfare 79:*3–9.

Manlove, J. (1998). The influence of high school dropout and school disengagement on the risk of school-age pregnancy. *Journal of Research on Adolescence.*

Margolin, L. (1992). Deviance on record: Techniques for labeling child abusers in official documents. *Social Problems 39:*58–70.

Marie, A. (1954). Hematome sousdural du nourrisson associe a des fractures des membres. *Semaine hospitale Paris 30:*1757.

Marmor, T. R., Mashaw, J. L., and Harvey, P. L. (1990). *America's misunderstood welfare state: Persistent myths, enduring realities.* New York: Basic Books.

Marquezy, R. A., Bach, C., and Blondeau, M. (1952). Hematome sousdural et fractures multiplas des os longs chez un nourrisson de N. mois. *Archives Francaises de Pediatrie 9:*526.

Martin, H., and Fox, S. (2003). Cuts imperil child-support checks. *Los Angeles Times,* B1 (June 8).

Martin, C. A., Hill, K. K., and Welsh, R. (1998). Adolescent pregnancy a stressful life event: Causes and consequences. In T. W. Miller, ed., *Child of trauma: Stressful life events and their effects on children and adolescents.* Madison, CT: International Universities Press.

Martin, M. (1985). Poverty and child welfare. In K. L. Levitt and B. Wharf, eds., *The challenge of child welfare,* 53–65. Vancouver: University of British Columbia.

Marx, K. (1862). *The theory of surplus value.* New York: Prometheus Books.

Marx, K. (1867). *Capital: A critique of political economy,* translated by Ben Fowkes. New York: Penguin, 1992.

Massey, D. S., and Denton, N. A. (1993). *American apartheid: Segregation and the making of the underclass.* Cambridge, MA: Harvard University Press.

Mathewes-Green, F. (1996). Pro-life dilemma: Pregnancy centers and the welfare trap. *Policy Review* (July).

Matza., D. (1964). *Delinquency and drift.* New York: Wiley.

Max, S. (2001). The pros and cons of 529s. *Money,* October 15.

Mayer, S. E. (1997). *What money can't buy: Family income and children's life chances.* Cambridge, MA: Harvard University Press.

Mayer, S. E., and Jencks, C. (1989). Poverty and the distribution of material hardship. *Journal of Human Resources 24:*88.

McCabe, A. (1967). *The pursuit of promise.* New York: Community Service Society.

McCurdy, M. A., and Daro, D. (1993). *Current trends in child abuse reporting and fatalities: The results of the 1992 annual fifty state survey.* Chicago: National Committee for the Prevention of Child Abuse.

McDonald, T., and Marks, J. (1991). A review of risk factors assessed in child protective services. *Social Service Review 65:*112–132.

McDonald, W. R., and Associates. (1992). *Evaluation of AB 1562 in-home care demonstration projects.* Final report. Sacramento, CA: Author.

McGowan, B. G. (1990). Family-based services and public policy: Context and implications. In J. K. Whittaker, et al., eds., *Reaching high risk families: Intensive family preservation services in human services,* 65–87. Hawthorne, NY: Aldine de Gruyter.

McGowan, B., and Meezan, W., eds. (1983). *Child welfare.* Itasca, IL: Peacock Publishing.

McKenzie, R. B., ed. (1999). *Rethinking orphanages for the 21st century.* Thousand Oaks, Calif.: Sage Publications.

McKenzie, R. B. (2003). The impact of orphanages on the alumni's lives and assessments of their childhoods. *Children and Youth Services Review 25:*703–745.

McLanahan, S. (1988). The consequences of single parenthood for subsequent generations. *Focus 11:*16–21.

McLanahan, S., and Garfinkel, I. (1993). Single mothers in the United States: Growth, problems and policies. In J. Hudson, and B. Galaway, eds., *Single parent families: Perspectives on research and policy,* 15–29. Toronto: Thompson Educational Publishing.

McNeil, J. (1998). *Changes in Median Household Income: 1969 to 1996.* United States Census Bureau, Series P23-196. Washington, DC: U.S. Government Printing Office. Online at www.census.gov.

Mead, L. M. (1985). The hidden jobs debate. *Public Interest 95:*40–58.

Mead, L. M. (1986). *Beyond entitlement: The social obligations of citizenship.* New York: Free Press.

Mech, E. (1970). Decision analysis in foster care practice. In H. D. Stone, ed., *Foster care in question,* 26–51. New York: Child Welfare League of America.

Meersman, L. (1999). End to social promotion is scaled back. *Los Angeles Times,* December 1, A26.

Meezan, W., and McCroskey, J. (1993). Family centered home based interventions for abusive and neglectful families in Los Angeles. Unpublished paper. Los Angeles: University of Southern California School of Social Work.

Meissner, M. (1975). No exit for wives: Sexual division of labour and the cumulation of household demands. *Canadian Review of Sociology and Anthropology 12:*424–439.

Merrill Lynch and Gemini Consulting. (2001). *World Wealth Report 2000.* Figure 3. New York: Merrill Lynch.

Merrill Lynch and Cap Gemini Ernst and Young. (2002). *World wealth report 2001.* Figure 1. New York: Merrill Lynch.

Metcalf, C. E., and Thornton, C. (1992). Random assignment. *Children and Youth Services Review 14:*145–156.

Meyer, C. H. (1984). Can foster care be saved? *Social Work 29:*499.

Meyer, H. S., Borgatta, E., and Jones W. (1965). *Girls at vocational high: An experiment in social work intervention.* New York: Russell Sage Foundation.

Michigan Department of Social Services. (1993). *Report to the House Appropriations Subcommittee on Social Services, May 25.* Lansing, MI: Author.

Miller, D. S. (1959). Fractures among children—1, parental assault as causative agent. *Minnesota Medicine 42:*1209–1213.

Miller-Johnson, S., Winn, D., Coie, J., Maumary-Gremaud, A., Hyman, C., Terry, R., and Lochman, J. (1999). Motherhood during the teen years: A developmental perspective on risk factors for adolescent childbearing. *Developmental Psychology 11:*85–100.

Mills, C. W. (1959). *The sociological imagination.* New York: Oxford University Press.

Mills, L. G. (2000). Woman abuse and child protection: A tumultuous marriage (Part I). *Children and Youth Services Review 22:*199–205

Mincy, R. B., and Dupree, A. T. (2001). Welfare, child support and family formation. *Children and Youth Services Review 23:*577–601.

Mitchell, C., Tovar, P., and Knitzer, J. (1989). *The Bronx Homebuilders program: An evaluation of the first 45 families.* New York: Bank Street College of Education.

Mlyniec, W. J. (1983). Prosecuting a termination of parental rights case. In M. Hardin, ed., *Foster children in the courts,* 193–228. Boston: Butterworth Legal Publishers.

Mnookin, R. H. (1973). Foster care: In whose best interest? *Harvard Educational Review 43:*599–638.

Mnookin, R. H. (1985). *In the interest of children: Advocacy, law reform, and public policy.* San Francisco: Freeman.

Moffitt, R. A. (2002). From welfare to work: What the evidence shows. Washington, DC: Brookings Institution.

Montgomery, S. (1982). Correspondence. *British Journal of Social Work 12:*669–672.

Moore, K. A., Nord, C. W., and Peterson, J. L. (1989). Non-voluntary sexual activity among adolescents. *Family Planning Perspectives 21:*110–114.

Moore, A., Beverly, S., Schreiner, M., Sherraden, M., Lombe, M., Cho, E. Y. N., Johnson, E., and Vonderlack, R. (2001). *Saving, IDA programs, and effects of IDAs: A survey of participants,* research report. St. Louis: Center for Social Development, Washington University.

Moynihan, D. P. (1965). *The Negro family: The case for national action.* Washington, DC: Office of Policy Planning and Research, U.S. Department of Labor.

Moynihan, D. P. (1973). *The politics of a guaranteed annual income: The Nixon administration and the Family Assistance Plan.* New York: Random House.

Moynihan, D. P. (1981). Children and welfare reform. *Journal of the Institute for Socioeconomic Studies 6:*1–8.

Moynihan, D. P. (1986). *Family and nation.* San Diego: Harcourt Brace Jovanovich.

Moynihan, D. P. (1990). Towards a post-industrial social policy. *Families in Society 71:*51–56.

Mullen, E. J, and Dumpson, J. R., eds. (1972). *Evaluation of social intervention.* San Francisco: Jossey-Bass.

Mullen, E., Chazin, R., and Feldstein, D. (1970). *Preventing chronic dependency.* New York: Community Service Society.

Murphy, P. T. (1997). *Wasted: The plight of America's unwanted children.* Chicago: Ivan R. Dee.

Murray, C. (1984). *Losing ground.* New York: Basic Books.

Murray, C. (1993). The coming white underclass. *Wall Street Journal,* October 29.

Myers, J.E.B. (2000). Medicolegal aspects of child abuse. In R. M. Reece, ed., *Treatment of child abuse: Common ground for mental health, medical, and legal practitioners,* 313–335. Baltimore: Johns Hopkins University Press.

Myrdal, G. (1944). *An American dilemma.* New York: Harper and Brothers.

Nagi, S. Z. (1977). *Child maltreatment in the United States: A challenge to social institutions.* New York: Columbia University Press.

Nasar, S. (1992). The 1980s: A very good time for the very rich. Data show the top 1% got 60% of gain in decade's boom. *New York Times,* March 5, A1 and C13.

Nasar, S. (1994). Economics of equality: A new view. *New York Times,* January 8, A17 and 26.

National Black Child Development Institute. (1989). *Who will care when parents don't? A study of Black children in foster care.* Washington, DC: Author.

National Center for Children in Poverty. (1990). *Five million children: A statistical profile of our poorest young citizens.* New York: Author, School of Public Health, Columbia University.

National Center for Comprehensive Emergency Service to Children. (1976). *Comprehensive emergency services training guide, 2d ed.* Nashville, TN: Author.

National Center for Health Statistics. (1969). *Divorces: Analysis of changes in the United States, 1969. Vital and healh statistics.* Series 21, No. 22 (4/73). Washington, DC: Author.

National Center for Health Statistics. (1989). *Vital statistics of the United States, Vol. II. Mortality, Part A.* Washington, DC: U.S. Department of Health and Human Services.

National Center for Health Statistics. (1999). Births, marriages, divorces, and deaths: Provisional data for 1998. *National vital statistics reports 47*(21). Hyaattsville, MD: U.S. Department of Health and Human Services.

National Center for Health Statistics. (2001). *Teen pregnancy rate reaches a record low in 1997.* Hyattsville, MD: National Center for Health Statistics.

National Commission on Children. (1991). *Beyond rhetoric a new American agenda for children and families: Final report of the National Commission on Children.* Washington, DC: Author.

National Council on Welfare. (1985). *Opportunity for reform, a response by the National Council of Welfare to the consultation paper on child and elderly benefits.* Ottawa: Minister of Supply and Services Canada.

National Council on Welfare. (1989). *Social spending and the next budget.* Ottawa: Health and Welfare Canada.

National Council on Welfare. (1993). *Poverty profile update for 1991.* Ottawa: Author.

National Research Council. (1993). *Understanding child abuse and neglect.* Washington, DC: National Academy Press.

Native Council of Canada. Crime and Justice Commission. (1978). *Metis and non-status Indians.* Ottawa: Supply and Services Canada.

Needell, B., Webster, D., Cuccaro-Alamin, S., Armijo, M., Lee, S., Brookhart, A., Lery, B., Shaw, T., Dawson, W., Piccus, W., Magruder, J., & Kim, H. (2003).

Child welfare services reports for California. Retrieved [June 30, 2003], from University of California at Berkeley Center for Social Services Research website. 2001 Caseload Children in Child Welfare Supervised Foster Care by Placement Type. Online at cssr.berkeley.edu/CWSCMSreports/.

Nelson, B. J. (1984). *Making an issue of child abuse: Political agenda setting for social problems.* Chicago: University of Chicago Press.

Nelson, K., and Landsman, M. J. (1992). *Alternative models of family preservation: Family-based services in context.* Springfield, IL: Charles C. Thomas.

Nelson, K., Emlen, A., Landsman, M. J., and Hutchinson, J. (1988). *Factors contributing to success and failure in family-based child welfare services: Final report.* Iowa City: National Resource Center on Family Based Services, University of Iowa School of Social Work.

Norman, A. J., and Glick, P. C. (1986). One-parent families: A social and economic profile. *Family Relations 35:*9–17.

Norris, M., and Wallace, B., eds. (1965). *The known and the unknown in child welfare research: An appraisal.* New York: Child Welfare League of America.

Norton, A. J. and Miller, L. F. (1992). *Marriage, divorce and remarriage in the 1990's.* Current Population Reports, Series P-23, No. 180. U.S. Bureau of Census. Washington, DC: U.S. Government Printing Office.

O'Neill, W. L. (1967). *Divorce in the progressive era.* New Haven, CT: Yale University Press.

O'Neill, W. L., and O'Neill, G. (1972). *Open marriage: A new life style for couples.* New York: Evans.

Offord, D. R., Boyle, M. H., Szatmari, P., Rae-Grant, N. I., Links, P. S., Cadman, D. T., Byles, J. A., Crawford, J. W., Munroe-Blum, H., Byrne, C., Thomas, H., and Woodward, C. A. (1987). Ontario child health study: II. Six-month prevalence of disorder and rates of service utilization. *Archives of General Psychiatry 44:*832–836.

O'Higgins, M. (1988). The allocation of public resources to children and the elderly in OECD countries. In J. Palmer, T. Smeeding, and B. B. Torrey, eds., *The vulnerables: Americas's young and old in the industrial world,* 214–222. Washington, DC: Urban Institute Press.

O'Higgins, M., Schmaus, G., and Stephenson, G. (1985). *Income distribution and redistribution: A microdata analysis of seven countries.* Luxembourg Income Study, Working Paper No. 3.

Oliver, M. L., and Shapiro, T. M. (1995). *Black wealth and white wealth: A new perspective on racial inequality.* New York: Routledge.

Ontario. (1979). *The family as a form for social policy.* Toronto: Provincial Secretary for Social Development.

Orshansky, M. (1965). Counting the poor: Another look at the poverty profile. *Social Security Bulletin 28:*3–29.

Orshansky, M. (1967). Who was poor in 1966? In E. M. B. Burns, ed., *Children's allowances and the economic welfare of children,* 19–57. New York: Citizen's Committee for Children of New York.

Ozawa, M. N. (1977). Social insurance and redistribution. In A. Schorr, ed., *Jubilee for our times: A practical program for income equality,* 123–177. *New York: Columbia University Press.*

Ozawa, M. N. (1991a). Child welfare programs in Japan. *Social Service Review 65:1–21.*

Ozawa, M. N. (1991b). Unequal treatment of children by the Federal government. *Children and Youth Services Review 13:255–268.*

Ozawa, M. N. (1993). America's future and her investment in children. *Child Welfare 72:517–529.*

Ozment, S. E. (2001). *Ancestors: The loving family in old Europe.* Cambridge, MA: Harvard University Press.

Packman, J., Randall, J., and Jacques, N. (1986). *Who needs care? Social work decisions about children.* Oxford: Basil Blackwell.

Page, R. M. (1987). Child abuse: The smothering of an issue-A British perspective. *Children and Youth Services Review 9:51–65.*

Pardue, M. G. (2003). Sharp reduction in Black child poverty due to welfare reform. *Backgrounder* #1661. Washington, DC: Heritage Foundation.

Parton, N. (1985). *The politics of child abuse.* London: Macmillan.

Pate A. M., and Hamilton, E. E. (1992). Formal and informal deterrents to domestic violence: The Dade county spouse assault experiment. *American Sociological Review 57:691–697.*

Patterson, J. T. (1994). *America's struggle against poverty, 1900–1994.* Cambridge, MA: Harvard University Press.

Pear, R. (2002). U.S. agents arrest dozens of fathers in support cases. *New York Times,* August 19.

Pearce, D. (1990). Welfare is not for women: Why the War on Poverty cannot conquer the feminization of poverty. In L. Gordon, ed., *Women, the state, and welfare.* Madison, WI: University of Wisconsin Press.

Pechman, J. A. (1989). *Tax reform, the rich and the poor.* Washington, DC: Brookings Institution.

Pecora, P. J., Fraser, M. W., and Haapala, D. A. (1991). Client outcomes and issues for program design. In K. Wells and D. Biegel, eds., *Family preservation services: Research and evaluation.* 3–32. Newbury Park: Sage.

Pecora, P. J., Fraser, M. W., and Haapala, D. A. (1992). Intensive home-based family preservation services: An update from the FIT project. *Child Welfare 71:177–188.*

Peddle, N., and Wang, C. T. (2001) *Current trends in child abuse prevention, reporting, and fatalities: The 1999 fifty state survey.* Prevent Child Abuse America. Working paper 808.

Peddle, N. Wang, C. T., Diaz, J., and Reid, R. (2001) *Current trends in child abuse prevention and fatalities: The 2000 fifty state survey.* Prevent Child Abuse America. Working paper 808.

Pelton, L. H. (1981). Child abuse and neglect: The myth of classlessness. In L. H. Pelton, ed., *The social context of child abuse and neglect,* 23–38. New York: Human Sciences Press.

Pelton, L. H. (1989). *For reasons of poverty: A critical analysis of the public child welfare system in the United States.* New York: Praeger.

Pelton, L. H. (1991). Beyond permanency planning: Restructuring the public child welfare system. *Social Work 36:*337–434.

Pelton, L. H. (1992). A functional approach to reorganizing family and child welfare interventions. *Children and Youth Services Review 14:*298–304.

Perkins, F. (1946). *The Roosevelt I knew.* New York: Harper and Row.

Perrucci, R., and Wysong, E. (2002). *New class society: Goodbye American dream?* 2d ed. New York: Rowman and Littlefield Publishers, Inc.

Peters, J., Shackelford, T. K., and Buss, D. M. (2002). Understanding domestic violence against women: using evolutionary psychology to extend the feminist functional analysis. *Violence and Victims 17:* 255–64.

Phelps, E. (1997). *Rewarding work.* Cambridge, MA: Harvard University Press.

Phillips, K. (1990). *The politics of rich and poor: Wealth and the American electorate in the Reagan aftermath.* New York: Random House.

Phillips, K. (1993). *Boiling point: Republicans, Democrats and the decline of middle-class prosperity.* New York: Random House.

Phillips, K. (2002). *Wealth and democracy: A political history of the American rich.* New York: Broadway Books.

Phillips, M. H., Haring, B. L., and Shyne, A. W. (1972). *A model for intake decisions in child welfare.* New York: Child Welfare League of America.

Phillips, R. (1991). *Untying the knot: A short history of divorce.* Cambridge: Cambridge University Press.

Pierce, W. (1992). Adoption and other permanency considerations. *Children and Youth Services Review 14:*61–66.

Pike, V. (1976). Permanent planning for foster children: The Oregon Project. *Children Today 5:*22–25.

Pike, V., and Downs, S. (1977). *Permanent planning for children in foster care: A handbook for social workers.* DHEW Publication No. (OHD) 77-30124. Washington, DC: U.S. Government Printing Office.

Pine, B. A. (1986). Child welfare reform and the political process. *Social Service Review 60:*339–360.

Piven, F. F., and Cloward, R. A. (1970). *Regulating the poor: The function of public welfare.* New York: Pantheon.

Plotnick, R. (2000). Economic security for families with children. In P. J. Pecora, J. K. Whittaker, A. N. Maluccio, and R. P. Barth (with R. D. Plotnick), eds., *The child welfare challenge: Policy practice, and research.* 2d ed., 95–127. Hawthorne, NY: Aldine de Gruyter.

Polakow, V. (1993). *Lives on the edge: Single mothers and their children in the other America.* Chicago: University of Chicago Press.

Porter, K. H., and Dupree, A. (2001). Poverty trends for families headed by working single mothers. Washington, DC: Center on Budget and Policy Priorities.

Powers, E., and Witmer, H. L. (1951). *An experiment in the prevention of delinquency-The Cambridge Somerville youth study.* New York: Columbia University Press.

Presser, H. B. (1994). Employment schedules among dual-earner spouses and the division of household labor by gender. *American Sociological Review 59*:348–364.

Presser, H. B. (1999). Toward a 24-hour economy. *Science 284*:177–179.

Presser, H. B. (2000). Nonstandard work schedules and marital instability. *Journal of Marriage and the Family 62*:93–110.

Proch, K., and Howard, J. A. (1986). Parental visiting of children in foster care. *Social Work 31:*178–181.

Pryor, R. C. (1991). *New York State Central Register reporting highlights, 1974–1990*. Albany, NY: State Central Register for Reports of Child Abuse and Maltreatment.

Quinn, M. (1996). Family preservation: It can kill. *Newsday* (New York), January 11, A33.

Radbill, S. X. (1974). History of child abuse and infanticide. In R. E. Helfer and C. H. Kempe, eds., *The battered child*, 3–21. Chicago: University of Chicago Press.

Rainwater, L., and Smeeding, T. M. (1995). *Doing poorly: The real income of children in a comparative perspective*. Working paper No. 127. Syracuse, NY: Syracuse University, Maxwell School of Citizenship and Public Affairs.

Rainwater, L., and Yancey, W. L. (1967). *The Moynihan report and the politics of controversy*. Cambridge, MA: MIT Press.

Ramirez, L. P. (2002). 529 plans: The best way to start investing for college. *Parent Child Development*.

Ratiner, C. (2000). Child abuse treatment research: Current concerns and challenges. In R. M. Reece, ed., *Treatment of child abuse: Common ground for mental health, medical, and legal practitioners*, 362–370. Baltimore: Johns Hopkins University Press.

Ravetz, J. (1971). *Scientific knowledge and its social problems*. London: Oxford University Press.

Rector, R. (2001). *Implementing welfare reform and restoring marriage*. Washington, DC: Heritage Foundation.

Rector, R. E. and Fagan, P. F. (2001). The good news about welfare reform. *Backgrounder* No. 1468. Washington, DC: Heritage Foundation.

Rector, R. E., Johnson, K. A., and Fagan, P. F. (2001). *Understanding differences in Black and White child poverty rates*. Center for Data Analysis Report #01-04. Washington, DC: Heritage Foundation.

Rector, R. E., and Youssef, S. E. (1999). The determinants of welfare caseload decline. Heritage Foundation Center for Data Analysis Report CDA99-04, May 11. Washington, DC: Heritage Foundation.

Reich, R. (1998). My dinner with Bill. *The American Prospect* 9(38).

Reich, R. (2000). The great divide. *The American Prospect* 11(12).

Regional Research Institute for Human Services. (1978). *Permanent planning in foster care: Resources for training*. Portland, OR: Author.

Reid, J. H. (1959). Action called for—recommendation. In H. S. Maas and R. E. Engler, *Children in need of parents*, 378–397. New York: Columbia University Press.

Reid, W. J., and Hanrahan, P. (1981). The effectiveness of social work: Recent evidence. In E. M. Goldberg and N. Connelly, eds., *Evaluative research in social care: Papers from a workshop on recent trends in evaluative research in social work and the social services, May 1980*, 9–20. London: Heinemann.

Rein, M., and Rainwater, L. (1978). Patterns of welfare use. *Social Service Review 52:*511–534.

Rein, M., Nutt, T. E., and Weiss, H. (1974). Foster family care: Myth and reality. In A. Schorr, ed., *Children and decent people*, 24–52. New York: Basic Books.

Rejda, G. E. (1970). Family allowances as a program for reducing poverty. *Journal of Risk Insurance 37:*539–554.

Report on Business Magazine. (1993). 1993 in Figures. Supplement to *Globe and Mail*, January, 94–98.

Rich, L. M. (2001). Regular and irregular earnings of unwed fathers: Implications for child support practices. *Children and Youth Services Review 23:*353–376.

Richmond, M. E. (1912). *Relation of output to intake. Charity Organization Bulletin, New Series, 3*(9).

Richmond, M. E. (1917). *Social diagnosis.* New York: Russell Sage Foundation.

Richmond, M. E. (1986). *The friendly visitor: General suggestions to those that visit the poor.* Philadelphia: Society for Organizing Charity.

Ringwalt, C., and Caye, J. (1989). The effects of demographic factors on perceptions of child neglect. *Children and Youth Services Review 11:*133–144.

Roberts, D. (2002). *Shattered bonds: The color of child welfare.* New York: Basic Books.

Roberts, P. (2002). *The importance of child support enforcement: What recent social science research tells us.* Washington, DC: Center for Law and Social Policy.

Rodham, H. (1977). Children's policies: Abandonment and neglect. *The Yale Law Journal 86:*1522–1531.

Ross, D. P., and Shillington, R. (1989). *The Canadian fact book on poverty, 1989.* Ottawa: Canadian Council on Social Development.

Rossi, P. H. (1987). The iron law of evaluation and other metallic rules. In J. Miller and M. Lewis, eds., *Research in social problems and public policy, Vol. 4, 3–20.* Greenwich, CT: JAI Press.

Rossi, P. H. (1992a). Assessing family preservation programs. *Children and Youth Services Review 14:*77–97.

Rossi, P. H. (1992b). Strategies for evaluation. *Children and Youth Services Review 14:*167–191.

Rossi, P., and Wright, J. D. (1984). Evaluation research: An assessment. *Annual Review of Sociology 10:*331–352.

Rossi, P. H. (1994). Review of "Families in Crisis." *Children and Youth Services Review 16:*461-465.

Rubin, A. (1985). Practice effectiveness: More grounds for optimism. *Social Work 30:*469–476.

Rubin, A. (1986). Tunnel vision in the search for effective interventions: Rubin responds. *Social Work 31:*403–404.

Rutter, M. (1972). *Maternal deprivation reassessed.* London: Penguin.

Rzepnicki, T. L., and Stein, T. J. (1985). Permanency planning for children in foster care: A review of projects. *Children and Youth Services Review 7:*95–108.

St. Onge, A., and Elam, M. L. (2000). Legal intervention for the physically abused. In R. M. Reece, ed., *Treatment of child abuse: Common ground for mental health, medical, and legal practitioners,* 107–116. Baltimore: Johns Hopkins University Press.

Sarri, R., and Finn, J. (1992a). Child welfare policy and practice: Rethinking the history of our certainties. *Children and Youth Services Review 14:*219–236.

Sarri, R., and Finn, J. (1992b). Introduction to special issue on child welfare policy and practice: Rethinking the history of our certainties. *Children and Youth Services Review 14:*213–216.

Sawhill, I. V., and Haskins, R. (2002). Welfare reform and the work support system. WRandB Brief #17, March. Washington, DC: Brookings Institution.

Sawhill, I. V. (1998). Teen pregnancy prevention: Welfare reform's missing component. *Policy Brief #38,* November, Washington, DC: Brookings Institution.

Scannapieco, M. (1994). Home-based services program: Effectiveness with at-risk families. *Children and Youth Services Review 16:*363-377.

Schafer, R., and Erickson, S. D. (1993). Evolving family preservation services: The Florida experience. In E. S. Morton and R. K. Grigsby, eds., *Advancing family preservation practice.* 56–69. Newbury Park: Sage.

Schloesser, P., Pierpont, J., and Poertner, J. (1992). Active surveillance of child abuse fatalities. *Child Abuse and Neglect 16:*3–10.

Schneider, P. (1987). Lost innocents: The myth of missing children. *Harpers,* February, 47–53.

Schorr, A. L. (1966). *Poor kids.* New York: Basic Books.

Schorr, A. L. (1986). *Common decency.* New Haven, CT: Yale University Press.

Schorr, A. L. (2000). The bleak prospect for public child welfare. *Social Service Review 74:*124–136.

Schorr, A. L., ed. (1974). *Children and decent people.* New York: Basic Books.

Schram, S. F. (1991). Welfare spending and poverty: Cutting back produces more poverty, not less. *American Journal of Economics and Sociology 50:*129–141.

Schram, S. F., and Wilken, P. H. (1989). It's no 'Laffer' matter: Claim the increasing welfare aid breeds poverty and dependency fails statistical test. *American Journal of Economics and Sociology 48:*203–217.

Schram, S. F., Turbett, J. P., and Wilken, P. H. (1988). Child poverty and welfare benefits: A reassessment with state data of the claim that American welfare breeds dependence. *American Journal of Economics and Sociology 47:*409–422.

Schreiner, M., Clancy, M., and Sherraden, M. (2003). *Savings performance in the American Dream demonstration, Research report.* Center for Social Development. St. Louis, MO: Washington University.

Schuerman, J. R., and Vogel, L. H. (1986). Computer support of placement planning: The use of expert systems in child welfare. *Child Welfare 65:*531–543.

Schuerman, J. R., Rzepnicki, T. L., and Littell, J. H. (1991). From Chicago to Little Egypt: Lessons from an evaluation of a family preservation program. In K.

Wells and D. Biegel, eds., *Family preservation services: Research and evaluation.* 33–46. Newbury Park: Sage.

Schuerman, J. R., Rzepnicki, T. L., Littell, J. H., and Budde, S. (1992). Implementation issues. *Children and Youth Services Review 14:*193–206.

Schuerman, J., Rzepnicki, T. L., Littell, J. H., and Chak, A. (1993). *Evaluation of the Illinois Family First Placement Family Preservation Program: Final Report.* Chicago, IL: Chapin Hall Center for Children.

Schwab, J. A., Bruce, M. E., and McRoy, R. G. (1986). Using computer technology in child placement decisions. *Social Casework 67:*359–368.

Schwartz, I. M., and AuClaire, P. (1989). *Intensive home-based service as an alternative to the out-of-home placement: The Hennepin county experience.* Unpublished paper.

Schwartz, I. M., AuClaire, P., and Harris, L. J. (1991). Family preservation services as an alternative to the out-of-home placement of adolescents: The Hennepin county experience. In K. Wells and D. Biegel, eds., *Family preservation services: Research and evaluation,* 187–206. Newbury Park: Sage.

Scott, P. D. (1973). Fatal battered baby cases. *Medicine, Science and the Law 13:*197–206.

Scott, P. D. (1978). The psychiatrist's viewpoint. In S. M. Smith, ed., *The maltreatment of children,* 175–203. Baltimore, MD: University Park Press.

Sedlak, A. (1989). *The supplementary analyses of data on the national incidence of child abuse and neglect.* (p. 2-2, Table 2-1). Rockville, MD: Westat.

Sedlak, A. (1991). *The supplementary analyses of data on the national incidence of child abuse and neglect.* Revised August 30, 1991. Rockville, MD: Westat.

Sedlak, A. (1991). *The supplementary analyses of data on the national incidence of child abuse and neglect.* Revised August 30, 1991. Rockville, MD: Westat.

Sedlak, A., and Broadhurst, D. D. (1996). *Third national incidence study of child abuse and neglect: final report.* Washington, DC: U.S. Dept. of Health and Human Services, Administration for Children and Families, Administration on Children, Youth and Families, National Center on Child Abuse and Neglect.

Sedlak, A. J. (1988). *Study of national incidence and prevalence of child abuse and neglect: Final report.* Washington, DC: U.S. Dept. of Health and Human Services, National Center on Child Abuse and Neglect, Administration for Children and Families, Administration on Children, Youth and Families.

Segal, S. P. (1972). Research on the outcomes of social work therapeutic interventions: A review of the literature. *Journal of Health and Social Behavior 13:*3–17.

Segalman, R., and Basu, A. (1981). *Poverty in America: The welfare dilemma.* Westport, CT: Greenwood Press.

Select Committee on Children, Youth, and Families. (1987). *Abused children in America: Victims of official neglect.* U.S. House of Representatives. Washington, DC: U.S. Government Printing Office.

Select Committee on Children, Youth, and Families. (1989a). *No place to call home: Discarded children in America.* U.S. House of Representatives. Washington, DC: U.S. Government Printing Office.

Select Committee on Children, Youth, and Families. (1989b). *U.S. children and their families: Current conditions and recent trends, 1989.* U.S. House of Representatives. Washington, DC: U.S. Government Printing Office.

Seltzer, J. A., and Brandreth, Y. (1994). What fathers say about involvement with children after separation. *Journal of Family Issues 15:* 49-77.

Steuerle, C. E., and Bakija, J. M. (1994). *Retooling Social Security for the 21st century: Approaches to reform.* Washington, DC: Urban Institute.

Shapiro, I. (2001). *The latest IRS data on after-tax income trends.* Washington, DC: Center on Budget and Policy Priorities.

Shapiro, I., Greenstein R., and Primus, W. (2001). *Pathbreaking CBO study shows dramatic increases in income disparities in 1980s and 1990s: An analysis of the CBO data.* Washington, DC: Center on Budget and Policy Priorities.

Sharpe, R., and Lundstrom, M. (1991). SIDS sometimes used to cover up child abuse deaths. *USA Today,* January 10, 2.

Sheldon, B. (1986). Social work effectiveness experiments: Review and implications. *British Journal of Social Work 16:*223–242.

Sherman, E. A., Neuman, R., and Shyne, A. (1973). *Children adrift in foster care: A study of alternative approaches.* New York: Child Welfare League of America.

Sherman, L. W., and Smith, D. A. (1992). Crime, punishment, and stake in conformity: Milwaukee and Omaha experiments. *American Sociological Review 57:*680–690.

Sherman, L. W., and Berk, R. (1984). The specific deterrent effects of arrest for domestic assault. *American Sociological Review 49:*261–272.

Sherraden, M. (1990). Rethinking social welfare: Towards assets. *Social Policy 18:*37–43.

Sherraden, M. (1991). *Assets and the poor: A new American welfare policy.* New York: M. E. Sharpe.

Sherraden, M. (2002a). *Individual development accounts: A summary of research.* Center for Social Development. St. Louis, MO: Washington University.

Sherraden, M. (2002b). *Asset-based policy and the Child Trust Fund.* St. Louis: Center for Social Development, Washington University.

Shlonsky, A., and Gambrill E. (2001). The need for comprehensive risk management systems in child welfare. *Children and Youth Services Review 23:*79–107.

Shyne, A. W., and Schroeder, A. G. (1978). *National study of social services to children and their families.* (DHEW Publication No. OHDS 78-30150). Washington, DC: United States Children's Bureau.

Siegal, M. (1994). *Children, parenthood, and social welfare: In the context of developmental psychology.* Oxford: Oxford University Press.

Silverman, F. N. (1953). The Roentgen manifestations of unrecognized skeletal trauma in infants. *American Journal of Roentgenology 69:*413–427.

Sinanoglu, P. A. (1981). Working with parents: Selected issues and trends as reflected in the literature. In A. N. Maluccio and P. A. Sinanoglu, eds., *The challenge of partnership: Working with parents of children in foster care,* 3–21. New York: Child Welfare League of America, Inc.

Sisman, H. (1990). One of the saddest jobs on earth. This World section of *The San Francisco Chronicle,* November 4, 13–16.

Skocpol, T. (1992). *Protecting soldiers and mothers: The political origins of social policy in the United States.* New York: Belknap Press.

Skocpol, T. (1997). The next liberalism. *The Atlantic Monthly 279:*118–120.

Skocpol, T. (2000). *The missing middle: Working families and the future of American social policy.* New York: W.W. Norton.

Smith, A. (1937). *An inquiry into the nature and cause of the wealth of nations.* [1776]. New York: Modern Library.

Smith, C. J., and Devore, W. (forthcoming). African American children in the child welfare and kinship system: From exclusion to over inclusion. *Children and Youth Services Review.*

Smith, M. J. (1950). Subdural hematoma with multiple fractures. *American Journal of Roentgenology 6:*343–344.

Smith, P. B., and Poertner, J. (1993). Enhancing the skills of adolescents as individuals and as parents. *Children and Youth Services Review 15:*275–280.

Social Security Administration. (2002). *Social security programs throughout the world: Europe, 2002.* Online at www.ssa.gov/policy/docs/progdesc/ssptw/2002/europe/index.html.

Solomon, J. (1989). Managers focus on low-wage workers. *Wall Street Journal,* May 9, B1.

Song, Y., and Lu, H. H. (2001). *Low-income children in the United States: A brief demographic profile.* New York: National Center for Children in Poverty. Online: www.nccp.org.

Sosin, M. R., Piliavin, I., and Westerfelt, H. (1991). Toward a longitudinal analysis of homelessness. *Journal of Social Issues 46:*157–174.

Specht, H. (1990). Social work and the popular psychotherapies. *Social Service Review 64:*345–357.

Specht, H., and Courtney, M. E. (1997). *Unfaithful angels: How social work has abandoned its mission.* New York: Simon and Schuster.

Spector, M., and Kitsuse, J. I. (1977). *Constructing social problems.* Menlo Park: Cummings.

Spencer, J. W., and Knudsen, D. D. (1992). Out-of-home maltreatment: An analysis of risk in various settings for children. *Children and Youth Services Review 14:*485–492.

St. Pierre, R. G., Layzer, J. I., Goodson, B. D., and Bernstein, L. S. (1997). *The effectiveness of Comprehensive, Case Management Interventions: Findings from the National Evaluation of the Comprehensive Child Development Program.* Cambridge, MA: Abt Associates.

Stanley, T. J. (1988). *Marketing to the affluent.* Homewood, IL: Dow Jones-Irwin.

Stark, E. (1992). Framing and reframing battered women. In E. Buzawa and C. Buzawa, eds., *Domestic violence: The criminal justice response,* 271–292. Dover, MA: Auburn House.

Starr, P. (1982). *The social transformation of American medicine.* New York: Basic Books.

Starr, R. H. (1982). *Child abuse prediction: Policy implications.* Cambridge, MA: Harper and Row, Ballinger Publishing.

Steering Committee, Study of Out-Of-Home Care Placement Trends and Costs. (1990). *Ten reasons to invest in the families of California.* Sacramento: Author.

Stein, T. J. (1985). Projects to prevent out-of-home placement. *Children and Youth Services Review 7:*109–122.

Stein, T. J. (1991a). *Child welfare and the law.* New York: Longman.

Stein, T. J. (1991b). Personal communication, September 11.

Stein, T. J. (2003). The Adoption and Safe Families Act: How Congress overlooks available data and ignores systemic obstacles in its pursuit of political goals. *Children and Youth Services Review 25:*669-682.

Stein, T. J., and Gambrill, E. D. (1976). *Decision making in foster care: A training manual.* Berkeley, CA: University Extension Publications.

Stein, T. J., and Rzepnicki, T. L. (1984). *Decision-making in child welfare services: Intake and planning.* Hingham, MA: Kluwer-Nijoff Publishing, Kluwer Academic Publications.

Stein, T. J., Gambrill, E. D., and Wiltse, K. T. (1978). *Children in foster homes: Achieving continuity of care.* New York: Praeger Publishers.

Steiner, G. Y. (1976). *The childrens' cause.* Washington, DC: Brookings Institution.

Stingle, K. (2002). Competing responsibilities: Who will care for the children. In T. E. Lengyel and D. Campbell, eds., *Welfare policy through the lens of personal experience,* 43–62. Milwaukee, WI: Alliance for Children and Families.

Straus, M., and Gelles, R. (1986). Societal change and change in family violence from 1975–1985 as revealed by two national surveys. *Journal of Marriage and the Family 48:*465–479.

Straus, M., Gelles, R. J., and Steinmetz, S. (1980). *Behind closed doors: Violence in the American family.* Garden City, NY: Doubleday.

Stuart, A. (1986). Rescuing children: Reforms in the child support payment system. *Social Service Review 60:*201–217.

Sussman, A., and Cohen, S. (1975). *Reporting child abuse and neglect: Guidelines for legislation.* Cambridge, MA: Ballinger Publishing.

Szykula, S. A., and Fleischman, M. J. (1985). Reducing out-of-home placements of abused children: Two controlled field studies. *Child Abuse and Neglect 9:*277–283.

Tatara, T. (1983). *Characteristics of children in substitute and adoptive care.* Washington, DC: Voluntary Cooperative Information System, American Public Welfare Association.

Tatara, T., and Pettiford, E. K. (1985). *Characteristics of children in substitute and adoptive care.* Washington, DC: Voluntary Cooperative Information System, American Public Welfare Association.

Taylor, P. (1991). Tax cuts can help our kids: Relief for families benefits society. *Washington Post,* June 16, 1B.

Testa, M. F., and Goerge, R. M. (1988). *Policy and resource factors in the achievement of permanency for foster children in Illinois.* Unpublished paper. Chapin Hall Center for Children at the University of Chicago, Chicago.

Testa, M.F., and Slack, K.S. (2002). The gift of kinship foster care. *Children and Youth Services Review 24*:79–108.

Theiman, A. A., Fuqua, R., and Linnan, K. (1990). *Iowa family preservation three year pilot project: Final evaluation report*. Ames, IA: Iowa State University.

Theis, S. (1924). *How foster children turn out*. New York: State Charities Aid Association.

Thomlison, R. J. (1984). Something works: Evidence from practice effectiveness studies. *Social Work 29*:51–56.

Thoburn, J., Brandon, M., and Lewis, A. (1997). Need, risk, and significant harm. In N. Parton, ed., *Child protection and family support: Tensions, contradictions and possibilities*, 165–192. London: Routledge.

Thurow, L. C. (1975). *Generating inequality: Mechanisms of distribution in the U.S. economy*. New York: Basic Books.

Thurow, L. C. (1987). *Declining American incomes and living standards*. New York: Economic Policy Institute.

Thurow, L. C. (1992). *Head to head: The coming economic battle among Japan, Europe, and America*. San Francisco: William Morrow and Company.

Titmuss, R. (1968). *Commitment to welfare*. New York: Pantheon Books.

Tobin, J. (1968). Raising the incomes of the poor. In K. Gordon, eds., *Agenda for the nation: Papers on diplomatic and foreign policy issues*, 77-116. Washington, DC: Brookings Institution.

Tobin, J., Wu, D. Y. H., and Davidson, D. (1989). *Preschool in three cultures: Japan, China and the United States*. New Haven: Yale University Press.

Todd, A. J. (1919). *The scientific spirit in social work*. New York: Macmillan.

Trattner, W. I. (1990). *From poor law to welfare state: A history of social welfare in America*. New York: Free Press.

Trotzkey, E. (1930). *Institutional care and placing-out*. Chicago: Marks Nathan Jewish Orphan Home.

Turner, D., and Shields, B. (1985). The legal process of brining children into care in British Columbia. In K. L. Levitt and B. Wharf, eds., *The challenge of child welfare*, 108–124. Vancouver: University of British Columbia.

Turner, M. D. (2001). Child support enforcement and in-hospital paternity establishment in seven cities. *Children and Youth Services Review 23*:557–575.

Tyler, A. H., and Brassard, M. R. (1984). Abuse in the investigation and treatment of intrafamiliar child sexual abuse. *Child Abuse and Neglect 8*:47–53.

United States Census Bureau. (1998). Marital status and living arrangements: March 1998 (Update). *Current Population Reports*. Series P-20-514. Washington, DC: U.S. Census Bureau.

UNICEF. (2000). *Child poverty in rich nations*. Florence, Italy: United Nations Children's Fund. (see www.unicef-icdc.org)

United States Advisory Board on Child Abuse and Neglect. (1990). *Child abuse and neglect: Critical first steps in response to a national emergency*. Washington, DC: Author.

United States Advisory Board on Child Abuse and Neglect. (1991). *A caring community: Blueprint for an effective federal policy on child abuse and neglect*. Washington, DC: Author.

United States Bureau of the Census. (1987). *Child support and alimony, 1985. Current population reports.* Series P-23, No. 152. Washington, DC: Author.

United States Bureau of the Census. (1987). *Children with single parents—how they fare.* CENBR/97-1. Washington, DC: Author.

United States Bureau of the Census. (1987). *Money income of households, families and persons in the United States: 1987.* Washington, DC: Author.

United States Census Bureau. (1993). *Survey of Income and Program Participation (SIPP), 1993 Wave 9.* Internet release date: October 31, 2000.

United States Census Bureau. (1997). *Current population reports.* Series P-6. Washington, DC: U.S. Government Printing Office.

United States Census Bureau. (1998). Marital status and living arrangements: March 1998 (Update). *Current Population Reports.* Series P-20-514. Washington, DC: U.S. Census Bureau.

United States Census Bureau. (1999). *Current population reports,* Series P-6. Washington, DC: U.S. Government Printing Office.

United States Census Bureau. (2000). *Poverty in the United States: 2000,* Current Population Reports. Series P60-214 and data published online at www.census.gov/hhes/www/poverty.html.

United States Census Bureau. (2001a). *America's families and living arrangements: 2000. Population characteristics.* Series P20-537. Washington, DC: U.S. Government Printing Office. (See www.census.gov)

United States Census Bureau. (2001b). Poverty in the United States: 2000. *Current population reports,* Series P60-214. Washington, DC: U.S. Government Printing Office. (see www.census.gov)

United States Census Bureau. (2002). Poverty in the United States: 2002. *Current population reports.* Series P60-219. Washington, DC: U.S. Government Printing Office. (see www.census.gov)

United States Department of Health and Human Services, National Center on Child Abuse and Neglect. (1981). *Study findings: National study of the incidence and severity of child abuse and neglect.* DHHS Publication No. (OHDS) 81-30325. Washington, DC: U.S. Government Printing Office.

United States Department of Health and Human Services, National Center on Child Abuse and Neglect. (1988). *Study findings, study of national incidence and prevalence of child abuse and neglect,* 5–29. Washington, DC: U.S. Government Printing Office.

U.S. Department of Health and Human Services. (2001). *Child maltreatment 1999: Reports from the states to the national child abuse and neglect data system.* Washington, DC: U.S. Government Printing Office.

United States General Accounting Office. (1989). *Children and youths: About 68,000 homeless and 186,000 in shared housing at any given time.* Washington, DC: U.S. Government Printing Office.

United States General Accounting Office. (2001). *Moving hard-to-employ recipients into the workforce.* GA)-01-368. (March) Washington, DC: author.

United States House of Representatives. (1981). *Missing children's act.* Hearings held by the Subcommittee on Civil and Constitutional Rights, Committee on the Judiciary. 97th Congress, 1st session, 18, November 30.

United States House of Representatives. (1998). *Green Book: Background material and data on programs within the jurisdiction of the Committee on Ways and Means.* Washington, DC: U.S. Government Printing Office.

United States House of Representatives. (2000). *Green Book: Background material and data on programs within the jurisdiction of the Committee on Ways and Means.* 106th Congress. Washington, DC: U.S. Government Printing Office.

United States Senate. (1983). *Child kidnapping.* Hearings held by the Subcommittee on Juvenile Justice, Committee on the Judiciary. 98th Congress. 1st session, February 2.

University Associates. (1992). *Evaluation of Michigan's Families First program: Summary of results.* Lansing, MI: Author.

University Associates. (1993). *Evaluation of Michigan's Families First program: Summary report.* Lansing, MI: Author.

University of California, Office of the President. (2003). *Undergraduate access to the University of California after the elimination of race-conscious policies.* Oakland, CA: Author. Online at www.ucop.edu/sas/publish/aa_final2.pdf. Also see www.ucop.edu/news/factsheets/mayfr2.pdf.

USA Today. (2003). Household net worth declines. *Money,* June 7, B1.

Usdansky, M. L. (2003). *Single parent families and their impact on children: Changing portrayals in popular magazines in the U.S., 1900–1998.* Working Paper, 03-04. Princeton, NJ: Center for Research on Child Wellbeing.

Van Voorhis, R. A., and Gilbert, N. (1998). The structure and performance of child abuse reporting systems. *Children and Youth Services Review 20:* 207–221.

Vasaly, S. M. (1976). *Foster care in five states: A synthesis and analysis of studies from Arizona, California, Iowa, Massachusetts, and Vermont.* Washington, DC: Social Research Group, George Washington University.

Ventura, S. J., and Bachrach, C. A. (2000). Nonmarital childbearing in the United States, 1940–99, *National Vital Statistics Reports 48*(16).

Ventura, S. J., Mathews, T. J., and Hamilton, B. E. (2001). Births to teenagers in the United States, 1940–2000, *National Vital Statistics Reports 49*(10).

Vleminckx, K., and Smeeding, T. M., eds., (2001). *Child well-being, child poverty and child policy in modern nations.* Abingdon: The Policy Press.

von Hoffman, N. (1985). Pack of fools. *New Republic 193:*9–11.

Wald, M. S. (1988). Family preservation: Are we moving too fast? *Public Welfare 46:*33–37.

Wald, M. S., and Woolverton, M. (1990). Risk assessment: The emperor's new clothes? *Child Welfare 69:*483–511.

Wald, M. S., Carlsmith, J. M., and Leiderman, P. H. (1988). *Protecting abused and neglected children.* Stanford, CA: Stanford University Press.

Wall Street Journal. (1985). May 9, p. 1.

Wall Street Journal. (1991). Wealth of U.S. households stayed flat. January 11.

Wallerstein, J. S., and Kelly, J. B. (1979). Children and divorce: A review. *Social Work 24:*468–475.

Wallerstein, J. S., Lewis, J. M., and Blakeslee, S. (2000). *The unexpected legacy of divorce.* New York: Hyperion.

Washington Post. (1995). The welfare fade. Editorial. *Washington Post,* November 3, 1995.

Weaver, R. K., and Armacost, M. H. (2000). *Ending welfare as we know it.* Washington, DC: Brookings Institution Press.

Weicher, J. (1996). *The distribution of wealth: Increasing inequality.* Washington, DC: American Enterprise Institute.

Weitzman, L. J. (1985). *The divorce revolution: The unexpected social and economic consequences for women and children in America.* New York: Free Press.

Welch, W. M. (1994). Two-thirds back a costly welfare overhaul: Many fear cheating is widespread. *USA Today,* April 22, 7A.

Wells, K., and Biegel, D. E., eds. (1991). *Family preservation services: Research and evaluation.* Newbury Park, CA: Sage.

Wells, K., and Whittington, D. (1993). Child and family functioning after intensive family preservation services. *Social Services Review 67:55–83.*

Wemmerus, N. E., Forkosh, E. S., and Almond, D. (1996). *Characteristics of National School Lunch and School Breakfast Program participants.* Washington, DC: U.S. Department of Agriculture, Food and Consumer Service, Office of Analysis and Evaluation.

Wenocur, S., and Reisch, M. (1989). *From charity to enterprise: The development of American social work in a market economy.* Urbana: University of Illinois Press.

Wertheimer, R. (2001). *Working poor families with children: Leaving welfare doesn't necessarily mean leaving poverty* (Research brief). Washington, DC: Child Trends.

Westat. (1991). *A national evaluation of Title IV-E Foster Care Independent Living Program for Youth: Phase II final report,* vols. I and II. Rockville, MD: Westat, Inc.

Weston, J. T. (1974). The pathology of child abuse. In R. E. Helfer and C. H. Kempe, eds., *The battered child, 2d ed.,* 61–86. Chicago: University of Chicago Press.

Wexler, R. (1995). *Wounded innocents: The real victims of the war against child abuse.* Amherst, NY: Prometheus Books.

Wheeler, C. E. (1992). *Intensive family support services: Catalyst for systems change.* Sacramento, CA: Walter R. McDonald and Associates.

Wheeler, C. E., Reuter, G., Struckman-Johnson, D., and Yuan, Y. T. (1992). *Evaluation of the State of Connecticut intensive family preservation services: Phase V annual report.* Sacramento, CA: Walter R. McDonald and Associates.

Whitebook, M., Howes, C., and Phillips, D. (1998). *Worthy work, unlivable wages: The national child care staffing study, 1988–97.* Washington, DC: Center for the Child Care Workforce.

Whitehead, B. D. (1993). Dan Quayle was right. *Atlantic Monthly,* April. Available online www.theatlantic.com/politics/family/danquayl.htm.

Wilensky, H. L. (2002). *Rich democracies: Political economy, public policy, and performance.* Berkeley: University of California Press.

Wilensky, H. L., and Lebeaux, C. N. (1958). *Industrial society and social welfare.* New York: Russell Sage Foundation.

Wilhelm, M. (1998). *Revenue estimates and distributional analysis for "Stakeholder Society."* Unpublished manuscript.

Will, G. (1988). What Dukakis should be saying. *Washington Post,* September 15.

Will, G. (1991). Society challenged to break poverty cycle that traps kids. *Register Guard* (Eugene, Oregon), B2.

Willems, D. N., and DeRubeis, R. (1981). *The effectiveness of intensive preventive services for families with abused, neglected, or disturbed children: Hudson county project final report.* Trenton, NJ: Bureau of Research, Division of Youth and Family Services.

Wilson, J. (1990). U.S. child abuse shame increases as poverty grips more children. *Register Guard (Eugene, Oregon),* November 20, 10A.

Wilson, J. O. (1985). *The power economy.* Boston: Little, Brown, and Company.

Wilson, J. Q. (2002). *The marriage problem: How our culture has weakened families.* New York: HarperCollins.

Wilson, W. J. (1987). *The truly disadvantaged: The inner city, the underclass, and public policy.* Chicago: University of Chicago Press.

Wilson, W. J. (1997). *When work disappears: The world of the new urban poor.* Chicago: University of Chicago Press.

Wilson, W. J., and Neckerman, K. M. (1987). Poverty and family structure: The widening gap between evidence and public policy issues. In S. H. Danziger and D. H. Weinberg, eds., *Fighting poverty,* 232–259. Cambridge: Harvard University Press.

Wiltse, K. (1976). Decision making needs in foster care. *Children Today 5:*1–5.

Wires, E. W., and Drake, E. W. (1952). Use of statistics in testing practice. *Child Welfare 31:*17–18.

Wolff, E. N. (2000). *Recent trends in wealth ownership, 1983–1998.* Table 3 and note to Table 5. Working Paper No. 300.
Online at www.levy.org/docs/wrkpap/papers/300.html.

Wolff, E. N. (2001). Recent trends in wealth ownership. In T.M. Shapiro and E. Wolff, eds., *Benefits and mechanisms for spreading asset ownership in the United States.* Conference Volume. New York: Russell Sage Foundation.

Wolins, M, and Piliavin, I. (1964). *Institution of foster family: A century of debate.* New York: Child Welfare League of America.

Wood, S., Barton, K., and Schroeder, C. (1988). In-home treatment of abusive families: Cost and placement at one year. *Psychotherapy 25:*409–414.

Woolley, P. V., and Evans, W. A. (1955). Significance of skeletal lesions in infants resembling those of traumatic origin. *Journal of the American Medical Association 181:*17–24.

Wright, E. O., Shire, K., Hwang, S. L., Dolan, M., and Baxter, J. (1992). The non-effects of class on the gender division of labor in the home: A comparative study of Sweden and the United States. *Gender and Society 6:* 252–282.

Yanez, L. (2003). County weighs handling child-abuse calls. *Miami Herald*, April 22.

Yuan, Y. T., McDonald, W. R., Wheeler, C. E., Struckman-Johnson, D., and Rivest, M. (1980). *Evaluation of AB 1562 in-home care demonstration projects: Final report.* Sacramento: Walter R. McDonald and Associates.

Yuan, Y. T. (1990). *Evaluation of AB 1562 in-home care demonstration projects.* Volumes I and II. Sacramento, CA: Walter R. MacDonald and Associates.

Zietz, D. (1964). *Child welfare: Principles and methods.* New York: John Wiley.

Zigler, E. (1979). Controlling child abuse in America: An effort doomed to failure? In R. Bourne and E. H. Newberger, eds., *Critical perspectives on child abuse,* 171–213. Lexington, MA: Lexington Books.

Zill, N., and Rogers, C. C. (1988). Recent trends in the well-being of children in the United States and their implications for public policy. A. J. Cherlin, ed., *The changing American family and public policy,* 31–115. Washington, DC: Urban Institute Press.

Author Index

Subject Index

abandoned children, 12, 13, 14, 18, 30, 106
abducted children, 184, 185, 389
ability to pay, 328, 329
abortion, 97, 246, 247, 251, 252, 260, 392, 395
accumulation of wealth, 210
accused parents' perspective, 127–129, 157
adequacy of income, 168, 170, 175, 400
adjusted gross income, 324
administrative supervision, 15, 44, 46
adopted, 74, 79, 84–89, 378
adoption, 25, 26, 44, 68, 75, 78–82, 84–89, 105, 251, 377, 378
  color of, 88
  disruption, 87
  foster parent, 80
  freed for, 78, 79, 81, 82, 85, 87
  give child up for, 251, 252
  legislation, 84–87
  placements, 84
  subsidies, 86, 88, 316
  waiting for, 87, 89
Adoption Assistance and Child Welfare Act, 82, 83, 377
Adoptions and Safe Family Act (ASFA), 84–87, 377, 415
advance maintenance payment, 331–338, 373
advocacy research, 55, 56
African American children, 59, 233, 234, 253–255, 259, 262, 263, 266–268, 273, 283
African American families, 99, 212, 244, 254, 256, 257, 262, 266

  marriage rates, 258
  two-parent, 259, 266
Aid to Dependent Children (ADC), 22, 23, 226, 243
Aid to Families with Dependent Children (AFDC), 23, 203, 226, 244, 266–269, 277, 281, 313, 318, 354
  Kadushin's treatment of, 27
  payment amount, 251, 266, 271, 338
Alabama, 172, 173, 271, 279, 307
Alameda Project, 68, 73–82, 389
Alaska, 147, 279
alcoholism, 17, 134, 191
alienation of youth, 349
alimony, 100, 171, 417
almshouses, 12, 13
American Association of Retired Persons (AARP), 110
American Civil Liberties Union, 57
American dream, 354, 361, 408
American Enterprise Institute, 261, 419
American Humane Association, 144, 151, 178
American Society for the Protection of Animals, 124
Annie E. Casey Foundation, 57, 232, 378
apprentice training, 355, 362
Argentina, 271, 359
Arizona, 133, 147, 173, 279, 418
Arkansas, 131, 146, 173, 279
asset holders, 218, 272, 371
asset-based welfare, 354, 359
Australia, 18, 238, 315, 373
Austria, 115, 333

437